AF879031

Building Data Products

Introduction to Data and Analytics Engineering

For non-programmers

Brian McMillan
minimumviablearchitecture.com

Version: 0.9.9_pdf
ISBN: 978-1-7375365-3-6

Building Data Products:
Introduction to Data and Analytics Engineering for non-programmers

Copyright © 2021 Brian McMillan. All rights reserved

Published by: Brian McMillan, Tucson, AZ USA

Author: Brian McMillan
Editors: Nicole Davis, Emily Seinz, William McMillan
Illustrator: Brian McMillan
Cover Design: Brian McMillan

Release History:
Initial release August 2021

Comments and Questions

Please address any comments and questions directly to the author.

Brian McMillan
brian@minimumviablearchitecture.com
https://twitter.com/brianmcmillan01/

Websites

General information about this book, including errata and discussions will be posted to:
https://www.minimumviablearchitecture.com/

All code samples will be hosted on GitHub:
https://github.com/brianmcmillan/intro_to_data_and_analytics_engineering.git

To all those who were never given the chance
to bring something into the world.

Table of Contents

> **TL;DR** THIS BOOK IS ABOUT KEEPING THE DAY-TO-DAY WORK OF A DATA AND ANALYTICS ENGINEER BORING.
>
> IT'S ABOUT LEARNING AND HONING THE SKILLS NEEDED TO APPROACH ANY NEW DATA SET WITH CONFIDENCE AND LEARNING HOW TO BUILD RESILIENT AND FLEXIBLE DATA SYSTEMS FROM SCRATCH.
>
> I HOPE THIS BOOK PROVIDES YOU WITH A NEW SET OF TOOLS AND SKILLS TO ADDRESS THE MOST COMMON ISSUES FACING ANYONE WORKING WITH DATA, AS WELL AS A COUPLE OF NEW WAYS TO LOOK AT COMMON BUSINESS AND TECHNOLOGY ISSUES.

Who Shouldn't Read This Book?

This book isn't for someone looking for the latest and greatest shiny thing. We're not going to learn how to use the latest open-source software from a giant tech company. We're not going to learn about processing petabytes of data in real time. We're not going to rely on commercial software costing tens of thousands of dollars or people with specialized skills.

This book also isn't for the data scientist looking to deploy a new AI/ML model, nor is it for a manager looking for an AI/ML/Predictive/Big Data/Cloud silver bullet.

Who Should Read This Book?

This book is for current and future frustrated data analysts who want to become skilled enough to approach any data problem with confidence and competence. Additionally, this book is for IT organizations realizing that their old policies, practices, and architectures no longer achieve the value they once did. If you are struggling with evolving and modernizing your business intelligence offering, this book provides a framework to start that transition.

This book offers a systematic approach to developing data products focused on improving any business. It is the culmination of years of intense hands-on practice, frustration, and experimentation in and around small analytics teams.

Learn How to:

- Measure value based on the financial maturity of a company, including measuring improvement activity.
- Apply principles and strategies to improve the development speed, reliability, and usability of data.
- Develop a toolbox of open-source software tools to dramatically reduce the time needed to deliver data products.
- Build solutions with sustainable and flexible life cycles.
- Become a self-sufficient data or analytics engineer.
- Realign the IT value proposition with core business goals and financial capacity.
- Improve the speed and predictability of delivering data products to business stakeholders.
- Reduce risk through incremental migration strategies.
- Build tools to automate the development and ongoing support of products.
- Create a dramatically less costly and more flexible information-management system stack.

Prologue

I have always been suspicious about kids who knew what they wanted to do when they grew up. I never had that clarity. As a child, I easily dove into whatever was in front of me, and I was extremely passionate about some of those things. But I lacked clarity, and being a herpetologist, oceanographer, or astronomer never felt like a possible career path.

However, looking back, I admit that I've always known my path, but there wasn't a way to describe it. That's because my perfect occupation didn't exist (yet).

Forty years ago[1], at age 12, I spent several weekends with my Dad at work *"helping"* him develop a VisiCalc[2] spreadsheet. The spreadsheet modeled if the bank he worked for should purchase their building or continue to lease the property. Today, this doesn't seem like a big deal, but at the time this was the first small computer ever purchased by the bank. According to my dad, it was quite a controversial investment.

I'll never forget going into the office and seeing a small sea of tidy desks, each with a 10-key adding machine, blotter, and uncomfortable-looking chair. At the back wall sat a single Apple III computer. My dad told me, "Someday, there will be one of these on every desk, and half of these people will be doing something else."

A seed was planted at that moment.

Growing up, we were one of two families I knew who had a computer in the house. Even when I went to college, I only had one other friend with a computer. He was a physics major, and he wrote planetary simulations that ran for weeks. I wrote papers, created balance sheets for my side business, and occasionally ran econometric software for classes. At no point did I ever consider becoming a computer science major. I wanted to run a business, and computers were a useful tool.

Fast-forward several years, and I rejoined Electronic Data Systems (EDS)[3] as the "business guy" on a team rewriting a server monitoring database into the company's first data warehouse. In the beginning, there were only five of us. Eventually, multiple teams were developing and supporting two different data warehouses deployed into three global regions. We supported detailed server performance metrics for over 200,000 servers, all the regional call distribution switches, and over twenty help desk instances. Only three part-time workers provided the day-to-day support for the entire global infrastructure.

Working with that team introduced me to the power of databases and the importance of doing the right thing, at the right time, in the right way. Our technical lead impressed upon everyone this mantra: *"I don't care."* His mantra didn't mean "*That's not important*." Instead, "I don't care" meant "*We've got it covered*." It's the same as Postal's law:

Be conservative in what you do,
be liberal in what you accept from others.
- Jon Postal[4]

As the "business guy," I learned from the developers the value of evolving complex systems incrementally by re-implementing simple design patterns. I saw how maintaining clear system boundaries makes it easy to swap out significant components as needed.

Need to migrate from Business Objects to reporting services? *"I don't care."* Need to report on different platform metrics from two new performance agents? *"I don't care."* Need to report on corporate SLAs? *"I don't care."* Need to port from DB2 to Vertica and SQL Server? *"I don't care."* A well-principled system gives you that level of flexibility.

Looking back, I've always been a systems architect with a strong leaning toward data. Hopefully, this book and the associated ideas can shape a new way of thinking about the value of data and your relationship to it.

---

[1] The Apple III was released November 1980 (https://en.wikipedia.org/wiki/Apple_III).

[2] VisiCalc was the first spreadsheet developed to work on the new personal computers. (https://en.wikipedia.org/wiki/VisiCalc).

[3] Electronic Data Systems (EDS) (https://en.wikipedia.org/wiki/Electronic_Data_Systems).

If you want a taste of the company culture, you need to watch some of the commercials. (https://youtu.be/L2zqTYgcpfg and https://youtu.be/m_MaJDK3VNE).

[4] Postal's Law (https://en.wikipedia.org/wiki/Robustness_principle).

If you really want to geek out, read RFC1958: Architectural Principles of the Internet for a taste of the early design principles of the Internet (https://tools.ietf.org/html/rfc1958).

Chapter 1: 99 Problems[5]

Most technology books are focused on explaining a process (agile)[6], methodology (Test Driven Development)[7], or technology (Kubernetes)[8] with the hope that you will learn enough to apply it in the day-to-day world. If you are lucky, solving or improving the technical problem has a measurable impact on the business. Unfortunately, most technology-focused books provide little guidance on how to assess whether these technologies are appropriate to your business problems and, if they are, how would you know?

This chapter begins with an overview of the major technology issues all software development teams face. These problems are not solvable with technology but instead are almost exclusively related to a lack of understanding of common business issues. Next, we'll dive into those business problems and present a financial life cycle model that focuses improvement efforts on the right metrics at the right time. The final section introduces the critical importance of product life cycles.

By using financial and product life cycle models and a real-world data set, we will identify core problems. We will build a tool to structure any data development project. Then, we will analyze a real-world data set. By the end of the book, we will have built and fully automated a data discovery web site, a dynamically generated sales report, and a core DataVault data warehouse all fully automated, scheduled, and deployed to the cloud.[9]

Seem intimidating? Impossible? If you have competent Excel skills and a basic understanding of SQL, it is achievable. While we will be writing programs that accomplish complicated tasks written in C and Python, you won't personally be writing in either of those languages. In fact, the technical challenges can be easier to overcome than the business challenges. Working with people and developing the ability to know what to do next can be infinitely more difficult than deploying a relational database in a container to the cloud.

Identifying the Technology Problems

When discussing technical problems, we should start with the issues facing all software development projects. These issues are well known and have been articulated by many authors. In *eXtreme Programming eXplained*,[10] Kent Beck describes software development as managing risk. Beck highlights eight points:

- Schedule slips
- Projects canceled
- The system goes sour
- The defect rate limits its use
- Business misunderstandings
- Business changes
- False feature-rich
- Staff turnover

Look at these issues and how they interrelate to understand which of these problems are most significant. To make these problems visible, we'll use a decision-making tool called a Current Reality Tree (CRT).[11] It's a powerful way to communicate a shared understanding of a problem space, leveraging our innate ability to recognize undesirable things. Once we have a few of the undesirable effects (UDEs) described, we can chain them together and build a tree describing the most critical problems and their causes.

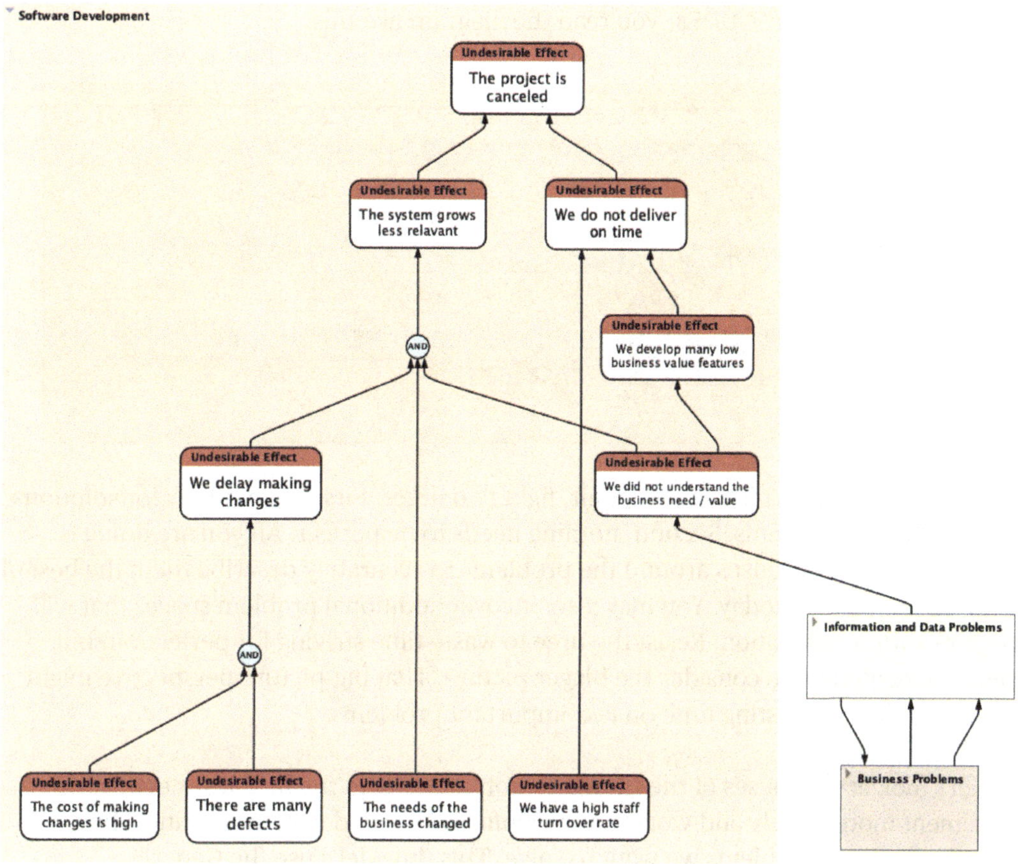

Software development problems

In this tree, we've decided (or discovered) that the primary UDE is that the current project is canceled. How did we get to that point? The Current Reality Tree should be read in a specific way: IF...THEN, starting from the lowest level and working up. In reading the tree this way, you have a clear way of communicating the likely causes.

Looking at one of the UDEs, you read the diagram like this:

```
IF THE NEEDS OF THE BUSINESS CHANGED
AND IF WE DELAY MAKING CHANGES
AND IF WE DO NOT UNDERSTAND THE BUSINESS NEED/
VALUE
THEN THE SYSTEM GROWS LESS RELEVANT

IF THE SYSTEM GROWS LESS RELEVANT
THEN THE PROJECT IS CANCELED
```

Programmatic, isn't it?! At this point, fight two urges. First, do not look for solutions to any of these problems. Second, nothing needs to be perfect. All you are doing is gaining enough consensus around the problems to accurately describe them the best of your understanding today. You may also uncover additional problem spaces that will require your investigation. Resist the urge to waste time striving for perfection, but spend enough time to consider the bigger picture. That big-picture perspective might prevent you from wasting time on less-important problems.

Let's look at the causes of the "IF we do not understand the business need/value" statement more closely and work out why information and data are a critical bridge into the business problems we want to solve. This time, let's use the Generic Manufacturing CRT described in *Manufacturing at Warp Speed*[12] rather than building our own from scratch.

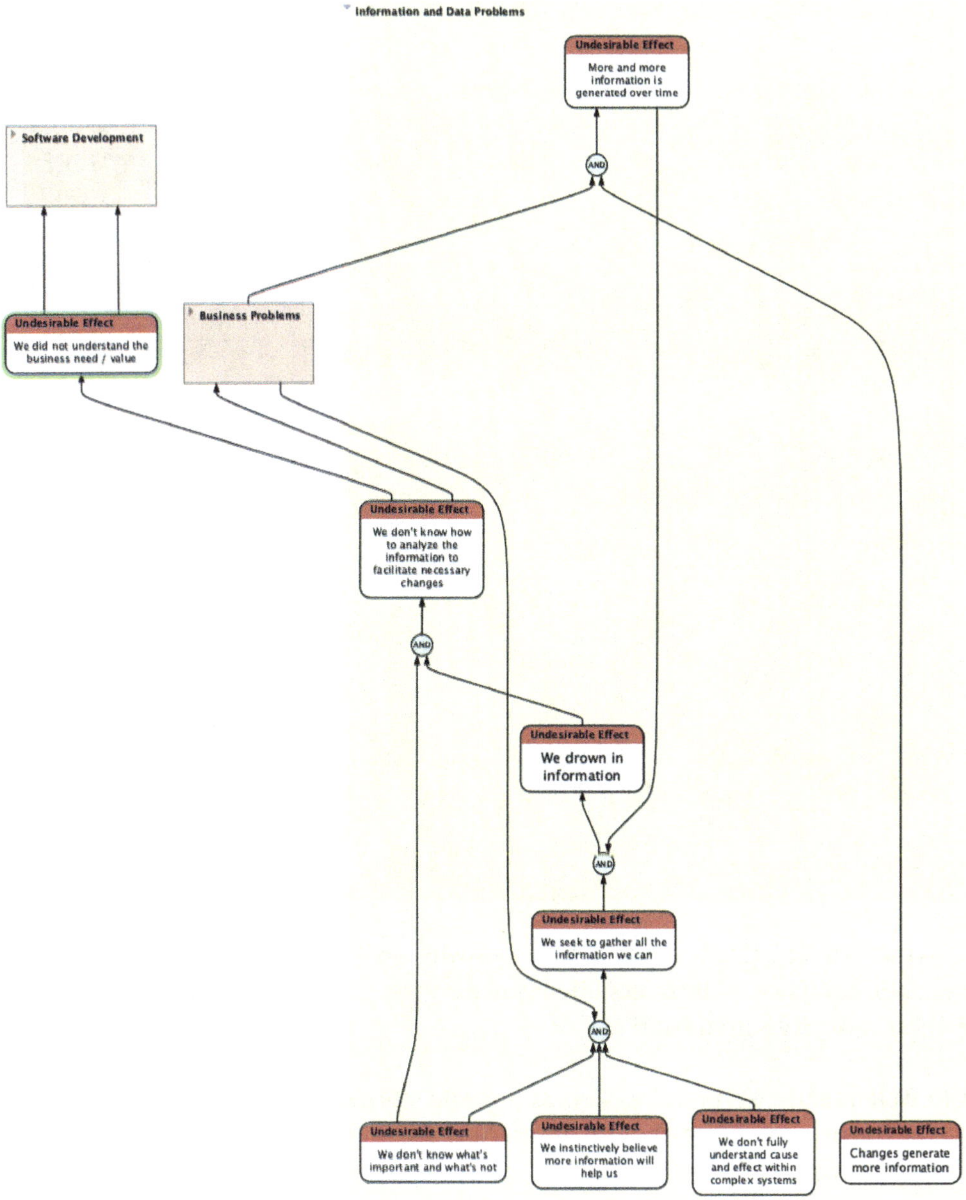

Information and Data Problems

```
IF WE DON'T FULLY UNDERSTAND CAUSE AND EFFECT
WITHIN COMPLEX SYSTEMS
AND IF WE DON'T KNOW WHAT'S IMPORTANT AND
WHAT IS NOT
AND IF WE INSTINCTIVELY BELIEVE MORE INFORMATION
WILL HELP US
THEN WE SEEK TO GATHER ALL THE INFORMATION WE
CAN

IF WE SEEK TO GATHER ALL THE INFORMATION WE CAN
AND IF CHANGES GENERATE MORE INFORMATION OVER
TIME
THEN WE DROWN IN INFORMATION

IF WE ARE DROWNING IN INFORMATION
AND IF WE DON'T KNOW WHAT'S IMPORTANT AND WHAT
IS NOT
THEN WE DON'T KNOW HOW TO ANALYZE THE
INFORMATION TO FACILITATE NECESSARY CHANGES

IF WE DON'T KNOW HOW TO ANALYZE THE INFORMATION
TO FACILITATE NECESSARY CHANGES
THEN WE CAN'T UNDERSTAND THE BUSINESS NEED/VALUE
```

This one is interesting because it describes why we think we need Data Warehouses, Data Lakes, complicated Business Intelligence systems, Data Science initiatives, and why these initiatives often fail.[13]

Our well-intentioned practice of collecting and storing as much data as possible might be the primary cause of our failures! Now the only question is, what does a business find valuable?

Identifying the Business Problems

Once we realize that the root cause of our software and development issues might be a lack of understanding of shared business problems, we need to spend time identifying the core types of problems.

All happy families are alike; each unhappy family is unhappy in its own way.
- Leo Tolstoy

To paraphrase the opening line of *Anna Karenina,*[14] all successful businesses are alike because they have figured out a business model that allows them to make more money than they spend (*Net Profitable*). While the superficial details of those business models may look different, the underlying details are amazingly similar.

We're going to adopt the Theory of Constraints definition of a business goal as "[making] money by [continuously] increasing net profit, while simultaneously increasing return on investment for all constituents, and simultaneously increasing cash flow."[15]

There is a lot to unpack in that definition. First, sales need to be greater than your total costs. Second, any investment the company makes should lead to increased net profit through an increase in sales.

While this seems obvious and relatively simple, maintaining profitability over an extended period is quite an accomplishment. The needs and wants of customers, owners, and employees shift dramatically over time, and the inability to adapt to any of these changes makes it difficult to maintain the goal. Companies also need to manage their impact on the larger world and consider the external impacts of their operations and products.

Fortunately, it is easy to identify the most common failure modes of a company.

The Throughput Economic Model

Throughput Economics[16] is an evolution and refinement of the concept of Throughput Accounting first introduced in *The Goal*. The basic theory is that by monitoring and managing a limited number of metrics, it is possible to identify and leverage the financial, customer, and operational issues constraining company performance. Even without analytic measurement, these constraints are unambiguous business problems.

The authors present a clear model of business problems grouped into what they term Financial Levels. These reflect the financial maturity of the company, which ranges from a company in deep trouble that cannot pay suppliers on time and therefore cannot make deliveries on time, to a highly evolved company capable of generating growing cash reserves.

The key here is to identify the financial level your company is likely operating within. At this initial stage, it is enough to have a hypothesis as to your level; quantifying that level comes later. The objective at this point is to begin a discussion with your stakeholders about what they perceive as the problem. Elevate the focus to the entire company rather than starting with the loudest or highest paid person in the room.[17]

Level 1 - Unable To Meet Financial Commitments

Companies at Level 1 are unable to meet their financial commitments to their creditors and occasionally miss a delivery because they are unable to purchase raw materials. Additional warning signs include:

- An unexpected drop in revenue.
- The use of personal funds to bolster cash reserves.
- Committing to additional debt.
- Considering reducing the number of employees.
- Considering closing the business.

All new businesses are examples of Level 1 companies. Their free cash flow and cash reserves are the only things keeping them afloat, and the rate of cash creation is the primary metric to manage.

If you are a new company, you need to escape Level 1. Accomplish this by operating as lean as possible while identifying a viable business model to get you through this phase quickly.[18]

Suppose you are an established company that finds itself back in Level 1 due to extraneous circumstances. It is critical that you identify this and focus on cash flow rather than profitability. This may not be an easy transition because decisions that preserve cash flow negatively impact profitability. An example is buying from a supplier that charges more but offers longer payment terms. However, at this level, staying in business longer, even if not profitable, may be the best strategy to weather a severe revenue hit.

Exit this level by figuring out a stable business model and continuously maintaining enough cash to stay in business until you can reach the next plateau.

The details are covered in later chapters, but here is a summary of the most important metrics to focus on at this level, as well as the metrics to ignore.

Metrics to measure:

- Free cash flow (cash velocity)
- Months of survival cash (cash runway)
- Overdue receivables
- Overdue payments

Metrics to ignore:

- Sales
- Net profit
- Traditional financial ratios (ROI, ROCE)
- Traditional theory of constraints metrics (T, OE)
- All financial ratios

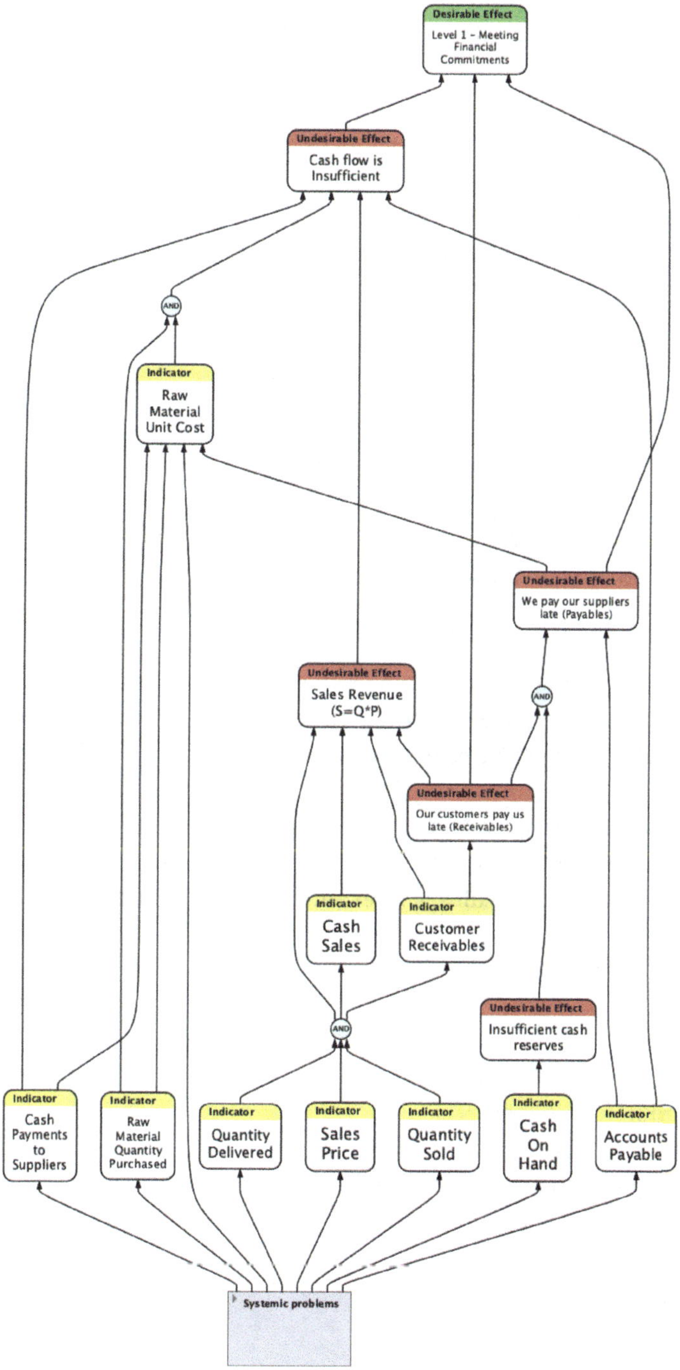

Business Problems - Level 1

Level 2 - Meeting All Financial Commitments but Not Profitable

As a company implements and iterates on their first successful business model, they enter Level 2. At this level, a business continues to be not profitable, but they are not likely to run out of cash.

The focus at this level is generating profits by any means necessary because you are losing money. Consider any opportunity to increase sales and production capacity. Pay attention to externalities that may impact your viability in the future; do nothing illegal, immoral, or unethical. This can be extended to not negatively impacting quality, overworking employees, or polluting the environment.

The key warning signs at this level are:

- Company is not profitable, but cash flow is somewhat reliable.
- Orders are occasionally late.
- Orders are occasionally delivered incomplete.

Improvement at this level requires you to first actively monitor receivables and cash to make sure you do not slip back into Level 1. Next, identify why orders may have been missed.

- Are customers looking for something you could offer but don't currently?
- Are the orders late because you couldn't produce all that was requested?
- Did you make delivery promises you couldn't keep?

In this and all subsequent levels, focus on whether the constraint is within the ordering or operations value streams. This is the level where it is important to look at net profit, which is the value of all sales revenue less all expenses.

Metrics to measure:

- Net profit
- Free cash flow (cash velocity)
- On-time and in full deliveries
- Missed delivery cause
- Protective capacity on the constrained resource (CCR)
- Overall equipment effectiveness on the constrained resource

Metrics to ignore:

- Sales
- Traditional financial ratios (ROI, ROCE)
- Traditional theory of constraints metrics (T, OE)
- Non-CCR utilization
- Manpower productivity

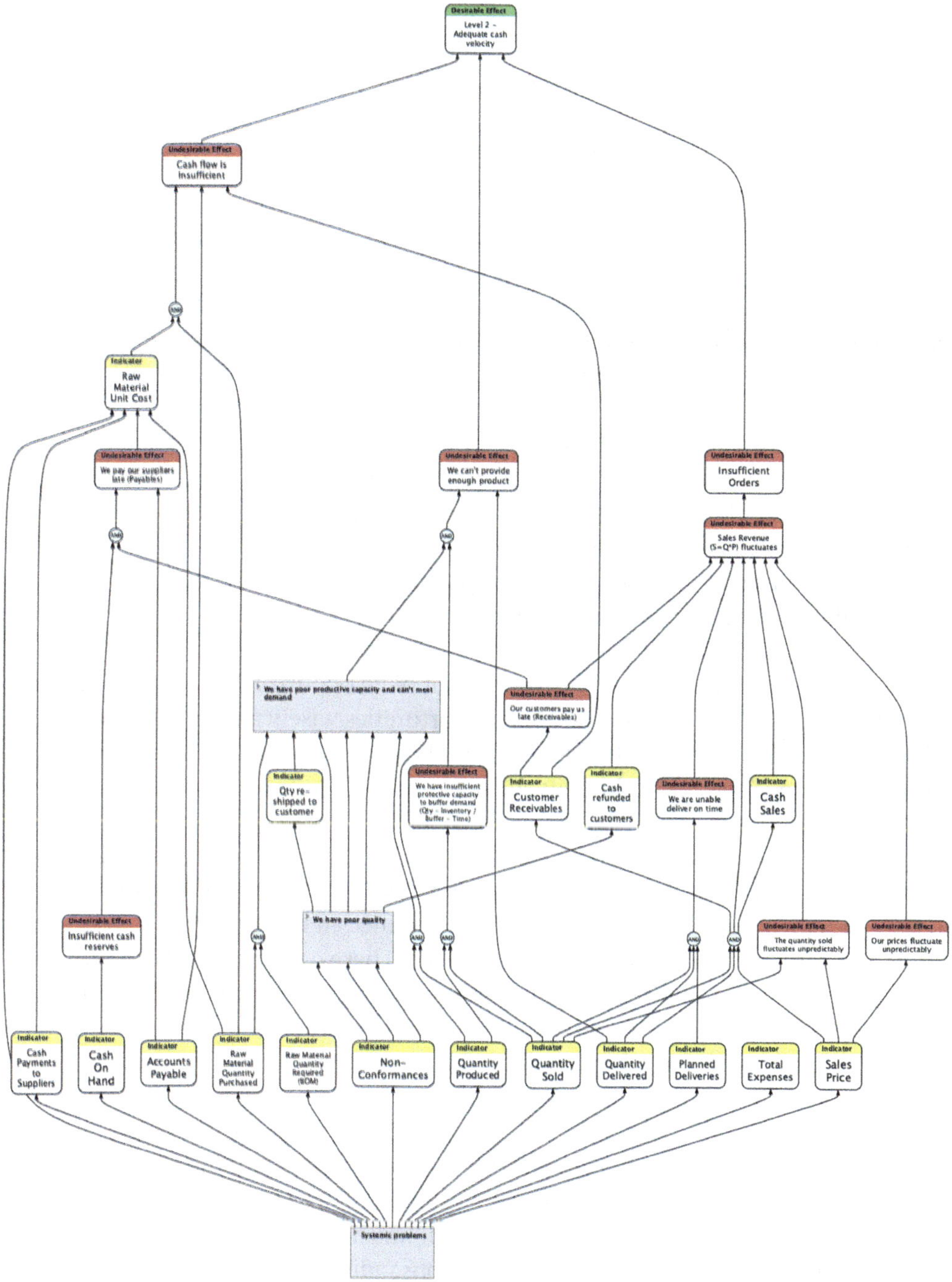

Business problems - Level 2

At this point, it should be obvious that different problems require different solutions. This is one of our core principles. Trying to measure Level 2 metrics in a Level 1 situation will be, at best, a waste of time and likely have a significant negative impact.

Level 3 - Meeting All Financial Commitments, Not Losing Money, but Profits Are Fluctuating

Now we've reached the financial level of the majority of companies. They are meeting all their financial commitments, but profits fluctuate unpredictably. Business is doing well but could be better. New initiatives and products may or may not meet expectations. This is what we would call a mature company.

The key indicators of this level are:

- Net Profit is positive but fluctuates from period to period.
- Net Profit growth from period to period is slowing.
- Orders are infrequently late or incomplete.
- New opportunities are not always as profitable as expected.
- It is difficult to identify and retire less profitable products.

In Level 2, the pursuit of profits drives pursuit of all opportunities. At this financial level, improvement depends on choosing opportunities wisely and being willing to retire less profitable opportunities as needed. The problem is having a reliable and easy-to-understand method to identify what you should focus on.

Here is where we need to introduce the idea of throughput. Throughput, like net profit, is a measure of the financial contribution of sales, but it considers only the variable expenses associated with the sale of a product. In the Theory of Constraints world, these are referred to as truly variable costs. These costs can include raw materials, packaging, shipping, certain marketing, and discount costs. All other costs are considered operating expenses. Calculating these costs can become pretty contentious, and the recommendation is to focus on raw material cost as the only truly variable cost to consider.[19]

The logic is that the raw material cost makes up the majority of the costs that vary with each sale, and it is sufficient to ignore the others. There are exceptions and complications to this rule, such as products with unusually high shipping costs, services, and content products. In these situations, adjust your definition of what constitutes a raw material.

How is throughput a more useful decision-making tool than net profit? First, it's simple. It is the difference between sales revenue (customer price x quantity sold) less the cost of the raw materials used to produce the product. It's an uncomplicated measure of money generated by each unit sold. It's not an accounting measure loaded up with value-added and marginal costs. It's simple enough to explain to anyone quickly and is easy to calculate.

Importantly, it provides enough information to quickly make sufficient decisions about product mix. In this case, of the products we sell, which ones are effective at turning raw materials into revenue? At this level, emphasize products that accomplish this goal and deemphasize less-effective products.

Metrics to measure:

- Net profit growth
- Throughput percent
- On-time and in full deliveries
- Protective capacity on the constrained resource (CCR)
- Overall equipment effectiveness on the constrained resource
- Free cash flow (cash velocity)

Metrics to ignore:

- Sales
- Traditional financial ratios (ROI, ROCE)
- Operating expense reduction
- Non-CCR utilization
- Manpower productivity

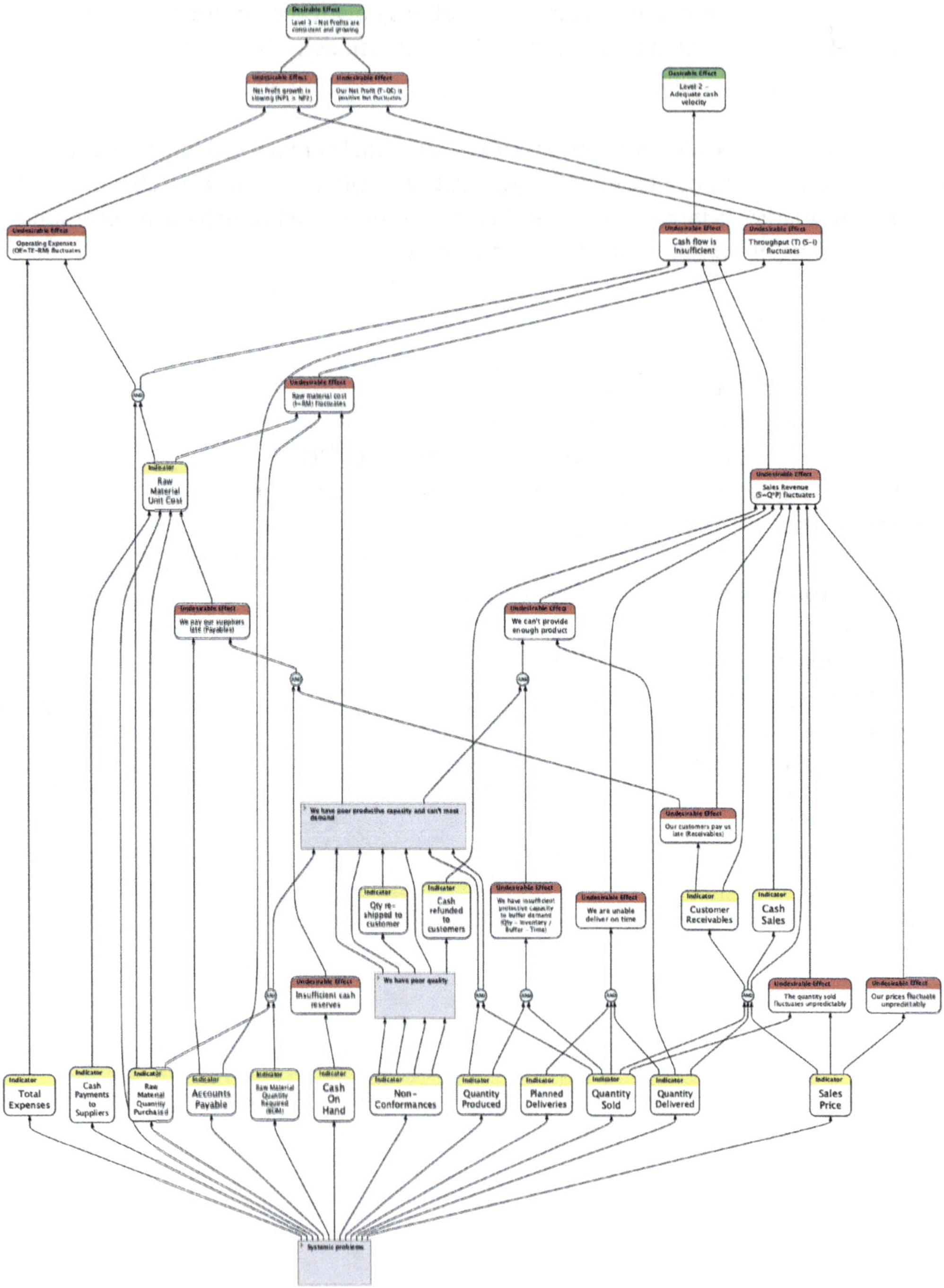

Business problems - Level 3

Level 4 - Net Profits Are Continuously Increasing

Companies at this stage are performing remarkably well. The only worry is whether their products, practices, and external factors can continue to support company growth.

The key indicators of this level are:

- Net Profit is reliably and consistently improving.
- The focus on orders is on improving delivery execution.
- New opportunities are effectively assessed and implemented.
- Product mix decisions are effectively assessed and implemented.

Here is where the full suite of Theory of Constraint, Lean, and Six Sigma practices come into play. Applying them earlier wastes valuable time and energy by sub-optimizing things that don't maximize performance of the entire system. That being said, the focus continues to be on identifying and exploiting either the order/product/customer constraint or the operational constraint.

If the company is order-constrained, deliver on time and in full over 95% of the time. Fine-tune your product mix and grow the number of units sold, increase the number of units produced, and decrease the cost of raw materials.

In an operations-constrained situation, the limiting factors are the systems supporting throughput. All the other factors besides raw material cost limit the creation of more throughput. These could be staffing allocation and factory size, as well as layout, rework, and sub-optimal process flows. The company makes these operating expenses to generate throughput.[20] [21]

Note the huge risk here in shifting the focus to cost-cutting in order to lower operating expenses. By keeping the operational productivity ratio (throughput/operating expense) at the company level and never allocating operating expenses to products and services, you can understand whether a local cost-cutting or investment decision will have a global benefit.

Metrics to measure:

- Throughput growth
- On-time and in full deliveries
- Protective capacity on the constrained resource (CCR)
- Overall equipment effectiveness on the constrained resource
- Operational productivity ratio at the company level
- Free cash flow (cash velocity)

Metrics to ignore:

- Sales
- Traditional financial ratios (ROI, ROCE)
- Operating expense reduction
- Non-CCR utilization
- Manpower productivity

Word of warning: At this level, things are operating smoothly and should be boring if you have identified and optimized the constraint. Resist the urge to create additional work to *improve* things that are not constraints.

Here are indicators of corporate IT sub-optimization:

- Increasing work in process inventory.
- Increased IT spending without clear alignment to improving Throughput (e.g., Data Science teams with nebulous artificial intelligence and machine learning objectives, the use of bleeding-edge technologies).
- Increased engineering and operations spend on automation.[22]

NOTE: These indicators may occur at lower levels of financial maturity. If they do, their impact is even more detrimental because the improvement opportunities are more obvious and less technology-driven. This is not to say that you should not use these advanced technologies to make improvements. If you choose to do so, target their adoption and critically assess their value and long-term run cost.[23]

Level 5 - Profits and Return on Capital Employed Are Increasing Continuously

Few companies reach this level. They have a refined product life cycle strategy and begin accumulating capital. The problem at this level is determining what to do with that capital.

The key indicators of this level are:

- Net profits are continuously improving.
- Product mix decisions are effectively assessed and implemented.
- Difficulties in deciding how to allocate capital, and as a result, cash reserves are either held in reserve or paid out in dividends.

At this level, refine the granularity of the data used to make decisions. Previously, you looked at sales revenue and raw material costs (throughput) and total costs less raw material costs (operating expense). Now, you have the luxury of making specific investment decisions about new products and services. To do this, begin tracking investment in new assets required to generate additional throughput.

Metrics to measure:

- Capital productivity (ROI)
- Throughput growth
- Operational productivity ratio at the company level
- On-time and In full deliveries
- Protective capacity on the constrained resource (CCR)
- Overall equipment effectiveness on the constrained resource

Metrics to ignore:

- Sales
- Operating expense reduction
- Non-CCR utilization
- Manpower productivity

Level 6 - Profits and Return on Capital Employed and Free Cash Flow Are Increasing Continuously

Simple. Keep refining the execution of your Level 5 processes. This level is what Eli Goldratt referred to as an *Ever-Flourishing Company* and this is the long-term goal of any business.

From a management perspective, you might be uncomfortable with looking at your business through this lens. Getting out of your specific process or product silo and actively thinking about the performance of the company as a whole can be both disorienting and threatening. The key to working through this discomfort is realizing where you are now and realistically orienting yourself and your expectations.

From the data and analytics engineering side, this model might be disorienting because it focuses on unsophisticated financial measurements and small and simple data sets. As we'll see later, this simplicity opens significant opportunities to provide clear and unambiguous value to the business.

Hopefully, you will see several purely technological parallels to these financial levels as we walk through the details of delivering this information to our business partners. It will help them make the best business decisions possible, at the right time, in the right order.

What's the Business Problem?

Where do you think your company is at? Assume that we're working at and with a company at Financial Level 3. We are meeting all our financial commitments and not losing money, but our profits are fluctuating.

As evidence, we have verbal confirmation and concrete evidence from existing financial and operational reports of the following:

- Net profit (sales revenue minus total expenses) are positive but fluctuates from period to period.
- Net profit growth (month over month) is slowing and inconsistent.
- Orders are infrequently late or incomplete.

Who Are our Business Stakeholders?

At this point, the primary stakeholders are our small team of one to two people, our manager, one senior executive, and another manager from the finance department.

We're not defining what department we work in, nor are we making any assumptions about our skills. The only requirement at this point is having the ear of someone in senior management to test a few hypotheses and an interest and curiosity about business improvement and decision-making.

Product Life Cycle

All the world's a stage,
And all the men and women merely players;
They have their exits and their entrances,
And one man in his time plays many parts,
His acts being seven ages.
- William Shakespeare[24]

Now that we understand our business and technology problems, we must consider the product life cycle. This is easy: products start with an idea, grow, and then die. Understanding this process is the most important concept about product development. Once again, we are indebted to Kent Beck for articulating how to leverage the product life cycle to produce more value.25

Explore, Expand, and Extract

The 3X model defines the level of value delivered at a given level of maturity. At the start of the curve, you are delivering little value. Over time, that value increases exponentially as the number of users increases. Then user growth and new value creation level off. Inevitably, the product reaches its end of life and fades into history. The 3X model defines the goal of each phase.

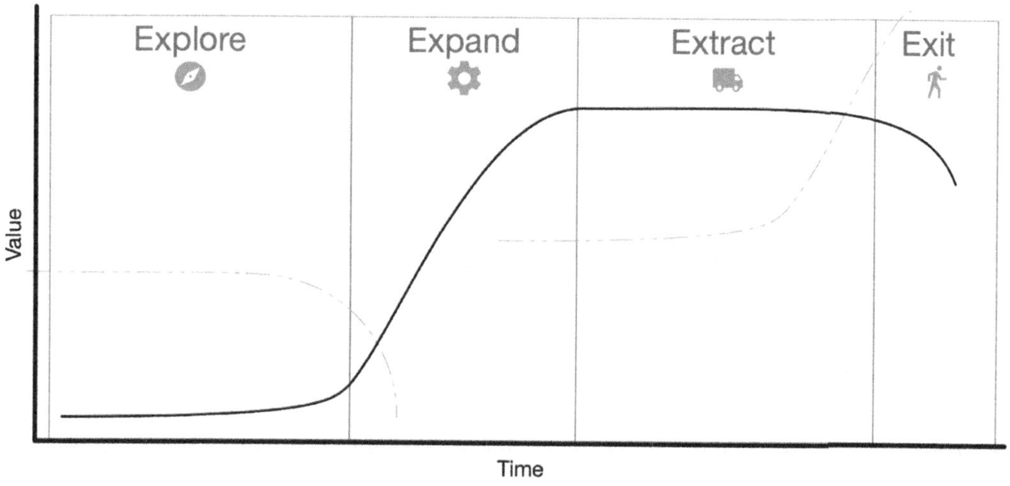

3X Curve

Explore - Finding that one idea that has high potential to deliver significant value to a customer.

Expand - Expanding the value of the new product by addressing and exploiting bottlenecks to growth as they appear.

Extract - This phase is about maximizing the value of your product by stabilizing and optimizing all aspects of the product.

Exit - All good things come to an end, and this phase is about shutting down.[26]

The most valuable aspect of this model is its universality. It can be applied across all industries, services, and products. It is less important to identify where you are at a point in time. Instead, the value in these maturity models is understanding how each maturity level has a distinct character. Leverage this character to maximize the value delivered to your customers.

Working counter to the practices of the maturity level negatively impacts that value significantly. Here are the most common ways of working counter to where you are in the product life cycle:

	Explore	Expand / Exit	Extract
Character	Chaos	Growth	Stability
Focus	Customer	Product	Process

General 3X attributes

Build it, and they will come: Acting like you are in Expand when you are in Explore by scaling a product without having clear feedback and understanding of customers' needs. That being said, asking your customers what they want may not generate the innovation you need.

Caring deeply about what customers want is much different from continually asking them what they want; it requires intuition and instinct about desires that have not yet formed.
"Our task is to read things that are not yet on the page. "
- Steve Jobs[27]

Does the customer invent a new product or service? The customer generates nothing. No customer asked for pneumatic tires. Tires are made of rubber. It is silly to think of riding on air. The first pneumatic tires in the United States were not good. The user had to carry with him rubber cement, plugs, and a pump and know how to use them.
- Dr. W. Edwards Deming[28]

One size fits all: Assuming that a new and successful methodology (e.g., agile) is appropriate in all situations. Agile is fantastic when you are exploring possibilities or trying to find solutions. It's chaotic when you know what needs to be done and when. If you know what needs to be done and you have confidence to do it, why wouldn't you make your best estimate of when you can deliver? In Explore, you don't have enough information or experience to make any promises. In Extract, you need to reliably deliver on all your promises. Wouldn't you prefer to buy from a company that can reliably deliver in two days over one that promises to deliver in one to five days?

Focusing on the wrong problem: Building a solution capable of supporting thousands of simultaneous users when your maximum expected user base is in the hundreds. This situation is extraordinarily common in large companies that allow their IT organization to build solutions on technologies developed at companies several orders of magnitude larger than they are.[29]

3X Influence on Investment

Explore is all about quickly finding an idea with solid payout and growth potential. Fresh ideas don't start with an assurance of amounting to anything. Fresh ideas are frequently bad or impossible. The trick is quickly finding the most valuable idea out of a pool of poor ones. Do this by making many small investments in a large number of ideas. Clearly articulate and critically assess the expected value of each of these opportunities. Most will fail quickly, and it is important to recognize this as soon as possible. One of the best ways is to minimize the investment of finances and time. The hope here is that inside of many small losses there will be a few big payouts.

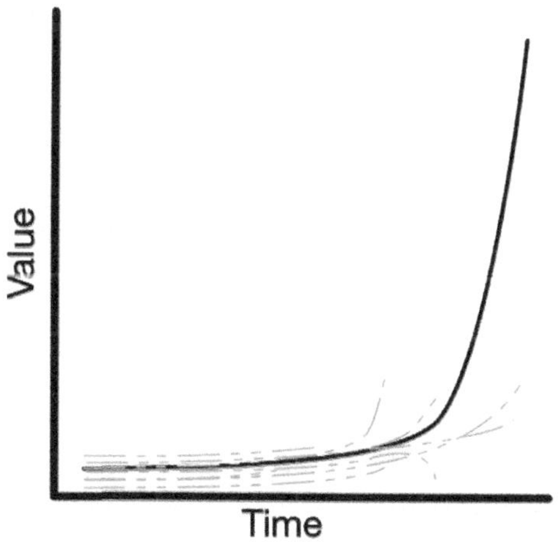

Many small investments, a few pay off

During the Expand phase, turn that big idea into something scalable and resilient. Invest in fixing what is broken. You are growing, and unlike in Explore, you can't spend money on every problem that arises. In this phase, capture that payout and build the future. This phase will be costly and significantly impact cash flow. Unfortunately, the investment cannot be avoided. The trick here is identifying the constraint and then investing in it until it has been exploited and controlled. Need more people? Hire them. Need more servers for the holidays? Pay for the elastic provisioning. Identify the additional features limiting wider adoption.

The Extract phase is all about achieving scale and fine-tuning the product. You are bigger now, with many customers, and everything requires large investments. Fortunately, you know how the system works and what is required. The risk of failure should be low. These investments focus on increasing revenue, decreasing costs, and achieving a predictable ROI. Make large investments for small but guaranteed payouts.

The Exit period begins when another higher-value product entering its Expand phase replaces the value of the original product. You might have missed a valuable opportunity and are figuring out what investments (or divestments) are needed to reflect your new reality. Controlling cost is key, but there is a fantastic opportunity to strategically invest in repurposing subcomponents to generate value elsewhere, including investments made to refactor the product into something smaller but still profitable.

	Explore	**Expand / Exit**	**Extract**
Horizon	Short term	Mid term	Long term
Reward	High potential Low likelihood	Increasing potential Increasing likelihood	Low potential High likelihood
Risk	Likely to occur Hard to detect Low impact	Less common Detectable Variable impact	Uncommon Preventable High impact

3X Investment

3X Influence on People

People are the key to any successful product, and they profoundly impact each phase. Everyone has their preferences, and the 3X model recognizes that different people are suited for different phases.

In the Explore phase, look for people with great ideas who have a high tolerance for risk and failure. Unfortunately, great ideas alone are not enough; Explorers need to execute and deliver something valuable as quickly as possible. They need to honestly assess success versus failure. The ideal candidate would be like a scientist: knowledgeable, curious, creative, inventive, and analytically critical.

Expanders start as engineers, turn into firefighters, and then back into engineers. In the early transition from Explore to Extract, you need people who know how to get things done and turn proof of concepts and minimum viable products into a real product. They possess skills to build products that meet the current needs without over-building unnecessary features and capacity.

As the product grows, it enters a phase where it is growing faster than you can keep up with. This is a critical time to have people who make quick prioritization decisions and have the discipline to stick with the problem until completion. Due to the frequency of the problems, they also need a high tolerance for imperfection. The goal here is to find problems, fix them, and move on. Exiters have many of the same traits as Expanders, except they are working in reverse. Their job is to shrink the system down in a controlled fashion rather than build it up.

Extractors have one goal: take something that is working, improve it, and make it as operationally efficient as possible. The systems, processes, procedures, practices, and policies developed in earlier phases get optimized here.

You need people with attention to detail, a critical quality mindset, and patience. These are the people who turn good products into great products.

How does this work in practice when you have an existing team working in the current phase? The first step is to have each person assess where they might be most comfortable in the 3X model. Not everyone will align with where the product is in the life cycle. This is perfectly acceptable because it is unlikely that every aspect of the product is at the same level of maturity. A mature product (Extract) has new features in early development, which call for someone with an Explorer mindset to define. Likewise, many features in Expand are not the constraint and should transition to the more stable Extract phase. Look critically at every feature and capability and, if possible, find people with natural behaviors suited to that phase. This creates development opportunities for people to stretch their boundaries and develop new behaviors.

	Explore	**Expand / Exit**	**Extract**
Personality	Scientist	Engineer	Manager
Driver	The possible	Find and fix	Good to great

People in 3X

3X Influence On Management Processes

Each of the phases requires different management focuses and practices. The issues between agile and waterfall project management are well known, and both systems have their place. However, project management is a small portion of the management process.

We've covered investments, people, and how to leverage different strategies across the product life cycle. When it comes to getting work done, three major management philosophies were developed and refined over decades in product manufacturing. Why manufacturing? At its core, product manufacturing provides the clearest link between raw materials, complex processes, and a finished product. Any reduction in the time it takes to convert raw materials into something a customer buys directly impacts profitability.

Similarly, a more predictable process makes it possible to evaluate whether a process performs as expected. Higher levels of predictability *may* even make it possible to predict what happens in the future. In manufacturing, as products move from raw, to simple sub-assemblies, to complex sub-assemblies, and on to finished products, it becomes harder to find and fix any nonconformance to standards. The longer a defect goes undetected, the harder it is to address and the more costly it becomes.[30]

	Explore	Expand / Exit	Extract
Management philosophy	Start-up	Lean / TOC	Six Sigma
Business planning	Customer and product discovery	Continuous improvement Flow management	Future focused
Product planning	POCs and MVPs	Custom to product	Product to commodity
Project planning	(A)gile	Critical Chain	Waterfall

Management in 3X

3X Influence on Technology

Because the 3X model is a product life cycle model, it applies to technology. We refer to technology in this case in the broadest possible terms, meaning the general qualities of a product. These include how a user perceives the product value: are they looking for something that provides a unique competitive advantage, or are they looking for the low-cost provider everyone uses?

The knowledge space refers to the type of knowledge required to use the product. Is the user familiar with the functionality of the product but needs to learn a new feature? A great example of this is a web site that teaches customers how to use Excel PowerQuery to transform data coming from multiple sources.[31]

Finally, the product space defines the type of product and how it's sold and consumed. When you think of technology, this is likely what you're referring to. Is it *high tech* or *low tech*? Does it require a lot of customization to work, or is it like a light that just works.[32]

This dimension is the core of the product life cycle. Because it is so obvious, we overlook how powerful the technology space is in locating our current phase. Knowing what phase we are in and where we are headed ensures that we are using the right methods at the right time. If we are honest about our location on the curve, we can assess where we might not be using appropriate methods. The technology space can indicate where our competitors might be in relation to us. Articulating where we are relative to our competitors is a huge competitive advantage.

Power comes from realizing that a valuable product is seldom a single thing. It consists of many interdependent individual components. This is the "customer value chain," depicted as a linked set of services required to deliver the desired value. This diagram depicts the services needed to help a manager make an informed business decision. Enabling an informed business decision requires many dependencies, the majority of which are invisible to the customer.

	Explore	Expand / Exit	Extract
User value perception	Leading edge Competitive advantage	Common Feature rich	Standard Low cost
Ubiquity	Rare	Increasing consumption	Widespread
Knowledge space	Learning to use	Learning about operations and features	Usability
Product space	Emergent Custom	Product Rental	Commodity Utility

3X and Technology

Consider our product to be an analytics platform that includes an analytics user interface and all the required data and analytics. Where does it sit in the product life cycle? Before answering this question, we need to make some assumptions about our situation. We will use these to work with this example throughout the rest of the book.

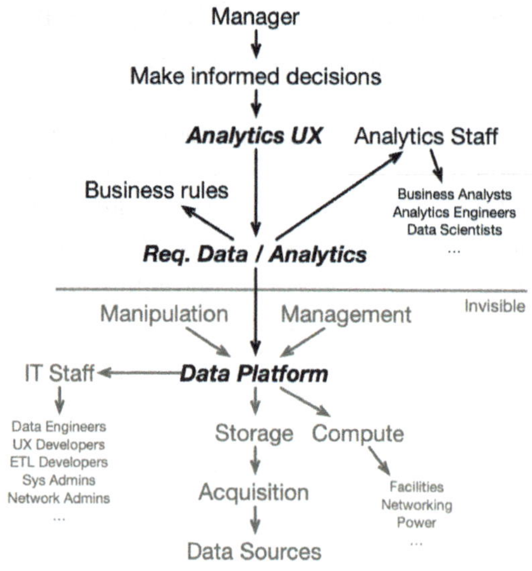

Analytics Value Chain

State of Play

It's 2011, and we are the largest online wholesaler of home decorations in Europe. Though we sell primarily to other businesses, we also sell to consumers through our online store, eBay, and Amazon. We have a High Street flagship store in London as well. Almost all of our management systems are internally built and managed. Unfortunately, a significant amount of manual reporting is done in spreadsheets, and we are spending a significant amount of time manually managing and integrating this data.

NOTE: Getting access to actual business data for demonstration purposes is difficult. However, the University of California Irvine Machine Learning Repository[33] has made a data set from a UK retailer freely available. One of the advantages to using real data for this book is that even today, the scenario where you are handed a file and expected to do magic is familiar to all data analysts.

We will make a few modernizations to the architecture and assume we could be getting this data from a SaaS provider in the future. Assume we've been given an extract of data in Excel to work with. Given this scenario, we can start to place the pieces of our value chain into the 3X Phases.

Simplifying Simon Wardley's take on the product life cycle,[34] split the Extract phase into three categories: in-house developed, purchased, and service products. Since the reporting is ad-hoc and manual, consider this either a proof of concept (POC) or minimum viable product (MVP) that belongs in the Explore phase.

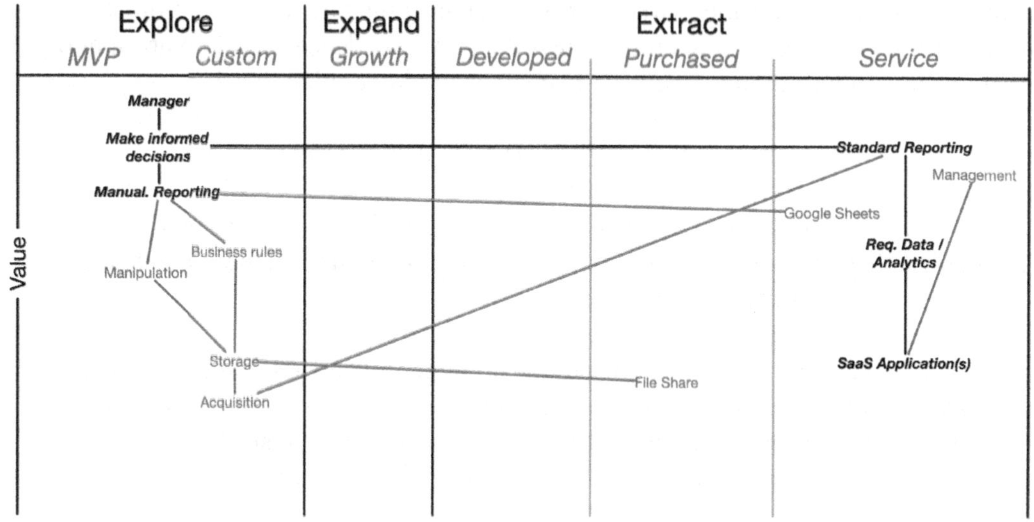

Simplified Wardley Map

The purchased and custom services sit on distinct ends of the life cycle curve, and should be handled differently. Manage standard services using the techniques and strategies for products in the Extract phase. The goal for items in the Explore column is to move them toward Extract. To accomplish this, we'll work quickly with agile techniques and follow agile principles and strategies.

---

[5] With all due respect to Jay-Z (https://en.wikipedia.org/wiki/The_Black_Album_(Jay-Z_album)).

[6] Agile Software Development (https://en.wikipedia.org/wiki/Agile_software_development).

[7] Test Driven Development (https://martinfowler.com/bliki/TestDrivenDevelopment.html).

Test Driven Development: By Example (https://www.oreilly.com/library/view/test-driven-development/0321146530/).

[8] kubernetes.io (https://kubernetes.io).

[9] I hate the terms "Cloud", "Cyber", "AI/ML", and "Big Data". They are marketing terms meant to mystify the underlying reality of easily simplified concepts. Usually for the purpose of scaring you into buying something you probably don't need.

Cloud -> Someone else's computers.
Cyber -> Protect your valuable assets from malicious people.
AI/ML -> Codifying the biases of developers into a black box and blindly trusting the results as something magical.
Big Data -> Collecting and curating "all the data" for some future undefined purpose.

[10] eXtreme Programming eXplained, 2000, Kent Beck, Reading MA, Addison Wesley Longman, Inc.

[11] The Logical Thinking Process, Dettmer, W. H., 2007, Milwaukee WI, ASQ Press.

[12] Manufacturing at Warp Speed, Schragenheim, E., Dettmer, W. H., 2001, Boca Raton, FL, CRC Press.

[13] Between 70% to 80% of corporate business intelligence projects fail, according to research by analyst firm Gartner., https://www.computerweekly.com/news/1280094776/Poor-communication-to-blame-for-business-intelligence-failure-says-Gartner.

[14] Anna_Karenina (https://en.wikipedia.org/wiki/Anna_Karenina).

[15] Goldratt, E. M. and J. Cox. (1984, 1992, 2004). The Goal: A Process of Ongoing Improvement. New York: North River Press.

[16] Schragenheim, E., Camp, H., Surace, R. 2019. Throughput Economics, Making Good Management Decisions. New York: Routledge/Productivity Press.

[17] HIPPO - Highest Paid Person's Opinion

[18] There are numerous resources to help you frame a viable business model. The most popular is the Business Model Canvas (Osterwalder, Alexander; Pigneur, Yves; Clark, Tim (2010). Business Model Generation: A Handbook For Visionaries, Game Changers, and Challengers. Strategyzer series. Hoboken, NJ: John Wiley & Sons.) and the Lean Canvas (Maurya, Ash (2012).

Running lean: iterate from plan A to a plan that works. The lean series (2nd ed.). Sebastopol, CA: O'Reilly.).

I think the Lean Canvas is the most appropriate tool for searching for a viable business model from scratch and the Business Model Canvas is better for established businesses needing to focus on specific products and suppliers.

[19] This idea of simplifying the definition of Truly Variable Costs is introduced in Srikanth, M. L., Robertson, S.. (1995). Measurements for Effective Decision Making. Guilford, CT: The Spectrum Management Group.

[20] The Theory of Constraints does something interesting with labor cost. It considers it an overhead operating expense and explicitly avoids associating it with product costs. Not only does this simplify decision-making, but it also drives behaviors that treat employees as capable of fluidly moving around. It drives you to ask, "What is the smartest thing everyone should be working on?".

[21] Likewise, in the simplified definition of Throughput, investments are treated as Operating Expense. One interesting side effect is that you begin to look at investments as needing to be flexible and general purpose. You never know when you might benefit from redeploying an underutilized CNC machine to increase the productive capacity of a constrained work center.

[22] My first exposure to the implementation of Theory of Constraints was at a General Motors engine plant in the mid-90s. In the back of the plant was a robot graveyard where we stored the decommissioned robots that were installed in the late 80s robot automation boom. Once we saw the impact the excess in process inventory was having on our ability to produce engines and components, we systematically went back to the old *inefficient* production methods.

[23] Run cost as architecture fitness function (https://www.thoughtworks.com/radar/techniques/run-cost-as-architecture-fitness-function).

[24] As You Like It, Shakespeare, W., 1599, (https://en.wikipedia.org/wiki/As_You_Like_It).

[25] eXtreme Programming eXplained, 2000, Kent Beck, Reading MA, Addison Wesley Longman, Inc. YOW! Conference 2018 - Kent Beck - 3x Explore, Expand, Extract, Beck, K., (https://www.youtube.com/watch?v=FlJN6_4yI2A).

Kent graciously credits Facebook with executing this model well before, and independent of, his joining the company in 2011. However, these ideas are explained in the book as Exploration, Productionizing, Maintenance, and Death.

Fast/Slow in 3X: Explore/Expand/Extract, Beck, K., (https://medium.com/@kentbeck_7670/fast-slow-in-3x-Explore-Expand-Extract-6d4c94a7539).

[26] The 3X model doesn't explicitly define a separate Exit phase, but I think it's useful to understand that everything must eventually come to an end.

[27] The Real Leadership Lessons of Steve Jobs, Walter Isaacson (https://hbr.org/2012/04/the-real-leadership-lessons-of-steve-jobs).

[28] Deming.org (https://deming.org/quotes/10144/).

[29] Oz Nova sums this up best in his post "You Are Not Google" (https://blog.bradfieldcs.com/you-are-not-google-84912cf44afb).

[30] Cost in this situation can be expressed as either time invested, time required, raw material cost, or lost sales.

[31] There is a good reason Microsoft Excel is the #1 business intelligence and analytics tool in the world. PowerQuery builds a robust data automation and integration tool directly into Excel. Excel is now capable of replacing a database and ETL tool in many situations. (https://docs.microsoft.com/en-us/power-query/power-query-what-is-power-query/).

[32] How I built a toaster, 2010, Thomas Thwaites, TEDSalon London2010, (https://www.ted.com/talks/thomas_thwaites_how_i_built_a_toaster_from_scratch?language=en).

[33] UC Irvine Machine Learning Repository (https://archive.ics.uci.edu/ml/index.php).

[34] The technique we are using here comes from Simon Wardley.
Wardley Maps, 2016, Simon Wardley, (https://medium.com/wardleymaps/on-being-lost-2ef5f05eb1ec).

My Basics for Business Strategy, 2017, Simon Wardley, (https://medium.com/hackernoon/my-basics-for-mapping-a-business-5b20f364b216).

Wardley Maps Community Hub, (https://github.com/wardley-maps-community/awesome-wardley-maps#templates)

Chapter 2: Principles and Strategies

As to methods, there may be a million and then some, but principles are few. The man who grasps principles can successfully select his own methods. The man who tries methods, ignoring principles, is sure to have trouble.
- Harrington Emerson[35]

Principles

Common principles and strategies lead to better, faster, more consistent decisions by quickly establishing agreed-upon guidelines. Rather than invent our own, consider portions of the principles the Open Group proposed to guide decision-making (The Open Group Architecture Framework (TOGAF)).[36] Focus on identifying high-level guidelines for managing information to improve company performance.

Open Group Business Principles

Maximize Benefit to the Enterprise: Information management decisions provide maximum benefit to the business as a whole.

Change Management: Make changes to applications and technology only in response to business needs and value.

Business Continuity: Maintain enterprise operations despite system interruptions.

Compliance with Law: Enterprise information management processes comply with all relevant laws, policies, and regulations.

Data and Information Principles

Data is an Asset: Data is an asset that has value to the enterprise and is managed accordingly.

Data is Shared: Users can access and share data necessary to perform their duties.

Data is Accessible: Data is accessible for users to perform their functions.

Information Management is Everybody's Business: All organizations participate in information management decisions needed to accomplish business objectives.

Data Trustee: Each data domain has trustees accountable for data definition, utilization, security, quality, and value.

Application Principles

Technology Independence: Applications are independent of specific technology choices and can operate on various technology platforms.

Ease-of-Use: Applications are easy to use. The underlying technology is transparent to users so that they can concentrate on the tasks at hand.

Common Use Applications: Prefer the development of applications used across the business over the development of similar or duplicative applications.

Technology Principles

Interoperability: Software and hardware should conform to defined standards that promote interoperability for data, applications, and technology.

Service Orientation: Base the architecture on services that mirror real-world business activities comprising the enterprise (or inter-enterprise) business processes.

Control Technical Diversity: Control technological diversity to minimize the non-trivial cost of maintaining expertise in and connectivity between multiple processing environments.

In the Exploration phase, where there are many unknowns, these principles serve as a broad guideline for developing proofs of concept. Considering future interoperability and technological diversity requirements early in developing a solution eases the Expand phase transition.

Consciously using new technologies in new ways to test the feasibility and value of a new idea is different than using new technologies because you want to. Change in the first case is driven by the desire to reduce risk by testing ideas. In contrast, the second case increases risk because the value doesn't align with maximizing the enterprise's benefit. Avoid this trap by always tying everything you develop back to the business value and product life cycle phase.

Unfortunately, principles can also stifle innovation and change, but using a defined set of general principles can mitigate this problem. There will be situations where you have two groups who disagree on whether something complies with a principle or even if a principle is valid. Rather than focusing on winners and losers, take the opportunity to refine the offending principle to clarify the disagreement.

Periodically revisit each principle by challenging it with an adversarial situation as a thought experiment. Consider a centralized data warehouse that supports all the information and technology principles and the principle of controlling technological diversity. Does it support interoperability and service orientation? How easy is it to change? If information is an asset, but the system responsible for managing it cannot easily change, it doesn't maximize the enterprise's benefit.

The rest of the book investigates how to maximize the organization's benefit. From a traditional business intelligence perspective, the best practice solution to this problem is building a data warehouse to centralize information. However, before we declare this as the default solution, we should look at an alternative set of principles.

UNIX Principles

Those who do not understand UNIX are condemned to reinvent it poorly.
~ Henry Spencer[37]

The first UNIX operating system was developed at Bell Labs in the 1960s and has survived and evolved to become the cornerstone of every computer we encounter, from the vast majority of servers powering the Internet to the operating system in your watch. Even Microsoft includes UNIX in Windows 10 as Windows Services for Linux (WSL). One of the reasons the UNIX operating system has persisted is its design philosophy (principles)[38]

Doug McIlroy, the inventor of the pipe command | suggests these four rules: [39] [40]

1. *Make each program do one thing well. To do a new job, build afresh rather than complicate old programs by adding new features.*
2. *Expect every program's output to become the input to another, as yet unknown, program. Don't clutter output with extraneous information. Avoid stringently columnar or binary input formats. Don't insist on interactive input.*
3. *Design and build software, even operating systems, to be tried early, ideally within weeks. Don't hesitate to throw away the clumsy parts and rebuild them.*
4. *Use tools in preference to unskilled help to lighten a programming task, even if you have to detour to build the tools and expect to throw some of them out after you've finished using them.*

Eric Raymond suggests seventeen rules of UNIX philosophy.[41] [42]

1. ***Rule of Modularity:*** *Write simple parts connected by clean interfaces.*
2. ***Rule of Clarity:*** *Clarity is better than cleverness.*
3. ***Rule of Composition:*** *Design programs to be connected to other programs.*
4. ***Rule of Separation:*** *Separate policy from mechanism; separate interfaces from engines.*
5. ***Rule of Simplicity:*** *Design for simplicity; add complexity only where you must.*
6. ***Rule of Parsimony:*** *Write a big program only when it is clear by demonstration that nothing else will do.*
7. ***Rule of Transparency:*** *Design for visibility to make inspection and debugging easier.*
8. ***Rule of Robustness:*** *Robustness is the child of transparency and Simplicity.*
9. ***Rule of Representation:*** *Fold knowledge into data so program logic can be stupid and robust.*
10. ***Rule of Least Surprise:*** *In interface design, always do the least surprising thing.*
11. ***Rule of Silence:*** *When a program has nothing surprising to say, it should say nothing.*
12. ***Rule of Repair:*** *When you must fail, fail noisily and as soon as possible.*
13. ***Rule of Economy:*** *Programmer time is expensive; conserve it in preference to machine time.*
14. ***Rule of Generation:*** *Avoid hand-hacking; write programs to write programs when you can.*
15. ***Rule of Optimization:*** *prototype before polishing. Get it working before you optimize it.*
16. ***Rule of Diversity:*** *Distrust all claims for "one true way."*
17. ***Rule of Extensibility:*** *Design for the future because it will be here sooner than you think.*

To get a true flavor for this philosophy and how it could directly influence Data and Analytics Engineers' work, read the full text of rules 15-17.

> ***(15) Rule of Optimization: Prototype before polishing. Get it working before you optimize it.***
>
> *The most basic argument for prototyping first is Kernighan & Plauger's; "90% of the functionality delivered now is better than 100% of it delivered never". Prototyping first may help keep you from investing far too much time for marginal gains.*
>
> *For slightly different reasons, Donald Knuth (author of The Art Of Computer Programming, one of the field's few true classics) popularized the observation that "Premature optimization is the root of all evil."[11] And he was right.*
>
> *Rushing to optimize before the bottlenecks are known may be the only error to have ruined more designs than feature creep. From tortured code to incomprehensible data layouts, the results of obsessing about speed or memory or disk usage at the expense of transparency and Simplicity are everywhere. They spawn innumerable bugs and cost millions of man-hours - often just to get marginal gains in the use of some resource much less expensive than debugging time.*
>
> *Disturbingly often, premature local optimization hinders global optimization (and hence reduces overall performance). A prematurely optimized portion of a design frequently interferes with changes that would have much higher payoffs across the whole design, so you end up with both inferior performance and excessively complex code.*
>
> *In the Unix world, there is a long-established and very explicit tradition (exemplified by Rob Pike's comments above and Ken Thompson's maxim about brute force) that says: Prototype, then polish. Get it working before you optimize it.*

Or: Make it work first, then make it work fast. 'Extreme programming' guru Kent Beck, operating in a different culture, has usefully amplified this to: ***"Make it run, then make it right, then make it fast."***

The thrust of all these quotes is the same: get your design right with an un-optimized, slow, memory-intensive implementation before you try to tune. Then, tune systematically, looking for the places where you can buy big performance wins with the smallest possible increases in local complexity.

Prototyping is important for system design as well as optimization – it is much easier to judge whether a prototype does what you want than it is to read a long specification. I remember one development manager at Bellcore who fought against the "requirements" culture years before anybody talked about "rapid prototyping" or "agile development." He wouldn't issue long specifications; he'd lash together some combination of shell scripts and awk code that did roughly what was needed, tell the customers to send him some clerks for a few days, and then have the customers come in and look at their clerks using the prototype and tell him whether or not they liked it. If they did, he would say, "you can have it industrial strength so many months from now at such-and-such cost." His estimates tended to be accurate, but he lost out in the culture to managers who believed that requirements writers should be in control of everything.

- Mike Lesk

Using prototyping to learn which features you don't have to implement helps optimization for performance; you don't have to optimize what you don't write. The most powerful optimization tool in existence may be the delete key.

- Ken Thompson

The *Rule of Optimization* speaks directly to constraint management and the Explore and Expand portions of the Product Life Cycle curve. There is no sense in building a big beautiful product no one will use. Nor is there any benefit in optimizing a non-constrained process or system.

> ***(16) Rule of Diversity: Distrust all claims for "one true way."***
>
> *Even the best software tools tend to be limited by the imaginations of their designers. Nobody is smart enough to optimize for everything, nor to anticipate all the uses to which they might put their software. Designing rigid, closed software that won't talk to the rest of the world is an unhealthy form of arrogance.*
>
> *Therefore, the Unix tradition includes a healthy mistrust of "one true way" approaches to software design or implementation. It embraces multiple languages, open, extensible systems, and customization hooks everywhere.*
>
> ***(17) Rule of Extensibility: Design for the future because it will be here sooner than you think.***
>
> *If it is unwise to trust other people's claims for "one true way," it's even more foolish to believe them about your designs. Never assume you have the final answer. Therefore, leave room for your data formats and code to grow; otherwise, you will often find that you are locked into unwise early choices because you cannot change them while maintaining backward compatibility.*

When you design protocols or file formats, make them sufficiently self-describing to be extensible.

Always, always either include a version number or compose the format from self-contained, self-describing clauses in such a way that new clauses can be readily added and old ones dropped without confusing format-reading code. Experience tells us that the extra marginal overhead of making data layouts self-describing is paid back a thousandfold by the ability to evolve them forward without breaking things.

When you design code, organize it so future developers will be able to plug new functions into the architecture without having to scrap and rebuild the architecture.

This rule is not a license to add features you don't yet need; it's advised to write your code so that adding features later when you do need them is easy. Make the joints flexible, and put "If you ever need to..." comments in your code. You owe this grace to people who will use and maintain your code after you.

You'll be there in the future, too, maintaining code you may have half-forgotten under the press of more recent projects. When you design for the future, the sanity you save may be your own.

Keep these three principles in mind with this book. They represent one way to solve a problem. There are many others. Even if this book strikes you as unrealistic or not applicable, I hope at the very least it opens a crack in the way you think about business and data problems.

Compared to TOGAF, the UNIX philosophy feels less prescriptive and more broadly applicable. Interestingly, both reflect the desire to improve interoperability between systems. They just approach the problem from completely different ends of the spectrum. The Open Group is concerned with improving closed systems interoperability, written by and for big companies. UNIX (Linux and Open Source Software) is concerned about the interoperability of open systems, written by individuals, not driven by a profit motive.[43]

Applying the UNIX Principles to Data Management

In Applying the Unix Philosophy, [44] Eric Raymond derives a few suggested strategies from the UNIX principles which directly apply to data and information management. How might these strategies play out if they were adopted to build data products? What could a possible solution look like?

Everything that can be a source and a destination independent filter should be one.

Break the solution down into its smallest possible components with well-defined inputs and outputs. Think about how the UNIX pipe[45] and tee[46] commands work. Their single job is passing input from one process to other processes. This allows for building arbitrary combinations of systems. Every system is constructed so as not to be dependent upon other systems. As a result, systems are composed of smaller independent components. This is precisely the strategy behind microservices.

Data streams should, if at all possible, be textual (That is, they can be viewed and filtered with standard tools).

Information passed between those small services should be human readable. For instance, give preference to CSV or JSON files over database connections and Excel files. Utilizing CSV files as the default data interchange format opens an entire ecosystem of free command-line-driven tools, many of which perform better than proprietary commercial software.[47]

Database layouts and application protocols should, if at all possible, be textual (human-readable and human-editable).

Again, human readability is the key. Use human-readable table names and field names that accurately reflect data. Different users may need items to be named differently, and data may be duplicated and denormalized. This may be a technical challenge, but the benefit to the system's users far outweighs the cost.

Complex front ends (user interfaces) should be cleanly separated from the complex back ends.

Keep the front ends decoupled from the back ends. Provide simple, textural front ends or application programming interfaces (APIs) to a back-end system and treat front-end user interfaces as separate systems with their own interfaces.

Whenever possible, prototype in an interpreted language before coding C. Mix languages if and only if using a single language will overcomplicate the program.

For data systems, this means using SQL and native command-line interfaces before Python, R, or a graphical database client. When it comes to analytical work, native Python and tools written in Python are more robust and scalable.

Be generous in what you accept, rigorous in what you emit.

The best example of this is the way SQLite handles dates and timestamps. In SQLite, there is no date or timestamp data type; everything is text. A robust set of functions freely and intelligently convert dates into any format. The same is true for all data typing. As a result, one of the most problematic areas in analytics is one of the most pleasant features of SQLite.[48]

When filtering, never throw away information unless you need to.

Yes, storage is cheap, and you should store everything—but that is not what this refers to. It refers to never destroying data. Destroying data was common in data warehousing, but then if someone needed to rebuild a fact table because the grain of data changed, the raw data was no longer in an accessible format. Hence, the suggestion to implement a persistent staging layer under star schema data marts[49] or the Raw Satellite and Business Satellites in a Data Vault.[50]

Small is beautiful. Write programs that do as little as possible to get the job done.

Again, think of `bash`, `make`, `cat`, `diff`, and `csvkit` before Informatica. They might get the job done faster, cheaper, and provide more visibility to what happens with the data. On the database side, while you wouldn't use SQLite as your enterprise data warehouse, it makes a fantastic local analytical database and a convenient way to share complex relational data sets.

Strategies

Now that we have defined some core principles and problems, we need to identify a few strategies to address those problems and bring the value we expect. Again, we are not going to reinvent the wheel. Developing the solution to these problems is, at its core, software development. We will be starting in Exploration. Therefore, we should adopt agile development practices until we transition services to Expand.

Unfortunately, adopting agile isn't so simple. There are hundreds of *Agile* techniques and frameworks we could adopt.[51] For the sake of Simplicity, we are going to stick to the original agile framework, Extreme Programming (XP).

The Agile Manifesto

Before we discuss the details of XP (or any agile framework), it is important to visit the *Manifesto for Agile Software Development*, commonly referred to as the *Agile Manifesto*.[52] This list outlines the desired way a development team should operate to quickly deliver customer value and manage the risks associated with changing requirements.

> ***We follow these principles:***
> - *Our highest priority is to satisfy the customer through early and continuous delivery of valuable software.*
> - *Welcome changing requirements, even late in development. Agile processes harness change for the customer's competitive advantage.*
> - *Deliver working software frequently, from a couple of weeks to a couple of months, with shorter timescale preference.*
> - *Business people and developers must work together daily throughout the project.*
> - *Build projects around motivated individuals. Give them the environment and support they need, and trust them to get the job done.*

- *The most efficient and effective method of conveying information to and within a development team is face-to-face conversation.*
- *Working software is the primary measure of progress.*
- *Agile processes promote sustainable development. The sponsors, developers, and users should be able to maintain a constant pace indefinitely.*
- *Continuous attention to technical excellence and good design enhances agility.*
- *Simplicity - the art of maximizing the amount of work not done - is essential.*
- *The best architectures, requirements, and designs emerge from self-organizing teams.*
- *At regular intervals, the team reflects on becoming more effective, then tunes and adjusts its behavior accordingly.*

These principles are distilled down into four values:

> *We are uncovering better ways of developing software by doing it and helping others do it. Through this work, we have come to value:*
>
> 1. *Individuals and interactions over processes and tools.*
> 2. *Working software over comprehensive documentation.*
> 3. *Customer collaboration over contract negotiation.*
> 4. *Responding to change over following a plan.*
>
> *That is, while there is value in the items on the right, we value the items on the left more.*

Agile, then, can be defined as a set of software development principles focused on iteratively delivering value through close collaboration. It's as simple as that.

Extreme Programming (XP)

Extreme programming (XP) was initially implemented in 1996, and the experience gained from implementing these practices was incorporated into the *Manifesto* in 2001. If you have been exposed to other agile frameworks like SCRUM, KANBAN, or SAFe, many of these values, principles, and practices will be familiar.[53]

XP holds five values (I'd propose a sixth), five basic principles, and twelve core practices. The values define important beliefs and actions each team member must embody to become an effective team. The principles provide the guidance needed to prioritize among many possible decisions. The core practices provide the working techniques.

~~Five~~ Six Values

> ***Communication:*** *Everyone is part of the team, and we will communicate face to face daily.*
>
> ***Simplicity:*** *We will do what is needed and asked for but no more.*
>
> ***Feedback:*** *We will take every iteration commitment seriously by delivering working software.*
>
> ***Respect:*** *Everyone gives and feels the respect they deserve as a valued team member.*
>
> ***Courage:*** *We will tell the truth about progress and estimates.*

A glaring omission from these values is diversity. Diversity in this context means encouraging a wide range of genders, ages, races, sexual orientations, abilities, levels of training, expertise, and other attributes. The importance of this value cannot be overstated.

For example, as a team is coming together, people will naturally recruit the most skilled and experienced members possible because they assume this will allow them to deliver more value faster. While this may be true in the short term, it can backfire in the long term as the solution grows and team members change. A non-diverse team tends to require its new members to be effectively identical to the original team. On the other hand, incorporating members with diverse skill levels to work alongside each other naturally forces Simplicity. Those with more experience will teach the less-skilled team members. As new programmers become more proficient, the risk of being reliant on one or two key people is greatly reduced.

More importantly, a narrow team composition reduces the ability to solve difficult problems. Multiple studies demonstrate that a randomly selected group of people is more effective in solving problems than a group of experts.[54] Rather than looking for the most skilled person, instead look for people interested in the problem. Worry less about the skills and more about discovering the broad types of problems a person is interested in solving. This is directly related to the aptitudes described in the *3X influence on people* section. It frees you to challenge biases with the confidence that more diversity is one of the tools available to solve complicated problems.

However, the previously mentioned studies acknowledge that diverse groups will have issues with communication and conflict. Fortunately, the agile principles directly address these issues.

> ***Diversity:*** *A diverse group of problem solvers is more likely to outperform a team of the best and brightest problem solvers.*

XP also defines its own set of principles, all focused on reducing the risks associated with change and the unknown. Change is frustrating but inevitable. One central theme of XP (and all agile practices) is that there are ways to balance the disruption change brings by minimizing the scope of the things affected by that change. If you start with smaller components with well-understood functionality, then changing them is easy. If changes are easy to make and validate, then you can make more changes in a given period. If your ability to change and confidence in your changes is high, then change is no longer a risk. It transforms into the thing that is required to bring value.

Five Basic Principles

> ***Rapid feedback:*** *Effective learning requires clear and quick feedback.*
>
> ***Assumed Simplicity:*** *Assume every problem can be solved with a simple solution. Do a good job on today's problem, and rest assured the remaining issues can be solved when it's needed.*
>
> ***Incremental changes:*** *Big changes don't work. Make many small changes and correct them as needed.*
>
> ***Embracing change:*** *The best strategy preserves the most future options. Minimize the number of irreversible decisions you make.*
>
> ***Quality work:*** *Quality isn't optional, strive for excellence.*[55]

Values and principles don't mean much if you don't also provide guidance on how the work should be done.

Twelve Practices

> ***On-Site Customer:*** *Include a real, live user on the team, available full-time to answer questions.*[56]
>
> ***Pair Programming:*** *All production code is written with two programmers and one machine.*
>
> ***40-Hour Week:*** *Work no more than 40 hours a week as a rule. Never work overtime a second week in a row.*
>
> ***Metaphor:*** *Guide all development with a simple shared story of how the whole system works.*
>
> ***The Planning Game:*** *Quickly determine the scope of the next release by combining business priorities and technical estimates. As reality overtakes the plan, update the plan.*
>
> ***Simple Design:*** *The system should be designed as simply as possible at any given moment. Remove extra complexity as soon as it is discovered.*
>
> ***Small Releases:*** *Put a simple system into production quickly, then release new versions on a very short cycle.*
>
> ***Testing:*** *Programmers continually write unit tests, which must run flawlessly for development to continue. Customers write tests demonstrating that features are finished.*
>
> ***Continuous Integration:*** *Integrate and build the system many times a day, every time a task is completed.*
>
> ***Refactoring:*** *Programmers restructure the system without changing its behavior to remove duplication, improve communication, simplify, or add flexibility.*
>
> ***Collective Code Ownership:*** *Anyone can change any code anywhere in the system at any time.*
>
> ***Coding Standards:*** *Programmers write all code following rules emphasizing communication through code.*

A Practical Example

We will be incorporating these 12 Practices in detail in the technical portion of the book to demonstrate how to apply them. As an introduction to these practices, let's walk through a small example.

Customer: Editor.
Team: Writer 1, Writer 2, Writer 3, Dev Team 1.
Metaphor: Automagically combine multiple edited documents into a single edited document.

Planning game: Define a few high-level stories taking 1-2 days to complete. We will use a standard story and acceptance criteria format, which seems rigid at first. Still, as you become familiar with the format, you will see how powerful it is when it comes time to determine whether you have met the requirements. The GIVEN... WHEN... THEN... format becomes the starting point for your tests.

Small Releases: In the example below, we start with a high-level outcome and then create two supporting stories. Because we agree that these are 1-2 day stories, we don't need to break them down any further. As this is our first iteration and is foundational to the solution, we agree to keep it simple and ensure we can get the minimum viable product (MVP) delivered before adding functionality.

S1: FINISHED DOCUMENT IS VIEWABLE ONLINE.

AS AN EDITOR
I NEED TO BE ABLE TO VIEW A DOCUMENT ONLINE.
IN ORDER TO APPROVE IT FOR LAYOUT.

GIVEN EDITED SUB-DOCUMENTS ARE COMPLETE,
WHEN I NAVIGATE TO A URL
THEN I CAN VIEW THE DOCUMENTS.

S1.1: COMBINE DOCUMENTS
AS AN EDITOR,
I NEED TO COMBINE MULTIPLE DOCUMENTS IN A SPECIFIC ORDER
IN ORDER TO HAVE A SINGLE DOCUMENT TO EDIT

GIVEN TWO OR MORE DOCUMENTS
AND AN ORDERED LIST OF THOSE DOCUMENTS
AND THE NAME OF THE TARGET DOCUMENT
AND A METHOD TO COMBINE DOCUMENTS

WHEN DOCUMENTS NEED TO BE COMBINED
THEN THEY ARE JOINED IN THE CORRECT ORDER
AND WRITTEN OUT AS THE TARGET DOCUMENT

S1.2: PUBLISH SUB-DOCUMENTS
AS A WRITING TEAM,
I NEED TO PUBLISH MY DOCUMENTS TO A SPECIFIC LOCATION
IN ORDER TO HAVE THEM EDITED.

GIVEN A COMPLETED SUB-DOCUMENT
AND A PUBLISHING LOCATION
WHEN WE FINISH OUR DOCUMENT
AND SAVE OR COPY IT TO THE PUBLISHING LOCATION
THEN THEY CAN BE JOINED TO THE FINAL DOCUMENT TO BE EDITED.

Simple Design: The team gets together to brainstorm the simplest solution they can devise, including sample documents of a few verses each. They determine that the simplest way to accomplish this is by writing a script to concatenate the files together. While not necessary, a simple block diagram can be useful to help communicate the solution components.

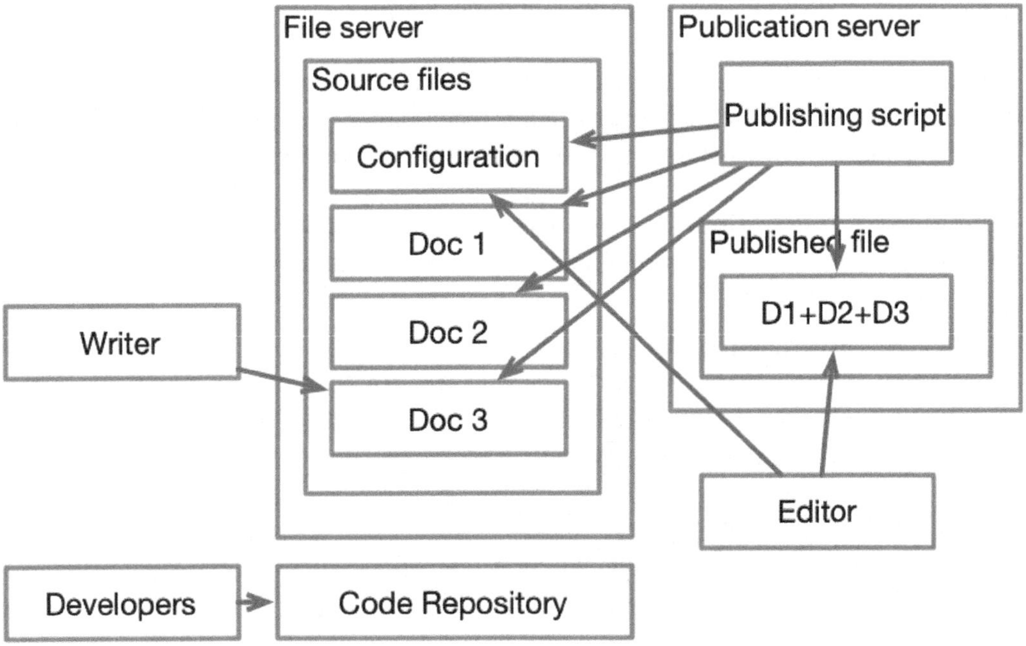

MVP Block Diagram

On-Site Customer, Pair Programming, 40 hour week: As an experiment, the team tries pair programming and agrees to work together to write the code rather than having each person working independently on a story. Pair programming seems like it might be slower. Working with the editor and their manager, everyone agrees to stick to a 40-hour week. The editor and writers agree to make themselves available over the next two weeks.

Coding Standards: The team realizes they have different ways of structuring their code as soon as they start working together. They decide to include a story in a future iteration to start to document coding standards. This story goes into the backlog.

Testing: They agree that testing requirements should be kept simple with checks for the existence of files and directories. Because this is easy, they agree that no additional stories are required.

Refactoring: The team is pretty confident that they will be able to complete the first release quickly and that as soon as these three stories are complete, they will clean up and reorganize the code to prepare for additional features.

Collective Code Ownership: Because the team is working closely together, they decide to use a trunk-based development approach rather than merging branches into the main codebase. Everyone's work will be in a shared repository.

Continuous Integration: The team agrees that they will be demoing in this first MVP iteration. The continuous integration functionality will require future stories.

AS A DEVELOPMENT TEAM
I NEED TO HAVE A LEGIBLE CODE BASE
IN ORDER TO MAKE IT EASIER TO CREATE, REFACTOR, AND MODIFY IN THE FUTURE.

GIVEN A SET OF CODE
WHEN THAT CODE IS WRITTEN
THEN IT WILL FOLLOW OUR CODING STANDARDS

NOTE: DIFFERENT STANDARDS FOR TYPES OF CODE (PYTHON, SQL, SHELL)? RESEARCH LINTERS AND CODE FORMATTERS?

AS A DEVELOPMENT TEAM
I NEED TO BE ABLE TO RELIABLY AND AUTOMATICALLY DELIVER CODE TO PRODUCTION.
IN ORDER TO ELIMINATE MANUAL AND ERROR-PRONE TASKS.

GIVEN A SET OF COMMITTED CODE
AND A CODE REPOSITORY
WHEN THAT CODE IS COMMITTED
THEN ASSESSED FOR STANDARDS COMPLIANCE (BUILD - LINT, PARSED)
AND COMBINED INTO WORKING CODE (BUILD - COMPILE)
AND ALL UNIT TEST WILL BE RUN AND MUST PASS (TEST)
AND ANY REQUIRED INFRASTRUCTURE CHANGES WILL BE EXECUTED (DEPLOY)
AND DEPLOYED TO AN INTEGRATION ENVIRONMENT (RELEASE)
AND ALL INTEGRATION TEST WILL BE RUN AND MUST PASS (TEST)
AND ALL PERFORMANCE TEST WILL BE RUN AND MUST PASS (TEST)
AND ANY REQUIRED INFRASTRUCTURE CHANGES WILL BE EXECUTED (DEPLOY)
AND WILL DEPLOY CODE TO PRODUCTION (DEPLOY)

NOTE: NEED TO SPLIT INTO MULTIPLE STEPS?

Team Size as a Core Strategy

The practice of pair programming establishes a minimum team size of two people. However, any significant project requires more people working on it as the number of features expands over time. Ignoring the earlier advice to avoid doing things the big Internet companies do, the agile advice about team size has now expanded to follow the Amazon rule of two pizza teams.[57] This means that to maintain optimal productivity, teams should keep their size down to what two (large) pizzas can feed. The reason for this comes down to the overhead of keeping everyone in the loop.

N = THE NUMBER OF PEOPLE
N(N-1)/2 = THE NUMBER OF LINKS BETWEEN PEOPLE

2 (2-1)/2 = 1 (1 PERSON ONLY NEEDS TO TALK TO 1 OTHER PERSON.)

3 (3-1)/2 = 3 (THERE ARE NOW THREE LINKS TO BE MAINTAINED.)
{A - B;
A - C;
B - C}

5 (5-1)/2 = 10 (SEEMS REASONABLE.)

8 (8-1)/2 = 28 (STILL NOT TOO BAD, BUT SOME PEOPLE ARE NOW BEING LEFT OUT.)

21 (21-1)/2 = 210 (COGNITIVE LOADING MAKES IT IMPOSSIBLE TO UNDERSTAND MOST OF THE DETAILS).

34 (34-1)/2 = 561 (THE MAJORITY ARE LEFT OUT OF THE COMMUNICATION.)

150 (150-1)/2 = 11175 (NO POSSIBLE WAY TO COMMUNICATE EVERYTHING. BUT THERE CAN STILL BE A COHESIVE GROUP.)

Dunbar number calculation

Maintaining social ties requires a great deal of effort, and as a result, you end up with layers of social relationships.[58] Robin Dunbar's research posits that you can have around five close intimate friends because maintaining those relationships is costly.

One interesting side note in his research is that the key for maintaining those relationships for women is communication, and for men, it is shared activity! Keep this in mind when working through communication problems. Perhaps the solution might be to break up a large team into smaller groups of 5-8 people to improve the value of the communication and at the same time allow focused interaction around a clear activity.

Technology Strategies

With the proper values and practices, Amazon has shown that small teams can scale up and work across the product life cycle. They accomplish this by ensuring that their two-pizza teams own and are responsible for their product through the entire life cycle. As a result, products are intentionally kept small enough for the team to support them. This artificial limitation requires each of these small products to support communications with other products from the start.

Isn't this applying a *one-size-fits-all* strategy across the product life cycle? No. The earlier distinction of using agile, Lean, and Six Sigma still apply. In an earlier product life cycle diagram, we assigned the value chain sub-components to their respective phase and treated each sub-component separately. Multiple product life cycle phases do not mean that there are separate teams for each phase. The same team will apply different techniques to maximize the value, depending on where a product (sub-component) is in its life cycle.

Microservices

In short, the microservices architectural style is an approach to developing a single application as a suite of small services, each running in its process and communicating with lightweight mechanisms, often HTTP. These services are built around business capabilities and independently deployable by fully automated deployment machinery. There is a bare minimum of centralized management of these services, which may be written in different programming languages and use different data storage technologies.

- Martin Fowler[59]

Rather than having one large product which does many things, a more agile (as in agility and resilience) approach is to build many small interoperable components which can be combined to deliver a larger service. This is commonly referred to as the *microservices architecture.*

Traditionally, big applications (and smaller ones too) are self-contained and deliver broad functionality. They typically have a user interface, an application tier, and a database tier. If they integrate with other systems, it is either within a suite from the same vendor (e.g., SAP) or unofficially through an ESB or direct database connections. These applications are *monoliths*. From a deployment perspective, the monolithic application is a single entity. Seldom does an upgrade to the application not affect the database and user interface. This application complexity is not a problem in smaller applications, but as applications and organizations scale, this becomes a significant constraint to delivering changes quickly.

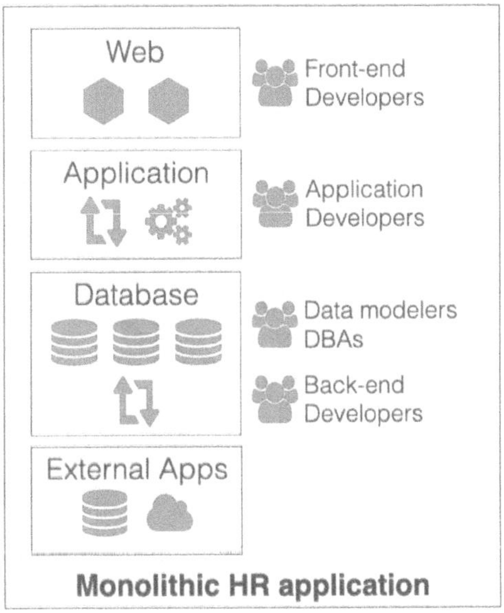

Monolith

Managing monolithic applications is further complicated in large companies because the support and development teams are often grouped by application tiers. In the most dramatic example, entire development teams may support multiple, unrelated applications.

The problem of the monolith applies to business intelligence and infrastructure functions as well. The default organizational response to complexity and size is to group people into dedicated roles and then split applications up the same way. Shared applications become common services and, even within application teams, you have roles like front-end and back-end developer. This organizational structure is not necessarily a problem, but it can impair flexibility and delivery.

Any organization that designs a system (defined broadly) will produce a design whose structure is a copy of the organization's communication structure.
- Mel Conway[60]

Breaking the Monolith

What then is an alternative structure? Align developers to customers and focus on delivering purposeful, small, flexible, composable, and compostable applications: one team, one service, total responsibility.

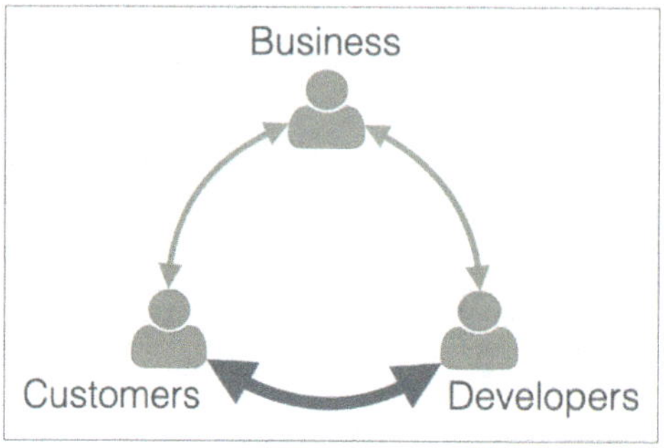

Developers, business, and customers

Small team size is the key. Small teams are better able to communicate with the customer and each other. The increased communication directly translates into agility to respond to changes; it instills ownership in the end product. The catch is that the complexity of products may limit how much small teams can produce. However, in an organization developing microservices, this is an advantage.

Consider the situation where a company wants to migrate from a dedicated local HR application to a hosted HR suite. There will likely be missing functionality in the new application, and as a result, a hard cut-over will be impossible. How can this be addressed? First, look at the required functionality. Perhaps the new application doesn't offer time recording as a feature. Acknowledge this fact, and prioritize attendance as an important business service. Second, dedicate a small team to the problem and focus on creating the best attendance system possible, as quickly as possible.

This team has complete ownership of the solution and the authority to work with all key customers. Most importantly, they own this service going forward. Utilizing another hosted service or writing their own is their decision.[61]

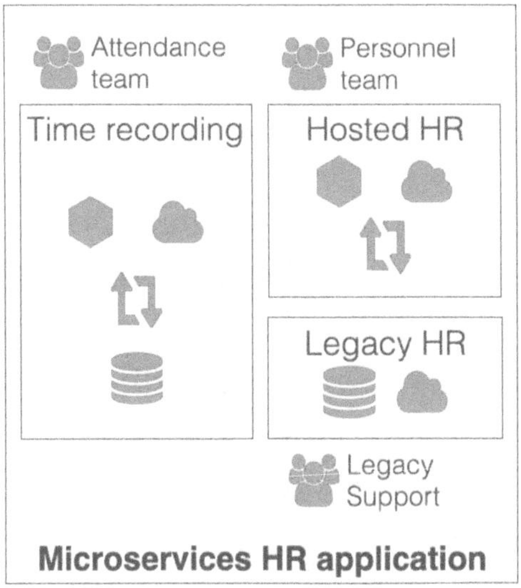

Microservice HR application

One of the key attributes of the microservices architecture is that every service is composable. Composability means that a service exposes key functionality to other services in a way that is stable, well-documented, and easy to interface with. Legibility makes it possible to consistently leverage the functionality in other services. Ease of use means that it is simple to build new services. For instance, it may now be trivial for a team to build "find a back-up service" by integrating multiple services into something new.

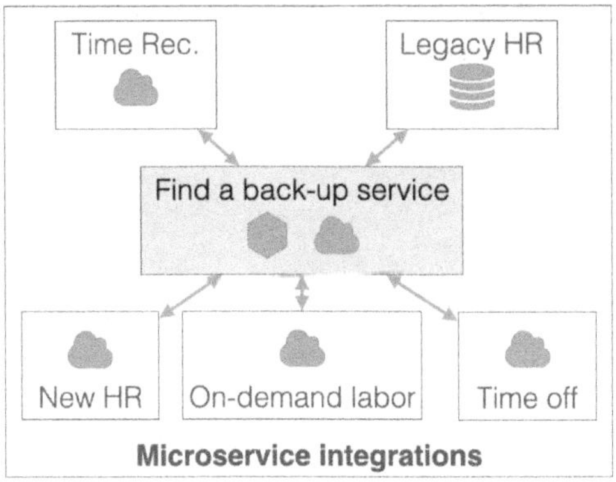

Microservice integrations

The final attribute, compostability, refers to the fact that these small, discrete services are under constant revision, and when they are no longer needed, they are turned off. It also refers to the ability to dynamically scale to meet consumer demand, increasing and decreasing the number of nodes as needed.

Unfortunately, microservices are not the answer to every problem. The added complexity is not appropriate for the initial versions of a product. It is much easier to build initial versions as monoliths. It is hard to imagine that Amazon started this way.

> *Amazon.com started ten years ago as a monolithic application, running on a Web server, talking to a database on the back end. This application, dubbed Obidos, evolved to hold all the business logic, all the display logic, and all the functionality that Amazon eventually became famous for similarities, recommendations, Listmania, reviews, etc. This went on until 2001, when it became clear that the front-end application couldn't scale anymore.*
> *- Werner Vogels*[62]

However, there are key design decisions we can comfortably make in early versions that make breaking up the monolith much easier in the future.[63]

DevOps

This feedback loop is the key motivation behind the DevOps movement. In practice, though, it isn't enough to tell a development team that they are free to build the best service using any tool they want and that support is up to them. Successful implementation of a continuous deployment pipeline requires many integrated tools and processes. Furthermore, these systems must be as automated as possible. If successfully implemented, the cycle time for a release can be brought down from months, typically, in monolithic corporate systems, to hours or less.[64]

Giving developers operational responsibilities has greatly enhanced the quality of the services, both from a customer and a technology point of view. The traditional model is that you take your software to the wall that separates development and operations, throw it over and then forget about it. Not at Amazon. You build it; you run it. Developers are in constant day-to-day contact with their customers and the operation of their products. This customer feedback loop is essential for improving the quality of the service.

You build it, you run it.
- Werner Vogles[65]

Common services have a place in a DevOps environment. However, they should supply the core server, networking, security, management infrastructure, and tooling to support the Continuous Build and Integration processes. The list of these required additional services is overwhelming. Still, the DevOps-centric development frameworks pre-integrate with many more common support tools such as GitHub for the code repository, and AWS AMI or Docker Hub for the image repository. The more mature frameworks have easy-to-use build, integration, and testing pipelines as well.[66]

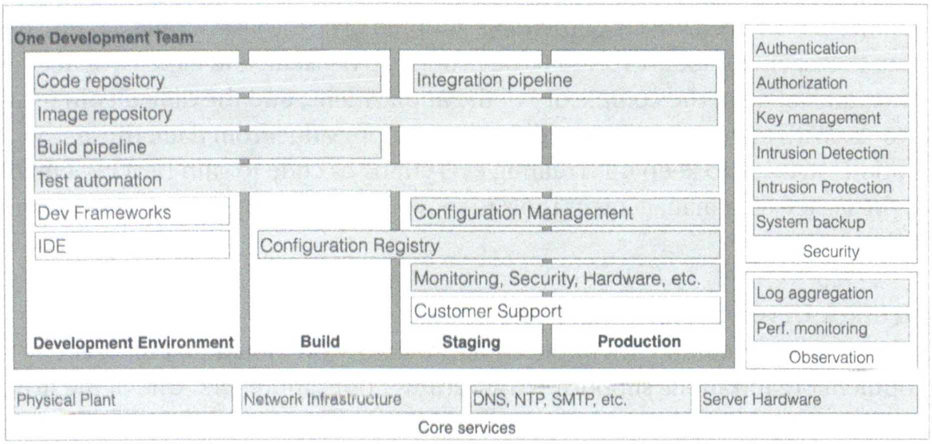

DevOps core services

One word of caution: if you are in the experimentation phase, many of these integration tasks can and should be done manually. The goal is to improve the product to the point where you need the underlying automation. Until then, you don't need to solve these problems. Fortunately, the common infrastructure support applications scale up well and support a high degree of interoperability. As a result, changing a monitoring and logging framework at a later date may have little impact on an application.

You don't have that problem yet.
- Anonymous

Creating a DevOps environment from scratch is a daunting task requiring many people with a wide range of skill sets and a significant investment. Fortunately, developers can handle these tasks with monolithic early versions at the early stages of a product, given the right development strategy and tools.

A phrase you may hear but can safely ignore is DataOps. Analytic models, business logic, database schema, ETL code, and data visualizations are all code that can be developed and deployed incrementally. Data sets need to be assembled (build), the business logic needs to be executed (run), data errors need to be found (test), and data needs to be removed (clean). Application developers have developed robust methods to address these issues, and there is no reason to reinvent the wheel.

One cynical word of caution about DataOps: many of the issues with data management (slow response to change, poor resiliency, poor scalability, specialized skill requirements) are artifacts of the tools adopted over the last decades. Databases and data management tools evolved to be proprietary, visual, and expensive due to the inherent value of data, the complexity of the applications, and the difficulty in using those tools. With an accelerating need to extract more value from data, those applications struggle to keep up. Treating everything as code to gain DevOps' benefits forces the legacy data management tools to move into the Exit phase of their product life cycles.

Full Stack Development

Looking at the monolithic HR application previously, we noted that different development organizations supported the various application tiers. One of the drivers for this differentiation is that each application tier is written in a different and unrelated language. While a senior developer may be fluent in more than one language, this is unlikely for a junior developer.

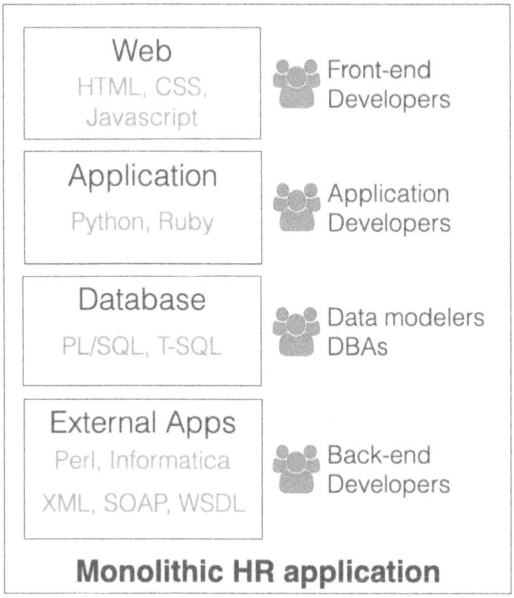

Monolithic development teams

There is a better solution to this issue. Due to advances in the JavaScript language, notably Node.js, it is now possible to write an entire application in one language, JavaScript. When this is coupled with a database that provides a native JavaScript interface, any developer can now participate in the delivery of new features within any portion of the application, at any time, with minimal disruption to the team. The benefit of this cannot be over-emphasized. Having one central language means that you have one unified development team who can take full responsibility for the application they have built.

Having a unified development stack means that support is greatly simplified. Node applications are inherently scalable, and Full Stack frameworks like AngularJS, Ember, Hapi, and Meteor support the development of everything from functional MVP web applications to world-class consumer e-commerce sites.[67] There is even a framework for building cross-platform desktop applications (nwjs.io)[68] and for converting these applications to native mobile apps (PhoneGap).[69]

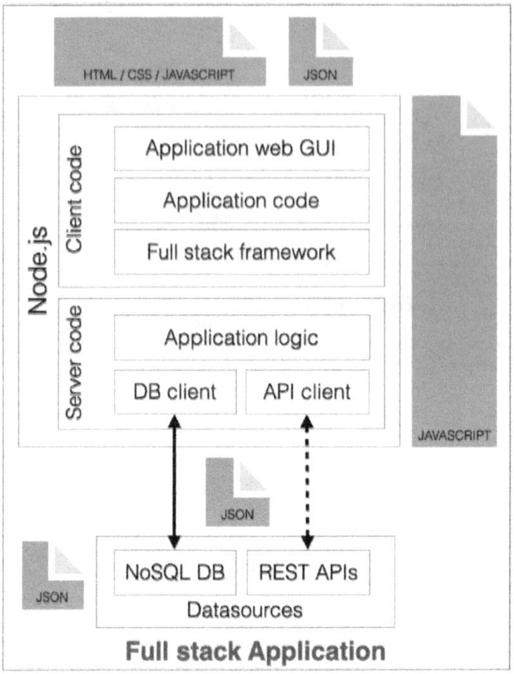

Full-Stack development

Under the covers, the web interface is traditional HTML, CSS, and JavaScript. Data exchanged with the server is in the standard JavaScript Object Notation (JSON) format. On the server side, all code is written in JavaScript. This provides an interesting advantage for a developer. It is not only possible, but it is a best practice to reuse server-side code on the client and vice versa.

Consider validation. It is now possible to write one validation function and execute it on the client to a pre-validate form input, then use the same code to validate the data before writing it to the server and again when reading data from the server and sending it to the user's browser or to another application through an application programming interface (API).

If you are familiar with traditional web applications, you might be wondering where the web server is. In a Node-based application, Node *is* the web server. Part of your application includes writing the server, yet another simplification to speed development and improve supportability.

```
var Hapi = require('hapi');

var server = new Hapi.Server();
server.connection({ port: 3000 });

server.route({
    method: 'GET',
    path: '/',
    handler: function (request, reply) {
        reply('Hello, world!');
    }
});

server.start(function () {
    console.log('Server running at:', server.info.uri);
});
```

A Hapi server

These frameworks, notably hapi.js[70], even support advanced web server features like proxying to allow you to seamlessly redirect traffic. This can redirect legacy web traffic to a new application, a critical technique for successfully breaking up monolithic applications. Another traditional web server feature built into hapi.js is caching. This allows a developer to easily manage complex caching behavior directly within the application without having to manage the configuration on an external web server, greatly simplifying the application architecture.[71]

Servers for Microservices

If large monolithic applications can be broken down into smaller microservices, you might want to break up large servers and virtual machines into even smaller servers.

Hypervisors

We have long been at a point in time where servers are more powerful than the applications we write. This presents a problem. How can we subdivide a server into smaller portions more properly matched to our capacity requirements? The answer is server virtualization. Virtualization offers the ability to locate many *guest* servers onto a single host server.

There are two ways to implement this. In type-2 virtualization, a host operating system runs virtualization software, genercically referred to as a hypervisor. The hypervisor is responsible for all of the resources (CPU, memory, and disk) assigned to the virtual machine (VM). Inside of this virtual machine, we have an operating system and associated applications.

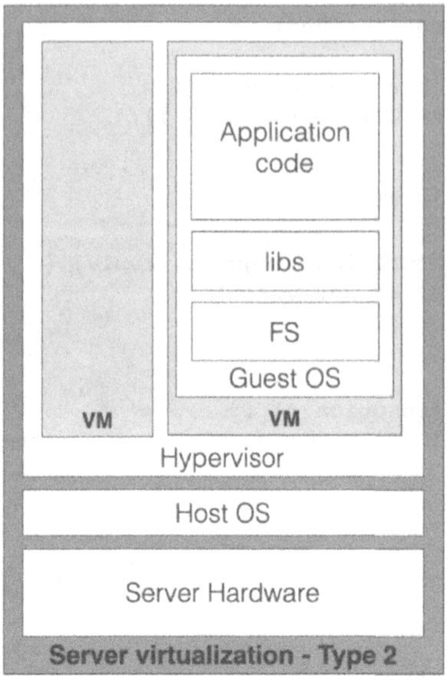

Type-2 VM

In type-1 virtualization, the hypervisor runs directly on the server hardware. In effect, it is a specialized operating system designed to manage virtual machines. The advantage of type-1 virtualization is that it provides more resources to the VM and hence greater server density.

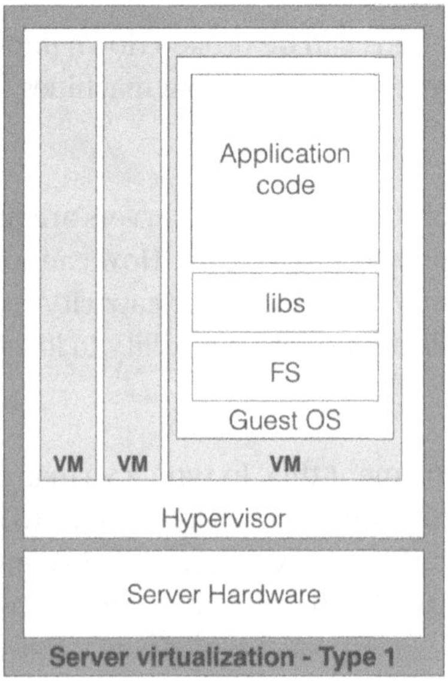

Type 1 VM

From an operations standpoint, virtual machines offer huge benefits: better capacity utilization, easier server provisioning, application isolation, and a familiar support interface (a virtual server resembles a physical server to operations). If the applications are written for it and the hypervisor management systems support it, provisioning a new virtual server can take a matter of minutes.

This is a perk for developers as they gain the ability to provision a server, deploy their code, and then test in a matter of hours. Consistency between the development, staging, and testing environments and extensive automation can cut this process down to minutes. The same goes for environments that can be dynamically scaled. Properly configured VM images can go online in minutes to meet additional demand. This is the way Amazon Web Services Elastic Beanstalk[72] works. However, there is room for dramatic improvement.

Containers

The UNIX-based operating systems have isolated system processes for years. What if you created isolated system processes capable of running a guest operating system, like a VM, but without all the overhead of a hypervisor? What if, rather than having dedicated and isolated system libraries, you shared dependencies and made the system images much smaller? Finally, what if you isolated system dependencies in a way that a container could run on any system?

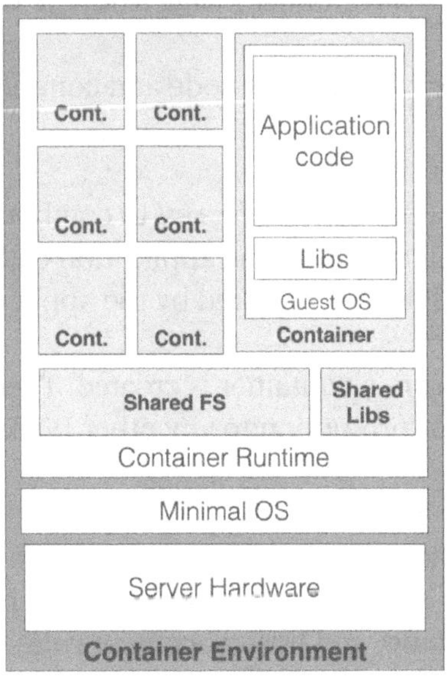

Container box diagram

If you accomplished these things, you would have a Container. Docker[73] is a popular implementation that exposes Linux containers in an incredibly easy-to-use way. A Docker-based development workflow looks like this:

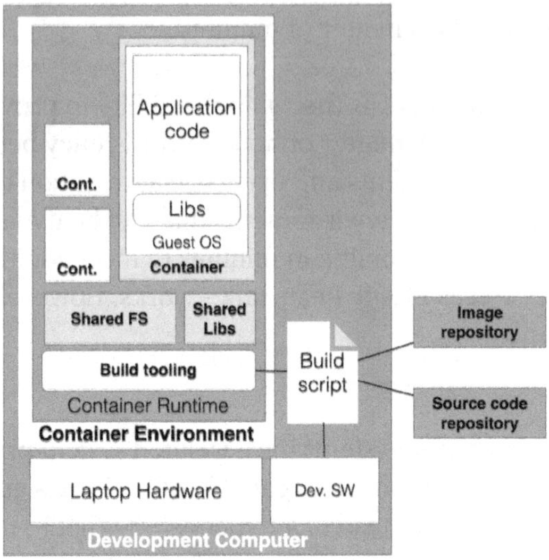

Container workflow

1. The developer downloads a container image from the image repository.

2. The developer writes their application code and commits it to the source code repository.

3. The developer writes a container *build script* to combine the source image, which is a small barebones Linux image, with the application code from the source code repository and any system libraries required by the application.

4. Once this build script is run, a container is created. This can now be uploaded into the image repository for promotion to any other Docker server or used as the basis for other applications.

5. If the application contains multiple applications, then another *composition script* can define how application components are grouped. This can include resource utilization, scaling, networking, and host placement rules. The developers manage both the build and composition scripts in the same source code control application as the application code. This makes it easy for them to manage the entire application life cycle.

6. When it comes time to deploy the application code, all that is required is for the build and composition scripts to be executed and for the build pipeline to deploy the containers to the appropriate servers.

Now, the magic of containers comes into play. Rather than take minutes to deploy on a host server, containers take seconds or less.[74] As a result, it is now feasible to enable fined-grained elastic scaling for every application.

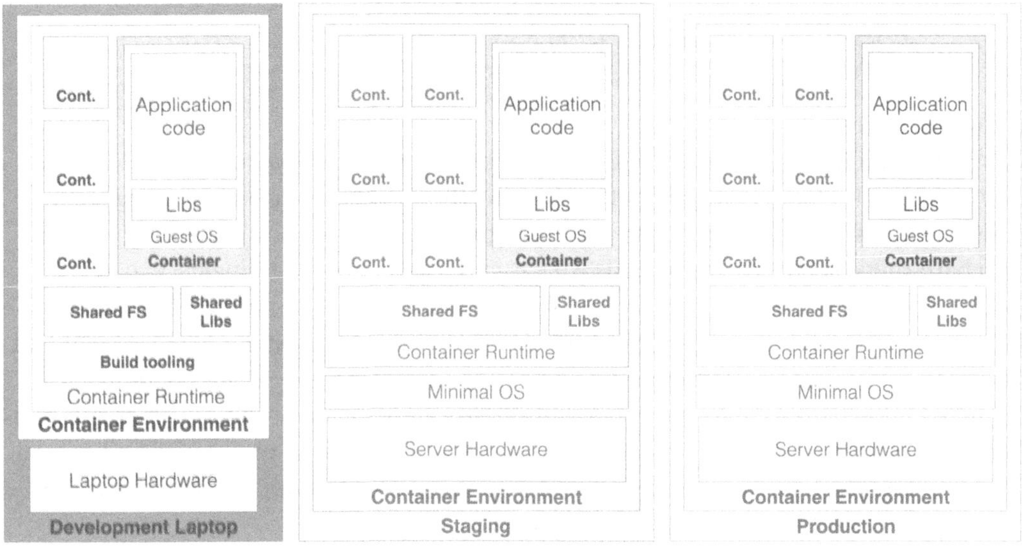

Container development

Containers are small and self-contained, so it is possible to create an application container on a developer laptop and run that same container in staging and production with no configuration changes. As a result, the continuous deployment process is greatly simplified because you no longer need to accommodate different server configurations. This is a miracle for production support because even slight differences in deployment environments can be a troubleshooting nightmare. Not to mention, you now can roll out or roll back different versions of an application in seconds.

This deployment flexibility extends to running containers in multiple container engines simultaneously. You could have containers at Amazon, Google, RackSpace, and a local ISP all running seamlessly! This a Hybrid Cloud[75] that works!

Of all the technologies outlined above, containers are the most recent. The 1.0 version of Docker was released in June 2014, and there have been constant improvements every month. It is a young technology, but this is how all applications will be managed and deployed in the future. As for the production readiness of Linux containers, here is what Google has to say:

> *Everything at Google, from Search to Gmail, is packaged and run in a Linux container. Each week we launch more than 2 billion container instances across our global data centers.*[76]

Microservers

Another radical option is to scale servers down to the workload of the application, using the smallest server capable of supporting the workload. Instead of using small VMs and containers to scale down, use small microservers like the Raspberry Pi (RPI)[77] as a bare-metal server platform. This isn't as crazy as it sounds. A single RPi can be configured to support 4CPU cores, 8GB RAM, 1GbE networking, and NVMe or SSD storage for $200. Because it is a bare-metal server, you can eliminate the overhead and complexity of virtual machines and container run times. This significantly reduces the complexity of the operating environment. Provisioning the environment, in this case, is no more difficult than is required with VMs or Docker. While an unpopular and radical opinion, for internal applications, self-hosting on the smallest appropriate hardware may be the easiest and least expensive option.[78]

Data and Analytics Engineering

As far back as 2014, ThoughtWorks[79] proposed the concept of an *Inverse Conway Maneuver* as a way to use team structure to drive the adoption of a desired architectural state. As discussed above, small independent development teams go hand in hand with the Microservices Architecture pattern.

> *Conway's Law asserts that organizations are constrained to produce application designs which are copies of their communication structures. This often leads to unintended friction points. The 'Inverse Conway Maneuver' recommends evolving your team and organizational structure to promote your desired architecture. Ideally, your technology architecture will display isomorphism with your business architecture.*[80]

Like application developers went from front end, back end, UX, testing, and production support roles to DevOps and full-stack developer roles, the traditional data roles of business analyst, ETL developer, data modeler, and production support can be transitioned into data engineering and analytics engineering roles.

This happens in concert with a move to transition the traditional business intelligence stack into the equivalent of a microservices stack. The transition to a microservices-based analytics platform requires reorganizing the team into more general-purpose roles. Both have a shared focus on data, but because the implementation is different, it will be helpful to initially identify two different roles.

Data Engineer

The first role is Data Engineer[81]. This is a software engineer role focused on building the data infrastructure and moving the data from sources to targets. Data infrastructure includes all the application infrastructure required to support the team's analytics requirements.

In smaller companies, this role has a lot of infrastructure requirements, and it requires recruiting someone with server management experience. If this isn't possible, keeping the infrastructure requirements to a bare minimum will be a necessary. Fortunately, if done properly, this minimum viable infrastructure can meet a surprising range of requirements. In larger companies with more established IT departments, much of the existing infrastructure can be leveraged, be it local or provided as a service. In either case, data engineers work toward building an automation framework that can be shared across multiple analytics products.

The data engineer is also responsible for moving data from various sources to targets as part of product development. This is traditionally the extract and load portion of the ETL flow. This may include performing basic data profiling and implementing the storage of historical data sets in preparation for later analytics. This ensures that the data engineer understands, and has visibility to the data, up to and including the base data sets used by the analytics engineer.

Analytics Engineer

Analytics Engineering[82] combines the traditional BI roles of analyst, ETL developer, DBA, dashboard/report developer, and web developer. The analytics engineer works closely with the data engineer and customer to establish the data and analytic features required for a product. While the data engineering role acquires (extract and load) data from the source systems and people, the analytics engineer manipulates the data into the required form. This includes data modeling, transformation, and building basic analytic models.

The joint responsibilities of these roles include performance monitoring and tuning, as well as developing data services that other products consume. It is important to understand that these roles are fluid and are intended to help structure and expose the types of work being done by the team.

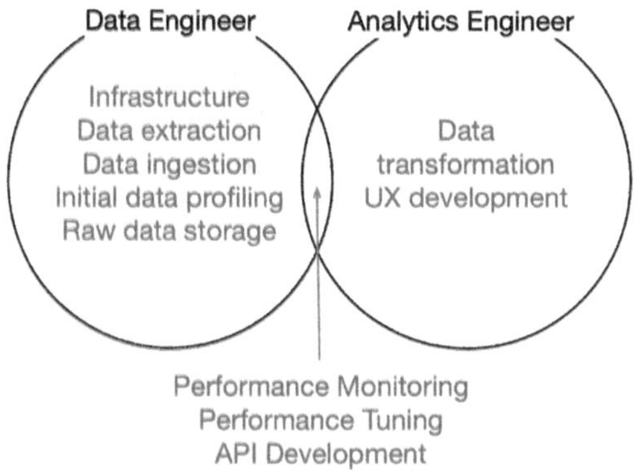

Data and Analytics Venn diagram

[35] Harrington Emerson (https://en.wikipedia.org/wiki/Harrington_Emerson).

[36] TOGAF Architecture Principles, The Open Group Architecture Framework (TOGAF) v9.2, (https://pubs.opengroup.org/architecture/togaf9-doc/arch/chap20.html).

[37] Henry Spencer Usenet signature, November 1987.

[38] The Art of Unix Programming, Raymond, E. S., 2003 (http://catb.org/~esr/writings/taoup/html/philosophychapter.html).

[39] man pipe (https://linux.die.net/man/8/pipe).

[40] Basics of the Unix philosophy (http://catb.org/~esr/writings/taoup/html/ch01s06.html#id2877537).

[41] Eric S. Raymond (https://en.wikipedia.org/wiki/Eric_S._Raymond).

[42] Basics of the Unix philosophy (http://catb.org/~esr/writings/taoup/html/ch01s06.html#id2877537)

[43] For an in-depth look at how this plays out in reality, see: Interoperability: Fix the Internet, Not the Tech Companies, Doctorow, 2019, Electronic Frontier Foundation, (https://www.eff.org/deeplinks/2019/07/interoperability-fix-internet-not-tech-companies).

[44] Applying the Unix Philosophy (http://catb.org/~esr/writings/taoup/html/ch01s08.html).

[45] pipe (https://linux.die.net/man/8/pipe).

[46] tee (https://man7.org/linux/man-pages/man1/tee.1.html).

[47] Over the years, I've seen numerous instances where we have had to resort to using tools like Python, Perl, sed, awk, and diff because ETL software costing hundreds of thousands of dollars could not process our data sets adequately. We hired someone passionate about Regular Expressions to write an ETL application from scratch to process a nasty proprietary server performance file when we couldn't find a commercial ETL application that could decompose the file. A decade later, that application was still faster and easier to use than Informatica.

[48] SQL Server is also liberal in the way it handles timestamps, a marked contrast to the gymnastics you need to perform in Oracle.

[49] The Kimball Group (https://www.kimballgroup.com).

[50] Data Vault Alliance (https://datavaultalliance.com).

[51] Deloitte published an infographic called The Agile Landscape. It's a tube map style visualization covering 21 agile frameworks and 257 tools. I have to assume this was part of a blog post discussing how ridiculous and redundant these frameworks have become. Thankfully it appears that they have removed this from their web site.

[52] Agile Manifesto (https://agilemanifesto.org/).

(https://en.wikipedia.org/wiki/Agile_software_development#The_Agile_Manifesto).

[53] eXtreme Programming eXplained, 2000, Kent Beck, Reading MA, Addison Wesley Longman, Inc. (http://www.extremeprogramming.org)

[54] Groups of diverse problem solvers can outperform groups of high-ability problem solvers, 2004, Hong, L., Page, S. E., PNAS, November 16, 2004, 101 (46) 16385-16389; (https://doi.org/10.1073/pnas.0403723101) (https://www.pnas.org/content/101/46/16385).

Diverse group is the best solution for problem-solving tasks, 2004, Wadley, J., The University Record Online, University of Michigan, (https://www.ur.umich.edu/0405/Nov22_04/23.shtml).

Teams Solve Problems Faster When They're More Cognitively Diverse, 2017, Reynolds, A., Lewis D., Harvard Business Review, (https://hbr.org/2017/03/teams-solve-problems-faster-when-theyre-more-cognitively-diverse).

[55] The original Macintosh team bought Steve Jobs a rubber stamp that said, "This is Shit!" to make it easier for him to comment on design submissions (https://www.asktog.com/columns/082iPad&Mac.html).

[56] Refer to the video in Footnote (https://en.wikipedia.org/wiki/Dunbar%27s_number) for a reference to why face-to-face and Skype interactions are so effective.

[57] Jeff Bezos' 2 Pizza Rule: Why Small Teams Work More Productively (https://blog.bufferapp.com/small-teams-why-startups-often-win-against-google-and-facebook-the-science-behind-why-smaller-teams-get-more-done).

[58] This mathematical relationship is directly reflected in the ideal and maximal group size for primates proposed by anthropologist Robin Dunbar. The natural, biologically limited number of "friends" appears to be 150 people.

Dunbar's Number, (https://en.wikipedia.org/wiki/Dunbar%27s_number)

TEDxObserver - Robin Dunbar - Can the Internet buy you more friends?, 2012, Dunbar, R., TEDx Talks, (https://www.youtube.com/watch?v=07IpED729k8&feature=emb_logo).

[59] Microservices, 2014, Fowler, M., (http://martinfowler.com/articles/microservices.html).

[60] Conway's Law, 1968, Conway M., (http://www.melconway.com/Home/Conways_Law.html).

[61] One of the Open Source tenets is that healthy discussion, debate, and competition are to be encouraged. In the short run, this may lead to duplicate effort, but a better system will evolve out of the struggle to best address the customer's needs in the long run.

[62] This is well worth the read, both as a history and as guidance. If you read only one paper, this interview with Amazon CTO Werner Vogels is the one to read. A Conversation with Werner Vogels - ACM Queue, (http://queue.acm.org/detail.cfm?id=1142065).

[63] Building Microservices provides a thorough overview of microservices and the secondary infrastructure needed to support them in production. (http://www.amazon.com/Building-Microservices-Sam-Newman-ebook/dp/B00T3N7XB4/ref=mt_kindle?_encoding=UTF8&me=).

[64] Challenges in Implementing Microservices by Fred George, (https://www.youtube.com/watch?v=yPf5MfOZPY0).

[65] A Conversation with Werner Vogels - ACM Queue, (http://queue.acm.org/detail.cfm?id=1142065).

[66] Continuous Delivery: Reliable Software Releases through Build, Test, and Deployment Automation is the foundational book on the DevOps process. (http://www.amazon.com/Continuous-Delivery-Deployment-Automation-Addison-Wesley-ebook/dp/B003YMNVC0/).

[67] Hapi Thanksgiving; It is about systems of nodes scaling, not node scaling, (https://medium.com/ben-and-dion/hapi-thanksgiving-it-is-about-systems-of-nodes-scaling-not-node-scaling-5d96d900d904).s

[68] nwjs.io (nwjs.io)

[69] Adobe PhoneGap (https://phonegap.com)

[70] hapi.dev (https://hapi.dev)

[71] Proxying Services With Hapi.js, (http://tech.opentable.co.uk/blog/2014/11/28/proxying-with-hapi/).

Dismantling the monolith - Microsites at Opentable - OpenTable Tech UK Blog, (http://tech.opentable.co.uk/blog/2015/02/09/dismantling-the-monolith-microsites-at-opentable/).

Caching (http://hapijs.com/tutorials/caching).

[72] AWS Elastic Beanstalk (https://aws.amazon.com/elasticbeanstalk/).

[73] Docker (https://www.docker.com/).

[74] Depending on the image size, a container can be spun up and removed in milliseconds. In fact, for certain workloads, it is preferable to spin up a container, run a process, and kill the container each time it is run rather than keep a container running. See: AWS Lambda (https://aws.amazon.com/lambda/).

[75] Hybrid clouds (https://www.thoughtworks.com/radar/platforms/hybrid-clouds).

[76] Google Container Engine is Generally Available, (http://googlecloudplatform.blogspot.com/2015/08/Google-Container-Engine-is-Generally-Available.html).

Kubernetes ([^https://cloud.google.com/kubernetes-engine/).

[77] Raspberry Pi (https://www.raspberrypi.org/products/raspberry-pi-4-model-b/).

[78] Falling from the Sky 2020 Self-Hosting Still Pays, 2020, Kennedy P., Server the Home, (https://www.servethehome.com/falling-from-the-sky-2020-self-hosting-still-pays/).

Benchmarking the Raspberry Pi 4, 2019, Halfacree G., (https://medium.com/@ghalfacree/benchmarking-the-raspberry-pi-4-73e5afbcd54b).

What performance can I expect from using a Raspberry Pi as a web server?, (https://raspberrypi.stackexchange.com/questions/194/what-kind-of-performance-can-i-expect-from-using-a-raspberry-pi-as-a-webserver).

Any research on containers will inevitably lead you down the Kubernetes path. Before you go any further, please spend some time understanding the overhead associated with this application. While it is powerful, remember that *You are not Google* and the overhead may far outweigh the benefits. See The Business Executive's Guide to Kubernetes, 2019. Frazelle, J., (https://blog.jessfraz.com/post/the-business-executives-guide-to-kubernetes/).

Expensify (expensify.com) has an interesting data infrastructure. They are using co-located commodity servers running a custom version of SQLite as their distributed data infrastructure (https://bedrockdb.com). It is worth the time to watch the founder of Expensify, David Barrett, explain the logic behind this decision (https://finovate.com/videos/findevr-silicon-valley-2016-expensify/), (https://www.youtube.com/watch?v=0pu6uZjFmQ4).

[79] Thoughtworks (https://www.thoughtworks.com).

[80] Inverse Conway Maneuver (https://www.thoughtworks.com/radar/techniques/inverse-conway-maneuver).

[81] First coined at Facebook in 2017 by Maxime Beauchemin. The Rise of the Data Engineer, 2017, Beauchemin, M., (https://www.freecodecamp.org/news/the-rise-of-the-data-engineer-91be18f1e603/).

The Downfall of the Data Engineer, 2017, Beauchemin, M., (https://medium.com/@maximebeauchemin/the-downfall-of-the-data-engineer-5bfb701e5d6b).

[82] When did analytics engineering become a thing? And why?, 2019, Carroll, C., (https://blog.getdbt.com/what-is-an-analytics-engineer/).

Chapter 3: Data Engineering

Sebastian: *Well, I am standing water.*
Antonio: *I'll teach you how to flow.*
Sebastian: *Do so: to ebb. Hereditary sloth instructs me.*
- William Shakespeare[83]

Data engineers make sure the plumbing is in place and functions correctly. They move the data into the analytics systems and set up those systems. This chapter covers a little history, and by the end, we will build, test, and run a robust data pipeline on our own.

The Data Pipeline

Data analytics work involves repetitively executing many tasks. This is simple if the tasks are strictly serial. However, most jobs have dependencies.

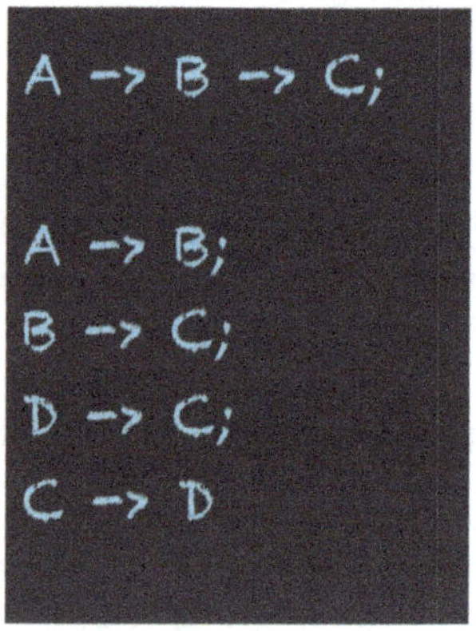

Dependency graph

If the dependencies are simple and the tasks are executed infrequently, it isn't necessary to do anything more complicated than running them manually. However, if the dependencies are complex or there are many steps, then consider adding automation. Once you make the shift to test-driven development (TDD), where you write tests before writing the code, you must have automation in place, even for simple serial workflows.

First Generation Data Management: ETL

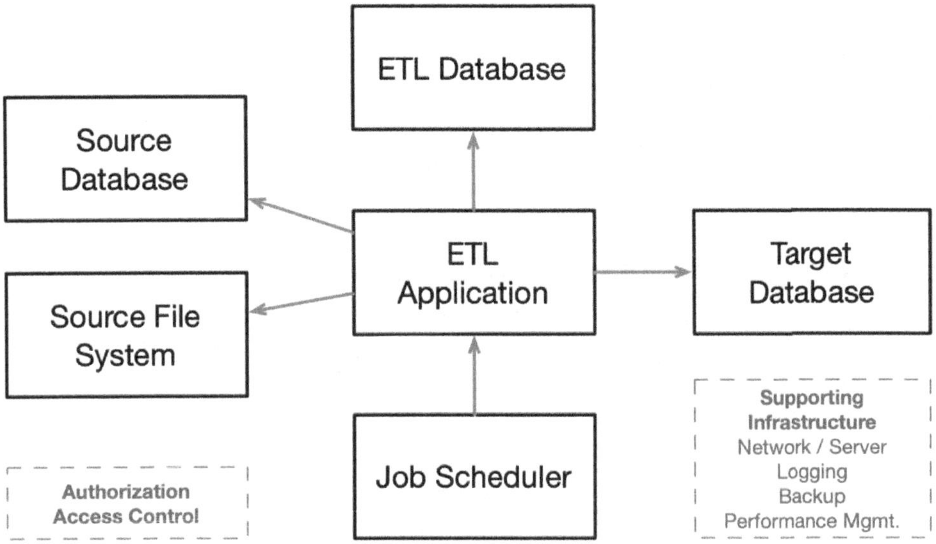

ETL Architecture

In the traditional data management space, we look to extract, transform, and load (ETL) tools to accomplish this. An entire industry is built around these complicated GUI-based ETL tools.[84]

One of the crucial things to understand about ETL applications is that they originated to meet the needs of data warehouse developers who were building under a specific design and implementation pattern, the star schema data warehouse.[85] In this pattern, data is extracted from source systems or a persistent staging area that mimics the source data structure, transforming it into fact and dimensional tables, and then loading it into a data mart in a database. Little to none of the transformation occurs in the database itself.

This is a historical artifact caused by the lack of features in early relational databases. Because they had limited storage capacity and could not perform complex aggregation grouping, date, or logical functions, it was necessary to implement this complex logic outside the database in an external application. This application needs to extract multiple data sets, store them in memory, apply complicated transformational logic, and then write the resulting data set into an external database requires infrastructure that is more complex than the target database. As a result, the software, hardware, and specialized dedicated support staff require significant investments in both capital and ongoing expenses.

These traditional ETL tools removed the complexity of the underlying code by giving developers an easy-to-use *drag and drop* interface to build complicated workflows. Theoretically, this made ETL jobs easy to develop and supportable by low-skilled analysts. For simple workflows, this holds true. The model holds up as long as the transformation logic is straightforward and can be done with tools provided within the application. Complex will require someone to write additional code using the proprietary application transformation language. Unfortunately, this now moves the support into the hands of specialized ETL developers.

Second Generation: Workflow Orchestration

As both data warehouse designs and the underlying databases have matured, the shortcomings of traditional ETL tools have necessitated new applications built to support new data integration workflows.

The first significant change is that databases themselves have evolved beyond basic relational data stores. All modern relational databases support complex Structured Query Language (SQL) statements such as common table expressions and window functions. These allow aggregations on complicated subsets of data, extensive support for complex date and time logic, and efficient indexing schemes to make queries faster. Most relational databases natively support non-tabular data structures like JSON and key-value pairs, eliminating the need for separate document databases like MongoDB.

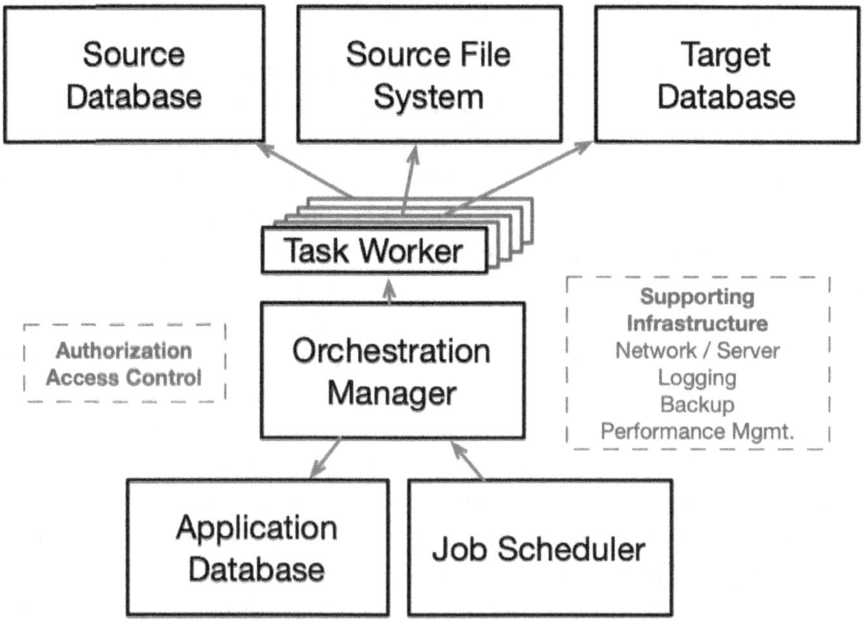

Airflow Architecture block diagram

The second major change is that databases have moved to the cloud. This creates numerous options to use specialized databases provided by Amazon[86], Google[87], Microsoft[88], Snowflake[89], and hosted versions of traditional databases like SQL Server and PostgreSQL. To further complicate matters, managing multiple databases means you can now break up data infrastructure into smaller, more easily tuned systems. This new multi-database and multi-platform data environment requires data flows that are multi-source and multi-target. Unfortunately, the management of dependencies across a diverse environment requires significant configuration and customization in the traditional ETL tools. Furthermore, the basic architecture of first-generation systems is fatally flawed because it requires transforming the movement of data into and out of source systems. Modern data architectures are just too complex to require this level of data movement.

One way to address this complexity is to clearly separate the extraction and load responsibilities from the transformation process. The vast majority of traditional transformations now occur inside the database, using native database functionality. All the workflow orchestration application needs to do is execute the query at the right time or when the right conditions have been met. Superficially, this is similar to implementing stored procedures, but without the dependence on the database-specific procedural language or the limitation of being executable within a single database. Any transformation that can be expressed as a SQL query can be executed by the database as a query triggered from the workflow engine. In cases where the logic exceeds the capabilities of SQL, such as a machine learning model in Python, it can be implemented in the workflow alongside SQL. As a result, all extraction, loading, and transformation code is now actual code rather than proprietary application logic.

Now that all the Extract Load Transform (ELT) tasks are handled as code, you can apply standard software development discipline. Applications like Apache Airflow[90] and Luigi[91] paved the way by providing an application to manage complex workflows across complex environments while still using code.

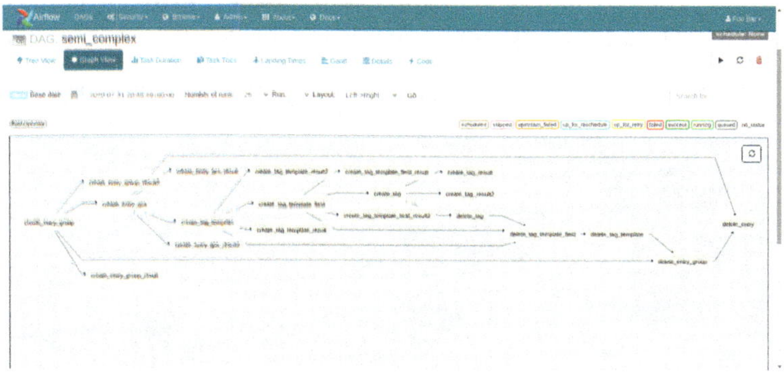

Apache Airflow GUI

Third Generation: DevOps for Data

While second-generation ELT tools broke the dependency on Graphical User Interface (GUI) applications, and network and memory-intensive monolithic ETL tools, they rely on application-specific Python dialects to express the tasks and dependencies.

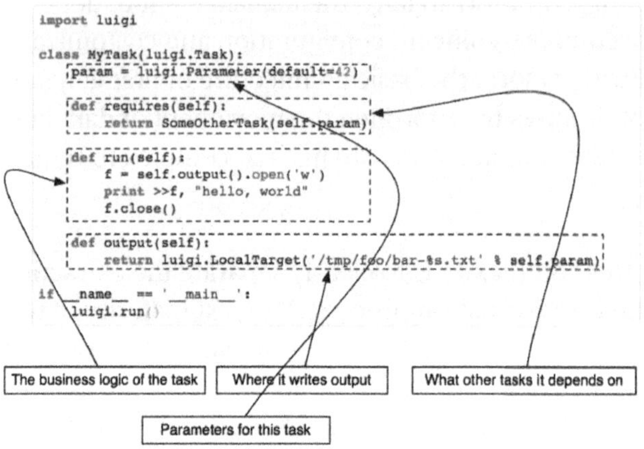

Python based task breakdown - Luigi

Newer 3rd Generation tools like dbt (Data Build Tool)[92] operate as full-featured applications. They manage data with the same level of engineering discipline as any other software application.

In practice, this means:

- Treating everything as code, including integration with version control systems.
- Writing and executing tests.
- Implementing configuration management for the environment.
- Managing schemas as part of the application rather than managing Data Definition Language (DLL) scripts in an external application like FlyWay[93] or Liquibase.[94]
- Implementing a build, test, deploy, run, clean workflow.

dbt Block Diagram

While the build, test, deploy, run, clean workflow executes the extract, load, and run process, it forces the developer to think more holistically about their entire data application. What is required to ***build*** the environment the way we need it (configuration management/set up)? Is there data we need to be in place before anything else (seed)? How would we know? We would execute ***tests*** to ensure everything is set up as needed and that we have everything necessary to execute the extractions, loads, and transformations. Once we have all the prerequisites, we ***deploy (install)*** the workflow to meet the application requirements. This includes successfully passing all integration tests and updating application documentation. Day-to-day operations are part of ongoing ***run*** tasks. These are the traditional ELT tasks and dependencies. Finally, the ***clean*** process is run to clean up stale data sets, temporary tables, and unneeded source data.

This shift encourages the developer to think of the application life cycle from the start of development through daily operations, making it easier to incrementally update and refactor the application in the future. It becomes easy to integrate tests to confirm that new features meet their requirements and have not broken any existing functionality. Data applications can be broken down into smaller independent data applications and referenced as dependencies in other code packages. The development team now has full visibility and responsibility for the entire data product.

dbt would be considered a Continuous Integration / Continuous Deployment (CI/CD) tool in the DevOps world,[95] much like Jenkins[96] or Bamboo.[97]

Continuous Integration is a software development practice where members of a team integrate their work frequently, usually each person integrates at least daily - leading to multiple integrations per day. Each integration is verified by an automated build (including test) to detect integration errors as quickly as possible. Many teams find that this approach leads to significantly reduced integration problems and allow a team to develop cohesive software more rapidly.
- Martin Fowler[98]

Continuous Integration allows the development team to focus on the iterative development of new features because the team is automating much of the tedious and error-prone tasks involved with building and testing software. Consistent and constant building and testing of the solution gives the team confidence to quickly modify the system and run it without defects.

The run phase of the process is slightly different for data products. "Running" in this case means day-to-day data management, extracting data sets, loading tables, updating the tables, and publishing data sets. As a result, there may be software development like core pipelines that manage the structure of the data product and separate operational data pipelines that resemble ELT pipelines.

Back to the Future: a Brief Introduction to the BASH Shell and MAKE

CI/CD for complex software projects was implemented long before Jenkins. If you have spent any time working in Linux or other UNIX derivatives, you will have inevitably had to make software. This command is using the Make application to execute all the steps required to compile and install an application from its source code.[99]

For instance, here is the procedure to install the SQLite database once the source files have been downloaded.[100]

```
./configure --prefix=/usr/local
make
make install
```

These commands spare you from having to run and understand the actual compile command.

```
gcc -Os -I. -DSQLITE_THREADSAFE=0 -DSQLITE_ENABLE_FTS4 \
   -DSQLITE_ENABLE_FTS5 -DSQLITE_ENABLE_JSON1 \
   -DSQLITE_ENABLE_RTREE -DSQLITE_ENABLE_EXPLAIN_COMMENTS \
   -DHAVE_USLEEP -DHAVE_READLINE \
   shell.c sqlite3.c -ldl -lreadline -lncurses -o sqlite3
```

What Make does is execute a set of tasks in the correct order while honoring each dependency. It is configured using a simple text file at the root of the project folder called `makefile`, although the developer can choose to name it something else.

```
<target>: <dependency>
[tab] <recipe>
```

The structure of the file is simple. Each task is defined by a set of rules with a specific but straightforward form.

The `<target>` is the name of the task. Traditionally, Make is meant to work with files in a directory, so the target is typically the name of the output file. The `<dependency>` is a list of one or more prerequisite `<tasks>` which must be successfully run before the `<recipe>` is run to build the `<target>`.

```
as_you_like_it.txt: spell_check
  CAT \
  as_you_like_it_001.txt \
  as_you_like_it_002.txt \
  > as_you_like_it.txt
```

NOTE: The structure of a makefile `<recipe>` must be preceded by a [tab] character. If you use `[spaces]`, you will see a `*** missing separator.` error.

Let's look at a simple example:

1. `as_you_like_it.txt:` is the name of the file being produced by the recipe.
2. `as_you_like_it_001.txt as_you_like_it_002.txt` is the name of the recipes that need to be completed before this recipe is executed.
3. This is a Command-Line Instruction (CLI) shell statement that combines two files in the order they are called and then writes out the target file. The backslash character \ allows you to wrap a single line command onto the next line for readability.

```
CAT \
  as_you_like_it_001.txt \
  as_you_like_it_002.txt \
  > as_you_like_it.txt
```

as_you_like_it_001.txt:

```
Alllll the world's a stage,
And all the men and women merely players;
They have their exits and their entrances,
And one man in his time plays many parts,
His acts being seven ages.
```

as_you_like_it_002.txt:

```
At first, the infant,
Mewling and puking in the nurse's arms.
Then the whining schoolboy, with his satchel
And shining morning face, creeping like snail
Unwillingly to school.
```

Now, let's look at the dependency:

```
spell_check:
  aspell -c as_you_like_it_001.txt
```

This recipe is simple. When the `spell_check` task is called, run the `aspell -c as_you_like_it_001.txt` command. If you run this command by itself, it looks like this:

```
aspell -c as_you_like_it_001.txt
```

```
Alllll the world's a stage,
And all the men and women merely players;
They have their exits and their entrances,
And one man in his time plays many parts,
His acts being seven ages.



1) All                              6) Alley
2) Ally                             7) Allow
3) Allah                            8) Alloy
4) Allie                            9) Allele
5) Allay                            0) AL
i) Ignore                           I) Ignore all
r) Replace                          R) Replace all
a) Add                              l) Add Lower
b) Abort                            x) Exit

?
```

Putting it all together, this simple makefile would look like this:

simple_makefile/makefile file contents:

```
as_you_like_it.txt: spell_check
  CAT \
  as_you_like_it_001.txt \
  as_you_like_it_002.txt \
  > as_you_like_it.txt

spell_check:
  aspell -c as_you_like_it_001.txt
```

Try to execute the file by running `make` using a terminal window inside the directory. The first screen you will see is from the spell_check recipe. This is identical to the command you ran earlier. Select `1) All` to correct the misspelling in the file. The output of the terminal will now look like this:

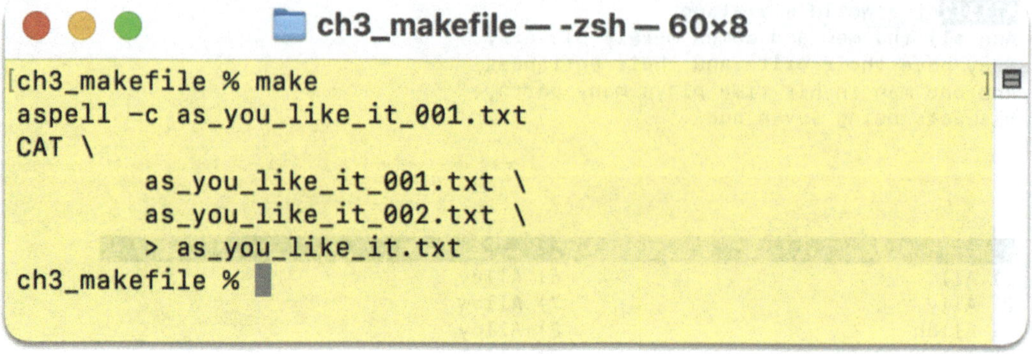

Make outputs the results of each script to the terminal window as it is being executed. In this case, it ran the `aspell -c as_you_like_it_001.txt` command, then `cat as_you_like_it_001.txt as_you_like_it_002.txt > as_you_like_it.txt`

NOTE: The BASH shell (terminal) normally outputs the results of a command to the terminal window. This is referred to as STDOUT (Standard Output). In the example above, we are using the special command > to output the results to a file. In this case, the > command creates the file if it doesn't exist. If the file does exist, the command replaces it with the output of the script. If you want to append the output of the script to the file, use the >> command.[101]

If you run the command `ls` you will see the file `as_you_like_it.txt.`

Running the command `nano as_you_like_it.txt` opens the nano text editor. `[ctrl]+[x]` will exit out of the editor without saving.

```
ch3_makefile — nano as_you_like_it.txt — 60×17

  GNU nano 2.0.6     File: as_you_like_it.txt

All the world's a stage,
And all the men and women merely players;
They have their exits and their entrances,
And one man in his time plays many parts,
His acts being seven ages.
At first, the infant,
Mewling and puking in the nurse's arms.
Then the whining schoolboy, with his satchel
And shining morning face, creeping like snail
Unwillingly to school.



^G Get Hel^O WriteOu^R Read Fi^Y Prev Pa^K Cut Tex^C Cur Pos
^X Exit   ^J Justify^W Where I^V Next Pa^U UnCut T^T To Spel
```

Alternatively, you can run the `cat as_you_like_it.txt` command to read the file, this time by sending it to STDOUT.

```
ch3_makefile — -zsh — 60×13

ch3_makefile % cat as_you_like_it.txt
All the world's a stage,
And all the men and women merely players;
They have their exits and their entrances,
And one man in his time plays many parts,
His acts being seven ages.
At first, the infant,
Mewling and puking in the nurse's arms.
Then the whining schoolboy, with his satchel
And shining morning face, creeping like snail
Unwillingly to school.
ch3_makefile %
```

Let's add the `aspell -c as_you_like_it_002.txt` to the makefile to spell check the next file. Running `make` again returns what you would expect.

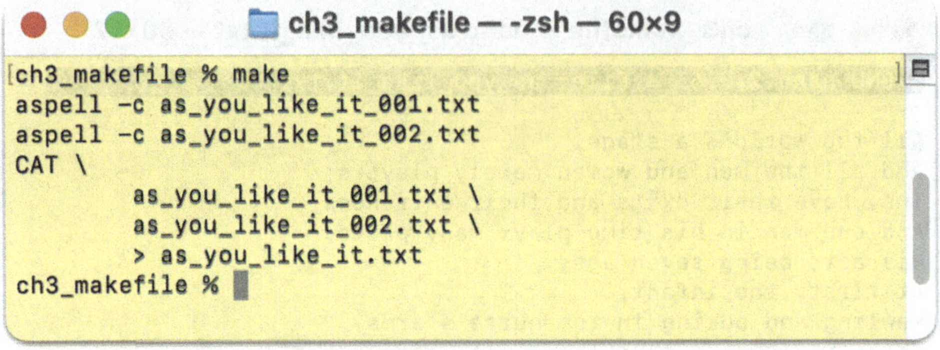

When `make` runs, we see the results of each of the recipes in the output. Notice that the dependencies are all run before the `as_you_like_it.txt` target.

Now we will modify the makefile and append a new file by adding a new line to the CAT recipe.

```
as_you_like_it.txt: spell_check
  CAT \
  as_you_like_it_001.txt \
  as_you_like_it_002.txt \
  new_file_003.txt \
  > as_you_like_it.txt

spell_check:
  aspell -c as_you_like_it_001.txt
  aspell -c as_you_like_it_002.txt
```

Rerunning `make` returns an error because the file we are adding does not exist yet. Read this error from the bottom up:

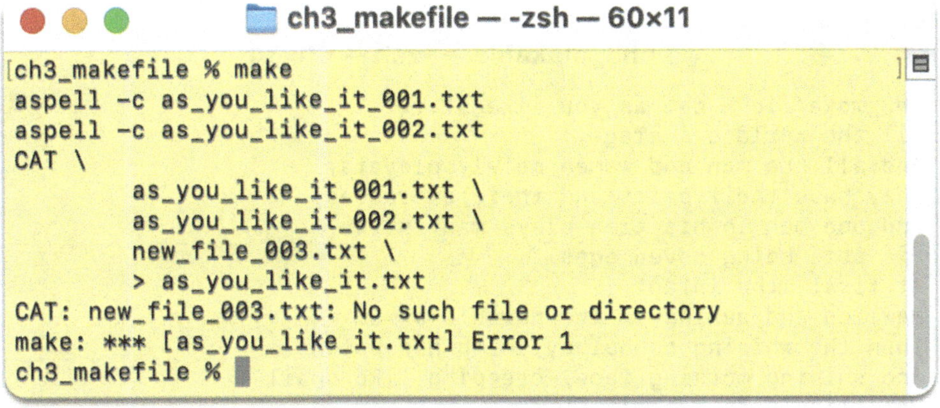

1. There is an error in the `[as_you_like_it.txt]` target.
2. It was thrown by the `CAT` command.
3. No such file or directory - `new_file_003.txt`

Now, create a new file in the directory from the terminal.

```
echo 'some more text\n' > new_file_003.txt
```

```
ls
```

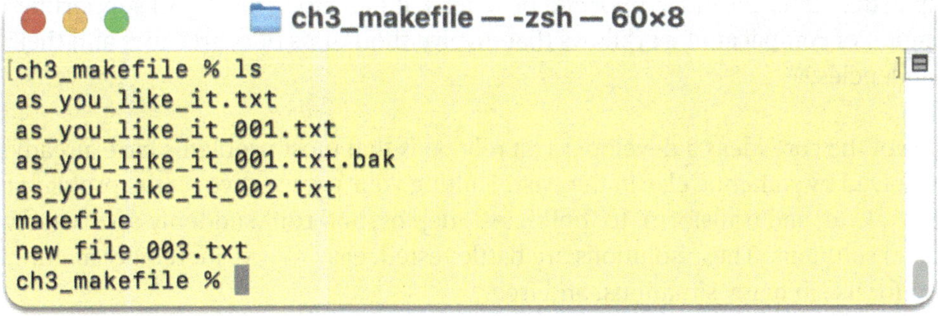

Now when we rerun, everything looks like we would expect.

```
cat as_you_like_it.txt
```

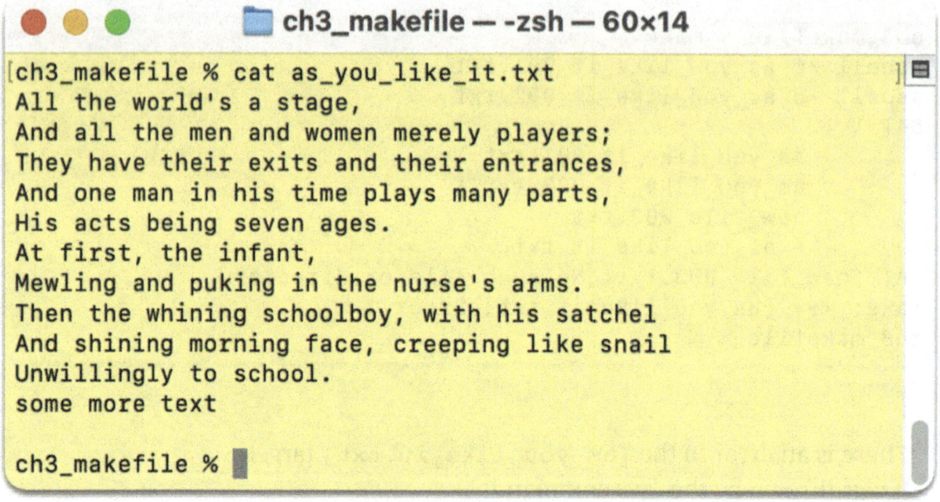

It may not seem like much at this point, but this small example sets the stage for solving one of the biggest problems every developer faces: How do I repeatedly execute a series of tasks without having to resort to manual labor or a complicated application?

The Make utility replaces the complicated and difficult-to-debug shell scripts used to compile the Linux OS and supporting programs. It has a long history of supporting the execution of complicated workflows that involve thousands of source files and their dependencies.[102]

One of the core ideas a developer can rely on is that most problems have already been solved by someone else in the past. Shifting your perspective on the problem from "extract, load, and transform" to "build, test, deploy, and run" suddenly opens a new world of solutions. These solutions are battle-tested, easy to use, incredibly mature, suited for use in many situations, and free.

If we map data transformation tools as a value chain, the power of this idea becomes clearer. Looking back at our value map, remember that products move from left to right as they become more mature, and they move toward the top as value increases. Keep in mind that the value assessment is purely subjective and will likely change over time or in different contexts, but it may be useful.

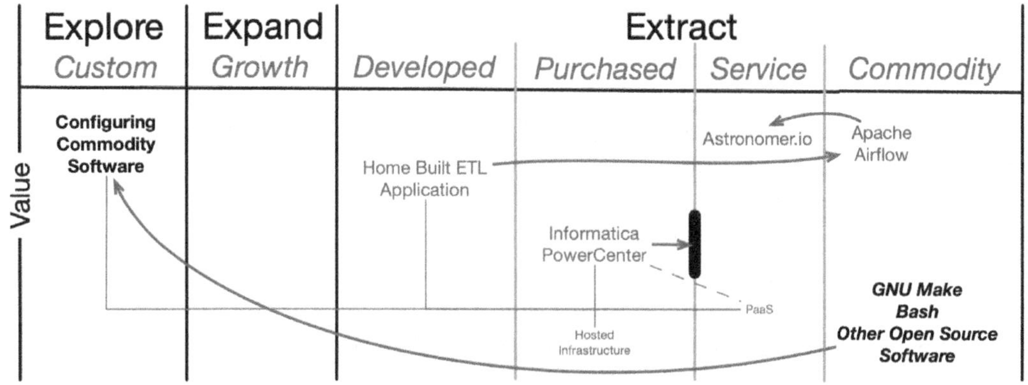

Build tools map

Starting with what is arguably most valuable, a home-built ETL application provides a solution capable of meeting all of our requirements because we have total ownership of the features. If new functionality is desired, we can add it as soon as the developers are available. Having total control means not suffering unneeded functionality or prioritization driven by outside requirements. If you host the application with a Platform as a Service (PaaS) provider like Amazon, you can replace a capital investment in infrastructure with an expense, shifting the financial burden to another accounting process. Assuming that this application is kept in-house, it never moves toward becoming a more broadly used commercial product.

However, you could make the leap, as many companies have, by open sourcing an in-house product and thereby gaining the benefit of broader adoption and development assistance from a vast user community. This is exactly how Airflow evolved from an internal orchestration tool at AirBnB to an Apache Foundation-supported open-source project. Astronomer[103] then built upon Airflow and created a hosted Software as a Service solution.

Informatica has a different trajectory. As a commercial product designed to meet particular requirements, and be deployed in particular ways, PowerCenter needs to overcome significant inertia to become a more modern data management platform. The only viable option to improve Informatica is to move from internally hosted infrastructure to a PaaS provider. This will move the capital investment in hardware to an expense for renting the platform. Unfortunately, it will also require addressing the complex problem of reaching into the company network to move data that was previously local onto the internet.

If we break down our data products into smaller, easier-to-manage pieces, we might get by with a home-built solution instead of spending money on an application built to address high volume and large-scale data issues. Rather than going down that road, investigate using commodity software to leapfrog the overhead of big systems in favor of smaller and more agile ones.

We take this same approach throughout the rest of the book. Rather than reinvent the wheel, look to industry-standard software, processes, patterns, and data structures as ways to accelerate creating customer value. The first step is building a tool to automate creating data products. This provides the core functionality for a robust product.

Creating a Project Build Tool

One of the key enablers for any development project is developing within a consistent and repeatable framework. First we will develop a simple program to initialize a new data project. This project build tool provides the following features:

1. It automates creating a complex directory structure.
2. Provides consistent project layouts across multiple projects.
3. It repopulates standard template files for core activities.
4. It is easy to use.
5. It is easy to understand how the tool was built and operates, which simplifies modifying to meet future needs.
6. It provides useful feedback and *help* documentation.
7. It is usable on multiple platforms (macOS, Linux, and Windows using Windows Subsystem for Linux).

Building a project build tool may seem premature, given that we haven't investigated any data for the data products we will be developing. Building this tool early accomplishes several critical goals. It allows us to design and build our standard project directory and file structure. It also validates that our basic development environment is working before we commit to further development. Most importantly, building this tool introduces us to the skills and techniques we will use later.

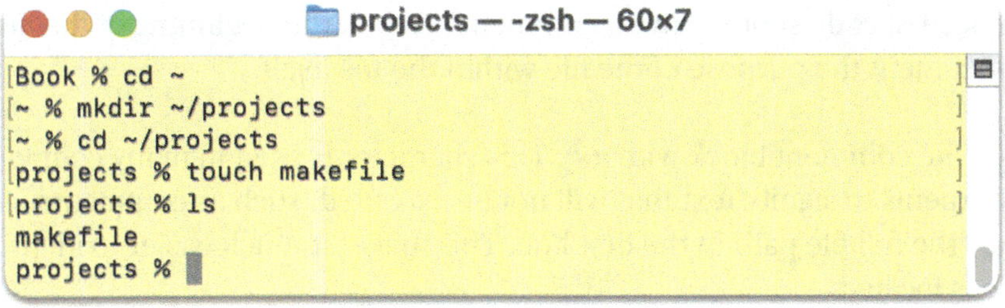

Setting Up the Environment

First, follow the installation instructions in the appendix for your operating system. From this point forward, we will work from the terminal window[104] and a text editor.[105] Create a project folder in a logical location on your local development computer. A reasonable default location is in the root of your home directory

`~/`"

```
cd ~
```

```
mkdir ~/projects
```

Within this directory, create a new file called `makefile`. There are numerous ways to accomplish simple tasks such as creating a new file in a new directory, but if you are unfamiliar or uncomfortable with the command line interface (CLI), this provides a good place to start.

1. `cd ~` changes your location in the terminal to your home directory.
2. `mkdir ~/projects` creates a new directory called projects.
3. `cd ~/projects` changes the directory you are working from to the projects directory.
4. `touch makefile` creates a new, empty file called makefile.
5. `ls` lists the contents of the directory. You can see the same thing in your computer file browser.

Open the makefile in a text editor, paste in or type the following code, and save the file.

Every piece of code should have a comment block at the beginning of the file to quickly document the purpose of the file within the file itself.

1. Start the comment block with a `#`. This character is used in many coding environments to signify text that will not be executed, such as comments.
2. Place the full file path in the first line. This makes it much easier to identify where the file is located.
3. Follow this with a brief description of what the code is intended to do and how it should be executed.

```
# ~/projects/makefile
# Initialize a new data project
#
# Initialize the project -> make check
#
##############################################################
```

It can be tempting to include other information like who created the file, when it was created, and the modification history. In practice, these are never kept up to date, and attaching a person's name to the file tends to promote ownership by a single person as opposed to reinforcing that the entire team owns the code. Knowing when code was edited and by whom is important. However, this information is best maintained in a Source Code Repository (SCM) and Version Control System (VCS).

Integrating our code into version control comes later once we have successfully created the basic system. Thinking back to the project life cycle, we are in Exploration, and setting up and integrating what we've created into version control is part of the Expand phase. In Explore, we focus on delivering the greatest value as soon as possible. Having a repeatable project initiation process is much more valuable than knowing who edited what code and when.

Where should this code be stored if it is too early to place under version control? At this point, the location isn't critical; the code can be stored wherever is convenient. However, keeping the code local means it cannot be easily shared, and backups may not be available. A good compromise may be to use Dropbox or Google File Stream.[106] The biggest advantage to services like these is that they synchronize your local files with the shared files automatically. They also make the files easy to share.

Notes about future features (TODOs) and bugs are also tempting to include in the comment block. These are best handled outside the code in a prioritized task list. This way, the team can prioritize decisions based on the value of all the work across the entire solution, rather than focusing on improving one small component.

The next step in creating the makefile will be to add the initial configuration variables and to write our first task. Add the following code to the file.

```
################################################################
# System variables and paths
SHELL := /bin/bash
ROOTDIR := $(shell pwd)

# Setup project
PROJECTNAME ?= test
PROJECTDIR := $(ROOTDIR)/$(PROJECTNAME)
```

This establishes our initial set of project variables. The first section of the code will define the variables we will be reusing throughout the program. These variables will make it easier to understand and modify the code later. The variables in makefiles are defined using the pattern `name = value`, where the name can be any case, and the value can be either a string or a shell command. As a convention to keep the code easier to read, we are defining the variable names in uppercase and any shell command in lowercase.

Note that we are using the `:=` variable assignment rather than the expected `=`. The `:=` assignment tells Make to assign the variable once, at the initial parsing of the file, rather than each time the variable is expanded. The values of these variables will not change. The `?=` operator assignment is shorthand for "if this value is not set, then use 'test'."

The next step is to add our first target and recipes to the file.
If we run the `make` command in the directory, the output looks like this:

```
projects — -zsh — 65×8
projects % make
/bin/bash
/Users/brianmcmillan/projects
test
/Users/brianmcmillan/projects/test
projects %
```

When Make runs, it executes the first target in the file, `check:`, by default. It parses the dependencies and then executes them. Here, we are simply using the `echo` command to print the value of the variables to the screen. There are two additional things to note. First, we are using the special `@` character at the start of the recipe line to prevent make from printing the recipe and then its results. This makes the output much cleaner. In order to understand the `.PHONY:` command[107], you need to remember that make is designed to process files. However, not all of our targets will be files. To keep Make from executing these, we can link them as dependencies to a `.PHONY:` target.

Add another recipe to the file.

```
test/project:
  @if test ! -d $(PROJECTDIR);\
  then echo [PASS] - Project \"$(PROJECTNAME)\" does not exist;\
  else echo [FAIL] - Project \"$(PROJECTNAME)\" already exists;\
  fi
```

This code introduces the IF...THEN...ELSE logic used by the bash shell. To understand the the logic, read the statement as:

1. Use the `test !` (not equal to) command to look for a directory `-d` that matches the value in `$(PROJECTDIR)`.
2. Then print a `[PASS]` message,
3. Else print a `[FAIL]` message.

NOTE: Make has its own `ifeq` and `ifneq` logic to control the flow of the makefile logic but **not** the logic of a recipe. For this, we need to use the bash conditional logic.

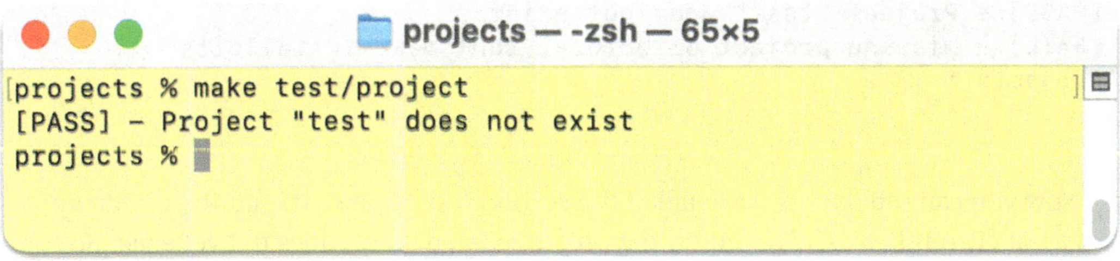

Now we can see the name of the project and the results of a simple test for the existence of a directory. Manually create a "test" directory and execute the `make test/project` command again.

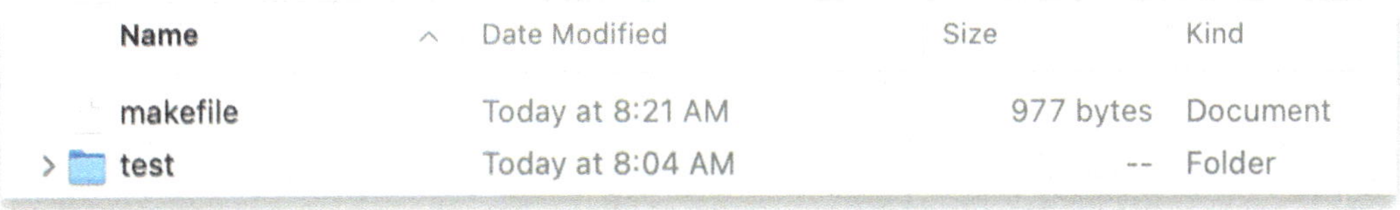

In this first test, we are testing for the nonexistence of a project based on the lack of a directory of the same name. We are not testing for the *existence* of the project or directory. For this, we need to add another test. We will also add an instruction on how to solve the issue.

```
test/project:
  @if test ! -d $(PROJECTDIR);\
    then echo [PASS] - Project \"$(PROJECTNAME)\" does not exist;\
    else echo [FAIL] - Project \"$(PROJECTNAME)\" already exists;\
    fi
  @if test -d $(PROJECTDIR);\
    then echo [PASS] - Project directory already exist;\
    else echo [FAIL] - Missing project directory, run \"make installdirs\";\
    fi
```

First, delete the `test/` directory with the `rm -r test` command. Then run the makefile again.

```
projects — -zsh — 65×5
projects % make test/project
[PASS] - Project "test" does not exist
[FAIL] - Missing project directory, run "make installdirs"
projects %
```

Now you can see that we have failed the second test because the `test/` directory does not currently exist. Therefore, the project named "test" does not yet exist. So the next step is to create an `installdirs:` target to make the directory.

```
installdirs:
  @mkdir -p $(PROJECTNAME)
```

If we run the make installdirs target, and then the ls command, we can see we created a target called "test".

```
projects — -zsh — 65x7
projects % make test/project
 [PASS] - Project "test" does not exist
 [FAIL] - Missing project directory, run "make installdirs"
projects % make installdirs
projects % ls
makefile        test
projects %
```

If we wan to remove the project directory, we can do so manually or we can write a target to do it for us.

```
uninstalldirs: ## Removes the project directories.
  @rm -r $(PROJECTNAME) && echo [PASS] - Removing project directory
```

The rm -r command is very powerful. It removes directories and all their contents without prompting for confirmation or providing any way to undo or recover the deleted files and directories. We could modify the uninstall task to be more friendly, but at this point, we *want* rm -r to delete everything. This recipe also uses the && command to execute the echo command after the rm command to provide feedback after the rm command executes.

The Linux functions we have used so far, test, echo, mkdir, rm, and make, all have flags that modify the behavior of the command. How do you learn which flag to use or what a command does? There are several ways to do so without going to the internet.[108] The first option is to call the man <function> command. The man (manual) command displays the online manual pages for a function. For instance, here is the man page for mkdir. We can see that the -p option creates intermediate directories as required.

projects — less ◂ man mkdir — 80×39

```
MKDIR(1)                  BSD General Commands Manual                 MKDIR(1)

NAME
     mkdir -- make directories

SYNOPSIS
     mkdir [-pv] [-m mode] directory_name ...

DESCRIPTION
     The mkdir utility creates the directories named as operands, in the order
     specified, using mode rwxrwxrwx (0777) as modified by the current
     umask(2).

     The options are as follows:

     -m mode
             Set the file permission bits of the final created directory to
             the specified mode.  The mode argument can be in any of the for-
             mats specified to the chmod(1) command.  If a symbolic mode is
             specified, the operation characters ``+'' and ``-'' are inter-
             preted relative to an initial mode of ``a=rwx''.

     -p      Create intermediate directories as required.  If this option is
             not specified, the full path prefix of each operand must already
             exist.  On the other hand, with this option specified, no error
             will be reported if a directory given as an operand already
             exists.  Intermediate directories are created with permission
             bits of rwxrwxrwx (0777) as modified by the current umask, plus
             write and search permission for the owner.

     -v      Be verbose when creating directories, listing them as they are
             created.

     The user must have write permission in the parent directory.

DIAGNOSTICS
     The mkdir utility exits 0 on success, and >0 if an error occurs.
:
```

Another common option is to use the `--help` or `-h` option, which prints a concise help page. The `man --help` command looks like this.

projects — -zsh — 80×29

```
projects % man --help
man, version 1.6g

usage: man [-adfhktwW] [section] [-M path] [-P pager] [-S list]
        [-m system] [-p string] name ...

  a : find all matching entries
  c : do not use cat file
  d : print gobs of debugging information
  D : as for -d, but also display the pages
  f : same as whatis(1)
  h : print this help message
  k : same as apropos(1)
  K : search for a string in all pages
  t : use troff to format pages for printing
  w : print location of man page(s) that would be displayed
      (if no name given: print directories that would be searched)
  W : as for -w, but display filenames only

  C file   : use `file' as configuration file
  M path   : set search path for manual pages to `path'
  P pager  : use program `pager' to display pages
  S list   : colon separated section list
  m system : search for alternate system's man pages
  p string : string tells which preprocessors to run
               e - [n]eqn(1)   p - pic(1)    t - tbl(1)
               g - grap(1)     r - refer(1)  v - vgrind(1)
projects % 
```

At this point, we can add help information to our own makefile by creating a new task called `help:` which we invoke by executing the `make help` command. Don't worry about the complexity of the recipe other than to notice that it introduces a few new commands: `grep`, `sort`, `awk`, and `printf`.

```
help: ## List of all makefile tasks.
  @grep -E '^[a-zA-Z_-]+:.*?## .*$$' $(MAKEFILE_LIST) | \
  awk 'BEGIN {FS = ":.*?## "};\
  {printf "\033[36m%-20s\033[0m %s\n", $$1, $$2}'
```

Next, add comments beside each target, prefixed by ##. Now, when you run the `make help` command, you will see a list of all the tasks you can perform.

```
##################################################################
all: help ## Executes the default make task. Initially, 'help'.

check: info/variables test/project ## Run the project test suite.
```

```
projects — -zsh — 65×7
projects % make help
check                      Run the project test suite.
installdirs                Creates the project directories.
uninstalldirs              Removes the project directories.
help                       List of all makefile tasks.
projects %
```

We now have a *mostly* functional tool to automate the creation of a consistent project directory structure. However, our makefile needs a few refinements. At its core, Make was designed to process files, and none of the tasks we've created operate on files. Make refers to these task targets as `.PHONY:`. A `.PHONY:` target is a task that is called outside the typical build process, and by explicitly designating them as such, you eliminate the risk of having a task like `uninstall:` run inadvertently.

```
.PHONY: installdirs
installdirs: ## Creates the project directories.
	@mkdir -p $(PROJECTNAME)
```

Another change we will make is to add the default task of `all:` to the makefile. This is the first task in the file and reflects the default behavior we expect to see when typing the `make` command without any parameters. Initially, the target executed by the `all` command will be `help`. Later, once we define a `run` task, the `all` command will run all the tasks required to build the solution.

As a result, if you type `make` again, you will see the following.

projects — -zsh — 72×7

```
projects % make
all              Executes the default make task. Initially, 'help'.
check            Run the project test suite.
installdirs      Creates the project directories.
uninstalldirs    Removes the project directories.
help             List of all makefile tasks.
projects %
```

We now have a solution which can run a few basic tests for the existence of a directory and some guidance on what to do if the directory doesn't exist. Now we need this logic to work automatically with any project name we might choose.

Changing the project name is easy to do. When we call make, we can pass a variable assignment in the command line. If we execute `make info/variables PROJECTNAME=sales` then we can see we are passing "sales" as the variable.

projects — -zsh — 72×6

```
projects % make info/variables PROJECTNAME=sales
/bin/bash
/Users/brianmcmillan/projects
sales
/Users/brianmcmillan/projects/sales
projects %
```

To automate the logic, we can modify our `test/project:` target to automatically create the `PROJECTNAME` directory if it doesn't already exist. This will replace our previous `installdirs:` target. With this change, we can simplify the test to just report back whether the project directory exists or not.

```
test/project:
  @if test -d $(PROJECTDIR);\
    then echo [PASS] - Project directory already exist;\
    else echo [FAIL] - Missing project directory, run \"make installdirs\";\
    fi

.PHONY: installdirs
installdirs:
  @if test -d $(PROJECTDIR);\
    then echo [WARNING] - Project directory already exist;\
    else mkdir -p $(PROJECTNAME) && echo [INFO] - Creating project directory;\
    fi
```

The GNU Make standard specifies a number of expected targets for every makefile. Before we begin building out our Project Build Tool, we will add these to the file to give us some structure to build from.[109]

target	Description
all	The default task. Typically, this will build the entire solution.
check	Executes the post-build tests.
info	Generates the informational files.
install	Builds the solution and copies the files to the location where they will be used.
uninstall	Deletes all of the installed files.
clean	Deletes any intermediate files created during the build.
dist	Creates a distribution for the solution.
installdirs	Creates the required directory structure.
installcheck	Performs the post-installation checks.

The `dist:` target isn't doing anything at the moment other than providing a minimal amount of feedback through an `echo` statement.

```
################################################################
all: help ## Executes the default make task. Initially, 'help'.
check: info/variables test/project ## Run the project test suite.
info: info/variables ## Generates the informational files.
install: installdirs installcheck ## Builds the project "make install PROJECTNAM
uninstall: uninstalldirs ## Uninstalls the project.

.PHONY: installcheck
installcheck: ## Run the installation test suite.
	@echo undefined

.PHONY: dist
dist: ## Create a distribution package.
	@echo undefined
```

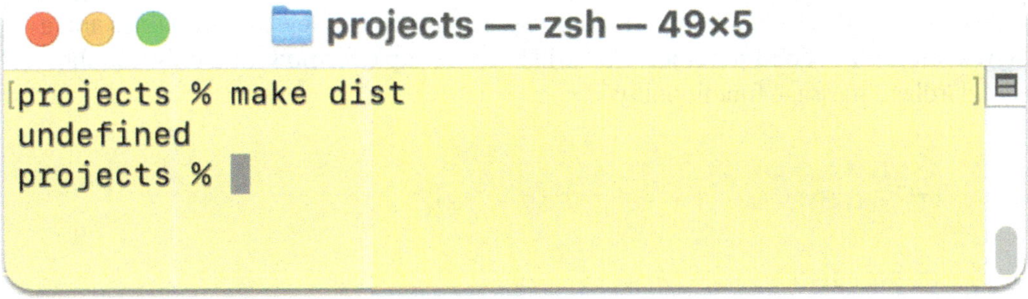

We can write anything after the `echo`, but it would be better to write something that provides useful feedback when we are looking at the terminal window. This feedback will be helpful now and in the future, once we have automated everything and need to look back at the history of previous runs saved to a log file. Fortunately, we have good industry standards to follow. For example, here is the "Logs" page in Google CloudRun.

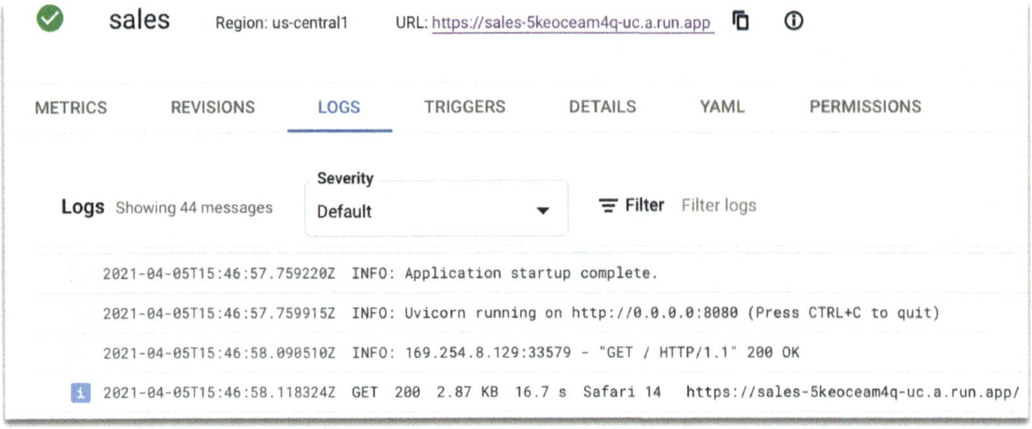

In the header, we have information on where the log information came from: the Sales application, us-central1 region, and the URL. This answers the question of who provided this data. The log activity is simply the data, timestamp, and a message. Embedded in some of the messages is text to indicate the severity of the issue (e.g., INFO). Adding this functionality into our makefile requires a few new variables and a new standardized echo statement. We will keep it simple for now, and only add the standardized message functionality.

```
# Utility variables
DTS = $(shell date +%Y-%m-%dT%H:%M:%S-%Z)

.PHONY: dist
dist: ## Create a distribution package.
	@echo $(DTS)    [INFO] - Executing dist.
```

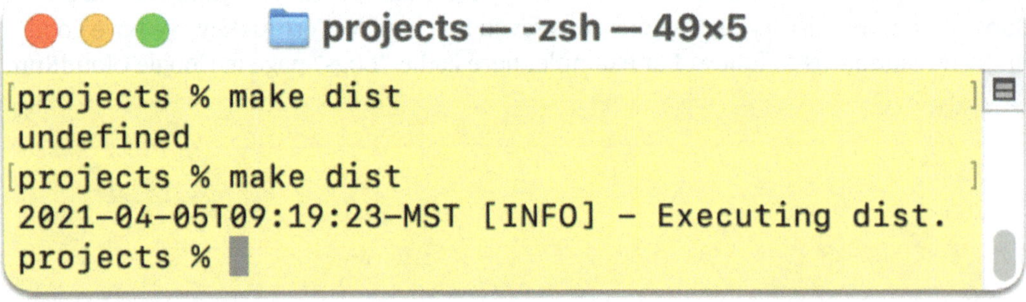

With a bit of restructuring, the makefile now contains a header section with the location of the file, some usage information, and the definitions of several variables. Some of these variables set as soon as the makefile is read by Make and some set as they are needed.

```
# ~/projects/projects/makefile
# Initialize a new data project
#
# make help
# make install PROJECTNAME=myproject
# make uninstall PROJECTNAME=myproject
#
##############################################################
# System variables and paths
SHELL := /bin/bash
ROOTDIR := $(shell pwd)

# Setup project
PROJECTNAME ?= test
PROJECTDIR := $(ROOTDIR)/$(PROJECTNAME)

# Utility variables
DTS = $(shell date +%Y-%m-%dT%H:%M:%S-%Z)
```

The next section in the file defines the standard targets, a number of which we will be discussing soon.

```
##############################################################
all: install ## Executes the default make task. Initially, 'help'.
  @echo $(DTS)    [INFO] - Executing all.
check: info/variables test/project ## Run the project test suite.
  @echo $(DTS)    [INFO] - Executing check.
info: info/variables ## Generates the informational files.
  @echo $(DTS)    [INFO] - Executing info.
install: installdirs installcheck ## Builds the project "make install PROJECTNAM
  @echo $(DTS)    [INFO] - Executing install.
uninstall: uninstalldirs ## Uninstalls the project.
  @echo $(DTS)    [INFO] - Executing uninstall.

.PHONY: installcheck
installcheck: ## Run the installation test suite.
  @echo $(DTS)    [INFO] - Executing installcheck.

.PHONY: dist
dist: ## Create a distribution package.
  @echo $(DTS)    [INFO] - Executing dist.
```

```

.PHONY: help
help: ## List of all makefile tasks.
  @echo $(DTS)     [INFO] - Executing help.
  @grep -E '^[a-zA-Z_-]+:.*?## .*$$' $(MAKEFILE_LIST) | \
  awk 'BEGIN {FS = ":.*?## "};\
  {printf "\033[36m%-20s\033[0m %s\n", $$1, $$2}'

.PHONY: info/variables
info/variables: ## List the variables in the makefile.
  @echo $(DTS)     [INFO] - Executing info/variables.
  @echo SHELL: $(SHELL)
  @echo ROOTDIR: $(ROOTDIR)
  @echo PROJECTNAME: $(PROJECTNAME)
  @echo PROJECTDIR: $(PROJECTDIR)
  @echo DTS: $(DTS)
```

The remaining targets cover the logic we need to execute in order to create and remove a project directory.

```

.PHONY: test/project
test/project: ## Test for a PROJECTNAME directory.
  @echo $(DTS)     [INFO] - Executing test/project.
  @if test -d $(PROJECTDIR);\
    then echo $(DTS)     [PASS] - Project directory already exist;\
    else echo $(DTS)     [FAIL] - Missing project directory, run \"make installdi
    fi

.PHONY: installdirs
installdirs: ## Creates the project directories.
  @echo $(DTS)     [INFO] - Executing installdirs.
  @if test -d $(PROJECTDIR);\
    then echo $(DTS)     [WARNING] - Project directory already exist;\
    else mkdir -p $(PROJECTNAME) && echo $(DTS)     [INFO] - Creating project dir
    fi

.PHONY: uninstalldirs
uninstalldirs: ## Removes the project directories.
  @echo $(DTS)     [INFO] - Executing uninstalldirs.
  @rm -r $(PROJECTNAME) && echo $(DTS)     [WARNING] - Removing project directory
```

The typical project creation workflow for a project named “myproject” looks like this:

projects — -zsh — 78×20

```
2021-04-05T09:57:39-MST [INFO] - Executing help.
all                     Executes the default make task. Initially, 'help'.
check                   Run the project test suite.
info                    Generates the informational files.
install                 Builds the project "make install PROJECTNAME=<proj>".
uninstall               Uninstalls the project.
installcheck            Run the installation test suite.
dist                    Create a distribution package.
help                    List of all makefile tasks.
installdirs             Creates the project directories.
uninstalldirs           Removes the project directories.
projects % make install PROJECTNAME=myproject
2021-04-05T09:58:16-MST [INFO] - Executing installdirs.
2021-04-05T09:58:16-MST [INFO] - Creating project directory
2021-04-05T09:58:16-MST [INFO] - Executing installcheck.
2021-04-05T09:58:16-MST [INFO] - Executing install.
projects % ls
makefile        myproject
projects %
```

Adding Additional Project Directories

Now that the initial template is done, it is time to create the additional directories we will need. Data projects have a large number of complex components, which are all required to make a solution work. Keeping all this code organized is not a simple task, and having a standardized directory structure helps.

Rather than spend time creating our own unique structure, we will leverage the tried and true UNIX standards. Initially, these will look cryptic, but if we familiarize ourselves with them early, future system administration tasks will make more sense.

Directory name	Purpose	Directory variable name
src/	Location for all source files we need for our project. This will include actual source code and templates.	SOURCEDIR
etc/	Configuration files for the project. Includes server configurations, database models, scripts, and schedules.	SYSCONFIGDIR

Directory name	Purpose	Directory variable name
svc/	The files we will be served to our users. Includes HTML pages, files to be loaded, and the database.	SERVICEDIR
opt/	Optional packages. This is the directory for the solution we are delivering. It includes both the results of a build (dist:) and files to be deployed.	OPTIONALPKGDIR
var/	Files we need to maintain as the application runs. Includes marker and log files.	LOCALSTATEDIR
tmp/	Purely temporary files.	TEMPSTATEDIR

With these six directories, we should be able to define and run just about any project we can think of. This may seem like overkill, but adopting the best practices from teams that have a mature data product practice allows you to leapfrog past the difficult transition from Exploration into Expansion. Other people have done the hard design work, which frees you from working through those decisions from scratch.

The UNIX structure guides all the components needed to support a data product past Expansion and into Extraction. In practice, we will slowly iterate through the solution, adding features incrementally as they are needed. Time to add a server to support additional API traffic? Now you don't need to decide where that code goes.

Continue following a development pattern called test-driven development (TDD), writing your test before your code. These tests answer simple questions (e.g., Does a specific directory exist?). As in our earlier tests, we can easily implement them in our makefile.

The idea is that we write a test to define our end-state. If we run the test, it will fail. Then, we write just enough code to pass the test. When we run the test, it should pass. Finally, we modify the test to reflect the next feature we need, write the new code, then rerun all the tests again.

By getting in the habit of writing a test, writing the code, and passing the test, we start to build confidence in the product. If we add a step to run all the tests over the entire product, we know we have a fully working solution we can confidently deploy at any time.

The first step to adding additional project directories is to define these directories as new variables. By using variables, we give ourselves the flexibility to redefine them as needed in the future. We will always need to know where the `SYSCONFIGDIR` is, but we don't need to be too rigid about what we call it. The new variables should also be added to the `info/variables:` target.

```
# Setup project
PROJECTNAME ?= test
PROJECTDIR := $(ROOTDIR)/$(PROJECTNAME)
SOURCEDIR := /src
SYSCONFIGDIR := /etc
SERVICEDIR := /svc
OPTIONALPKGDIR := /opt
LOCALSTATEDIR := /var
TEMPSTATEDIR := /tmp
```

The actual test leverages the IF...THEN logic we used to create the project directory.

```
test/dirs: ## Test for the existance of a directory_listing
  @echo $(DTS)    [INFO] - Executing test/dirs.
  @if test -d $(PROJECTDIR)$(SOURCEDIR);\
    then echo $(DTS)    [PASS] - Project directory $(PROJECTDIR)$(SOURCEDIR) exists.;\
    else echo $(DTS)    [FAIL] - Project directory $(PROJECTDIR)$(SOURCEDIR) does not exist;\
    fi
```

As expected, running `make test/dirs PROJECTNAME=myproject` fails because we have not written the code to create the directories.

```
projects — -zsh — 78x7
projects % make test/dirs PROJECTNAME=myproject
2021-04-05T11:15:01-MST [INFO] - Executing test/dirs.
2021-04-05T11:15:01-MST [FAIL] - Project directory /Users/brianmcmillan/projec
ts/myproject/src does not exist
projects %
```

The simplest solution is to add the additional directories to the `installdirs:` recipe we already have.

```
.PHONY: installdirs
installdirs: ## Creates the project directories.
  @echo $(DTS)    [INFO] - Executing installdirs.
  @if test -d $(PROJECTDIR);\
    then echo $(DTS)    [WARNING] - Project directory already exist;\
    else mkdir -p $(PROJECTNAME) \
      $(PROJECTNAME)/$(SOURCEDIR) \
      $(PROJECTNAME)/$(SYSCONFIGDIR) \
      $(PROJECTNAME)/$(SERVICEDIR) \
      $(PROJECTNAME)/$(OPTIONALPKGDIR) \
      $(PROJECTNAME)/$(LOCALSTATEDIR) \
      $(PROJECTNAME)/$(TEMPSTATEDIR) \
      && echo $(DTS)    [INFO] - Creating project directory;\
    fi
```

Executing the test/install/test workflow now produces exactly what we need. Use the tree command to list the directories.

The next step is to modify the default targets to reflect the tasks we want to be able to perform, including their dependencies.

```
####################################################################
all: install check ## Executes the default make task. Initially, 'help'.
info: help info/variables ## Generates the informational files.
check: installcheck ## Executes all test suites.
installcheck: info/variables test/project test/dirs ## Run the project test suite.
install: installdirs ## Builds the project "make install PROJECTNAME=<proj>".
uninstall: uninstalldirs ## Uninstalls the project.
```

Adding Default Text Files

Now that we have successfully implemented the project directory structure, the next step is adding the basic files that every project should include. Once again, don't worry about all this structure; it's there for guidance and to simplify the number of decisions you will need to make in the future. These files are also part of the standard GNU software project recommendations.

Files to include in every project:

File name	Purpose
AUTHORS.md	Contact names for the project.
README.md	General information for the project.
CHANGELOG.md	List of changes.
NEWS.md	General project news.
LICENSE.md	License documenting how the project can be shared and modified.

Adding these to the makefile is similar to the process for creating the directories. First, create the tests for both the new "src" directory and the individual files.

```
.PHONY: test/project_templates
test/project_templates:
	@if test -s $(PROJECTDIR)/AUTHORS.md; \
	  then echo $(DTS)    [PASS] - $(PROJECTDIR)/AUTHORS.md file exists; \
	  else echo $(DTS)    [FAIL] - $(PROJECTDIR)/AUTHORS.md file does not exist; fi
	@if test -s $(PROJECTDIR)/CHANGELOG.md; \
	  then echo $(DTS)    [PASS] - $(PROJECTDIR)/CHANGELOG.md file exists; \
	  else echo $(DTS)    [FAIL] - $(PROJECTDIR)/CHANGELOG.md file does not exist; fi
	@if test -s $(PROJECTDIR)/LICENSE.md; \
	  then echo $(DTS)    [PASS] - $(PROJECTDIR)/LICENSE.md file exists; \
	  else echo $(DTS)    [FAIL] - $(PROJECTDIR)/LICENSE.md file does not exist; fi
	@if test -s $(PROJECTDIR)/NEWS.md; \
	  then echo $(DTS)    [PASS] - $(PROJECTDIR)/NEWS.md file exists; \
	  else echo $(DTS)    [FAIL] - $(PROJECTDIR)/NEWS.md file does not exist; fi
	@if test -s $(PROJECTDIR)/README.md; \
	  then echo $(DTS)    [PASS] - $(PROJECTDIR)/README.md file exists; \
	  else echo $(DTS)    [FAIL] - $(PROJECTDIR)/README.md file does not exist; fi
```

Creating the actual template files from scratch expands on our earlier use of the `cat` command. Unfortunately, creating these files isn't as easy as it would be if we were using a shell script. Rather than resorting to a creative misuse of Make variables, we are going to create these through brute force.

```
.PHONY: installsrcdir
installsrcdir: ## Uninstalls the source directory and templates.
	@echo $(DTS)     [INFO] - Executing installsrcdir.
	@mkdir -p $(ROOTDIR)/src

src/AUTHORS.md:
	@echo $(DTS)     [INFO] - Executing src/AUTHORS.md.
	@echo "# Authors" >> src/AUTHORS.md
	@echo "| Name | Role | Email | Phone |" >> src/AUTHORS.md
	@echo "|:--|:--|:--|:--|" >> src/AUTHORS.md
	@echo "| Prospero | Lead Sorcerer | prince@milan.com | 555-444-3333 |" >> src/AUTHORS.md
	@echo "| Miranda | Prospero's daughter | princess@milan.com | 555-444-2222 |" >> src/AUTHORS.md
	@echo "| Caliban | Slave of Prospero | mooncalf@island.net | 555-867-5000 |" >> src/AUTHORS.md
	@echo "| Ariel | Spirit | spirit@island.net | 555-867-5309 |" >> src/AUTHORS.md

src/CHANGELOG.md:
	@echo $(DTS)     [INFO] - Executing src/CHANGELOG.md.
	@echo "# Change Log" >> src/CHANGELOG.md
	@echo "YYYY-MM-DD  Jane Doe  <mailto:johndoe@example.com>" >> src/CHANGELOG.md
	@echo "* file1.txt (function): Lorem ipsum dolor sit amet" >> src/CHANGELOG.md
	@echo "* file1.txt (unrelated_change): Lorem ipsum dolor sit amet" >> src/CHANGELOG.md

```

The final step involves moving these files from their shared location in the source directory into the newly created project directory and adding the targets to the `install:` target.

```
.PHONY: install/project_templates
install/project_templates:
	@echo $(DTS)     [INFO] - Executing install/project_templates.
	@cp -f $(ROOTDIR)/src/AUTHORS.md $(PROJECTDIR)
	@cp -f $(ROOTDIR)/src/CHANGELOG.md $(PROJECTDIR)
	@cp -f $(ROOTDIR)/src/LICENSE.md $(PROJECTDIR)
	@cp -f $(ROOTDIR)/src/NEWS.md $(PROJECTDIR)
	@cp -f $(ROOTDIR)/src/README.md $(PROJECTDIR)
```

```
.PHONY: install/src
install/src: \
	installsrcdir \
	src/AUTHORS.md \
	src/CHANGELOG.md \
	src/LICENSE.md \
	src/NEWS.md \
	src/README.md \
```

Reviewing the New Project Build Tool

We now have a robust tool to build the basic project structure for any new data product. It dramatically simplifies the work involved with establishing a project by automating the repetitive task of creating directories and moving files. More importantly, this standard structure relieves us from thinking about the necessary steps for each new project. Standardized structures make it easier to train new developers and assist other teams with their products.

Looking at the specific features, the Project Build Tool consists of a single configuration file written in the GNU Make language and a folder of template files that are included in every project.

```
.
├── makefile
├── new_project
│   ├── AUTHORS.md
│   ├── CHANGELOG.md
│   ├── LICENSE.md
│   ├── NEWS.md
│   ├── README.md
│   ├── etc
│   ├── opt
│   ├── src
│   ├── svc
│   ├── tmp
│   └── var
└── src
    ├── AUTHORS.md
    ├── CHANGELOG.md
    ├── LICENSE.md
    ├── NEWS.md
    └── README.md
```

The makefile includes a built-in help function to provide basic documentation and instructions for running the tool. View these instructions by typing `make help`.

```
projects — -zsh — 105×14
projects % make help
2021-04-06T07:56:28-MST [INFO] - Executing help.
all                 Executes the default make task. Initially, 'help'.
info                Generates the informational files.
check               Executes all test suites.
installcheck        Run the project test suite.
install             Builds the project "make install PROJECTNAME=<proj>".
uninstall           Uninstalls the project.
installcheck        Run the installation test suite.
dist                Create a distribution package.
help                List of all makefile tasks.
installdirs         Creates the project directories.
uninstalldirs       Removes the project directories.
projects %
```

When the `make` command is run, all the complicated steps and dependencies in the makefile are executed. Because the makefile was written using the test-driven development methodology, all important inputs and expected outputs are tested. The results of those tests provide feedback to the user when the build process is run.

projects — -zsh — 105×39

```
projects % make PROJECTNAME=new_project
2021-04-06T08:50:25-MST [INFO] - Executing installdirs.
2021-04-06T08:50:25-MST [INFO] - Creating project directories
2021-04-06T08:50:25-MST [INFO] - Executing installsrcdir.
2021-04-06T08:50:25-MST [INFO] - Executing install/project_templates.
2021-04-06T08:50:25-MST [INFO] - Executing info/variables.
SHELL: /bin/bash
ROOTDIR: /Users/brianmcmillan/projects
PROJECTNAME: new_project
PROJECTDIR: /Users/brianmcmillan/projects/new_project
DTS: 2021-04-06T08:50:25-MST
SOURCEDIR: /src
SYSCONFIGDIR: /etc
SYSCONFIGDIR: /svc
OPTIONALPKGDIR: /opt
LOCALSTATEDIR: /var
TEMPSTATEDIR: /tmp
2021-04-06T08:50:25-MST [INFO] - Executing test/project.
2021-04-06T08:50:25-MST [PASS] - Project directory already exist
2021-04-06T08:50:25-MST [INFO] - Executing test/dirs.
2021-04-06T08:50:25-MST [PASS] - Project directory /Users/brianmcmillan/projects/new_project/src exists.
2021-04-06T08:50:25-MST [PASS] - Project directory /Users/brianmcmillan/projects/new_project/etc exists.
2021-04-06T08:50:25-MST [PASS] - Project directory /Users/brianmcmillan/projects/new_project/svc exists.
2021-04-06T08:50:25-MST [PASS] - Project directory /Users/brianmcmillan/projects/new_project/opt exists.
2021-04-06T08:50:25-MST [PASS] - Project directory /Users/brianmcmillan/projects/new_project/var exists.
2021-04-06T08:50:25-MST [PASS] - Project directory /Users/brianmcmillan/projects/new_project/tmp exists.
2021-04-06T08:50:25-MST [INFO] - Executing installcheck.
2021-04-06T08:50:25-MST [PASS] - /Users/brianmcmillan/projects/src directory exists
2021-04-06T08:50:25-MST [PASS] - /Users/brianmcmillan/projects/src/AUTHORS.md file exists
2021-04-06T08:50:25-MST [PASS] - /Users/brianmcmillan/projects/src/CHANGELOG.md file exists
2021-04-06T08:50:25-MST [PASS] - /Users/brianmcmillan/projects/src/LICENSE.md file exists
2021-04-06T08:50:25-MST [PASS] - /Users/brianmcmillan/projects/src/NEWS.md file exists
2021-04-06T08:50:25-MST [PASS] - /Users/brianmcmillan/projects/src/README.md file exists
2021-04-06T08:50:25-MST [PASS] - /Users/brianmcmillan/projects/new_project/AUTHORS.md file exists
2021-04-06T08:50:25-MST [PASS] - /Users/brianmcmillan/projects/new_project/CHANGELOG.md file exists
2021-04-06T08:50:25-MST [PASS] - /Users/brianmcmillan/projects/new_project/LICENSE.md file exists
2021-04-06T08:50:25-MST [PASS] - /Users/brianmcmillan/projects/new_project/NEWS.md file exists
2021-04-06T08:50:25-MST [PASS] - /Users/brianmcmillan/projects/new_project/README.md file exists
projects %
```

Next Steps:

- Try creating a new project from scratch.
- Remove a specific project.
- Play with the other standard targets to develop a feel for how they operate.
- Add additional templates you might find useful.
- Add additional sub-directories.

---

[83] Shakespeare, W., The Tempest (A2, S2)

[84] Informatica PowerCenter (https://www.informatica.com/products/data-integration/powercenter.html)

Microsoft SQL Server Integration Services (https://docs.microsoft.com/en-us/sql/integration-services/sql-server-integration-services?view=sql-server-ver15)

IBM DataStage (https://www.ibm.com/products/infosphere-datastage)

Talend (https://www.talend.com/products/integrate-data/)

Pentaho (https://www.hitachivantara.com/en-us/products/data-management-analytics/pentaho.html)

[85] Star Schema (https://en.wikipedia.org/wiki/Star_schema)

[86] Amazon DynamoDB (https://aws.amazon.com/dynamodb/)
Amazon Relational Database Service (RDS) (https://aws.amazon.com/rds/)

[87] Google Cloud databases (https://cloud.google.com/products/databases)

[88] Azure Databases (https://azure.microsoft.com/en-us/product-categories/databases/)

[89] Snowflake (https://www.snowflake.com)

[90] Apache Airflow (https://airflow.apache.org)

[91] Luigi (https://luigi.readthedocs.io/en/stable/)

[92] dbt (https://www.getdbt.com)

[93] FlyWay (https://flywaydb.org)

[94] Liquibase (https://www.liquibase.org)

[95] Continuous Delivery, 2010, Humble J., Farley D., Addison-Wesley, (https://martinfowler.com/books/continuousDelivery.html)

[96] Jenkins (https://www.jenkins.io)

[97] Bamboo (https://www.atlassian.com/software/bamboo)

[98] Continuous Integration, 2006, Fowler, M., (https://martinfowler.com/articles/continuousIntegration.html)

[99] GNU Make (https://www.gnu.org/software/make/)

[100] SQLite download (https://sqlite.org/download.html)

[101] There are several other IO Redirections you can use, but “>” and “>>” are the most useful. (https://www.gnu.org/software/bash/manual/html_node/Redirections.html)

[102] Linux Kernel (https://git.kernel.org/pub/scm/linux/kernel/git/stable/linux.git/tree/?h=v5.1.3)

[103] Astronomer (https://www.astronomer.io)

[104] In the macOS, the default terminal window can be opened in the Terminal application (/Applications/Terminal)

[105] The default text editor on a Mac is TextEdit, but it is much more efficient to use a dedicated text editor designed for editing code. We will be using Atom for our examples.

[106] Dropbox (https://www.dropbox.com/)

Google File Stream (https://www.google.com/intl/en_cy/drive/download/)

[107] PHONY targets (https://www.gnu.org/software/make/manual/make.html#Phony-Targets)

[108] The man pages and --help flag will document the standard usage, but searching for the command online will provide numerous examples of how to use the function. Basic functionality will be sufficient in most cases.

[109] Standard Targets (https://www.gnu.org/prep/standards/html_node/Standard-Targets.html)

Chapter 4: Working with CSV files and Excel

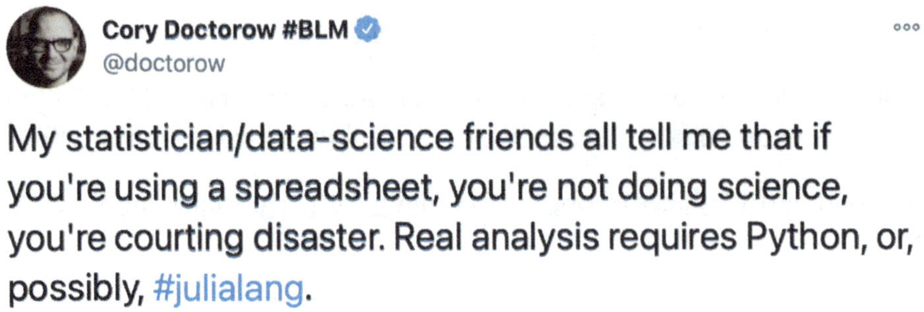

[110]

Now that we have a framework to contain our projects and the confidence to automate all of our future work, it's time to consider how to work with the raw data. What are the first steps when evaluating a new data set? How can we efficiently determine what data we have? Finally, how do we make the most effective use of our strategy to "leverage human-readable textual representations of our data as an application protocol"?

This next example begins where most data analysis activities start: with an Excel file. Fortunately, just because we are given an Excel file doesn't mean we have to use Excel. Instead, we will use command-line driven utilities to convert, profile, and manipulate large spreadsheets of sales data from an online store.[111]

The online_retail_II.xlsx file is a 46MB Microsoft Excel file with eight columns and 1,067,371 records of sales transactions split into two workbook tabs. This is a great data set to study because it comes from actual sales invoice data covering multiple years of transactions. For the vast majority of companies, most data sets fall within this magnitude. Small data management systems can easily process data sets with less than 10 million records. If we limit the data sets to the current financial life cycle, the useful data volumes are significantly less. In this simple example, we are only concerned with three hundred thousand records out of the million we started with.

Deciding What To Work on

Before we start, we will create a few agile stories to learn how to clearly describe the work. Unlike when we created the Project Build Tool, where we added feature after feature, we want to quickly define the scope of our data research activity to avoid spending too much time over-analyzing the data set.

One of the most common ways to define an agile story is to use the tried-and-true user story template first defined in 2001.[112]

```
AS A <SOME ROLE>
I CAN (WANT) <SOME CAPABILITY>
SO THAT <SOME BENEFIT>
```

This template concisely defines who the user is, what they aim to accomplish, and the resulting goal or benefit. However, there are other alternatives. One of the best turns the "AS A..." format on its head to emphasize the stakeholder business value.[113]

```
IN ORDER TO <BUSINESS OBJECTIVE>
AS A <PERSON RESPONSIBLE>
I WANT <ACTION TO ACHIEVE OBJECTIVE>
```

The traditional "AS A..." story emphasizes the user and what they want. It's a subtle difference, but if stories follow the "IN ORDER TO..." format, the focus shifts to satisfying the desired business outcome. When defining acceptance criteria and whether a story is finished, the focus is meeting the business objective, not completing a specific task for a specific user.

Unfortunately, this complicates the, "we completed the 'I CAN do X', so this story is complete" statement. If the business objective is not met, then the story is incomplete. This will drive your Scrum Master crazy because closing stories will be difficult until the team can clearly define the actions necessary to reach the business objective.

Developing an effective story description is difficult and most stories will require additional information to describe what a complete story should look like. One of the most common methods to define the acceptance criteria, is to clearly define how the system behaves when these feature are complete. This process is called Behavior Driven Development (BDD)[114] and the story acceptance criteria are written in Gherkin Syntax.[115]

```
IN ORDER TO <BUSINESS OBJECTIVE>
AS A <PERSON RESPONSIBLE>
I WANT <ACTION TO ACHIEVE OBJECTIVE>

GIVEN <THE STARTING CONDITION>
WHEN <TRIGGERING EVENT>
THEN <EXPECTED OUTCOME>
```

If you are able to write your acceptance criteria in this very specific syntax, it is even possible to automate the creation and execution of the test cases. Unfortunately, to get the full benefits, you need to have the automated testing tools and know how to execute Gherkin test cases.[116] Additionally, it requires stakeholders to interpret these developer-focused acceptance criteria. While a great technique, don't wait for technology to be in place before you start defining good acceptance criteria. You can get the benefits without technological maturity. For lower maturity levels, using a simple checklist to define the acceptance criteria may sufficiently communicate what "done" looks like to both the stakeholders and the development team.[117]

```
IN ORDER TO IDENTIFY THE TOP 10
PRODUCTS
AS A SALES MANAGER
I WANT A LIST OF THE TOP PRODUCTS FOR
THE LAST SIX MONTHS.
```

IN ORDER TO FOCUS ON THE PRODUCTS WITH THE HIGHEST REVENUE.
AS A SALES MANAGER
I WANT A LIST OF THE TOP 10 PRODUCTS WITH SIMILAR PRODUCT ATTRIBUTES, BY TOTAL REVENUE, OVER THE LAST SIX MONTHS.

What does this look like in our online retail data set?

This may be a good start, but what does "top 10 products" mean? Is this by quantity, price, or revenue? Assuming products have multiple sizes and colors, should they be grouped? Can we do that with the current data set? Most importantly, why do you need to know the top 10 products? Let's clarify that story.

A story generates a conversation between the person looking to get incremental value and the people working to achieve that value. The story format does not matter as much as identifying the work to achieve the objective.

One word of caution when developing acceptance criteria: avoid defining every small task. Keep it at the level needed to know when the story ends, plus any indicators of risk or sub-story milestones. Carefully consider the story complexity because you might want to split up the story to make milestones visible.

```
IN ORDER TO FOCUS ON THE PRODUCTS WITH
THE HIGHEST REVENUE.
AS A SALES MANAGER
I WANT A LIST OF THE TOP 10 PRODUCTS
WITH SIMILAR PRODUCT ATTRIBUTES, BY
TOTAL REVENUE, OVER THE LAST SIX
MONTHS.

[] DATA SET RECEIVED FROM THE SALES
DEPT
[] PERFORM INITIAL ANALYSIS
[] GO/NO GO AGREEMENT
[] GROUP PRODUCTS BY ATTRIBUTE
[] DERIVE DATA SET: PRODUCT NAME
GROUP, REVENUE, SALES DATE, LIMIT TOP
10
[] PROVIDE TOP 10 PRODUCTS BY REVENUE
IN AN EMAIL TO THE SALES MANAGER.
```

A checklist process allows us to easily communicate progress to all the stakeholders. If the sales manager notices no activity past the GO/NO GO agreement, it will be clear that the developers are stuck on the group products task. The picture below reflects how this could be communicated as an imdone[118] kanban board.[119]

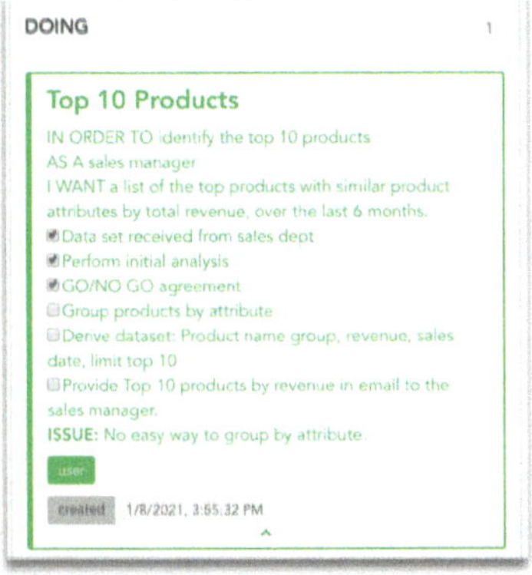

Creating stories and their acceptance criteria is about prioritizing and communicating the work for the next couple of weeks. Initially, defining the work will be painful and time consuming. Over time, it becomes much easier, and the stories become simpler, as communication and processes improve. Strive to find the sweet spot where you have just enough detail to know what to do.

Exploring the Data

```
├── makefile
├── new_project
│   ├── AUTHORS.md
│   ├── CHANGELOG.md
│   ├── LICENSE.md
│   ├── NEWS.md
│   ├── README.md
│   ├── etc
│   ├── opt
│   ├── src
│   ├── svc
│   ├── tmp
│   └── var
```

Now that we know what we are doing and have defined what done looks like, it's time to get to work. Excel performs this analysis easily. Filter out the last six months of data, calculate total sales revenue, and return the file to the sales manager, perhaps with a chart or two. Wait, our story didn't specify a chart, just the data. Perhaps that can be done later. However, what if we group the data by different periods, or by country, or other groupings? More importantly, what if we need to rebuild the filtering logic from the updated file next month? How long will that take and what additional work might we be asked to do in the mean time?

Sidestep this issue by first separating the data from the inevitable cleanup and business logic. Following our strategy of textual representation. First get the data out of Excel and take a quick look at it. For that initial data exploration, we examine two different approaches.

Establishing the Project

Before we begin our exploration, we're eating our own dog food by creating a new project with our Project Build Tool. Run the `make PROJECTNAME=sales` command from within the project folder created earlier. Name the project "sales" for now. It's too early to say if it might evolve into a sales data product, but at least we know where to put our work.

Since we're early in the exploration process, one bit of advice.: don't worry about README files or much of anything else. Let that technical debt build up for now.[120]

However, it seems we missed something. Where should we place the data? We expected our sources to be remote and in a database or on a network file share. Yet in this case, we were handed the files.

We have two options: use an existing directory like the service directory (`svc/`), or create a new one called `data/`. Since the `svc/` directory was intended for serving files, let's copy the files there.

Why Wouldn't We Use Excel?

Spreadsheets are fantastic data stores and analytics applications if used appropriately. Unfortunately, this is seldom the case and sometimes comes with great consequences. There is even a European Spreadsheet Risk Interest Group (EuSpRig)[121] that collects examples of how errors in spreadsheets have had real-world impacts. Our spreadsheets won't directly affect people's lives and livelihood, but they do cost us valuable time as we struggle with issues like these:

- Complicated formulas hidden in cells
- Inconsistent formulas in the same column
- Inconsistent formats, especially dates in the same column
- Manual reformatting of data sets rather than making use of features like pivot tables.
- Difficulty identifying duplicate data.
- Using Excel as a form or report, making it difficult to extract data.
- Emailing as the only simple way to share files.
- Inability to identify and merge changes across multiple spreadsheets.
- Inability to automate data manipulation tasks outside a hidden programming interface.[122]
- Frequent data corruption, either through user error, solution complexity, or application defects.

Regardless, spreadsheets make fantastic prototyping tools. If the team follows simple rules like separating the data from the interface and proficiently using esoteric features like Pivot Tables, Slicers, and PowerQuery, they can quickly develop fantastically capable applications.

Unfortunately, due to the issues mentioned, you may end up with a mission-critical application that can't exit out of Explore and enter Expand without being completely reimplemented. If you make the conscious decision to implement a Proof of Concept or Minimum Viable Product in a spreadsheet, make it very clear that this is used only to clarify requirements and to assess the impact of assumptions, not to build a production application.

However, you will frequently work with and deliver spreadsheets as part of your analysis. The appendix includes a spreadsheet style guide derived from an article in The American Statistician[123] to help minimize these risks. The next section presents several alternative tools to break the reliance on spreadsheets as a data and business logic store.

Extracting Excel Tables Into CSV Files

Verify that `in2csv` is properly installed by running `in2csv -V`. This should return something like `in2csv 1.0.5`. If it does not, follow the software installation instructions in the appendix. Before we begin, look at the help information by typing `in2csv -h` or by looking online.[124]

CSVKit is a suite of command-line tools to make working with CSV files easy. It contains many separate utilities which can be combined to process and manipulate data in files.

Command	Purpose
in2csv	Converts various tabular data formats into CSV.
csvclean	Cleans a CSV file of common syntax errors.
csvstat	Prints descriptive statistics for all columns in a CSV file. Will intelligently determine the type of each column and then print analysis relevant to that type (ranges for dates, mean and median for integers, etc.
csvsort	Sort CSV files. Like the Unix "sort" command, but for tabular data.
csvstack	Stack up the rows from multiple CSV files, optionally adding a grouping value to each row.
csvsql	Generate SQL statements for a CSV file or execute those statements directly on a database. In the latter case, it supports both creating tables and inserting data.
sql2csv	Executes arbitrary commands against a SQL database and outputs the results as a CSV.

The first step is verifying file access using the `-n` or `--names` argument. The `-f` argument tells `in2csv` that this is an Excel file, but `in2csv` can be used to process CSV, DBF, XLS, fixed-width files, and several JSON-formatted files. Additionally, `in2csv` performs basic data type inferences for columns that appear to be dates and a few other basic data format validation checks.

sales — -zsh — 53×5

```
sales % in2csv -f xlsx -n svc/online_retail_II.xlsx
Year 2009-2010
Year 2010-2011
sales %
```

The most basic extraction on an Excel spreadsheet is to extract a single workbook sheet using the `--sheet command`. Use the > command to write out that data to another file.

sales — -zsh — 74×6

```
sales % in2csv -f xlsx --sheet "Year 2010-2011" svc/online_retail_II.xlsx
> "svc/online_retail_II_-_Year_2010-2011.csv"
sales % ls svc/
online_retail_II.xlsx
online_retail_II_-_Year_2010-2011.csv
sales %
```

The same function converts an Excel file with variable tabs into CSV, creating multiple files named `[source file]_#.csv`. The - command writes out all tabs, which is useful if you expect new tabs to appear in the file over time.

sales — -zsh — 74×9

```
sales % in2csv -f xlsx --write-sheets "-" svc/online_retail_II.xlsx > "svc
/online_retail_II.csv"
sales % ls svc/
online_retail_II.csv
online_retail_II.xlsx
online_retail_II_-_Year_2010-2011.csv
online_retail_II_0.csv
online_retail_II_1.csv
sales %
```

Data files are full of difficult-to-identify errors, and it should be standard practice to perform routine data quality checks. CSVkit has a `csvclean` utility for this purpose. Fortunately, in our sample data set, there are no gross errors. If there are errors, it will create a `.err` file.

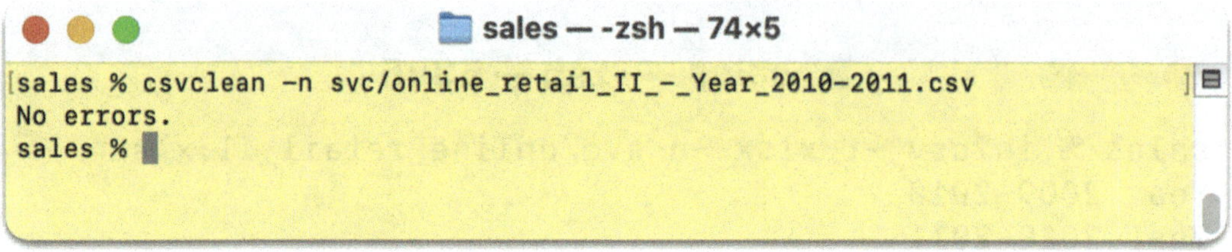

Let's look into each file to get a statistical profile of each field. Even if you were continuing to work in Excel, this feature alone is worth the effort. This is life saver if you have to explicitly model your database tables before loading data into them.

Looking through this analysis, we have all the basic data: price, quantity, description, and data from 2010-12-01 to 2011-12-09. If you run `csvstat` against the other file `csvstat data/online_retail-_II_0.csv`, the invoice data range is from 2009-12-01 to 2010-12-09, so the data overlaps in December 2010. Fortunately, that does not affect our required data analysis from 2011-06-09 to 2011-12-09.

Manipulating our Data Set

Now that we know where our data is located, let's perform a few basic manipulations like filtering the data to the requisite period.

```
sales — -zsh — 100×8
sales % csvsort -c "InvoiceDate" svc/online_retail_II_-_Year_2010-2011.csv
Invoice,StockCode,Description,Quantity,InvoiceDate,Price,Customer ID,Country
536365,85123A,WHITE HANGING HEART T-LIGHT HOLDER,6,2010-12-01T08:26:00,2.55,17850,United Kingdom
536365,71053,WHITE METAL LANTERN,6,2010-12-01T08:26:00,3.39,17850,United Kingdom
536365,84406B,CREAM CUPID HEARTS COAT HANGER,8,2010-12-01T08:26:00,2.75,17850,United Kingdom
536365,84029G,KNITTED UNION FLAG HOT WATER BOTTLE,6,2010-12-01T08:26:00,3.39,17850,United Kingdom
536365,84029E,RED WOOLLY HOTTIE WHITE HEART.,6,2010-12-01T08:26:00,3.39,17850,United Kingdom
536365,22752,SET 7 BABUSHKA NESTING BOXES,2,2010-12-01T08:26:00,7.65,17850,United Kingdom
```

We can take the steps above and string them together into a data flow pipeline.

```
in2csv -f xlsx --sheet "Year 2010-2011" svc/online_retail_II.xlsx \
| csvcut -c InvoiceDate,Invoice,StockCode,Description,\
Quantity,Price,"Customer ID",Country \
| csvsort -c "InvoiceDate" -r > "svc/online_retail_II_-_Year_2010-2011.csv"
```

1. `in2csv` command extracts the "Year 2010-2011" workbook tab.
2. The results are *piped* to the `csvcut` command using the | command to reorder the columns.
3. The results are sorted by the `csvsort`. This sorted data set is then written using > redirection to the "data/online_retail_II_-_Year_2010-2011.csv" file.

Now that we have our data set, filter it to a subset of the invoice dates.

`csvgrep` and the standard UNIX commands like `grep`, `awk`, and `sed` work on strings and do not understand dates. While complicated code accomplishes this, databases make this query remarkably easy. Fortunately, we don't have to load this data into a database before we can query it.[125] The `csvsql` command can execute SQL queries directly against CSV files.

Filter the data to the last six months and write the results to another CSV file. This command is slow. It is much faster to import the data into a database, but you need to weigh the time savings against convenience.

Having a filtered data set is great, but we want a data set that calculates the total price (quantity * price) and aggregates it by description. Do this by modifying the SQL query.

```
csvsql --query "\
SELECT Description AS description\
,SUM(Quantity) AS quantity\
,ROUND(AVG(Price),2) AS price\
,ROUND(SUM(Quantity * Price),2) AS total_sales_revenue \
FROM 'online_retail_II_-_Year_2010-2011' \
WHERE InvoiceDate >= ( 
SELECT DATE(MAX(InvoiceDate), '-6 months', 'localtime') \
FROM 'online_retail_II_-_Year_2010-2011'\
) \
GROUP BY Description \
ORDER BY 4 DESC \
LIMIT 100" \
"svc/online_retail_II_-_Year_2010-2011.csv" > \
"svc/online_retail_II_last_6_months_filtered.csv"
```

```
csvsql --query "<sql query>" "<source file>" >
"<output file>"
```

Here is the SQL query reformatted to make it easier to read.

```sql
SELECT
  Description AS description
  ,SUM(Quantity) AS quantity
  ,ROUND(AVG(Price),2) AS price
  ,ROUND(SUM(Quantity * Price),2) AS total_sales_revenue
FROM 'online_retail_II_-_Year_2010-2011'
WHERE InvoiceDate >= (
  SELECT
    DATE(MAX(InvoiceDate), '-6 months', 'localtime')
  FROM 'online_retail_II_-_Year_2010-2011'
)
GROUP BY Description
ORDER BY 4 DESC
LIMIT 100
```

If you are unfamiliar with SQL, the basic structure is that you `SELECT` data `FROM` a table. This data can be `GROUPED BY` some columns and filtered by a `WHERE` and `LIMIT` statements. Finally, the data can be sorted by the `ORDER BY` command.

Under the covers, the query is being executed like this:

1. `FROM` “online_retail_II_-_Year_2010-2011"
2. `WHERE` InvoiceDate is greater than or equal to the largest InvoiceDate minus six months
3. `GROUP BY` Description
4. `SUM()` Quantity
5. `AVG` (average) Price
6. Calculating `SUM`(Quantity * Price)
7. Rename the fields with the `AS` clause
8. `ORDER DESC`[ending] BY the 4th column (total_price)
9. `LIMIT` to the top 100 records

Don't get intimidated by the query. It is possible to derive almost any data set without using any external application other than a few simple command-line tools.

We can quickly look at the data by using the `csvlook` command to render the CSV data into an easier-to-read format.

```
sales — -zsh — 87×17
sales % csvlook svc/online_retail_II_last_6_months_filtered.csv
| description                         | quantity |  price | total_sales_revenue |
| ----------------------------------- | -------- | ------ | ------------------- |
| DOTCOM POSTAGE                      |      321 | 384.91 |          123,556.41 |
| REGENCY CAKESTAND 3 TIER            |    5,429 |  14.07 |           68,685.31 |
| RABBIT NIGHT LIGHT                  |   29,486 |   2.37 |           64,326.29 |
| PAPER CHAIN KIT 50'S CHRISTMAS      |   16,341 |   3.30 |           54,166.87 |
| JUMBO BAG RED RETROSPOT             |   27,351 |   2.40 |           54,088.32 |
| PARTY BUNTING                       |    8,638 |   5.77 |           47,966.06 |
| WHITE HANGING HEART T-LIGHT HOLDER  |   15,925 |   3.27 |           45,406.65 |
| PICNIC BASKET WICKER 60 PIECES      |       61 | 649.50 |           39,619.50 |
| POSTAGE                             |    1,754 |  25.17 |           39,163.10 |
| ASSORTED COLOUR BIRD ORNAMENT       |   21,812 |   1.71 |           34,980.04 |
| POPCORN HOLDER                      |   36,334 |   1.01 |           33,969.46 |
| SPOTTY BUNTING                      |    6,456 |   5.56 |           32,706.56 |
| CHILLI LIGHTS                       |    5,629 |   7.18 |           30,925.76 |
| SET OF 3 REGENCY CAKE TINS          |    6,253 |   5.84 |           30,687.15 |
```

Looking at our acceptance criteria, now is the time to have the review of the initial results with our Sale Manager. We have a few questions.

1. Does the data look like you were expecting? Are the top products what you expected to see?
2. Are there products we should be filtering from the data set (e.g., postage, Manual)
3. Are there any other filters or groups you need to help make decisions about the products?
4. What product decisions are you making?

Using CSVKIT Load Data Into a Database

As we've seen, `csvkit` allows us to query files with SQL queries, but `csvkit` can load data and extract data from databases. Starting with our extracted CSV file, it is a simple matter to load files into a database.[126]

Insert the CSV file into our database with the following statement:

1. `--db sqlite:///svc/sales.db` - Create a SQLite database called sales.db.

```
csvsql \
--db sqlite:///svc/sales.db \
--create-if-not-exists --overwrite \
--no-inference --no-constraints \
--chunk-size 10000 \
--tables online_retail_II_-_Year_2010-2011 \
--insert svc/online_retail_II_-_Year_2010-2011.csv
```

2. `--create-if-not-exists --overwrite` - Drops and recreates the table before loading the data.
3. `--no-inference --no-constraints` - Assigns all fields to the text data type without any length limits.
4. `--chunk-size 10000` - Bulk inserts 10,000 rows at a time.
5. `--tables online_retail_II_-_Year_2010-2011` - The name of the table to be created.
6. `--insert svc/online_retail_II_-_Year_2010-2011.csv` - The name of the source file to be loaded.

This script creates a new database and populates a new table with all the fields and data in the source file using a number of script parameters to control how this task is executed. Creating a table automatically eliminates the need to model the table schema before loading the data, dramatically simplifying the integration of new data sources. This feature is natively supported on PostgreSQL, MySQL, Oracle, Microsoft SQL Server, and SQLite databases.

However, only SQLite supports automated database creation. This is because the database runs locally and does not require any configuration or the assistance of a database administrator (DBA). This ease of use makes SQLite the preferred database for early-stage data analysis tasks.

This database can be opened up and queried in any database client software supporting SQLite databases.

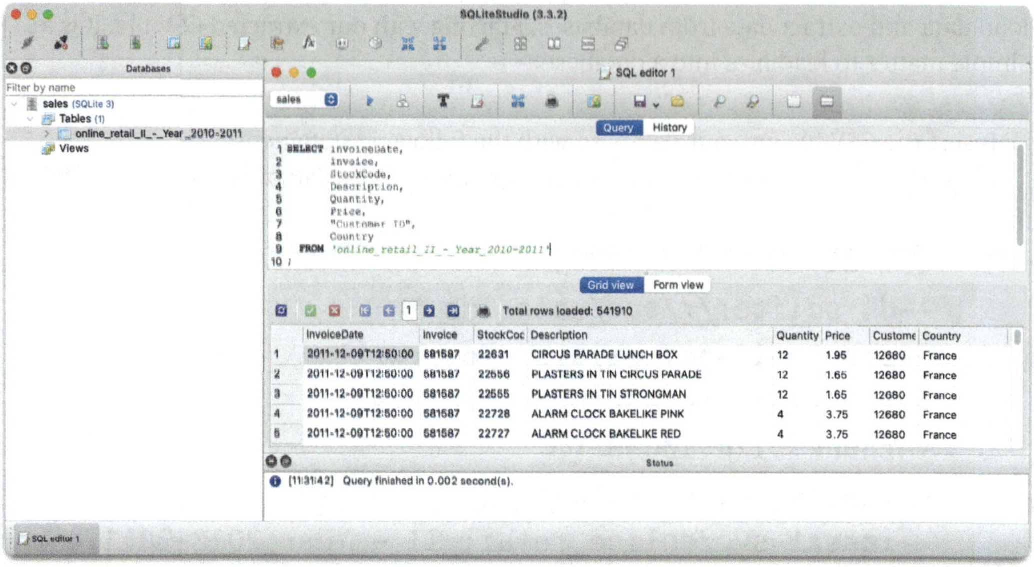

Modifying our Analysis

Now that we have the table in the database, we can refactor our earlier query and reproduce the results. As expected, when this query executes against the new database, it is multiple orders of magnitude faster.[127]

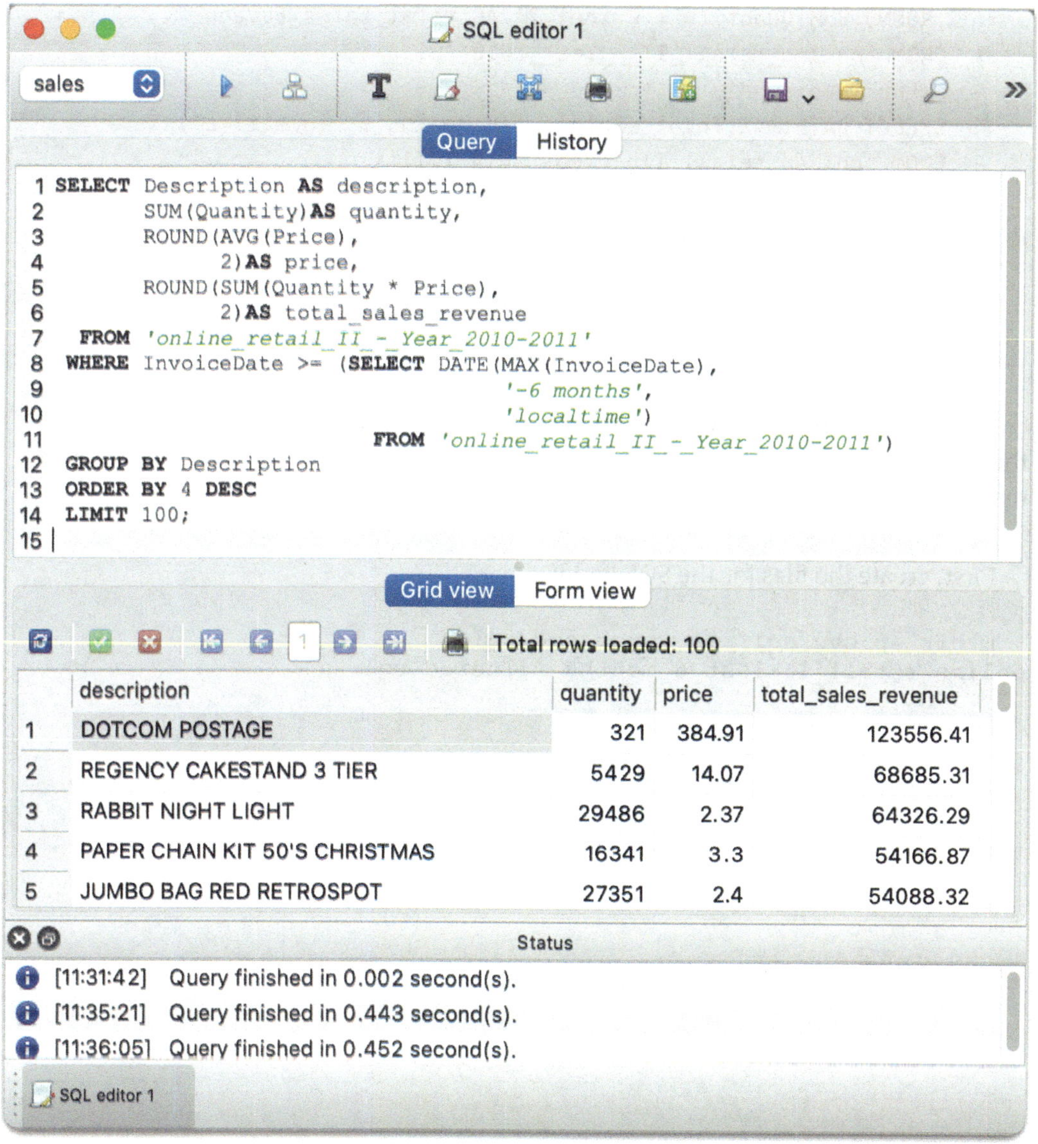

We can use `sql2csv` to query the database and write the results to a file.

```
sql2csv --db sqlite:///svc/sales.db --query "\
SELECT Description AS description\
,SUM(Quantity) AS quantity\
,ROUND(AVG(Price),2) AS price\
,ROUND(SUM(Quantity * Price),2) AS total_sales_revenue \
FROM 'online_retail_II_-_Year_2010-2011' \
WHERE InvoiceDate >= (
SELECT DATE(MAX(InvoiceDate), '-6 months', 'localtime') \
FROM 'online_retail_II_-_Year_2010-2011'\
) \
GROUP BY Description \
ORDER BY 4 DESC \
LIMIT 100" \
"svc/sales.db" > "svc/online_retail_II_last_6_months_filtered.csv"
```

If we save the query above as a separate file, we can separate the query logic from the code used to execute the query. This makes the code more modular and easier to maintain and modify.

First, create the files for the SQL code:

```
mkdir -p svc/sql/ && touch svc/sql/
online_retail_II_last_6_months_filtered.sql
```

Then update the file with:

```sql
-- sales/svc/sql/online_retail_II_last_6_months_filtered.sql
---------------------------------------------------------------

SELECT Description AS description
,SUM(Quantity) AS quantity
,ROUND(AVG(Price),2) AS price
,ROUND(SUM(Quantity * Price),2) AS total_sales_revenue
FROM 'online_retail_II_-_Year_2010-2011'
WHERE InvoiceDate >= (
SELECT DATE(MAX(InvoiceDate), '-6 months', 'localtime')
FROM 'online_retail_II_-_Year_2010-2011'
)
GROUP BY Description
ORDER BY 4 DESC
LIMIT 100
;
```

Now run the `sql2csv` commands to query the database and refresh the CSV files.

```
sql2csv \
--db sqlite:///svc/sales.db \
"svc/sql/online_retail_II_last_6_months_filtered.sql" \
> "svc/online_retail_II_last_6_months_filtered.csv"
```

If you edit the `online_retail_II_last_6_months-_filtered.sql` query to limit the data to 10 records and rerun the statement, you would see ten records in the file. Cleanly separating the SQL code from the system executing the code is a critical feature. It allows you to update the business logic without needing to modify the command executing the query.

```
sales — -zsh — 81×14
sales % csvlook svc/online_retail_II_last_6_months_filtered.csv
| description                         | quantity |  price | total_sales_revenue |
| ----------------------------------- | -------- | ------ | ------------------- |
| DOTCOM POSTAGE                      |      321 | 384.91 |          123,556.41 |
| REGENCY CAKESTAND 3 TIER            |    5,429 |  14.07 |           68,685.31 |
| RABBIT NIGHT LIGHT                  |   29,486 |   2.37 |           64,326.29 |
| PAPER CHAIN KIT 50'S CHRISTMAS      |   16,341 |   3.30 |           54,166.87 |
| JUMBO BAG RED RETROSPOT             |   27,351 |   2.40 |           54,088.32 |
| PARTY BUNTING                       |    8,638 |   5.77 |           47,966.06 |
| WHITE HANGING HEART T-LIGHT HOLDER  |   15,925 |   3.27 |           45,406.65 |
| PICNIC BASKET WICKER 60 PIECES      |       61 | 649.50 |           39,619.50 |
| POSTAGE                             |    1,754 |  25.17 |           39,163.10 |
| ASSORTED COLOUR BIRD ORNAMENT       |   21,812 |   1.71 |           34,980.04 |
sales %
```

In the spirit of keeping our data streams in a human-readable text format so they can be easily viewed and filterable, now is a good time to introduce basic meta-data to our file. By adding the timestamp of the data load and information about where the file came from, we make it easier to know where a record originated and enables us to combine data from multiple sources and times without losing that context or requiring separate database tables and load directories.

To accomplish this, we need to force the inclusion of two new columns of data in our files with the `csvstack` command. This command creates a new column named `load_dts` and populates it with the shell `date` command formatted as a date timestamp. This new data set is then piped into another `csvstack` command that adds a string into a new `provider_code` column. This is then written to a temporary file which is then renamed with the `mv` command to replace the original file.

The value in adding this data about our data (meta-data) at the CSV file stage is that if and when these source files are reused, we know where they originated. By doing this, even our source data maintains independence from the system doing the processing without hiding where it came from.

```
csvstack -n load_dts -g \
$(date +%Y-%m-%dT%H:%M:%S-%Z) \
"svc/load/online_retail_II_-_Year_2010-2011.csv" | \
csvstack -n provider_code -g \
"sales/svc/load/online_retail_II_-_Year_2010-2011.csv" > \
"tmp/online_retail_II_-_Year_2010-2011.tmp" && \
mv "tmp/online_retail_II_-_Year_2010-2011.tmp" \
"svc/load/online_retail_II_-_Year_2010-2011.csv"
```

```
sales — -zsh — 163×12
sales % head -10 svc/load/online_retail_II_-_Year_2010-2011.csv
provider_code,load_dts,InvoiceDate,Invoice,StockCode,Description,Quantity,Price,Customer ID,Country
sales/svc/load/online_retail_II_-_Year_2010-2011.csv,2021-04-07T14:47:09-MST,2011-12-09T12:50:00,581587,
sales/svc/load/online_retail_II_-_Year_2010-2011.csv,2021-04-07T14:47:09-MST,2011-12-09T12:50:00,581587,
sales/svc/load/online_retail_II_-_Year_2010-2011.csv,2021-04-07T14:47:09-MST,2011-12-09T12:50:00,581587,
sales/svc/load/online_retail_II_-_Year_2010-2011.csv,2021-04-07T14:47:09-MST,2011-12-09T12:50:00,581587,
sales/svc/load/online_retail_II_-_Year_2010-2011.csv,2021-04-07T14:47:09-MST,2011-12-09T12:50:00,581587,
```

Building the Project Automation Tool

While waiting for feedback on our outstanding questions, take this time to perform cleanup and reorganization of the project. This makes it easier to support in the future.

Modifying the Data Build Tool

As we've seen, not only do we have files to be loaded, and a local database, we have intermediary and published files. If we map out the files and steps against the base directories we can see we have a number of files that are part of the services we are building. These belong under the `svc/` directory. We could put them in the `opt/` directory but that is intended for our deployment artifacts, not our Work in Process (WIP). The same could be said for our database as well. Up until it is deployed, it is part of our WIP. The SQL queries are really code we are using to configure the database, so they belong in the `etc/` directory. Finally, while the load and extract scripts are part of the system configuration, they are implemented inside the makefile and therefore are not maintained separately.

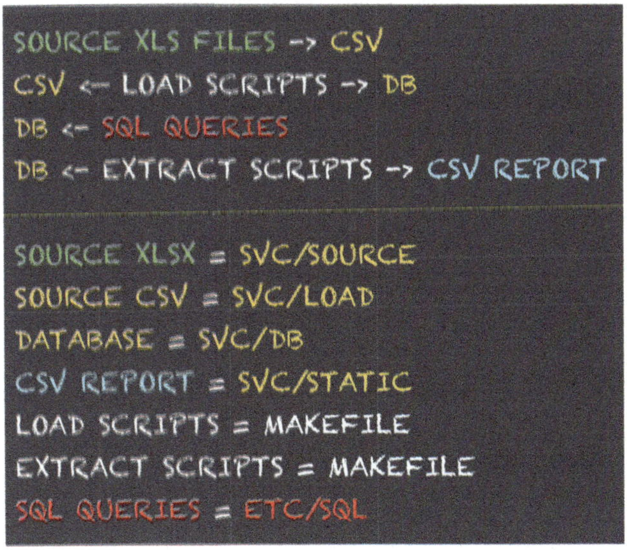

By adding these sub-directories to the Data Build Tool the project will be updated with these new directories and they will be added to every project thereafter.

The additional code looks like this:

```
test/dirs:
...
  @if test -d $(PROJECTDIR)$(SERVICEDIR)/source;\
    then echo $(DTS)    [PASS] - Project directory $(PROJECTDIR)$(SERVICEDIR) exists.;\
    else echo $(DTS)    [FAIL] - Project directory $(PROJECTDIR)$(SERVICEDIR) does not exist;\
    fi
  @if test -d $(PROJECTDIR)$(SERVICEDIR)/load;\
    then echo $(DTS)    [PASS] - Project directory $(PROJECTDIR)$(SERVICEDIR) exists.;\
    else echo $(DTS)    [FAIL] - Project directory $(PROJECTDIR)$(SERVICEDIR) does not exist;\
    fi
  @if test -d $(PROJECTDIR)$(SERVICEDIR)/db;\
    then echo $(DTS)    [PASS] - Project directory $(PROJECTDIR)$(SERVICEDIR) exists.;\
    else echo $(DTS)    [FAIL] - Project directory $(PROJECTDIR)$(SERVICEDIR) does not exist;\
    fi
  @if test -d $(PROJECTDIR)$(SERVICEDIR)/static;\
    then echo $(DTS)    [PASS] - Project directory $(PROJECTDIR)$(SERVICEDIR) exists.;\
    else echo $(DTS)    [FAIL] - Project directory $(PROJECTDIR)$(SERVICEDIR) does not exist;\
    fi
  @if test -d $(PROJECTDIR)$(SYSCONFIGDIR)/sql;\
    then echo $(DTS)    [PASS] - Project directory $(PROJECTDIR)$(SYSCONFIGDIR) exists.;\
    else echo $(DTS)    [FAIL] - Project directory $(PROJECTDIR)$(SYSCONFIGDIR) does not exist;\
    fi
```

```
installdirs:
  @mkdir -p $(ROOTDIR)/src \
  ...
  $(PROJECTNAME)$(SERVICEDIR)/source \
  $(PROJECTNAME)$(SERVICEDIR)/load \
  $(PROJECTNAME)$(SERVICEDIR)/db \
  $(PROJECTNAME)$(SERVICEDIR)/static \
  $(PROJECTNAME)$(SYSCONFIGDIR)/sql \
```

Now that we have the new directory structure, we can manually rearrange the old files in `svc/` to their new locations. The scripts we used to generate these files will be refactored to the new locations as we build a new makefile for our project.

```
.
├── makefile
├── sales
│   ├── AUTHORS.md
│   ├── CHANGELOG.md
│   ├── LICENSE.md
│   ├── NEWS.md
│   ├── README.md
│   ├── etc
│   │   └── sql
│   │       └── online_retail_II_last_6_months_filtered.sql
│   ├── opt
│   ├── src
│   ├── svc
│   │   ├── db
│   │   │   └── sales.db
│   │   ├── load
│   │   │   └── online_retail_II_-_Year_2010-2011.csv
│   │   ├── source
│   │   │   └── online_retail_II.xlsx
│   │   └── static
│   │       └── online_retail_II_last_6_months_filtered.csv
│   ├── tmp
│   └── var
```

Building our Project Makefile Template

Now it's time to begin developing a new makefile to automate this work. This file will also become a new template in our project build tool and will be automatically included in all future projects.

The project makefile serves as the framework to hold our tasks, their dependencies, and our method of reliably executing those tasks. Not surprisingly, it has similar features as the Data Build Tool.

1. Automate the execution of complex data flows.
2. Provide pre-populated standard code blocks for core activities.
3. Is easy to use.
4. Is easy to understand how the tool was built and operates, which makes modifying future needs easier.
5. Provides useful feedback and helps with user documentation.
6. Is usable on multiple platforms (macOS, Linux, and Windows using Windows Subsystem for Linux).

Before we dig into creating the new makefile, we should be reminded of the a few of the Rules of UNIX philosophy.

> 1. ***Rule of Modularity:*** *Write simple parts connected by clean interfaces.*
> 2. ***Rule of Clarity:*** *Clarity is better than cleverness.*
> 5. ***Rule of Simplicity:*** *Design for Simplicity; add complexity only where you must.*
> 7. ***Rule of Transparency:*** *Design for visibility to make inspection and debugging easier.*
> 8. ***Rule of Robustness:*** *Robustness is the child of transparency and Simplicity.*
> 11. ***Rule of Silence:*** *When a program has nothing surprising to say, it should say nothing.*
> 12. ***Rule of Repair:*** *When you must fail, fail noisily and as soon as possible.*

For many of us, this may be the longest and most complicated program we've ever written, and it will feel intimidating at first. Take heart that it gets easier with practice and there are many features common to all programming languages designed to make the process easier.

If we were to distill those seven rules down even further, into something more practical, we could restate them as:

1. *First, do the simplest thing that works.*
2. *Break features down into small understandable chunks.*
3. *Make your work obvious.*
4. *Catch the most common failure modes early. If things are working, don't inform me unless it is necessary.*
5. *Look for and eliminate repetition.*

Of these, the biggest opportunity lies in balancing making the work obvious with eliminating repetition. Much of the work of a Data Engineer is repetitive and Data Pipelines tend to break down into a few basic tasks: extract data, move data, load data, manipulate data. Look for opportunities to break the process down into small identical tasks where possible.

One indicator of success will be logically organized code with obvious blocks of logic. While, the code within these blocks may be repetitive, it should be obvious you are performing the same tasks in the same way. This repetition actually makes the code easier to read because the non-repetitive, non-standardized sections are now obvious.

Let's walk through an example. Consider these variables from the Project Build Tool.

```
# System variables and paths
SHELL := /bin/bash
ROOTDIR := $(shell pwd)

# Setup project
PROJECTNAME ?= test
PROJECTDIR := $(ROOTDIR)/$(PROJECTNAME)
SOURCEDIR := /src
SYSCONFIGDIR := /etc
```

These variables could be rewritten in the project makefile as:

```
# Project directory paths
SHELL := /bin/bash
ROOTDIR := $(shell pwd)
PROJECTDIR := $(ROOTDIR)
PROJECTNAME := $(notdir $(ROOTDIR))
SYSCONFIGDIR := $(PROJECTDIR)/etc
SOURCEDIR := $(PROJECTDIR)/src
```

If we run make info/variables, we see:

```
sales % make info/variables
SHELL := /bin/bash
ROOTDIR := /Users/brianmcmillan/projects/sales
PROJECTDIR := /Users/brianmcmillan/projects/sales
PROJECTNAME := sales
SOURCEDIR := /Users/brianmcmillan/projects/sales/src
SYSCONFIGDIR := /Users/brianmcmillan/projects/sales/etc
sales %
```

There are a couple of points to look at more closely. First, because we are in a project directory, the path to the sub directories is defined by including the $(PROJECTDIR) by doing this assignment here, we minimize the need to join multiple variables together in other targets (e.g., $(ROOTDIR)/$(PROJECTNAME)$(SYSCONFIGDIR)). The second thing to note is the use of the $(notdir $(ROOTDIR)) statement. This is one of many special variables we will be introducing as we build out the makefile. Looking closer, the statement expands to this:

1. $(notdir $(ROOTDIR))
2. $(notdir (/Users/brianmcmillan/projects/sales))
3. $(sales)

The $(notdir $()) variable interprets its input as a directory path and outputs the end of that path as the text that is not a directory. Logically, the $(dir $()) variable would return just the directory portion.

Our next step is to write our tests. In the Build tool we explicitly tested for each directory and returned either a [PASS] or a [FAIL]. 99% of the time we expect the directory to exist so why should we provide feedback if nothing is wrong?

```
.PHONY: test/dirs
test/dirs: ## Test for the existance of a directory_listing
	@echo $(DTS)	[INFO] - Executing test/dirs.
	@if test -d $(PROJECTDIR);\
	  then echo $(DTS)	[PASS] - Project directory $(PROJECTDIR) exists.;\
	  else echo $(DTS)	[FAIL] - Project directory $(PROJECTDIR) does not exist;\
	  fi
	@if test -d $(SYSCONFIGDIR);\
	  then echo $(DTS)	[PASS] - Project directory $(SYSCONFIGDIR) exists.;\
	  else echo $(DTS)	[FAIL] - Project directory $(SYSCONFIGDIR) does not exist;\
	  fi
```

```
sales — -zsh — 98×5
sales % make test/dirs
2021-04-08T10:43:31-MST [INFO] - Executing test/dirs.
2021-04-08T10:43:31-MST [PASS] - Project directory /Users/brianmcmillan/projects/sales exists.
2021-04-08T10:43:31-MST [PASS] - Project directory /Users/brianmcmillan/projects/sales/etc exists.
sales %
```

A better strategy would be to test for the absence the directory and only if it is missing, return a value.

```
.PHONY: test/dirs
test/dirs: ## Test for the existance of a directory_listing
	@echo $(DTS)	[INFO] - Executing test/dirs.
	@if ! test -d $(PROJECTDIR); \
	then echo $(DTS)	[FAIL] - $(PROJECTDIR) does not exist; else true; fi
	@if ! test -d $(SYSCONFIGDIR); \
	then echo $(DTS)	[FAIL]	$(SYSCONFIGDIR) does not exist; else true; fi
```

Now, when we run `make test/dirs`, no feedback is returned to the console. Note, the shell uses the `!` command to mean "not", just like in sql (e.g., `!=` means `NOT LIKE`).

We still have a lot of repetition and it is not easy to know what variable we are testing for because it's hidden in the statement. Remember that Make was intended to process files and directories. What if we thought of our variables as files and considered them to be a target with the dependency set to the directory path?

```
<variable name>: <$(variable name)>
```

```
.PHONY: PROJECTDIR
PROJECTDIR: $(PROJECTDIR)
	@if ! test -d $(PROJECTDIR); then echo $(DTS)    [FAIL] - $(PROJECTDIR) does n
.PHONY: SYSCONFIGDIR
SYSCONFIGDIR: $(SYSCONFIGDIR)
	@if ! test -d $(SYSCONFIGDIR); then echo $(DTS)    [FAIL] - $(SYSCONFIGDIR) do
```

This is now much more obvious, but there is still a lot of repetition. Fortunately, Make has a special variable to address this: `$<`. This symbol tells Make to refer to the first dependency of the target. Now we're getting close!

```
.PHONY: PROJECTDIR
PROJECTDIR: $(PROJECTDIR)
	@if ! test -d $<; then echo $(DTS)    [FAIL] - $< does not exist; else true; f
.PHONY: SYSCONFIGDIR
SYSCONFIGDIR: $(SYSCONFIGDIR)
	@if ! test -d $<; then echo $(DTS)    [FAIL] - $< does not exist; else true; f
```

We could easily have over a dozen directories and variables we need to manage in our solution, so it seems like there should be a way to eliminate the remaining repetition. There is. Make has the ability to define a "Canned Recipe".[128] These special recipes are really just variables that can be referenced by a target.

The first step in defining these recipes is to define a new multi-line variable. To make it easier to understand the output, we can remove the `@` character from the recipe.

```
define test_dir
  if ! test -d $<; \
  then echo $(DTS)    [FAIL] - $< does not exist; \
  else true; fi
endef

.PHONY: test/dirs PROJECTDIR SYSCONFIGDIR
test/dirs: PROJECTDIR SYSCONFIGDIR
PROJECTDIR: $(PROJECTDIR)
  $(test_dir)
SYSCONFIGDIR: $(SYSCONFIGDIR)
  $(test_dir)
```

1. We have defined a new multi line variable containing the logic to test for the absence of a directory.
2. We replace each recipe with that variable. When make evaluates the target, it will expand the text in the macro as if it were written into each recipe. This includes expanding the reference to the first dependency.
3. These targets are processed as dependencies for the `test/dirs:` target.
4. The values of each dependency is printed to the terminal window.
5. Combine the .PHONY: dependencies together for readability.

The code is now significantly easier to read, and when the logic needs to change in the future, we only need to change it in one location.

Another improvement we need to make is to explicitly define the paths for the nonstandard utilities we will be using. While we are working with our makefile locally and under our user name, everything should work fine. However, when we execute the Data Pipeline on another system or under another user name, the default locations will likely be different. Defining the paths this way also allows us to specify specific versions of a utility. As an example, rather than using the version of SQLite installed on the system, we could refer to a custom complied versions we bundle with out application. These paths can be found by executing the `which <command name>` command.

```
###############################################################
# Program locations (which <utility>)
SHELL := /bin/bash
PYTHON3PATH := /Users/brianmcmillan/.pyenv/shims/python
PIPPATH := /Users/brianmcmillan/.pyenv/shims/pip
SQLITE3PATH := /usr/local/bin/sqlite3
IN2CSVPATH := /Users/brianmcmillan/.pyenv/shims/in2csv
CSVSTACKPATH := /Users/brianmcmillan/.pyenv/shims/csvstack
SQLITEUTILSPATH := /Users/brianmcmillan/.pyenv/shims/sqlite-utils
SPLITPATH := /usr/local/bin/gsplit
```

NOTE FROM THE FUTURE: In the spirit of minimizing rework, we are going to pre-define a number of additional sub-directories we will need in future chapters. By implementing them now we will avoid interrupting development. These changes will need to be merged back into the Build Tool at a future date.

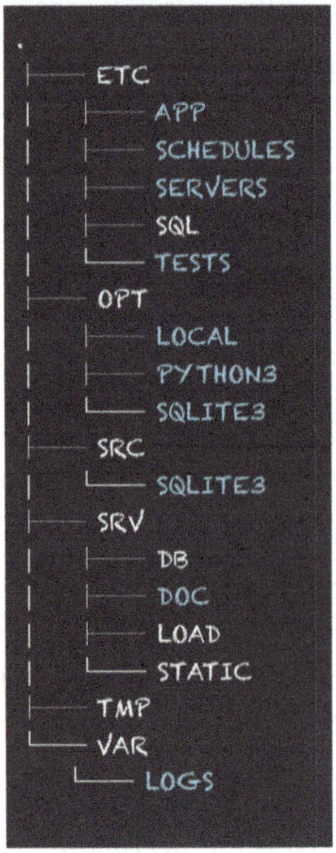

Not all of the variables are directories. Some of them refer to files that can be tested in exactly the same way. We just need to implement a new macro called `test_file` implementing the `test -s` command.

The standard Make `uninstall:` targets have not been addressed yet. Until we get further into the implementation, we should keep it as undefined. Ultimately, this target will completely delete the solution. If we execute make again, we should be able to rebuild the solution from nothing.

```
define test_file
  if ! test -s $<; \
  then echo $(DTS)     [FAIL] - $< does not exist; \
  else true; fi
endef
```

```
test/solution_files: SHELL PYTHON3 PIP SQLITE3 IN2CSV CSVSTACK SQLITEUTILS \
SPLIT GRAPHVIZDOT NODEGRAPH DBNAME LOGNAME
  @echo $(DTS)     [INFO] - Executing test/solution_files.
SHELL: $(SHELL)
  @$(test_file)
PYTHON3: $(PYTHON3)
  @$(test_file)
```

The last piece of our makefile template to build is some automatic documentation. This target uses the `tree` command we've used before to print a file listing all of the files in the project.

```
.PHONY: uninstalldirs
uninstalldirs: ## Removes the project directories. "make uninstall"
  @echo $(DTS)     [INFO] - Not defined.
  @#echo $(DTS)     [WARNING] - Removing project directory
  @#rm -r $(DIR_NAME)
```

```
.PHONY: documentation
documentation: ## Builds the documentation files for the build. (e.g. schema docs, da
  @echo $(DTS)     [INFO] - Executing documentation.
  @tree --prune > $(DOCUMENTATIONDIR)/directory_listing.txt
  @$(NODEGRAPH) --direction LR | dot -Tpng > $(DOCUMENTATIONDIR)/makefile_graph.png
```

```
directory_listing.txt
.
├── AUTHORS.md
├── CHANGELOG.md
├── LICENSE.md
├── NEWS.md
├── README.md
├── etc
│   └── sql
│       └── online_retail_II_last_6_months_filtered.sql
├── makefile
└── svc
    ├── db
    │   └── sales.db
    ├── doc
    │   ├── directory_listing.txt
    │   └── makefile_graph.png
    ├── load
    │   └── online_retail_II_-_Year_2010-2011.csv
    ├── source
    │   └── online_retail_II.xlsx
    └── static
        └── online_retail_II_last_6_months_filtered.csv

8 directories, 13 files
```

More interesting, is the command to run the `makefile2dot` python utility. This application reads the project makefile and then generates a graphviz[129] node graph of the relationships. This file will be indispensable when you need to figure out what all of these targets are doing.

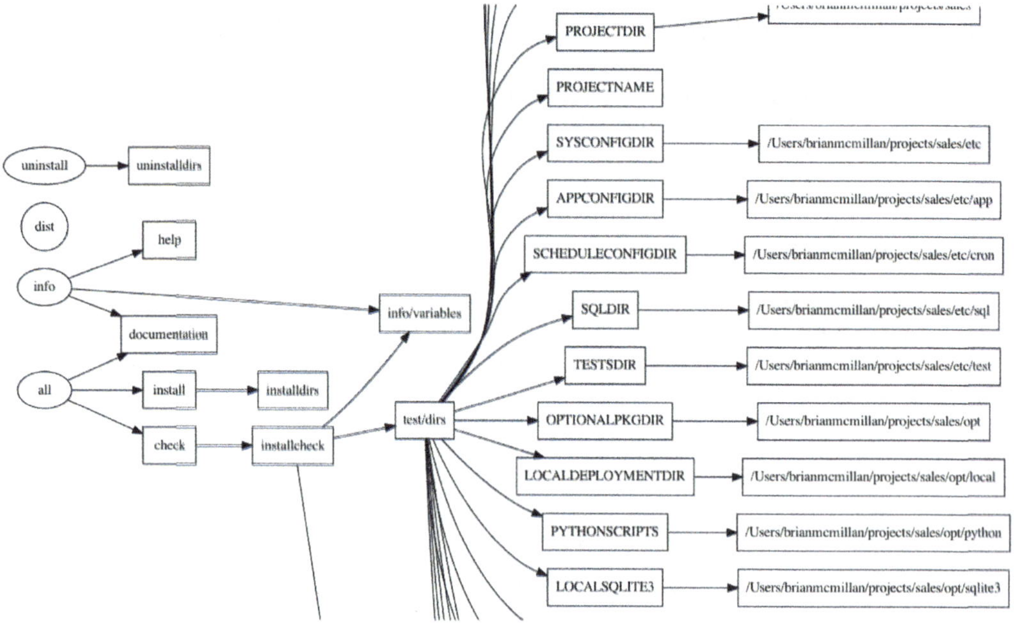

Makefile node graph

We can now run the make command and verify the basic makefile executes without any issues.

```
sales % make
2021-04-08T15:52:58-MST [INFO] - Executing installdirs.
2021-04-08T15:52:58-MST [INFO] - Creating or updating project directories
2021-04-08T15:52:58-MST [INFO] - Executing info/variables.
-- Program paths ----------------------------------------------------
SHELL: /bin/bash
PYTHON3: /Users/brianmcmillan/.pyenv/shims/python
PIP: /Users/brianmcmillan/.pyenv/shims/pip
sales % make
2021-04-08T15:53:31-MST [INFO] - Executing installdirs.
2021-04-08T15:53:31-MST [INFO] - Creating or updating project directories
2021-04-08T15:53:31-MST [INFO] - Executing info/variables.
-- Program paths ----------------------------------------------------
SHELL: /bin/bash
PYTHON3: /Users/brianmcmillan/.pyenv/shims/python
PIP: /Users/brianmcmillan/.pyenv/shims/pip
SQLITE3: /usr/local/bin/sqlite3
IN2CSV: /Users/brianmcmillan/.pyenv/shims/in2csv
CSVSTACK: /Users/brianmcmillan/.pyenv/shims/csvstack
SQLITEUTILS: /Users/brianmcmillan/.pyenv/shims/sqlite-utils
SPLIT: /usr/local/bin/gsplit
GRAPHVIZDOT: /usr/local/bin/dot
NODEGRAPH: /makefile2dot.py
-- Project directory paths ------------------------------------------
ROOTDIR: /Users/brianmcmillan/projects/sales
PROJECTDIR: /Users/brianmcmillan/projects/sales
PROJECTNAME: sales
-- Configuration paths (/etc) ---------------------------------------
SYSCONFIGDIR: /Users/brianmcmillan/projects/sales/etc
```

Building our First Pipeline

Our objective now is to reimplement the commands we ran earlier to extract the data from the Year_2010-2011 tab in the online_retail_II.xlsx file and then produce the online_retail_II_last_6_months_filtered.csv file. When developing these flows, it is helpful to write out the steps in the <verb> <– <subject> format. This helps organize the tasks to be performed and their inputs and outputs. Hopefully it's obvious that the verbs correspond to the recipes and the subjects correspond to the targets. This leave us to figure out what dependencies we need for each target.

```
TEST FILE <- ONLINE_RETAIL_II.XLSX
EXTRACT TAB <- ONLINE_RETAIL_II.XLSX (YEAR_2010-2011)
[WRITE CSV <- ONLINE_RETAIL_II_-_YEAR_2010-2011.CSV
  ADD METADATA <- LOAD_DTS + PROVIDER_CODE + CSV]
[CREATE DATABASE <- SALES.DB
  CREATE TABLE <- SRC_ONLINE_RETAIL_II_-_YEAR_2010-2011]
EXECUTE QUERY <- SALES_LAST_6_MONTHS_FILTERED_001.SQL
QUERY RESULTS <- FORMAT RESULTS TO CSV
WRITE CSV <- SALES_LAST_6_MONTHS_FILTERED_001.CSV
TEST FILE <- SALES_LAST_6_MONTHS_FILTERED_001.CSV
```

As always, our first step is to write the tests for the functionality we are developing. These test follow the same pattern as our earlier `$(test_file)` tests. In that recipe we introduced the `$<` automatic variable.[130]

```
###############################################################################
# Project content                                                             #
###############################################################################
# Input / Output Tests
.PHONY: test/io/online_retail

test/io/online_retail: \
  svc/source/online_retail_II.xlsx \
  svc/static/online_retail_II_last_6_months_filtered.csv
  @echo $(DTS)     [INFO] - Executing $@ on [$^].

svc/source/online_retail_II.xlsx:
  @$(test_file)
svc/static/online_retail_II_last_6_months_filtered.csv:
  @$(test_file)
```

```
define test_file
  if ! test -s $<; \
  then echo $(DTS)     [FAIL] - $< does not exist; \
  else true; fi
endef
```

This variable expands to the value of the first dependency of a target. There are a number of other useful variables we can leverage to make the code easier to use. If used creatively, with macros, it is possible to distill a complex set of tasks down to a target and a set of dependencies.

```
path/to/foo: a/b/bar c/baz qux.com quux quux
```

Variable	Purpose	Output
$@	The name of the target.	`path/to/foo`
$^	The name of all dependencies.	`a/b/bar c/baz qux.com quux`
$<	The name of the first dependency.	`a/b/bar`
$(@D)	Directory part of target.	`path/to`
$(@F)	File part of target.	`foo`
$(<D)	Directory part of first dependency.	`a/b`
$(<F)	File part of first dependency.	`bar`
$(^D)	Directory parts of all dependencies.	`a/b c . .`
$(^F)	File parts of all dependencies.	`bar baz qux.com quux`

Key automatic functions

These functions are similar to and can be compiled with the file name functions[131] to derive almost any text string from either the target or the dependency.

Variable	Output
`$(dir $@)`	`path/to`
`$(notdir $@)`	`foo`
`$(abspath $@)`	`/Users/brianmcmillan/projects/sales/path/to/foo`
`$(suffix $^)`	`.com`
`$(basename $^)`	`a/b/bar c/baz qux quux`
`$(addprefix new_, $(basename $(^F)))`	`new_bar new_baz new_qux new_quux`
`$(addsuffix .bak, $(basename $(^F)))`	`bar.bak baz.bak qux.bak quux.bak`
`$(word 2, $^)`	`c/baz`

Key file name functions

We can use these functions to make complicated features. For example, we can use the `cmp` utility to compare the old filtered CSV file to the new CSV file we will be creating when the pipeline is complete. We can use the `$(word #, $^)` variable to parse out specific dependencies based on their order. The `cmp -s` silently compares the contents of two files and if it fails, the `||` operator returns an error message.

```
define file_compare
  #<target>: <file 1> <file 2>
  @cmp -s $(word 1,$^) $(word 2,$^) || \
  echo $(DTS)    [FAIL] - $(word 2,$^) not equal to $(word 1,$^).
endef
```

This macro can be called whenever we need to compare two files by listing the two files as dependencies.

```
test/outputs: \
  etc/test/online_retail_II_last_6_months_filtered.csv \
  svc/static/online_retail_II_last_6_months_filtered.csv
  $(file_compare)
```

NOTE: Make requires each dependency to be defined as a target. If the dependency is not defined, Make will throw an error. In this example, we can solve this by defining a target to check for the existence of the test file.

Converting an Excel file into a CSV file is is our most complicate recipe yet. Fortunately, we're executing the same steps as before but this time we are going to use a number of Make variables to standardize the configuration of the extract with only targets and parameters.

```
287 touch_src/online_retail: svc/source/online_retail_II.xlsx
288   @touch $^ && echo [INFO] - Manually updating [$^] file date.
289
290 svc/load/online_retail_II_-_Year_2010-2011.csv: TABNAME = "Year 2010-2011"
291 svc/load/online_retail_II_-_Year_2010-2011.csv: svc/source/online_retail_II.xlsx
292   @echo [INFO] - Extracting data from $< [$(TABNAME)] into $@
293   @in2csv -f xlsx --sheet $(TABNAME) $< > $@
294   @csvstack -n load_dts -g $(DTS) $@ > $(TEMPSTATEDIR)/$(@F)_1.tmp
295   @csvstack -n provider_code -g $@ $(TEMPSTATEDIR)/$(@F)_1.tmp > $(TEMPSTATEDIR)/$(@F)_2.tmp
296   @mv $(TEMPSTATEDIR)/$(@F)_2.tmp $@
297   @rm $(TEMPSTATEDIR)/$(@F)_1.tmp
298   @$(test_file)
299   @echo [INFO] - record count = $(shell wc -l < $@)
300
```

1. (Line 290) We are setting are the names of the target CSV file and the name of the workbook tab. Here we are making use of the ability to set a variable value accessible only within this target.
2. (291) Set the dependency for the CSV file to the path and name of the Excel file.
3. (292) Logging statement to notify us the extraction process is beginning.
4. (293 - 297) Reimplementation of the previous extraction steps. Notice, we are writing the temporary files used by `csvstack` to the `/tmp` directory.
5. (298) Executes the canned variable to test for the presence of a file.
6. (299) Logging statement returning the number of lines in the new CSV file using the `wc` utility with the line count flag.

Here is the output when we run this target for the first time:

```
sales % make svc/load/online_retail_II_-_Year_2010-2011.csv
[INFO] - Extracting data from svc/source/online_retail_II.xlsx [Year 2010-2011] into svc/load/online_retail_II_-_Year_2010-2011.csv
[INFO] - record count = 541911
sales %
```

If we rerun the target again, Make returns a message that the target is up to date.

```
sales % make svc/load/online_retail_II_-_Year_2010-2011.csv
make: `svc/load/online_retail_II_-_Year_2010-2011.csv' is up to date.
sales %
```

This illustrates a fundamental feature of the way targets are processed. Make maintains an internal database of the modification timestamps of each of the files it manages. When a target is executed, the modification dates of the target and dependency files are evaluated, and only if a file is determined to be newer than the last run date will it be updated. In our example, because the Excel file had not been updated since the first run, it was not processed again.

Whenever the makefile is processed, Make will only execute the targets that need to be updated.[132] When it comes time to schedule the execution of the pipeline, we can safely set the schedule to run more frequently with the confidence that we will only process data when it has changed. As an example, if we expect the data to be updated once a day between 3 am and 7 am, rather than setting the schedule to 9 am to catch possible delays, we could run this pipeline to run every 2 hours and when the data arrives it is quickly processed. The runs without new data are quickly evaluated with no additional data processing.

To see how this works, line 285-286 uses the `touch` command to update the modification timestamp of a file. Running this target and then the extract target re-extracts the data.

```
sales — -zsh — 132×8
sales % make svc/load/online_retail_II_-_Year_2010-2011.csv
make: `svc/load/online_retail_II_-_Year_2010-2011.csv' is up to date.
sales % make touch_src/online_retail
[INFO] - Manually updating [svc/source/online_retail_II.xlsx] file date.
sales % make svc/load/online_retail_II_-_Year_2010-2011.csv
[INFO] - Extracting data from svc/source/online_retail_II.xlsx [Year 2010-2011] into svc/load/online_retail_II_-_Year_2010-2011.csv
[INFO] - record count = 541911
sales %
```

Loading this data into the database is simply a matter of creating a new target based on our earlier analysis.

```
svc/db/sales.db/SRC_online_retail_II_-_Year_2010-2011_001: svc/load/online_retail_II_-_Year_2010-2011.csv
  @echo [INFO] - Loading data into $(@F).$(@D) from $<
  @csvsql \
  --db sqlite:///$(@D) \
  --create-if-not-exists --overwrite \
  --no-inference --no-constraints \
  --chunk-size 10000 \
  --tables $(@F) \
  --insert $<
```

```
sales — -zsh — 87×13
sales % head -10 svc/online_retail_II_-_Year_2010-2011.csv
InvoiceDate,Invoice,StockCode,Description,Quantity,Price,Customer ID,Country
2011-12-09T12:50:00,581587,22631,CIRCUS PARADE LUNCH BOX ,12,1.95,12680,France
2011-12-09T12:50:00,581587,22556,PLASTERS IN TIN CIRCUS PARADE ,12,1.65,12680,France
2011-12-09T12:50:00,581587,22555,PLASTERS IN TIN STRONGMAN,12,1.65,12680,France
2011-12-09T12:50:00,581587,22728,ALARM CLOCK BAKELIKE PINK,4,3.75,12680,France
2011-12-09T12:50:00,581587,22727,ALARM CLOCK BAKELIKE RED ,4,3.75,12680,France
2011-12-09T12:50:00,581587,22726,ALARM CLOCK BAKELIKE GREEN,4,3.75,12680,France
2011-12-09T12:50:00,581587,22730,ALARM CLOCK BAKELIKE IVORY,4,3.75,12680,France
2011-12-09T12:50:00,581587,22367,CHILDRENS APRON SPACEBOY DESIGN,8,1.95,12680,France
2011-12-09T12:50:00,581587,22629,SPACEBOY LUNCH BOX ,12,1.95,12680,France
sales %
```

The recipe will create the database and table if they do not exist the first time it is run. On later runs, the data will be erased from the table and then rewritten.

Once the data is in the database, it will be useful to have some feedback on the number of records that are in the table, just like we reported the number of records in the CSV file. This will require a new target to open the database and execute a query to count the number of records in a table.

```
record_count/SRC_online_retail_II_-_Year_2010-2011_001: \
  svc/db/sales.db/SRC_online_retail_II_-_Year_2010-2011_001
  @echo [INFO] - record count = $(shell $(SQLITE3) $(<D) \
  "SELECT COUNT(*) || ' records in $(@F).$(<D)' FROM [$(@F)]" ".quit")

run: record_count/SRC_online_retail_II_-_Year_2010-2011_001
```

We can use the node graph from `make info` to visualize this flow. Looking at the flow, we can see that the `test/io` needs to be altered so we are testing the input and output files at the right time.

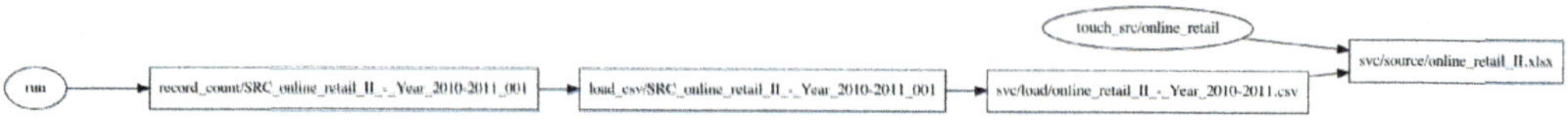

Data pipeline flow

We can safely remove the `svc/source/online_retail_II.xlsx` file from this flow because it is now being tested as part of our new flow. This leaves us with the the task to export the filtered CSV report file.

```
run: file_compare/online_retail ## Executes the primary data pipelines.

etc/sql/sales_last_6_months_filtered_001.sql:
  @$(test_file)

svc/db/sales.db: svc/db/sales.db/SRC_online_retail_II_-_Year_2010-2011_001

svc/static/online_retail_II_last_6_months_filtered.csv: \
  etc/sql/online_retail_II_last_6_months_filtered.sql \
  svc/db/sales.db
  @echo [INFO] - Executing $< and exporting to $@
  @sql2csv --db sqlite:///$(word 2,$^) $< > $@
```

Now the data is loaded into the database, we can refactor our SQL query to use this new table. This query can now be used to generate the extract and the `run:` target can be updated to use this extract as the last step in the pipeline. With a complete pipeline, the final task is to look at the tests we started with and convert them into something more valuable than checking for the existence of a file. The next logical step is to count the number of records in key files and tables.

```
-- sales/etc/sql/online_retail_II_last_6_months_filtered.sql
-----------------------------------------------------------

SELECT Description AS description
,SUM(Quantity) AS quantity
,ROUND(AVG(Price),2) AS price
,ROUND(SUM(Quantity * Price),2) AS total_sales_revenue
FROM 'SRC_online_retail_II_-_Year_2010-2011_001'
WHERE InvoiceDate >= (
SELECT DATE(MAX(InvoiceDate), '-6 months', 'localtime')
FROM 'SRC_online_retail_II_-_Year_2010-2011_001'
)
GROUP BY Description
ORDER BY 4 DESC
LIMIT 10
;
```

```
################################################################################
# Metrics                                                                      #
################################################################################
metrics: \
  metrics/online_retail_II_-_Year_2010-2011.csv \
  metrics/online_retail_II_last_6_months_filtered.csv \
  record_count/SRC_online_retail_II_-_Year_2010-2011_001

metrics/online_retail_II_-_Year_2010-2011.csv: \
  PATH=svc/load/online_retail_II_-_Year_2010-2011.csv
metrics/online_retail_II_-_Year_2010-2011.csv:
  $(record_count_csv)

metrics/online_retail_II_last_6_months_filtered.csv: \
  PATH=svc/static/online_retail_II_last_6_months_filtered.csv
metrics/online_retail_II_last_6_months_filtered.csv:
  $(record_count_csv)

record_count/SRC_online_retail_II_-_Year_2010-2011_001: \
  load_csv/SRC_online_retail_II_-_Year_2010-2011_001
  $(record_count_table)
```

```
define record_count_csv
  @#metrics/<csv_file.csv>(colon)(space)PATH = "<path/to/file.csv>"
  @#metrics/<csv_file.csv>(colon)(space)
  @echo $(DTS)     [INFO] - record count = $(shell wc -l < $(PATH)) $(PATH)
endef

define record_count_table
  @#record_count/<table name>(colon)(space)
  @echo $(DTS)     [INFO] - record count = $(shell $(SQLITE3) $(DBFILE) \
  "SELECT COUNT(*) || ' records in $(@F).$(notdir $(DBFILE))' FROM [$(@F)]" ".quit")
endef
```

sales — -zsh — 74×76

```
sales % csvstat svc/online_retail_II_-_Year_2010-2011.csv
  1. "Invoice"

        Type of data:          Text
        Contains null values:  False
        Unique values:         25900
        Longest value:         7 characters
        Most common values:    573585 (1114x)
                               581219 (749x)
                               581492 (731x)
                               580729 (721x)
                               558475 (705x)

  2. "StockCode"

        Type of data:          Text
        Contains null values:  False
        Unique values:         4070
        Longest value:         12 characters
        Most common values:    85123A (2313x)
                               22423 (2203x)
                               85099B (2159x)
                               47566 (1727x)
                               20725 (1639x)

  3. "Description"

        Type of data:          Text
        Contains null values:  True (excluded from calculations)
        Unique values:         4224
        Longest value:         35 characters
        Most common values:    WHITE HANGING HEART T-LIGHT HOLDER (2369x)
                               REGENCY CAKESTAND 3 TIER (2200x)
                               JUMBO BAG RED RETROSPOT (2159x)
                               PARTY BUNTING (1727x)
                               LUNCH BAG RED RETROSPOT (1638x)

  4. "Quantity"

        Type of data:          Number
        Contains null values:  False
        Unique values:         722
        Smallest value:        -80,995
        Largest value:         80,995
        Sum:                   5,176,451
        Mean:                  9.552
        Median:                3
        StDev:                 218.081
        Most common values:    1 (148228x)
                               2 (81829x)
                               12 (61063x)
                               6 (40868x)
                               4 (38484x)

  5. "InvoiceDate"

        Type of data:          DateTime
        Contains null values:  False
        Unique values:         23260
        Smallest value:        2010-12-01 08:26:00
        Largest value:         2011-12-09 12:50:00
        Most common values:    2011-10-31 14:41:00 (1114x)
                               2011-12-08 09:28:00 (749x)
                               2011-12-09 10:03:00 (731x)
                               2011-12-05 17:24:00 (721x)
                               2011-06-29 15:58:00 (705x)

  6. "Price"

        Type of data:          Number
        Contains null values:  False
        Unique values:         1630
        Smallest value:        -11,062.06
        Largest value:         38,970
        Sum:                   2,498,821.974
        Mean:                  4.611
        Median:                2.08
        StDev:                 96.76
        Most common values:    1.25 (50496x)
                               1.65 (38181x)
                               0.85 (28497x)
                               2.95 (27768x)
                               0.42 (24533x)

  7. "Customer ID"

        Type of data:          Number
        Contains null values:  True (excluded from calculations)
        Unique values:         4373
        Smallest value:        12,346
        Largest value:         18,287
        Sum:                   6,219,488,647
        Mean:                  15,287.684
        Median:                15,152
        StDev:                 1,713.603
        Most common values:    None (135080x)
                               17,841 (7983x)
                               14,911 (5903x)
                               14,096 (5128x)
                               12,748 (4642x)

  8. "Country"

        Type of data:          Text
        Contains null values:  False
        Unique values:         38
        Longest value:         20 characters
        Most common values:    United Kingdom (495478x)
                               Germany (9495x)
                               France (8558x)
                               EIRE (8196x)
                               Spain (2533x)

Row count: 541910
sales %
```

```
sales % make metrics
[INFO] - record count = 11 svc/static/online_retail_II_last_6_months_filtered.csv
[INFO] - record count = 541911 svc/load/online_retail_II_-_Year_2010-2011.csv
[INFO] - record count = 541910 records in SRC_online_retail_II_-_Year_2010-2011_001.svc/db/sales.db
sales %
```

Our primary data pipeline begins with a source Excel file, a sql script, and a target CSV file. All of these are executed whenever we run the `make run` command. If we run the `make touch_src/online_retail && make run` commands, the entire pipeline will start with re-extracting the data from Excel.

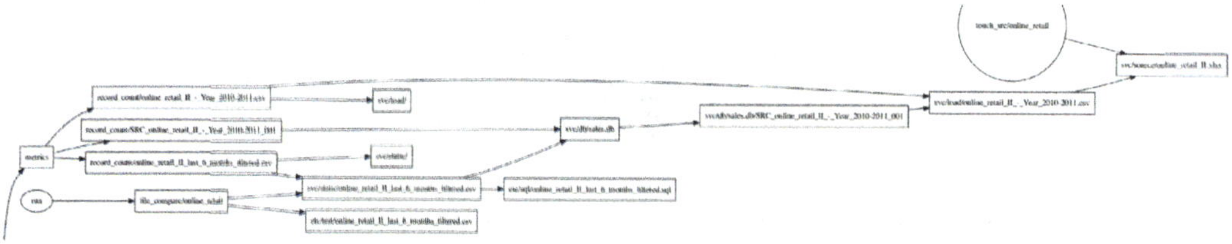

Modified flow

Our work isn't done. Once you have a working solution, set aside some time to refactor what you have so it is easier to understand, test, and expand in the future. The obvious candidates are moving complicated and repetitive recipes into macros and reorganizing the makefile to be more readable.

```
define extract_csv_from_excel
  @#<path/to/csv_file.csv>(colon)(space)TABNAME = "<name of XLS worksheet>"
  @#<path/to/csv_file.csv>(colon)(space)<path/to/source/excel_file.xlsx>
  @echo [INFO] - Extracting data from $< [$(TABNAME)] into $@
  @in2csv -f xlsx --sheet $(TABNAME) $< > $@
  @csvstack -n load_dts -g $(DTS) $@ > $(TEMPSTATEDIR)/$(@F)_1.tmp
  @csvstack -n provider_code -g $@ $(TEMPSTATEDIR)/$(@F)_1.tmp > $(TEMPSTATEDIR)/$(@F)_2.tmp
  @mv $(TEMPSTATEDIR)/$(@F)_2.tmp $@
  @rm $(TEMPSTATEDIR)/$(@F)_1.tmp
  @$(test_file)
endef

define load_csv_into_database
  @#<path/to/database_file.db>/SRC_<csv_file_name>_001(colon)(space)<path/to/csv_file.csv>
  @echo [INFO] - Loading data into $(@F).$(@D) from $<
  @csvsql \
  --db sqlite:///$(@D) \
  --create-if-not-exists --overwrite \
  --no-inference --no-constraints \
  --chunk-size 10000 \
  --tables $(@F) \
  --insert $<
endef
```

NOTE: As you make each refactor, be sure to test the solution by rerunning the pipeline.

Retrospective

At this point, we built a solid foundation to confidently take in any file, perform basic analysis, and return the results without harming the ability to expand our analysis capability. In the next chapter, we incorporate new data sources and transition from pure data engineering tasks, like building the plumbing, to more analytics engineering tasks focused on answering business questions.

Next Steps

- Continue to reorganize the order of the targets to make them even easier to navigate.
- Spend time comparing the makefile_graph and the makefile to practice following the execution of the pipeline.
- Move the `installdirs:` recipe into the Project Build Tool.

---

110 Twitter @doctorow (https://twitter.com/doctorow/status/1316421451805724677)

111 UCI Machine Learning Repository - Online Retail Data Set (https://archive.ics.uci.edu/ml/datasets/Online+Retail)

UCI Machine Learning Repository - Online Retail II Data Set (https://archive.ics.uci.edu/ml/datasets/Online+Retail+II)

112 User Story Template (https://www.agilealliance.org/glossary/user-story-template/)

113 OLD FAVORITE: FEATURE INJECTION USER STORIES ON A BUSINESS VALUE THEME (http://antonymarcano.com/blog/2011/03/fi_stories/)

114 Introducing BDD (https://dannorth.net/introducing-bdd/)

115 Applying BDD acceptance criteria in user stories (https://www.thoughtworks.com/insights/blog/applying-bdd-acceptance-criteria-user-stories)

116 Cucumber (https://cucumber.io)

117 The Checklist Manifesto: How to Get Things Right, Gawande, A., 2010, (https://www.amazon.com/gp/product/0312430000/)

[118] imdone (https://imdone.io)

[119] Making Work Visible: Exposing Time Theft to Optimize Work & Flow, DeGrandis, D. (https://www.amazon.com/Making-Work-Visible-Exposing-Optimize-ebook/dp/B076BYZ6VN/)

[120] Thinking in business terms, the value we create is like a credit to the overall value we are providing. Technical debts are all the decisions we made that will eventually reduce those credits in the form of rework, time spent resolving potential defects, and deferred but necessary features.

[121] EuSpRig (http://www.eusprig.org/horror-stories.htm)

[122] Excel VBA scripts and PowerQuery are largely unknown and utilize features most Excel users don't know exist.

[123] Karl W. Broman & Kara H. Woo (2018) Data Organization in Spreadsheets, The American Statistician, 72:1, 2-10, DOI: 10.1080/00031305.2017.1375989)

[124] CSVKit (https://csvkit.readthedocs.io/en/latest/index.html) (https://csvkit.readthedocs.io/en/latest/index.html)

[125] This is not entirely true. CSVKit utilizes the SQLite database internally to provide a SQL query interface to CSV files in addition to enabling SQL queries on STDIN.

[126] We are going to continue to use `csvkit` rather than using the `sqlite3` command line tool because it supports working with other databases.

[127] Back of the napkin test shows that the `csvsql` command against a file-based database is almost 1000x times faster than using the in-memory SQLite instance (.400ms vs. 330s).

[128] Canned Recipe (https://www.gnu.org/software/make/manual/make.html#Canned-Recipes). Canned Recipes are also referred to as macros.

[129] Graphviz (https://graphviz.org)

[130] Automatic variables (https://www.gnu.org/software/make/manual/make.html#Automatic-Variables)

[131] File Name Functions (https://www.gnu.org/software/make/manual/make.html#File-Name-Functions)

[132] This applies only to files, we don't have the same visibility to database tables. However, we can use marker files to trick Make into treating this hidden data as a file.

Chapter 5: Improving the Data Analysis

Now that we have automated our data pipelines into a database and provided our initial analysis, we take the next leap by performing a deeper data quality analysis on our initial data set, followed by developing a new set of data extracts and our first visualization.

Building a Solid Foundation

The first step in any new development iteration is reviewing the completed stories and then planning and prioritizing the additional work. The biggest opportunity we discovered was cleaning up the product descriptions to remove a few line items. Grouping products together into product families helped the sales team better focus on high-revenue product groups.

IN ORDER TO FOCUS ON THE PRODUCTS WITH THE HIGHEST REVENUE.
AS A SALES MANAGER
I WANT A LIST OF THE TOP 10 PRODUCTS WITH SIMILAR PRODUCT ATTRIBUTES, BY TOTAL REVENUE, OVER THE LAST SIX MONTHS.

[X] DATA SET RECEIVED FROM THE SALES DEPT.
[X] PERFORM INITIAL ANALYSIS
[X] GO/NO GO AGREEMENT
[-] GROUP PRODUCTS BY ATTRIBUTE
[X] DERIVE DATA SET: PRODUCT NAME GROUP, REVENUE, SALES DATE, LIMIT TOP 10
[X] PROVIDE TOP 10 PRODUCTS BY REVENUE IN AN EMAIL TO THE SALES MANAGER.

```
sales — -zsh — 80×15
sales % csvlook svc/static/online_retail_II_last_6_months_filtered.csv
| description                         | quantity |  price | total_sales_revenue |
| ----------------------------------- | -------- | ------ | ------------------- |
| DOTCOM POSTAGE                      |      321 | 384.91 |          123,556.41 |
| REGENCY CAKESTAND 3 TIER            |    5,429 |  14.07 |           68,685.31 |
| RABBIT NIGHT LIGHT                  |   29,486 |   2.37 |           64,326.29 |
| PAPER CHAIN KIT 50'S CHRISTMAS      |   16,341 |   3.30 |           54,166.87 |
| JUMBO BAG RED RETROSPOT             |   27,351 |   2.40 |           54,088.32 |
| PARTY BUNTING                       |    8,638 |   5.77 |           47,966.06 |
| WHITE HANGING HEART T-LIGHT HOLDER  |   15,925 |   3.27 |           45,406.65 |
| PICNIC BASKET WICKER 60 PIECES      |       61 | 649.50 |           39,619.50 |
| POSTAGE                             |    1,754 |  25.17 |           39,163.10 |
| ASSORTED COLOUR BIRD ORNAMENT       |   21,812 |   1.71 |           34,980.04 |
sales %
```

Working with the Sales Manager, we developed a few new stories. The highest priority story should be simple to complete. Modify our query with a basic `WHERE` clause filter and then rerunning the extract.

> **IN ORDER TO** FOCUS ON THE PRODUCTS WITH THE HIGHEST REVENUE.
> **AS A** SALES MANAGER
> **I WANT** A LIST OF THE TOP 10 PRODUCTS WITH SIMILAR PRODUCT ATTRIBUTES, BY TOTAL REVENUE, OVER THE LAST SIX MONTHS.
>
> [ ] FILTER OUT POSTAGE, MANUAL, ETC.
> [ ] PROVIDE TOP 10 PRODUCTS BY REVENUE IN AN EMAIL TO THE SALES MANAGER.
> [ ] PROVIDE A CHART OF PRODUCT SALES BY WEEK OVER THE LAST SIX MONTHS.

The next highest priority story can't be argued with. Providing data as CSV extracts to pull into Excel isn't very user-friendly, and even a basic data visualization would improve our analysis. The technical question is whether this can be done in code and with our automation system.

```
IN ORDER TO FOCUS ON THE PRODUCTS WITH THE
HIGHEST REVENUE.
AS A SALES MANAGER
I WANT A CHART OF PRODUCT SALES BY WEEK OVER THE
LAST SIX MONTHS. (ATTRIBUTES BY: TOTAL REVENUE,
OVER THE LAST SIX MONTHS.
```

With our business stories prioritized, we develop a technical story to improve the data quality by applying a set of standard data-cleaning steps. After a quick discussion, we work on this story first because it underlies all the other analyses.

```
IN ORDER TO PROVIDE A SINGLE SOURCE OF INVOICE
DATA
AS A SALES MANAGER
I WANT CONSOLIDATED DATA SET OF INVOICE DATA
AND NO DUPLICATE RECORDS
AND A RECORD OF CHANGES TO INVOICES OVER TIME
AND IDENTIFICATION OF POTENTIALLY MISSING DATA

[] BUILD OUT A DATA SET WITH ALL GROSS DATA
ERRORS REMOVED.
```

The final story begins the work of grouping products into product families. This was originally part of our first business story, but because it requires additional research and likely requires developing a solution to allow for user input, it was pushed to the end of this iteration.

IN ORDER TO FOCUS ON THE PRODUCTS WITH THE HIGHEST REVENUE.
AS A SALES MANAGER
I WANT TO BE ABLE TO GROUP SIMILAR PRODUCTS.

[] RESEARCH PRODUCT GROUPINGS, SUGGEST IDEAS.
[] POC - ALIAS TABLE FOR PRODUCT DESCRIPTIONS.
[] REVIEW TOP 10 DATA SET W/ GROUPINGS.

Basic Data Cleaning

The first step in processing our data is to evaluate whether there are any duplicate records in the data set. This step is critical if the data is from a reporting system or if it may have been aggregated or had fields removed. We must suspect that every data set has duplicates. The first step in determining whether this is the case is to execute a simple `SELECT DISTINCT` query on the table. In the first example, we execute the query in our visual query editor and then with a command-line tool. Unfortunately, our count of distinct records (536642) does not match our full record count (541910).

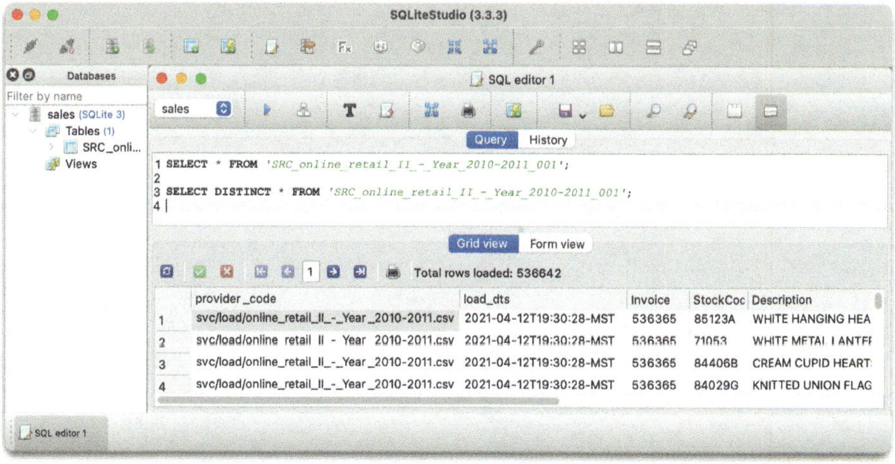

SELECT vs. SELECT DISTINCT

Now write a query against the `SRC_` table to return the unique records. There are many ways to do this, and the simplest is to write a sub-query selecting the distinct records.

```
SELECT DISTINCT
    provider_code,
    load_dts,
    Invoice,
    StockCode,
    Description,
    Quantity,
    InvoiceDate,
    Price,
    "Customer ID",
    Country
FROM SRC_online_retail_II_-_Year_2010-2011_001;
```

This accomplishes what we want, but now we need to analyze this data set in different ways to look for other basic data issues. Use a subquery to serve as the data set in a new query.

The problem with a subquery that is in-line with the FROM statement is its difficulty to read and to independently execute the subquery. This case is simple, but in more complicated analytic queries with many complex sources, this will be nearly impossible to figure out what a query is doing or where it has errors.

```
SELECT
provider_code,
load_dts,
Invoice,
StockCode,
Description,
Quantity,
InvoiceDate,
Price,
"Customer ID",
Country
FROM (
  SELECT DISTINCT
      provider_code,
      load_dts,
      Invoice,
      StockCode,
      Description,
      Quantity,
      InvoiceDate,
      Price,
      "Customer ID",
      Country
  FROM SRC_online_retail_II_-_Year_2010-2011_001
);
```

To fix this, we are going to rewrite the query using a technique called a Common Table Expression (CTE) (AKA a `WITH` statement).

```
WITH CTE_SOURCE AS (
  SELECT DISTINCT *
  FROM "SRC_online_retail_II_-_Year_2010-2011_001"
)

SELECT
  provider_code,
  load_dts,
  Invoice,
  StockCode,
  Description,
  Quantity,
  InvoiceDate,
  Price,
  "Customer ID",
  Country
FROM CTE_SOURCE;
```

A CTE allows you to create a temporary data set in your query that can be referenced later. It increases code legibility and makes it possible to step through the query logic as the query is built.

This query is now much easier to understand.

1. FROM `SRC_online_retail_II_-_Year_2010-2011_001`, `SELECT` all the `DISTINCT` records `AS CTE_SOURCE`.
2. FROM `CTE_SOURCE`, `SELECT` each named field.

Normally, SQL Style Guides[133] tell you to be explicit and never use the `*` shorthand for all fields, but in this `SELECT DISTINCT` case, it is an acceptable exception because the statement is unambiguous. Take the entire data set and filter out the duplicates.

Creating a RAW_ Table for Analysis

Now that our query contains distinct values, we write that data into a new table. Rather than ask a data modeler to design a table for us, we use the SQL language to build and populate the table using a query.

Modify the previous query in the SQL editor to add the standard header, basic data typing, and a `CREATE TABLE` statement. Save this file in the `etc/sql/` directory as `RAW_ONLINE_RETAIL_II_ - YEAR_2010_2011_001_create.sql` using the naming convention `RAW_<name_of_file>_###_<verb>.sql` to make it easier to identify the purpose of the SQL query.

This query builds on the previous one by adding a `CTE_BASE` block of code where we redefine the column types if they are not text.

NOTE: SQLite does not have a separate data type for dates; leave them as text. It is also a good practice to lowercase all the field names to distinguish them from uppercase table names and to separate *camelCase* words with an underscore to make them easier to read.

```
-- sales/etc/sql/RAW_ONLINE_RETAIL_II_YEAR_2010_2011_001_create.sql
------------------------------------------------------------
CREATE TABLE IF NOT EXISTS RAW_ONLINE_RETAIL_II_YEAR_2010_2011_001 AS

WITH CTE_SOURCE AS (
    SELECT DISTINCT *
    FROM "SRC_online_retail_II_-_Year_2010-2011_001"
    )
,
CTE_BASE AS (
    SELECT
        "provider_code",
        "load_dts",
        "Invoice" AS invoice,
        "StockCode" AS stock_code,
        "Description" description,
        CAST("Quantity" AS NUMERIC) AS quantity,
        "InvoiceDate" AS invoice_date,
        CAST("Price" AS NUMERIC) AS price,
        "Customer ID" AS customer_id,
        "Country" AS country
    FROM CTE_SOURCE
    )

SELECT * FROM CTE_BASE
;
```

Execute this query from the command line using the SQLite `sqlite3` database client. We are building the table in the database and inserting the records from the query results with the same query.

```
sqlite3 svc/db/sales.db ".read etc/sql/
RAW_ONLINE_RETAIL_II_YEAR_2010_2011_001_create.sql" ".quit"
```

Earlier, we used the `sql2csv` to execute SQL queries to load data into the database. This utility works with many databases, not just SQLite. When moving data into different destinations, the ability to connect to many different targets is an absolute necessity. This feature of being both source and destination independent is referred to as loose coupling. It is *loose* because it is easy to change either the source or target at any time. This is particularly true because we use a CSV file as an intermediate data set.

However, once we are within a specific database and executing queries against that database, using the database-specific command-line utility is faster, easier to use, and more feature rich. The cost of this *tight* coupling is that if you switch to a new database platform, the code will need to be changed. Unfortunately, due to variations in the SQL dialect used in every platform, you will modify significantly more than the command-line structure used to execute a query in the migration.

There are numerous ways to reduce this impact:

- Follow consistent coding standards as defined in shared style guides. The guides should be regularly updated to reflect the current best practices.
- Avoid database-specific syntax.
- Break complicated databases, tables, code, and supporting software into small manageable pieces rather than attempting to do everything at once. Like the Dunbar Number suggests, smaller teams reduce the cognitive load. Keeping the application smaller also reduces the load. Strive to keep everything as small, discrete, and easy to understand as possible.
- Change should happen in small, independent steps.
- Tests, even simple ones, make it possible to make changes with confidence.

Now that we have our first query creating a database table, we should add it to our automation script. Update the `run` target to process the `create/tables` target.

NOTE: Creating and loading a table this way is a one time event. If you rerun the query the table will not be created nor will data be reloaded.

Do not forget to add the record count test for this table to the `metrics:` target.

```
define create_table
  @#<table_name>(colon)(space)<path/to/<table_name>_create.sql>
  @echo $(DTS)    [INFO] - Creating table $@.
  @$(SQLITE3) $(DBFILE) ".read $<" ".quit"
endef
```

```
create/tables: RAW_ONLINE_RETAIL_II_YEAR_2010_2011_001

etc/sql/RAW_ONLINE_RETAIL_II_YEAR_2010_2011_001_create.sql:
  $(test_file)

RAW_ONLINE_RETAIL_II_YEAR_2010_2011_001: \
  etc/sql/RAW_ONLINE_RETAIL_II_YEAR_2010_2011_001_create.sql
  $(create_table)

test_table/RAW_ONLINE_RETAIL_II_YEAR_2010_2011_001:
  $(test_table)

```

```
metrics: \
  metrics/online_retail_II_-_Year_2010-2011.csv \
  metrics/online_retail_II_last_6_months_filtered.csv \
  record_count/SRC_online_retail_II_-_Year_2010-2011_001

record_count/RAW_ONLINE_RETAIL_II_YEAR_2010_2011_001: \
  RAW_ONLINE_RETAIL_II_YEAR_2010_2011_001
  $(record_count_table)
```

Creating a table based on the results of a query is an ideal way to make a new table available for one-time analysis. We're creating a new table and simultaneously adding the desired record set. What happens to this data in the future is unclear. This is also the reason we refer to these tables with the "RAW_" prefix. In future analysis we will be creating other types of tables.

As the data sources and our understanding of our needs become more stabilized, we will need to decide if the benefit of this ease of use outweighs the benefits of specifying a well-defined data structure. In particular, if we expect many sources to be providing data simultaneously, we will need to have a stable definition of the target table and the ability to update the data.

Creating an INFO_ Table for Reporting

The next logical step is to create a table to store the results of the query we used to produce our Top 10 analysis. This table will be prefixed with "INFO_" to identify that it provides information to end users. We also add the suffix "_001" to the table to denote that this is version one of the result set. This will allow is to modify the table logic in the future as a new version and still keep the old version available. As we build more tables, the usefulness of these naming conventions will become more obvious.

Create a new sql file in the `etc/sql/` directory and then modify it to create the new table. This file will resemble the previous CREATE TABLE query but the data being inserted will come from a modification of the `online_retail_II_last_6_months_filtered.sql` query.

```
touch etc/sql/INFO_SALES_LAST_6_MONTHS_FILTERED_001_create.sql
```

Copy the `transforms/info/sales_last_6_months_filtered_001.sql` query into the `create_INFO_SALES_LAST_6_MONTHS_FILTERED_001.sql` file and modify it to create a new table.

```
-- sales/etc/sql/INFO_SALES_LAST_6_MONTHS_FILTERED_001_create.sql
----------------------------------------------------------------
CREATE TABLE IF NOT EXISTS INFO_SALES_LAST_6_MONTHS_FILTERED_001 AS

WITH CTE_SOURCE AS (
  SELECT Description AS description
  ,SUM(Quantity) AS quantity
  ,ROUND(AVG(Price),2) AS price
  ,ROUND(SUM(Quantity * Price),2) AS total_sales_revenue
  FROM 'SRC_online_retail_II_-_Year_2010-2011_001'
  WHERE InvoiceDate >= (
  SELECT DATE(MAX(InvoiceDate), '-6 months', 'localtime')
  FROM 'SRC_online_retail_II_-_Year_2010-2011_001'
  )
  GROUP BY Description
  ORDER BY 4 DESC
  LIMIT 100
    )

SELECT * FROM CTE_SOURCE
;
```

Adding this table the makefile follows the same steps as the RAW_ONLINE_RETAIL_II_YEAR_2010_2011_001 table.

```
# Database and table tests--------------------
test_database: $(DBFILE)
  @#test_database(colon)(space)<path/to/database.db>
  @if ! test -s $<; \
  then echo $(DTS)    [FAIL] - $< file does not exist; \
  else echo $(DTS)    [INFO] - DB $(shell $(SQLITE3) $(DBFILE) ".databases"); fi

test_tables: \
  test_table/SRC_online_retail_II_-_Year_2010-2011_001

test_table/SRC_online_retail_II_-_Year_2010-2011_001:
  @#test_table/<table_name>(colon)
  @if ! test $(@F) = $(shell $(SQLITE3) $(DBFILE) ".tables $(@F)" ".quit"); \
  then echo [FAIL] - $(@F) table does not exist; \
  else true; fi
```

While these database record count test implicitly test for the existence of the database and tables we should create separate structural test for the database and individual tables. Of course, these recipes are to be converted into macros.

Now is also a good time to review and revise the master targets and rerun the solution.

```
#################################################################
all: run documentation ## Executes the default make task.
info: help info/variables test/dirs test/solution_files documentation ## Generat
check: test/outputs test_tables test_db metrics ## Executes all test suites.
installcheck: test/dirs test/inputs ## Run the project test suite.
install: create/tables ## Builds the database and application structure.
uninstall: uninstalldirs ## Uninstalls the project.
run: test/inputs test/outputs metrics ## Executes the data pipelines.
```

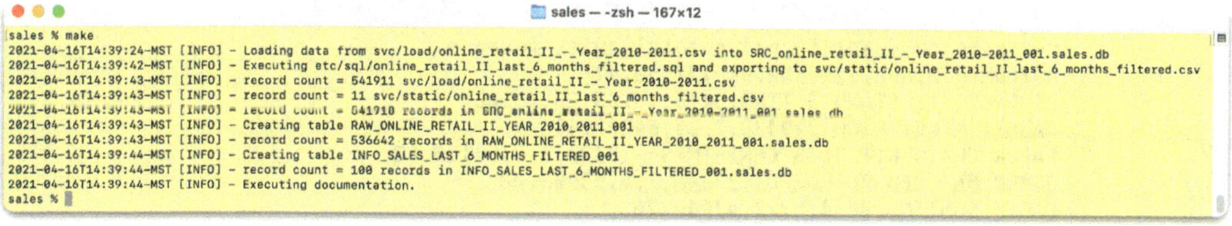

Updating the Old Deliverables

The next step is to modify our exported CSV file in the `svc/static/` directory by creating a new version of the `online_retail_II_last_6_months_filtered.sql` file named `online_retail_II_last_6_months_filtered_002.sql`. This query extracts data from the RAW_ table rather than the SRC_ table and returns the Top 100 products by total revenue.

```sql
-- sales/etc/sql/online_retail_II_last_6_months_filtered_002.sql
----------------------------------------------------------

SELECT description
,SUM(quantity) AS quantity
,ROUND(AVG(price),2) AS price
,ROUND(SUM(quantity * price),2) AS total_sales_revenue
FROM 'RAW_ONLINE_RETAIL_II_YEAR_2010_2011_001'
WHERE invoice_date >= (
SELECT DATE(MAX(invoice_date), '-6 months', 'localtime')
FROM 'RAW_ONLINE_RETAIL_II_YEAR_2010_2011_001'
)
GROUP BY description
ORDER BY 4 DESC
LIMIT 100
;
```

After adding the tests, metrics, and updating the `run/online_retail_II:` target, we can execute make to test the solution.

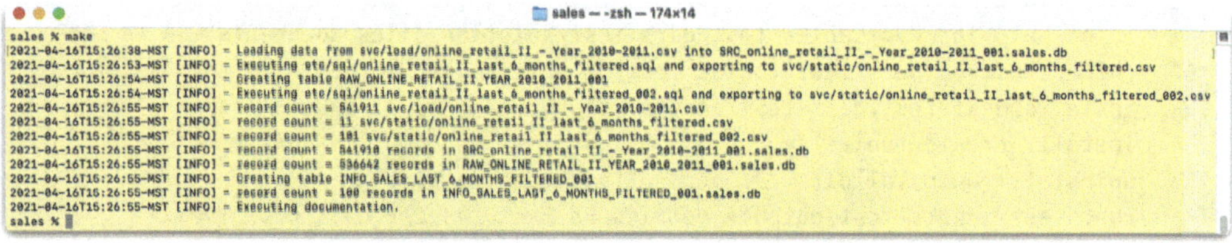

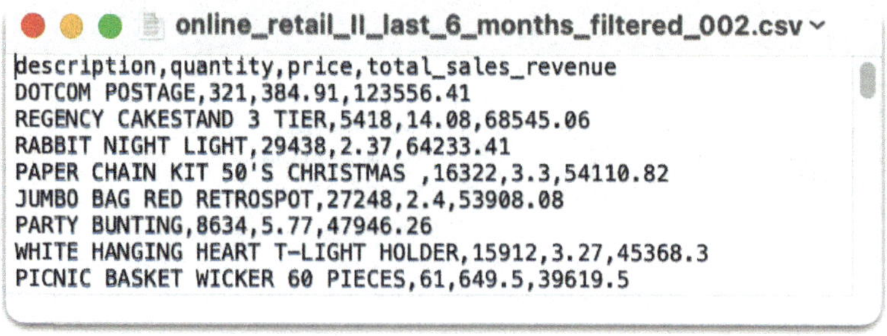

Confidence Check

At this point, we have:

- Modified our analysis to migrate our source Excel file into a database.
- Reproduced our original analysis.
- Fixed a major data quality issue.
- Automated the analysis workflow.

One of the benefits of this automation is that we can tear down all our previous work and rebuild it from scratch. If we were to lose our development workstation we can easily rebuild it. Or, if we made an error in our coding or data pipeline, it might be easier to intentionally delete everything and rebuild from scratch.

When deploying our solution to production servers, we need the confidence that if problems arise in that environment, we can re-deploy it from scratch. If we can deploy to one server, we can deploy to multiple systems. This scales the solution to support increased traffic by load balancing [134] or even A/B split testing.[135]

However, executing numerous steps isn't sufficient if you don't know that they are executed correctly. This is where all the tests come in. Executing tests and providing valuable feedback is critical to building confidence in the system. Simply stringing your tasks together gets you to your goal quickly, but without the tests, how would you know about issues introduced by other developers? Or if the system stopped working as expected?

Having confidence in your ability to quickly recover from disaster allows you to take a small investment in building a few simple up-front tests and leverage them into significantly faster delivery. This is because multiple changes can be made simultaneously, and this speed in turn lowers support costs.

If we want to test out our solution, we need to update the `uninstalldirs:` recipe to reflect this new need. Now, when we execute the `make uninstall` command, all of the files we've created will be removed.

```
├── makefile
└── svc
    ├── db
    │   └── sales.db
    ├── doc
    │   ├── directory_listing.txt
    │   └── makefile_graph.png
    ├── load
    │   └── online_retail_II_-_Year_2010-2011.csv
    ├── source
    │   └── online_retail_II.xlsx
    └── static
        ├── online_retail_II_last_6_months_filtered.csv
        └── online_retail_II_last_6_months_filtered_002.csv
```

Run `make uninstall` and then `make info` to update the file and directory listing. As you can see, we are back at square one, except for the new sql query files.

```
sales — -zsh — 64x38
sales % tree
.
├── AUTHORS.md
├── CHANGELOG.md
├── LICENSE.md
├── NEWS.md
├── README.md
├── etc
│   ├── app
│   ├── cron
│   ├── server
│   ├── sql
│   │   ├── INFO_SALES_LAST_6_MONTHS_FILTERED_001_create.sql
│   │   ├── RAW_ONLINE_RETAIL_II_YEAR_2010_2011_001_create.sql
│   │   ├── online_retail_II_last_6_months_filtered.sql
│   │   └── online_retail_II_last_6_months_filtered_002.sql
│   └── test
│       └── online_retail_II_last_6_months_filtered.csv
├── makefile
├── opt
│   ├── local
│   ├── python
│   └── sqlite3
├── src
│   └── sqlite3
├── svc
│   ├── db
│   ├── doc
│   ├── load
│   ├── source
│   │   └── online_retail_II.xlsx
│   └── static
├── tmp
└── var
    └── log

21 directories, 12 files
sales %
```

The solution now includes the source file, the SQL query files, and one CSV file we use to ensure the final output CSV file is exactly what we expect.

Now for the real test. Will running `make` rebuild the project? It appears that everything ran perfectly!

directory_listing.txt

```
.
├── AUTHORS.md
├── CHANGELOG.md
├── LICENSE.md
├── NEWS.md
├── README.md
├── etc
│   ├── sql
│   │   ├── INFO_SALES_LAST_6_MONTHS_FILTERED_001_create.sql
│   │   ├── RAW_ONLINE_RETAIL_II_YEAR_2010_2011_001_create.sql
│   │   ├── online_retail_II_last_6_months_filtered.sql
│   │   └── online_retail_II_last_6_months_filtered_002.sql
│   └── test
│       └── online_retail_II_last_6_months_filtered.csv
├── makefile
└── svc
    ├── db
    │   └── sales.db
    ├── doc
    │   ├── directory_listing.txt
    │   └── makefile_graph.png
    ├── load
    │   └── online_retail_II_-_Year_2010-2011.csv
    ├── source
    │   └── online_retail_II.xlsx
    └── static
        ├── online_retail_II_last_6_months_filtered.csv
        └── online_retail_II_last_6_months_filtered_002.csv

9 directories, 18 files
```

Looking at the diagram produced by `make info`, we can see that the default `all` target runs the entire build and the whole process starting with `svc/source/online_retail_II.xlsx`.

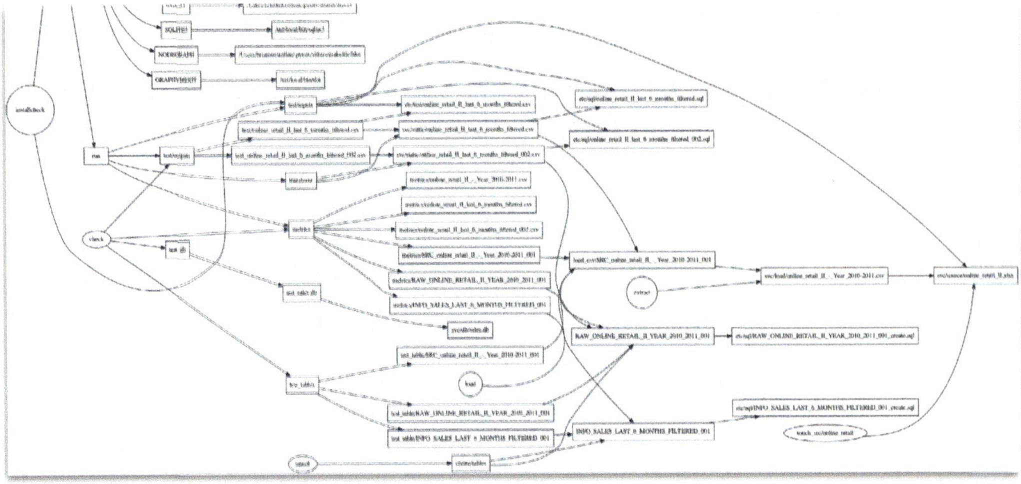

Don't underestimate the importance of having a programmatically generated view of the steps in your data pipeline. It is a critically necessary development tool. While you may think you can manage and maintain all the dependencies by force of logic and good coding practices, having a picture reveals structural inconsistencies hidden by your familiarity with the code. Carefully review each of the steps in both the diagram and the makefile. If a dependency is missing, add it to the makefile and then rerun the tasks `make` and rebuild the diagram `make info`. Keep the changes small and rerun them after each change.

As a general rule:

- Extracts should come before loads.
- Loads should be followed by runs.
- Inspect every SQL query and add any table in the FROM clause as a dependency.

TL,DR: *Testing at every step saves money and time in the long run.*

Starting the Analytics Engineering

Now that we have our data infrastructure established by moving the data into a database, it is time to start the analysis. Look at our stories and decide which one makes the most sense to start to work on.

```
IN ORDER TO FOCUS ON THE PRODUCTS WITH THE
HIGHEST REVENUE.
AS A SALES MANAGER
I WANT A LIST OF THE TOP 10 PRODUCTS WITH
SIMILAR PRODUCT ATTRIBUTES, BY TOTAL REVENUE,
OVER THE LAST SIX MONTHS.

[] FILTER OUT POSTAGE, MANUAL, ETC.
[] PROVIDE TOP 10 PRODUCTS BY REVENUE IN AN
EMAIL TO THE SALES MANAGER.
[] PROVIDE A CHART OF PRODUCT SALES BY WEEK ONE
THE LAST SIX MONTHS.
```

Looking at the acceptance criteria, the most logical place to start is to filter out the "postage" and "manual" records by making a simple change to our `etc/sql/online_retail_II_last_6_months_filtered_002.sql` query and then run the tasks to generate a new file.

```sql
-- sales/etc/sql/online_retail_II_last_6_months_filtered_002.sql
-------------------------------------------------------

SELECT description
,SUM(quantity) AS quantity
,ROUND(AVG(price),2) AS price
,ROUND(SUM(quantity * price),2) AS total_sales_revenue
FROM 'RAW_ONLINE_RETAIL_II_YEAR_2010_2011_001'
WHERE invoice_date >= (
SELECT DATE(MAX(invoice_date), '-6 months', 'localtime')
FROM 'RAW_ONLINE_RETAIL_II_YEAR_2010_2011_001'
) AND
UPPER(description) NOT LIKE '%MANUAL%' AND
UPPER(description) NOT LIKE '%POSTAGE%'
GROUP BY description
ORDER BY 4 DESC
LIMIT 10
;
```

online_retail_II_last_6_months_filtered_002.csv

```
description,quantity,price,total_sales_revenue
REGENCY CAKESTAND 3 TIER,5418,14.08,68545.06
RABBIT NIGHT LIGHT,29438,2.37,64233.41
PAPER CHAIN KIT 50'S CHRISTMAS ,16322,3.3,54110.82
JUMBO BAG RED RETROSPOT,27248,2.4,53908.08
PARTY BUNTING,8634,5.77,47946.26
WHITE HANGING HEART T-LIGHT HOLDER,15912,3.27,45368.3
PICNIC BASKET WICKER 60 PIECES,61,649.5,39619.5
ASSORTED COLOUR BIRD ORNAMENT,21745,1.71,34866.81
POPCORN HOLDER,36322,1.01,33959.26
SPOTTY BUNTING,6453,5.56,32691.71
```

How Do We Find the Unique Records?

However, we shouldn't send it without performing an additional analysis step to look for other data anomalies. Every single data set we work with, even data directly from a trusted source system, can hide nasty surprises. The process of determining what combination of records is required to make a single unique record is the most important analytic skill you could learn. Not only will you identify defects in the data, you will gain insights into the underlying business processes day-to-day users of the data don't possess.

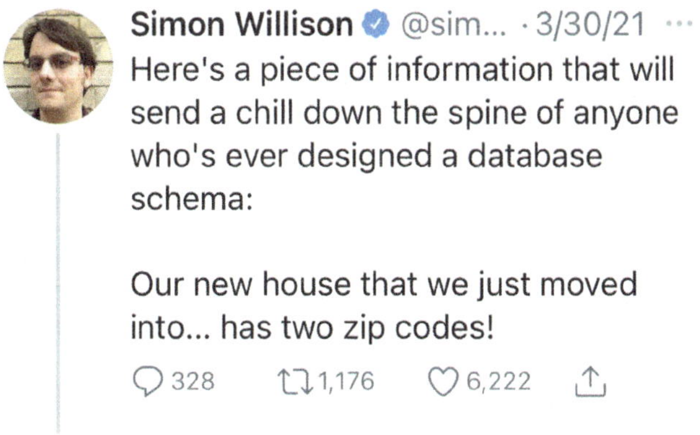

Create a new a new `svc/analysis/` directory. This analysis folder provides a location to store ad-hoc analysis queries and results we are not ready to include in the main solution.

Create a new SQL query in this directory called:
`RAW_ONLINE_RETAIL_II_YEAR_2010_2011_001_row_count.sql`

In this query, we will start with our `RAW_` table and apply our base six-month and manual filters.

```
--RAW_ONLINE_RETAIL_II_YEAR_2010_2011_001_row_count.sql
------------------------------------------------------------
WITH CTE_BASE AS (
  SELECT DISTINCT
  provider_code,
  load_dts,
  invoice,
  stock_code,
  description,
  invoice_date,
  quantity,
  price,
  customer_id,
  country
  FROM RAW_ONLINE_RETAIL_II_YEAR_2010_2011_001
  WHERE
      invoice_date >= (
          SELECT DATE(MAX(invoice_date), '-6 months', 'localtime')
          FROM RAW_ONLINE_RETAIL_II_YEAR_2010_2011_001
          ) AND
      UPPER(description) NOT LIKE '%MANUAL%' AND
      UPPER(description) NOT LIKE '%POSTAGE%'
)

SELECT * FROM CTE_BASE;

```

Based on this base data set, we begin the search for our key fields using an advanced SQL function called a Window Function.[136] These special functions are used to aggregate data by creating a *"window"* of data that can be applied across the entire data set. The `row_number()` window function counts the number of total records grouped by the fields in the partition.

Leveraging our `CTE_BASE` temporary data set, we will add fields to the window partition until we find the combination that yields a unique record. Along the way, we will likely uncover other issues with our data set.

Replace the initial `SELECT` query with a new one. This column will call the

```
--SELECT * FROM CTE_BASE;
SELECT
    row_number() OVER (PARTITION BY
            invoice,
            stock_code
        ORDER BY
            invoice DESC
        ) AS row_number,
    invoice_date,
    invoice,
    stock_code,
    description,
    customer_id,
    country,
    quantity,
    price
FROM CTE_BASE
ORDER BY 1 DESC;
```

`row_number()` window function and be called `row_number`. The window begins with the most logical records first (invoice and stock code).

The 6 means that there are six additional records with the same invoice and stock code combination.

	row_number	invoice_date	invoice	stock_code	description	customer_id	country	quantity	price
1	6	2011-06-28T14:47:00	C558347	S	SAMPLES	<NULL>	United ...	-1	9.9
2	5	2011-06-28T14:47:00	C558347	S	SAMPLES	<NULL>	United ...	-1	14.92
3	4	2011-08-05T16:10:00	562549	20829	GLITTER ...	17092	United ...	3	2.1
4	4	2011-09-25T14:33:00	568188	84879	ASSORTED ...	16049	United ...	4	1.69
5	4	2011-10-13T13:35:00	571046	22197	POPCORN ...	18096	United ...	4	0.85
6	4	2011-10-25T14:35:00	572703	21818	GLITTER ...	16110	United ...	13	0.39
7	4	2011-11-08T10:44:00	574965	23084	RABBIT ...	17964	United ...	7	2.08

Add a `WHERE` clause to look closer into those records.

```
FROM CTE_BASE
WHERE
    invoice = 'C558347' AND
    stock_code = 'S'
;
```

	row_number	invoice_date	invoice	stock_code	description	customer_id	country	quantity	price
1	1	2011-06-28T14:47:00	C558347	S	SAMPLES	<NULL>	United ...	-1	4.95
2	2	2011-06-28T14:47:00	C558347	S	SAMPLES	<NULL>	United ...	-1	6.15
3	3	2011-06-28T14:47:00	C558347	S	SAMPLES	<NULL>	United ...	-1	3.59
4	4	2011-06-28T14:47:00	C558347	S	SAMPLES	<NULL>	United ...	-1	16
5	5	2011-06-28T14:47:00	C558347	S	SAMPLES	<NULL>	United ...	-1	14.92
6	6	2011-06-28T14:47:00	C558347	S	SAMPLES	<NULL>	United ...	-1	9.9

For this invoice stock code combination, the prices are different. Unfortunately, we don't have an obvious reason why this would be happening on this invoice. There are a couple of possibilities. The first is that we are missing a field in the data set which would differentiate the prices. Notice that the quantities in this case are all "-1". The "C" in the invoice code means that these orders have been canceled. These prices are also associated with samples. Therefore, we might be dealing with an edge case.

It is easy to get distracted with edge cases. Early in the analysis the best strategy is to take note of them and then move on. Or, you could time box the additional research. The risk is that you waste valuable time pursuing perfection from imperfect data sources and delay delivering anything of value.

The best strategy in this situation is to take note that we have multiple prices for the same stock code on the same invoice and move on.

Add the price row to the window function and filter out the highest `row_number` record after running the query.

```
SELECT
    row_number() OVER (PARTITION BY
            invoice,
            stock_code,
            price
        ORDER BY
            invoice DESC
        ) AS row_number,
```

	row_number	invoice_date	invoice	stock_code	description	customer_id	country	quantity	price
1	4	2011-08-05T16:10:00	562549	20829	GLITTER ...	17092	United ...	3	2.1
2	3	2011-08-05T16:10:00	562549	20829	GLITTER ...	17092	United ...	1	2.1
3	2	2011-08-05T16:10:00	562549	20829	GLITTER ...	17092	United ...	2	2.1
4	1	2011-08-05T16:10:00	562549	20829	GLITTER ...	17092	United ...	5	2.1

We are now focused on a set of records on the same invoice with the same price but multiple quantities. Unfortunately, we don't have an obvious reason why this would be happening. There are a couple of possibilities. The first is that we are again, missing a field in the data set. It could also be that we do not have enough granularity on the invoice date field or that this files has been rounded up or down following some unknown business logic. Once again, the best course of action is to note the issue and move on.

The next column to add is quantity.

```
SELECT
    row_number() OVER (PARTITION BY
            invoice,
            stock_code,
            price,
            quantity
        ORDER BY
            invoice DESC
        ) AS row_number,
```

	row_number	invoice_date	invoice	stock_code	description	customer_id	country	quantity	price
1	2	2011-09-18T15:33:00	567183	22659	LUNCH BO...	14769	United ...	2	1.95
2	1	2011-09-18T15:32:00	567183	22659	LUNCH BO...	14769	United ...	2	1.95

Filtering on quantity leaves us with duplicate records having different invoice dates. We now need to add the invoice_date column.

```
SELECT
    row_number() OVER (PARTITION BY
            invoice,
            stock_code,
            price,
            quantity,
            invoice_date
        ORDER BY
            invoice DESC
        ) AS row_number,
```

	row_number	invoice_date	invoice	stock_code	description	customer_id	country	quantity	price
1	2	2011-11-09T13:56:00	575335	23203	JUMBO BAG VINTAGE DOILY	12931	United ...	300	1.79
2	1	2011-11-09T13:56:00	575335	23203	JUMBO BAG DOILEY PATTERNS	12931	United ...	300	1.79

This final filter illustrates precisely why we need to take the time to perform this analysis. There are multiple product descriptions for the same stock code, and if we try to aggregate by description, we will get the wrong answer, and if we aggregate by the code, it isn't clear what description we should use.

```
SELECT
    row_number() OVER (PARTITION BY
            invoice,
            stock_code,
            price,
            quantity,
            invoice_date,
            description
        ORDER BY
            invoice DESC
        ) AS row_number,
```

	row_number	invoice_date	invoice	stock_code	description	customer_id	country	quantity	price
1	1	2011-06-09T07:53:00	556109	21528	DAIRY MAID ...	13741	United ...	2	6.95
2	1	2011-06-09T07:53:00	556109	21530	DAIRY MAID ...	13741	United ...	18	0.79
3	1	2011-06-09T07:53:00	556109	21534	DAIRY MAID ...	13741	United ...	3	4.95
4	1	2011-06-09T07:53:00	556109	21775	DECORATIVE ...	13741	United ...	12	1.25
5	1	2011-06-09T07:53:00	556109	22283	6 EGG HOUSE ...	13741	United ...	2	7.95

Now we know that the customer and country fields are the only fields not required to make a unique record, and by inference, there is a one to one relationship between invoices and customers and customers and countries.

One additional query needs to be made to confirm that when an invoice has a "C" in it, the quantity is negative to reflect the part of the order that was canceled.

```
FROM CTE_BASE
WHERE
invoice LIKE 'C%'
--      invoice = '575335' AND
--       stock_code = '23203'
ORDER BY 1 desc
;
```

	invoice	quantity	price
1	C556117	-12	1.25
2	C556265	-1	28.04
3	C556268	-1	0.85
4	C556268	-2	9.95

This is an example of *overloading* a column with additional business logic that would be better handled as a separate column or leave as is. Since the canceled invoice line items are identifiable by their negative quantity, we can safely remove the "C" business code from the invoice and now we can accurately group by the invoice as well.

RAW_ONLINE_RETAIL_II_YEAR_2010_2011_001_row_count.sql:

```
--RAW_ONLINE_RETAIL_II_YEAR_2010_2011_001_row_count.sql
-----------------------------------------------------------
WITH CTE_BASE AS (
  SELECT DISTINCT
  provider_code,
  load_dts,
  --invoice as raw_invoice,
  REPLACE(invoice, 'C', '') AS invoice,
  stock_code,
  description,
  invoice_date,
  quantity,
  price,
  customer_id,
  country
  FROM RAW_ONLINE_RETAIL_II_YEAR_2010_2011_001
  WHERE
      invoice_date >= (
          SELECT DATE(MAX(invoice_date), '-6 months', 'localtime')
          FROM RAW_ONLINE_RETAIL_II_YEAR_2010_2011_001
          ) AND
      UPPER(description) NOT LIKE '%MANUAL%' AND
      UPPER(description) NOT LIKE '%POSTAGE%'
)

--SELECT * FROM CTE_BASE;
SELECT
    row_number() OVER (PARTITION BY
            invoice,
            stock_code,
            price,
            quantity,
            invoice_date,
            description
        ORDER BY
            invoice DESC
        ) AS row_number,
    invoice_date,
    --raw_invoice,
    invoice,
    stock_code,
    description,
    customer_id,
    country,
    quantity,
    price
FROM CTE_BASE
--WHERE
--raw_invoice LIKE 'C%'
--    invoice = '556277' --AND
--     stock_code = '23203'
ORDER BY 4 desc
;
```

Refining the Analysis

Going through the `row_number()` analysis is a laborious manual process, but it is the only way to develop an accurate feel for the contents of the entire data set. Becoming comfortable with window functions will dramatically simplify your queries in the same way pivot tables expand the analysis you can perform in Excel.

What are the next steps?

- Aggregations by week should not be affected by differences in price and quantity. Assume those are correct.
- Add date logic to convert the invoice date timestamp into a single date for the week. After discussing the weekly aggregation requirement with our customer, assume a Monday through Sunday reporting week. The date will be the Sunday of the week.
- Figure out a single description for each stock code.
- Group price and quantity by week, and calculate the total price for each stock code.
- Provide these results along with the previous six-month totals analysis.

The easiest place to start is building a new data set to calculate total sales revenue (price * quantity) by stock code and week as a sub-component of the analysis and a new common table expression.

Start by renaming and saving the previous query as `svc/analysis/INFO_WEEKLY_TOP_SALES_RANK.sql.` We can replace the row_number() query with a new CTE which calculates the total sales revenue by week, over the last six months.

```
--SELECT * FROM CTE_BASE;

CTE_SALES AS (
    SELECT
        --invoice_date,
        DATE(invoice_date, 'weekday 0', '-2 days') AS end_of_week_ssmtwtf,
        --invoice,
        stock_code,
        --description,
        --customer_id,
        --country,
        SUM(quantity) AS quantity,
        AVG(price) AS avg_price,
        ROUND(SUM(quantity) * SUM(price), 2) AS total_sales_revenue
    FROM CTE_BASE
    GROUP BY
        DATE(invoice_date, 'weekday 0', '-2 days'),
        stock_code
    ORDER BY 1,5 DESC
)

SELECT * FROM CTE_SALES;
;
```

	end_of_week_ssmtwtf	stock_code	quantity	avg_price	total_sales_revenue
1	2011-06-10	85123A	4098	3.0665	251330
2	2011-06-10	22502	67	191.61	89865.1
3	2011-06-10	23284	345	8.67437	47882.6
4	2011-06-10	22423	124	13.7511	32397.5
5	2011-06-10	21523	325	9.37111	27410.5

The next logical step is to determine the single best description for each stock code. We can use a new `row_number()` window function to determine if we have multiple names for a single stock code.

```
SELECT
    row_number,
    stock_code,
    UPPER(description) AS description,
    invoice_date
FROM (
    SELECT
        ROW_NUMBER () OVER (PARTITION BY
        stock_code
        ORDER BY
        invoice_date DESC
        ) AS row_number,
        stock_code,
        description,
        invoice_date
    FROM CTE_BASE
    ) A
WHERE
row_number = 1
ORDER BY 1 ASC;
```

We can immediately see that stock code "20713" has been described multiple ways, and it is unclear which description is correct.

	row_number	stock_code	description
1	8	20713	wrongly marked.23343 in box
2	7	20713	wrongly marked 23343
3	7	23084	website fixed
4	6	20713	wrongly coded-23343
5	6	23084	temp adjustment
6	5	20713	wrongly coded 23343

We have similar issues with "23343".

	row_number	stock_code	description
1	5	23343	wrongly coded 20713
2	4	23343	came coded as 20713
3	3	23343	JUMBO BAG VINTAGE CHRISTMAS
4	2	23343	20713 wrongly marked
5	1	23343	20713

There are two lessons to learn from this analysis. One, description fields are entered by people, and people will do things differently if they can't see what others have done before them. Two, even if you have all the history, the correct answer may not be clear. The best solution, in this case, may be to assume the latest description is the most accurate.

	row_number	stock_code	description	invoice_date
1	1	10080	GROOVY CACTUS INFLATABLE	2011-11-21T17:04:00
2	1	10120	DOGGY RUBBER	2011-12-04T13:15:00
3	1	10124A	SPOTS ON RED BOOKCOVER TAPE	2011-11-06T13:00:00
4	1	10124G	ARMY CAMO BOOKCOVER TAPE	2011-11-06T13:00:00
5	1	10125	MINI FUNKY DESIGN TAPES	2011-12-09T10:13:00
6	1	10133	damaged	2011-11-16T15:32:00

By filtering the stock codes by the latest invoice date, we reflect the latest description in the system. While not perfect, it is a good start, and it meets our need to have a single stock code and description in our reporting.

```
SELECT
    row_number,
    stock_code,
    UPPER(description) AS description,
    invoice_date
FROM (
    SELECT
        ROW_NUMBER () OVER (PARTITION BY
        stock_code
        ORDER BY
        invoice_date DESC
        ) AS row_number,
        stock_code,
        description,
        invoice_date
    FROM CTE_BASE
    ) A
WHERE
row_number = 1
ORDER BY 1 ASC;
```

	stock_code	description
1	10080	GROOVY CACTUS INFLATABLE
2	10120	DOGGY RUBBER
3	10124A	SPOTS ON RED BOOKCOVER TAPE
4	10124G	ARMY CAMO BOOKCOVER TAPE
5	10125	MINI FUNKY DESIGN TAPES
6	10133	DAMAGED

```
CTE_DESC AS (
    SELECT
        --row_number,
        stock_code,
        UPPER(description) AS preferred_description
        --invoice_date
    FROM (
        SELECT
            ROW_NUMBER () OVER (PARTITION BY
            stock_code
            ORDER BY
            invoice_date DESC
            ) AS row_number,
            stock_code,
            description,
            invoice_date
        FROM CTE_BASE
        ) A
    WHERE
    row_number = 1
    ORDER BY 1 ASC
)
```

Adding this query as a new stock code description CTE makes it possible to join it back with our sales CTE and ensure we have accurate descriptions.

```
SELECT
    A.end_of_week_ssmtwtf,
    A.stock_code,
    B.preferred_description,
    A.quantity,
    A.avg_price,
    A.total_sales_revenue
FROM CTE_SALES A
    INNER JOIN CTE_DESC B
    ON (A.stock_code = B.stock_code)
ORDER BY 1,6 DESC
;
```

	end_of_week_ssmtwtf	stock_code	preferred_description	quantity	avg_price	total_sales_revenue
1	2011-06-10	85123A	CREAM HANGING HEART T-LIGHT HOLDER	4098	3.0665	251330
2	2011-06-10	22502	PICNIC BASKET WICKER SMALL	67	191.61	89865.1
3	2011-06-10	23284	DOORMAT KEEP CALM AND COME IN	345	8.67437	47882.6
4	2011-06-10	22423	REGENCY CAKESTAND 3 TIER	124	13.7511	32397.5
5	2011-06-10	21523	DOORMAT FANCY FONT HOME SWEET HOME	325	9.37111	27410.5

There are numerous window functions[137] we can take advantage of to calculate things like Top 10 sales by stock code by week. The `row_number()` function, the `rank()` function calculates the rank order of the record, grouped by the window defined by the `PARTITION`.

	end_of_week_ssmtwtf	rank	stock_code	preferred_description	quantity	avg_price	total_sales_revenue
1	2011-06-10	1	85123A	CREAM HANGING HEART T-...	4098	3.0665	251330
2	2011-06-10	2	22502	PICNIC BASKET WICKER ...	67	191.61	89865.1
3	2011-06-10	3	23284	DOORMAT KEEP CALM AND ...	345	8.67437	47882.6
4	2011-06-10	4	22423	REGENCY CAKESTAND 3 TIER	124	13.7511	32397.5
5	2011-06-10	5	21523	DOORMAT FANCY FONT ...	325	9.37111	27410.5
6	2011-06-10	6	47566	PARTY BUNTING	198	5.40333	25676.6
7	2011-06-10	7	20685	DOORMAT RED RETROSPOT	330	8.35875	22067.1
8	2011-06-10	8	48187	DOORMAT NEW ENGLAND	314	7.46857	16415.9
9	2011-06-10	9	21955	DOORMAT UNION JACK GUN...	310	7.46857	16206.8
10	2011-06-10	10	48138	DOORMAT UNION FLAG	310	8.695	16172.7
11	2011-06-17	1	47566	PARTY BUNTING	507	5.47549	141580
12	2011-06-17	2	23245	SET OF 3 REGENCY CAKE TINS	465	5.48617	119900

Creating a View

Rather than create a table to store data, we can create a view, which is a query stored in the database. The advantage of a view is that it is easy to modify and does not store records in the database, keeping the database size small. The disadvantage to a view is that it is recalculated every time the query is executed. For large data sets which are queried frequently, this may have a dramatic impact on performance. This is remedied by materializing the query, which means the data is now stored as a regular table.[138]

The statement to create a view from a query is what you would expect.

```
CREATE VIEW IF NOT EXISTS <view_name> AS
<query>;
```

1. Save the previous file as `etc/sql/INFO_WEEKLY_TOP_SALES_001_create.sql`
2. Add `CREATE VIEW IF NOT EXISTS INFO_WEEKLY_TOP_SALES_RANK_001 AS` to the top of the file.
3. Save the file.
4. Add the creation of the view to the makefile and execute.

```
--etc/sql/INFO_WEEKLY_TOP_SALES_RANK_001_create.sql
-----------------------------------------------------
CREATE VIEW IF NOT EXISTS INFO_WEEKLY_TOP_SALES_RANK_001 AS

WITH CTE_BASE AS (
  SELECT DISTINCT
  provider_code,
  load_dts,
  --invoice as raw_invoice,
  REPLACE(invoice, 'C', '') AS invoice,
```

```
test_table/INFO_WEEKLY_TOP_SALES_RANK_001: \
  INFO_WEEKLY_TOP_SALES_001
  $(test_table)

etc/sql/INFO_WEEKLY_TOP_SALES_RANK_001_create.sql:
  $(test_file)

INFO_WEEKLY_TOP_SALES_001: \
  etc/sql/INFO_WEEKLY_TOP_SALES_RANK_001_create.sql
    $(create_table)
```

```
test_tables: \
  test_table/SRC_online_retail_II_-_Year_2010-2011_001 \
  test_table/RAW_ONLINE_RETAIL_II_YEAR_2010_2011_001 \
  test_table/INFO_SALES_LAST_6_MONTHS_FILTERED_001 \
  test_table/INFO_WEEKLY_TOP_SALES_RANK_001
```

Exporting Data in Other Formats

In preparation for publishing this new analysis and developing our first visualization, it is smart to understand how to extract data from the database in a wide variety of formats. Directly exporting data in human-readable and machine-readable formats dramatically reduces the work involved in incorporating the database into other systems. In Exploration, and even into Expand, exporting data to a file reduces the need to build complicated applications to move and process that data. If you can use the database to perform the aggregations and your automation system to build a sophisticated report, you may avoid investing in more complicated and expensive reporting infrastructure.

Comma Separated Values (CSV)

Earlier, we exported data from the database as CSV files using the `sql2csv` utility, but there are many other useful data export formats we can export with `sqlite-utils`.

```sql
--SELECT * FROM CTE_WEEKLY_SALES;

CTE_WEEKLY_TOP_SALES_RANK  AS (
    SELECT
    RANK() OVER (PARTITION BY
        end_of_week_ssmtwtf
        ORDER BY
        total_sales_revenue DESC
    ) AS rank,
    end_of_week_ssmtwtf,
    stock_code,
    preferred_description,
    quantity,
    avg_price,
    total_sales_revenue
    FROM CTE_WEEKLY_SALES
)

--SELECT * FROM CTE_WEEKLY_TOP_SALES_RANK ;

SELECT
    end_of_week_ssmtwtf,
    rank,
    stock_code,
    preferred_description,
    quantity,
    avg_price,
    total_sales_revenue
FROM CTE_WEEKLY_TOP_SALES_RANK
WHERE rank <= 10
ORDER BY 1,2;
```

CSV using `sql2csv` (in a makefile):

```
<target>: <dependency>
sql2csv --db sqlite:///<path/to/database.db> \
$< > $@
```

```
end_of_week_ssmtwtf,rank,stock_code,description,quantity,price,total_sales_revenue
2011-07-15,10,23284,DOORMAT KEEP CALM AND COME IN,117.0,219.99,25738.83
2011-06-24,10,85099F,JUMBO BAG STRAWBERRY,603.0,43.01,25935.03
2011-10-14,1,22423,REGENCY CAKESTAND 3 TIER,204.0,776.46,158397.84
```

CSV using `sqlite-utils` (in a makefile):

```
<target>: <dependency>
sqlite-utils <path/to/database.db> \
—csv[--no-headers] $< > $@
```

```
2011-07-08,9,48187,DOORMAT NEW ENGLAND,546.0,85.06,46442.76
2011-10-21,5,23344,JUMBO BAG 50'S CHRISTMAS ,586.0,107.46,62971.56
2011-10-21,8,23245,SET OF 3 REGENCY CAKE TINS,291.0,188.55,54868.05
```

Tab Separated Values (TSV) (in a makefile):

```
<target>: <dependency>
sqlite-utils <path/to/database.db> \
—table --fmt tsv $< > $@
```

```
end_of_week_ssmtwtf     rank    stock_code description                          quantity  price   total_sales_revenue
2011-11-04                 9         22910 PAPER CHAIN KIT VINTAGE CHRISTMAS          559  172.45              96399.6
2011-12-09                 7         23355 HOT WATER BOTTLE KEEP CALM                 432  323.12               139588
2011-07-29                 2         47566 PARTY BUNTING                              520  242.86               126287
```

Other formats

`sqlite-utils` is capable of saving the output of a query in many other formats. This is useful for quickly sending small result sets, producing documentation, and prototyping data sets for other systems to consume. By piping the output to the `convert` utility, you can even save the output to an image file.

Saving a query in other formats:

```
<target>: <dependency>
sqlite-utils <path/to/database.db> --table --fmt <type> $< > $@
```

Saving a query result as an image:

```
<target>: <dependency>
sqlite-utils <path/to/database.db> --table --fmt <type> $< |
convert -size 1800 -font Courier -border 10 -bordercolor white
label:@- $@
```

Tables

We can use the following query to demonstrate the most useful output formats. This query also demonstrates how to randomly select a limited number of rows.

Plain table:

```
sqlite-utils data/db/sales.db \
"SELECT * FROM INFO_WEEKLY_TOP_SALES_RANK_001 \
ORDER BY RANDOM() LIMIT 3" --table --fmt plain \
| convert -size 1800 -font Courier -border 10 \
-bordercolor white label:@- svc/static/fmt_plain.png
```

```
end_of_week_ssmtwtf        rank    stock_code  description
2011-07-08                    4         21523  DOORMAT FANCY FO
2011-11-11                    1         23084  RABBIT NIGHT LIG
2011-07-01                    8         23206  LUNCH BAG APPLE
```

Simple:

```
end_of_week_ssmtwtf        rank    stock_code  description
---------------------    ------  ------------  ----------------
2011-10-21                    6         22112  CHOCOLATE HOT W
2011-07-15                    2         22423  REGENCY CAKESTA
2011-11-18                    9         22112  CHOCOLATE HOT W
```

RST:

```
=====================  ======  ============  ===============
end_of_week_ssmtwtf      rank    stock_code  description
=====================  ======  ============  ===============
2011-09-23                 10         22114  HOT WATER BOTTI
2011-12-02                  5         23355  HOT WATER BOTTI
2011-06-10                  8         48187  DOORMAT NEW EN(
=====================  ======  ============  ===============
```

Orgtbl:

```
| end_of_week_ssmtwtf    |   rank | stock_code    | description
|------------------------+--------+---------------+---------------
| 2011-12-02             |      1 | 23084         | RABBIT NIGHT LI
| 2011-09-16             |      4 | 85123A        | CREAM HANGING H
| 2011-10-14             |      1 | 22423         | REGENCY CAKESTA
```

PSQL:

```
+------------------------+---------+---------------+----------------
| end_of_week_ssmtwtf    |    rank |    stock_code | description
|------------------------+---------+---------------+----------------
| 2011-08-12             |       4 |         22423 | REGENCY CAKESTA
| 2011-07-01             |       5 |         23173 | REGENCY TEAPOT
| 2011-11-04             |      10 |         84879 | ASSORTED COLOUR
+------------------------+---------+---------------+----------------
```

Pretty:

```
+---------------------+------+------------+----------------
| end_of_week_ssmtwtf | rank | stock_code |             des
+---------------------+------+------------+----------------
|      2011-07-29     |  9   |   23297    | SET 40 HEART SH
|      2011-06-24     |  4   |   22423    |     REGENCY CA
|      2011-09-09     |  1   |   21181    |   PLEASE ONE P
+---------------------+------+------------+----------------
```

Grid:

```
+------------------------+---------+---------------+----------------
| end_of_week_ssmtwtf    |    rank |    stock_code | description
+========================+=========+===============+================
| 2011-09-30             |       4 |         22423 | REGENCY CAKEST
+------------------------+---------+---------------+----------------
| 2011-10-21             |       4 |         23355 | HOT WATER BOTT
+------------------------+---------+---------------+----------------
| 2011-11-11             |       9 |         22910 | PAPER CHAIN KI
+------------------------+---------+---------------+----------------
```

Markdown / Wiki

Pipe:[139]

```
| end_of_week_ssmtwtf   |   rank | stock_code   | description              |   quantity
|:----------------------|-------:|:-------------|:-------------------------|----------:|---------:|--------
| 2011-11-25            |      7 | 22197        | POPCORN HOLDER           |      2754 |
| 2011-07-08            |      2 | 85099B       | JUMBO BAG RED RETROSPOT |
| 2011-10-07            |     10 | 23203        | JUMBO BAG VINTAGE DOILY |       7
```

GitHub:[140]

```
| end_of_week_ssmtwtf       |    rank | stock_code    | description
|---------------------------|---------|---------------|---------------
| 2011-08-05                |       6 | 23298         | SPOTTY BUNTIN(
| 2011-11-18                |       4 | 85123A        | CREAM HANGING
| 2011-08-19                |       4 | 47566         | PARTY BUNTING
```

MediaWiki:[141]

```
{| class="wikitable" style="text-align: left;"
|+ <!-- caption -->
|-
! end_of_week_ssmtwtf   !! align="right"|   rank !! align="right"|   stock_code !! description
|-
| 2011-07-29            || align="right"|      4 || align="right"|        23245 || SET OF 3 REGENCY C/
|-
| 2011-08-19            || align="right"|      8 || align="right"|        23202 || JUMBO BAG VINTAGE I
|-
| 2011-06-10            || align="right"|      9 || align="right"|        21955 || DOORMAT UNION JACK
|}
```

Jira:

```
|| end_of_week_ssmtwtf   ||    rank ||    stock_code || description
| 2011-06-24            |       1 |        47566 | PARTY BUNTING
| 2011-09-02            |       4 |        22423 | REGENCY CAKESTAND
| 2011-07-15            |       4 |        17003 | BROCADE RING PURSE
```

HTML Table:

```
<table>
<thead>
<tr><th>end_of_week_ssmtwtf  </th><th style="text-align: right;">  rank</th><th style="text-align: right;">  stock_code
</thead>
<tbody>
<tr><td>2011-06-10           </td><td style="text-align: right;">     3</td><td style="text-align: right;">         23284
<tr><td>2011-08-19           </td><td style="text-align: right;">     7</td><td style="text-align: right;">         22720
<tr><td>2011-10-21           </td><td style="text-align: right;">     6</td><td style="text-align: right;">         22112
</tbody>
</table>
```

JavaScript Object Notation (JSON)

While CSV files are the most common format for exchanging data sets (aside from Excel) with people, the most common data interchange format for applications is JavaScript Object Notation (JSON).[142] It is a lightweight data-interchange format based on the way the JavaScript language structures objects. Because JSON data structures are the native format expected by JavaScript code, exporting data directly into this structure makes it possible to separate the database from the application in the same way CSV files separate the database from both applications and people. This data can then be used directly in the JavaScript code within an HTML page or other applications.

CSV files are the perfect interchange format where the data is structured as a table with rows and columns. Unfortunately, this limits a CSV file to a single set of data. To combine multiple sets of data, you need multiple CSV files and some method to join them together. Unlike CSV, JSON can describe complex data relationships in a single data set. Rather than limit the data to a single set, JSON supports nesting of multiple objects and arrays of values. This provides almost unlimited flexibility in the types of data you can exchange. However, this comes at the expense of readability.

By default, the `sqlite-utils` utility outputs data as a JSON object.

```
sqlite-utils svc/db/sales.db "SELECT * FROM INFO_WEEKLY_TOP_SALES_RANK_001 ORDER BY RANDOM() LIMIT 3" > svc/static/json_001.json
```

```
sales % sqlite-utils svc/db/sales.db "SELECT * FROM INFO_WEEKLY_TOP_SALES_RANK_001 ORDER
sales % cat svc/static/json_001.json
[{"end_of_week_ssmtwtf": "2011-09-23", "rank": 3, "stock_code": "23243", "preferred_desc
 {"end_of_week_ssmtwtf": "2011-11-25", "rank": 5, "stock_code": "22423", "preferred_desc
 {"end_of_week_ssmtwtf": "2011-11-04", "rank": 5, "stock_code": "22423", "preferred_desc
sales %
```

The object is stripped of all whitespace and is not designed for human readability, but Python can be used to reformat the data to make it more readable.

```
sqlite-utils svc/db/sales.db "SELECT * FROM INFO_WEEKLY_TOP_SALES_RANK_001 ORDER BY RANDOM() LIMIT 3" | python -mjson.tool > svc/static/json_002.json && cat svc/static/json_002.json
```

sales — -zsh — 74×33

```
sales % sqlite-utils svc/db/sales.db "SELECT * FROM INFO_WEEKLY_TOP_SALES_
RANK_001 ORDER BY RANDOM() LIMIT 3" | python -mjson.tool > svc/static/json
_002.json && cat svc/static/json_002.json
[
    {
        "end_of_week_ssmtwtf": "2011-07-22",
        "rank": 5,
        "stock_code": "85099B",
        "preferred_description": "JUMBO BAG RED RETROSPOT",
        "quantity": 732,
        "avg_price": 2.54,
        "total_sales_revenue": 87217.8
    },
    {
        "end_of_week_ssmtwtf": "2011-09-02",
        "rank": 10,
        "stock_code": "23203",
        "preferred_description": "JUMBO BAG VINTAGE DOILY ",
        "quantity": 260,
        "avg_price": 2.74,
        "total_sales_revenue": 25638.6
    },
    {
        "end_of_week_ssmtwtf": "2011-07-08",
        "rank": 7,
        "stock_code": "22383",
        "preferred_description": "LUNCH BAG SUKI DESIGN ",
        "quantity": 539,
        "avg_price": 2.17,
        "total_sales_revenue": 46839.1
    }
]
sales %
```

The basic parts of a JSON object are objects { } composed of a collection of values, defined by pairs of *Keys* and *Values*. These are defined as "<key>": "<value>". Objects can be further grouped into arrays of objects ["<object1>", "<object2>", "<object3>"]

Looking at our data set, we can see it is an array [ ] made of three objects { }, { }, { } and each object contains many key-value pairs representing the columns of data in our query. If we run a more complex query, we can study a more complicated structure with values composed of arrays of arrays.

Extracting data from the database to JSON makes it possible to integrate our data with dynamic web pages. At first, we manually develop these pages to better understand the process. Later, when a web server publishes our data, we replace our static data sets with dynamic ones.

Building Visualizations With Code

IN ORDER TO FOCUS ON THE PRODUCTS WITH THE HIGHEST REVENUE.
AS A SALES MANAGER
I WANT A CHART OF PRODUCT SALES BY WEEK OVER THE LAST SIX MONTHS. (ATTRIBUTES: BY TOTAL REVENUE OVER THE LAST SIX MONTHS.

The next story in our backlog is to provide a chart of the weekly sales data. The easiest way to do this may be to import the data into a spreadsheet and build a chart. Unfortunately, publishing spreadsheet visualizations locks you into the spreadsheet software and requires additional steps to export the graphic. Following our pattern of treating all our work as code, we will look at the Vega-Lite[143] application to define our graphics with a simple JavaScript compatible visualization language.

Vega-Lite – A Grammar of Interactive Graphics

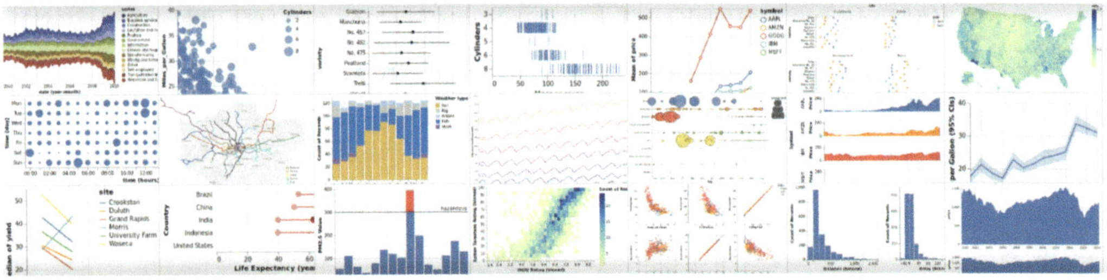

Vega-Lite is a high-level grammar of interactive graphics. It provides a concise, declarative JSON syntax to create an expressive range of visualizations for data analysis and presentation.

The key advantage of using Vega-Lite over other definition languages like D3, Python + Mathplotlib, R + ggplot2 is that it does not require expertise in the underlying low-level language. Nor does it require any additional software installation by the person developing or viewing the charts. Charts are configured by linking to a data set and defining the chart as a JSON object. This definition can then be embedded into a web page to be served from a web server or opened directly in a browser.

First, we are going to query the database and export a data set in JSON format. To get started, we will use a small sample of the data to make it easier to understand the mechanics behind creating our charts.

```
  sqlite-utils svc/db/sales.db "SELECT * FROM
INFO_WEEKLY_TOP_SALES_RANK_001 ORDER BY RANDOM() LIMIT 3" |
python -mjson.tool > svc/static/WEEKLY_TOP_SALES_RANK_001.json
```

```
[
    {
        "end_of_week_ssmtwtf": "2011-07-29",
        "rank": 2,
        "stock_code": "47566",
        "preferred_description": "PARTY BUNTING",
        "quantity": 520,
        "avg_price": 5.28,
        "total_sales_revenue": 126287.2
    },
    {
        "end_of_week_ssmtwtf": "2011-08-26",
        "rank": 1,
        "stock_code": "85099B",
        "preferred_description": "JUMBO BAG RED RETROSPOT",
        "quantity": 1418,
        "avg_price": 2.14,
        "total_sales_revenue": 130456.0
    },
    {
        "end_of_week_ssmtwtf": "2011-06-24",
        "rank": 6,
        "stock_code": "22386",
        "preferred_description": "JUMBO BAG PINK POLKADOT",
        "quantity": 611,
        "avg_price": 2.63,
        "total_sales_revenue": 46521.54
    }
]
```

This data set can be directly embedded into a Vega Lite visualization making it possible to specify and manage complicated graphics entirely in code.

```
{
  "data": {
    "values":
    [{"end_of_week_ssmtwtf": "2011-09-23", "rank": 9, "stock_code": "23203", "pr
     {"end_of_week_ssmtwtf": "2011-10-28", "rank": 7, "stock_code": "23344", "pr
     {"end_of_week_ssmtwtf": "2011-11-18", "rank": 10, "stock_code": "22423", "p
  },
  "mark": "bar",
  "encoding": {
    "x": {"field": "end_of_week_ssmtwtf", "type": "nominal"},
    "y": {"field": "total_sales_revenue", "type": "quantitative"}
  }
}
```

The Vega team provides a convenient online editor,[144] to assist in developing our chart. While designed to demonstrate the code behind their samples, it works perfectly with embedded JSON data. Once we have the code working properly, we can export the code into a web page.

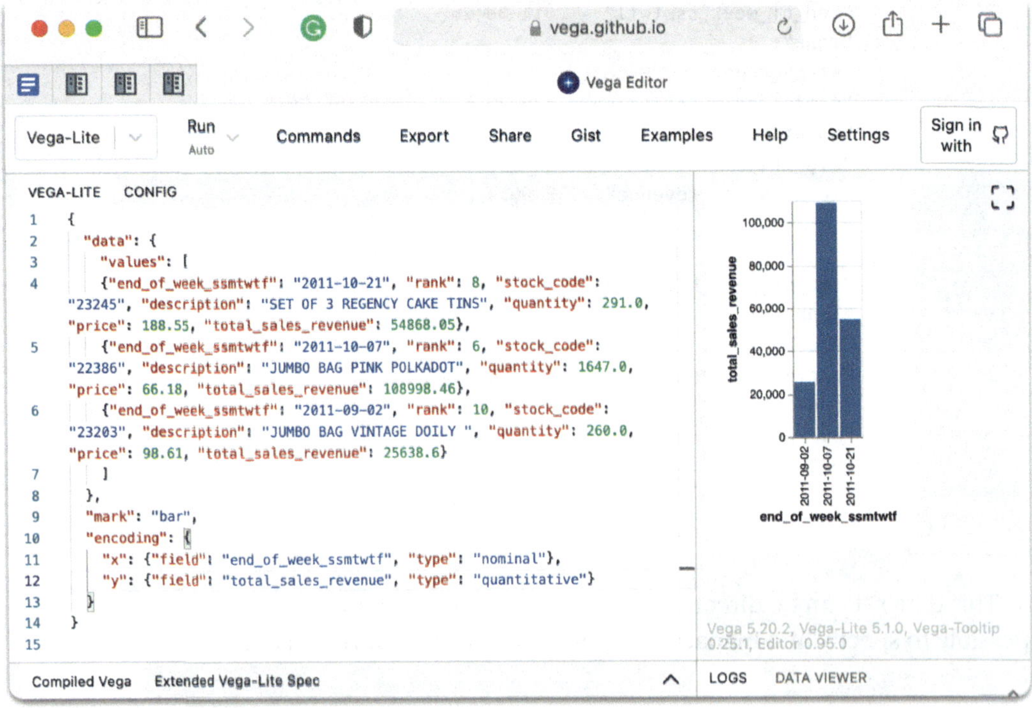

Vega Editor

If we embed the Vega code into an HTML document, the chart will be sharable as a self-contained web page. This visualization can then be exported to SVG, PNG, native Vega, or opened in the Vega-Lite editor to view the raw source code. Publishing the visualization and then modifying the definition after the publication, without requiring any special software, is a game-changing feature during the Exploration phase of data analysis. Even while the visualization is in production, freely experimenting with the data without worrying about affecting other viewers enables dropping back into the Exploration phase at any time.

```
<!DOCTYPE html>
<html>
  <head>
    <title>Vega-Lite Bar Chart</title>
    <meta charset="utf-8" />

    <script src="https://cdn.jsdelivr.net/npm/vega@5.17.0"></script>
    <script src="https://cdn.jsdelivr.net/npm/vega-lite@4.17.0"></script>
    <script src="https://cdn.jsdelivr.net/npm/vega-embed@6.12.2"></script>

    <style media="screen">
      /* Add space between Vega-Embed links  */
      .vega-actions a {
        margin-right: 5px;
      }
    </style>
  </head>
  <body>
    <!-- Container for the visualization -->
    <div id="vis"></div>
    <script>
      // Assign the specification to a local variable vlSpec.
      var vlSpec = {
        $schema: 'https://vega.github.io/schema/vega-lite/v4.json',
      <!-- Embed Vega-Lite Definition Here -->
      "data": {
        "values":
        [{"end_of_week_ssmtwtf": "2011-09-23", "rank": 9, "stock_code": "23203",
         {"end_of_week_ssmtwtf": "2011-10-28", "rank": 7, "stock_code": "23344",
         {"end_of_week_ssmtwtf": "2011-11-18", "rank": 10, "stock_code": "22423"
      },
      "mark": "bar",
      "encoding": {
        "x": {"field": "end_of_week_ssmtwtf", "type": "nominal"},
        "y": {"field": "total_sales_revenue", "type": "quantitative"}
      }
      <!-- Embed Vega-Lite Definition Here -->
      };

      // Embed the visualization in the container with id `vis`
      vegaEmbed('#vis', vlSpec);
    </script>
  </body>
</html>
```

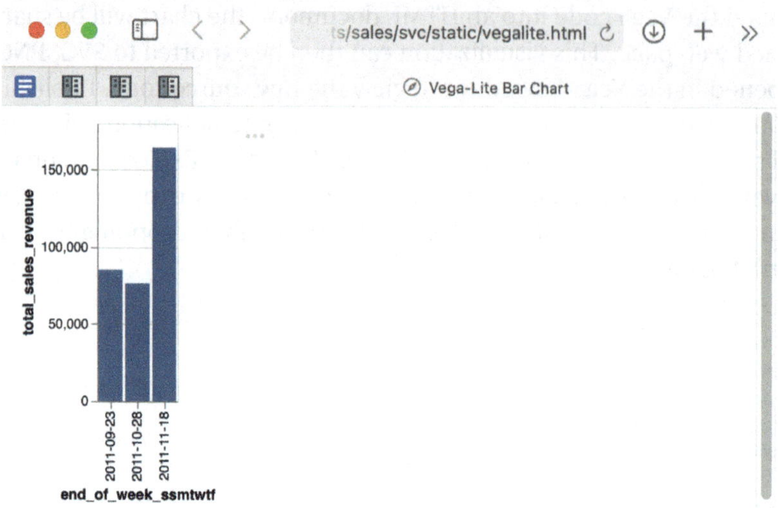

Developing a visualization requires us to write a JSON object to hold all of the properties we need. The most basic element of visualization is a `mark`. Marks are the objects to be plotted. These range from a simple point, bar, or circle to complex objects like maps, box plots, error bars, and rules.

```
        },
        "mark": "bar",
        "encoding": {
          "x": {"field": "end_of_week_ssmtwtf", "type": "nominal"},
          "y": {"field": "total_sales_revenue", "type": "quantitative"}
        }
```

The `key:value` pair: `"mark": "bar"` creates a bar chart. The encoding key defines how to plot the area of the chart. For basic charts, there are `"x":` and`"y":`objects. Within each, you can define multiple attributes like `"field":` and `" type":` , these attributes tie the data to the chart with the type defining the nature of the data in the field and how to process it.

Type	Description
Nominal	Names, classification, and groups
Quantitative	Numerical, quantity
Temporal	Dates, times, and timestamps
Ordinal	Ordering (requires a sort order to be defined)

To see how this affects the visualization, redefine the `"end_of_week_ssmtwtf"` field from `"nominal"` to `"temporal"` in the Vega Editor. The chart now reflects our sample sales revenue data more accurately.

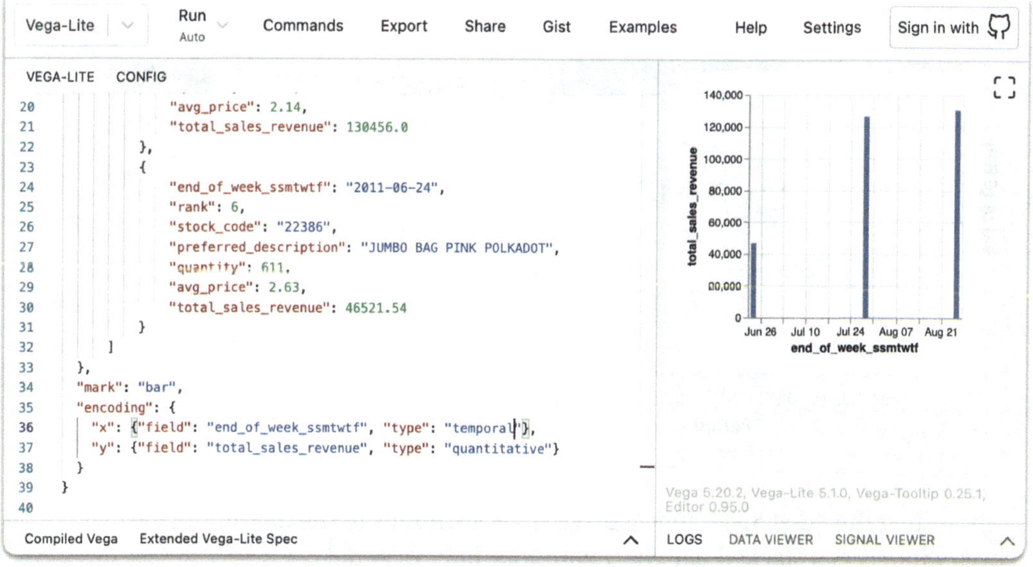

Following this pattern, we can continue to refine the visualization's encoding so that the basics of our data set are clearly defined.

```
"mark": "bar",
 "encoding": {
   "x": {"field": "end_of_week_ssmtwtf", "type": "temporal", "title": "Period", "timeUnit": "monthdate"},
   "y": {"field": "total_sales_revenue", "type": "quantitative", "title": "Value (GBP)", "aggregate": "sum" }
 }
```

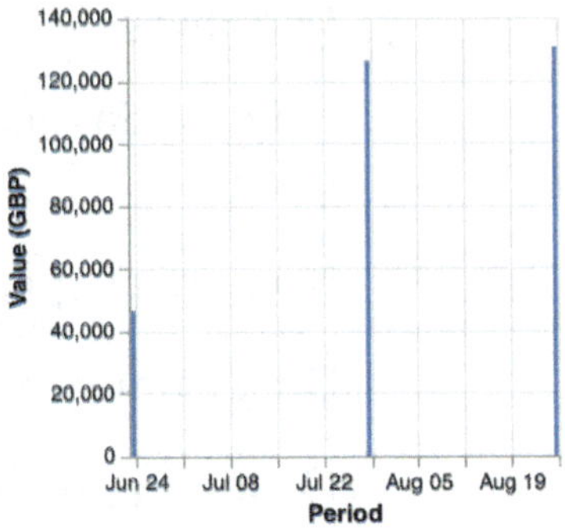

By modifying the encoding attributes, it is possible to create numerous variations on the presentation of the data. If we change the `"timeUnit":"monthdate"` value to `"month"` or `"quarter"`, Vega will handle re-aggregating the data for us.

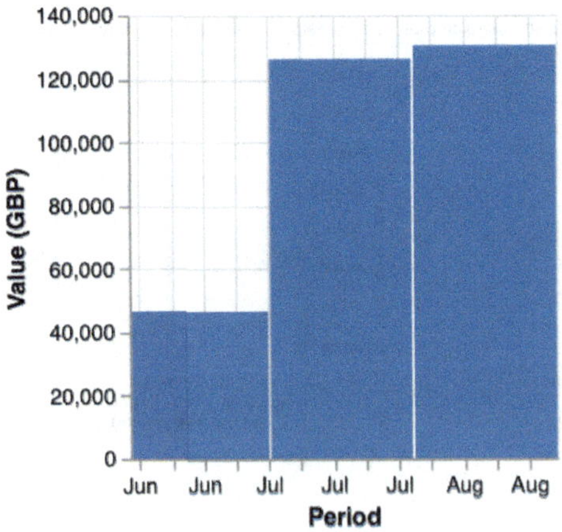

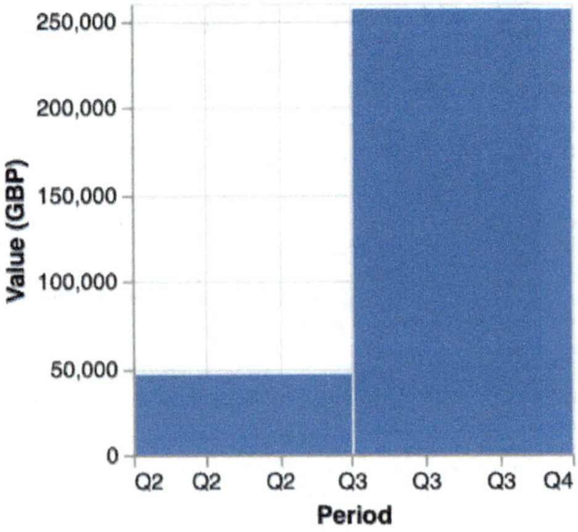

By adding the `"color":` and `"tooltip":` attributes to the definition, we can create a pretty functional stacked bar chart with four lines of code!

```
"mark": {"type": "bar", "tooltip": {"content": "data"}},
"encoding": {
  "x": {"field": "end_of_week_ssmtwtf", "type": "temporal", "title":
  "Period", "timeUnit": "month"},
  "y": {"field": "total_sales_revenue", "type": "quantitative", "title":
  "Value (GBP)", "aggregate": "sum" },
  "color": {"field": "preferred_description", "type": "nominal", "title":
  "Description", "sort": {"op": "sum", "field": "total_sales_revenue",
  "order": "descending"}}
}
```

If we update the data set to include all the data, the chart becomes pretty messy. However, it clearly shows the sales spike in November as our customers prepare for holiday sales in December. Even with all the complexity, we can still see our top-selling product in November is the Rabbit Night Light.

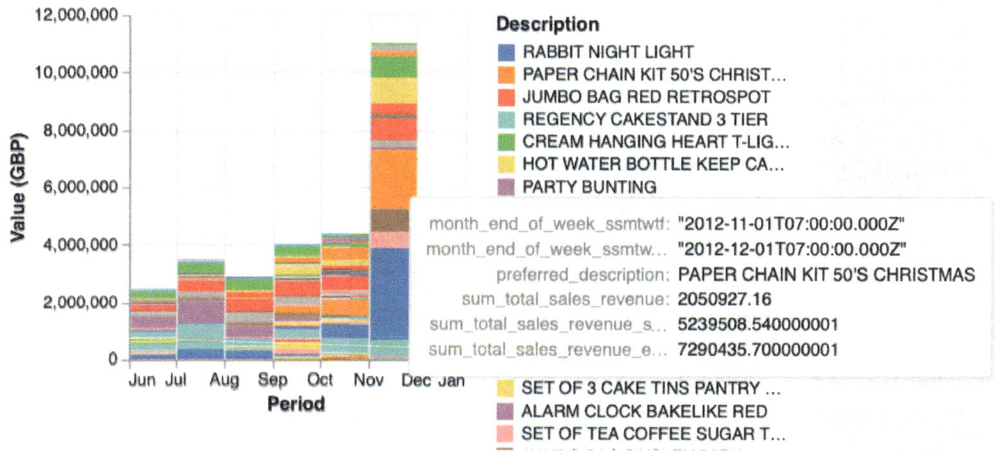

Addressing this issue is where Vega shines. One of the primary features of the language is its extensive support for programmatically composing multiple charts into groups.

This includes:

- Layering multiple charts together to make a single chart.
- Concatenating multiple different chart types together to provide side-by-side comparisons of different metrics.
- Repeating the same chart with different metrics.
- Faceting to draw a matrix of data, divided into rows and columns.[145]

Composing a visualization from multiple components is neither new nor unique to Vega and Vega-Lite. What is unique is Vega-Lite's simple code-driven approach. This is particularly well suited to automatically generating static and semi-dynamic visualizations where the structure is defined with standardized templates.

Solve this stacked bar problem by making a slight change to our visualization by adding a `"facet":` element to our encoding. This brings us up to eight lines of code! This visualization is impossible to build in Excel without resorting to complicated data staging, third-party plug-ins, or using PowerBI Desktop.

```
"mark": {"type": "bar", "tooltip": {"content": "data"}},
  "resolve": {"axis": {"x": "independent", "y": "independent"}},
  "encoding": {
    "facet": {"field": "preferred_description", "type": "ordinal",
    "columns": 3, "sort": {"op": "sum", "field": "total_sales_revenue",
    "order": "descending"}},
    "x": {"field": "end_of_week_ssmtwtf", "type": "temporal", "title":
    "Period", "timeUnit": "month"},
    "y": {"field": "total_sales_revenue", "type": "quantitative",
    "title": "Value (GBP)", "aggregate": "sum"},
    "color": {"field": "preferred_description", "type": "nominal",
    "title": "Description", "sort": {"op": "sum", "field":
    "total_sales_revenue", "order": "descending"}}
```

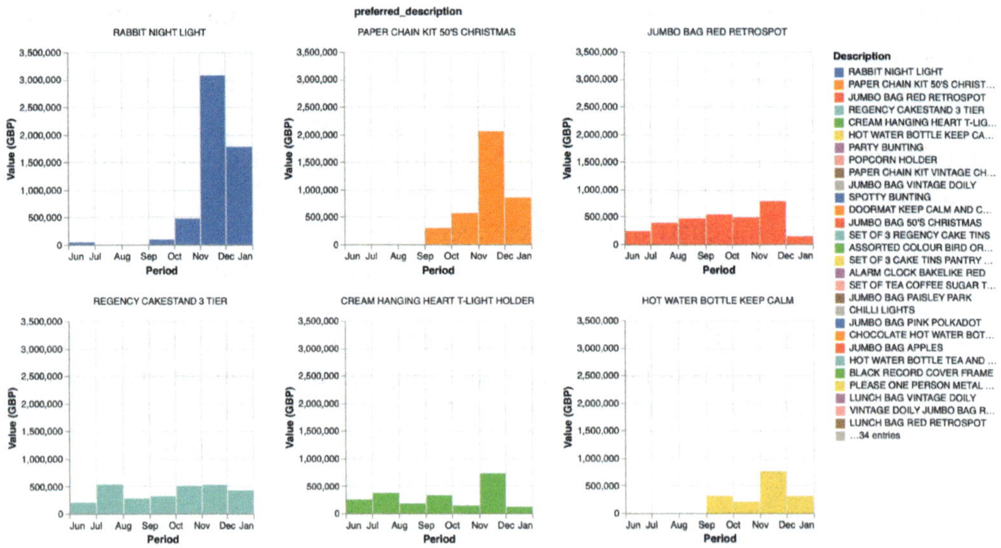

Faceted data set

Updating the Automation

Publishing this visualization involves two steps. First, publish the data set as a JSON document to leverage creating our HTML report. Second, dynamically rebuild the visualization using a standardized Make recipe. Once this data is available via a URL from a web server, replace this Make target with reference to the URL. The data will then automatically reflect the latest data without requiring an export step.

Creating our JSON data file requires a simple modification to the recipe we use to create our exported CSV files.

```
svc/static/WEEKLY_TOP_SALES_RANK_001.json: INFO_WEEKLY_TOP_SALES_RANK_001
	@#<path/to/export_file.csv>(colon)(space)<view_name>
	@echo $(DTS)      [INFO] - Executing $< and exporting to $@
	@sqlite-utils $(DBFILE) "SELECT * FROM $<" > $@
```

Building out a dynamic HTML template for the visualization is more complicated. But it demonstrates how to build more complicated files without resorting to another language like Python to produce the same results. Break down the HTML page with our visualization into its static and dynamic components. Because the static header and footer do not change with the data or the Vega-Lite specification, we pull them out of the file and use them as common templates.

NOTE: Add these templates to the Project Build Tool `src/` directory and makefile to leverage in future projects.

etc/app/vega_embed_header.viz:

```
<!DOCTYPE html>
<html>
  <head>
    <title>Vega-Lite</title>
    <meta charset="utf-8" />

    <script src="https://cdn.jsdelivr.net/npm/vega@5.17.0"></script>
    <script src="https://cdn.jsdelivr.net/npm/vega-lite@4.17.0"></script>
    <script src="https://cdn.jsdelivr.net/npm/vega-embed@6.12.2"></script>

    <style media="screen">
      /* Add space between Vega-Embed links  */
      .vega-actions a {
        margin-right: 5px;
      }
    </style>
  </head>
  <body>
    <!-- Container for the visualization -->
    <div id="vis"></div>
    <script>
      // Assign the specification to a local variable vlSpec.
      var vlSpec = {
        $schema: 'https://vega.github.io/schema/vega-lite/v4.json',
<!-- Embed Vega-Lite Definition Here -->

```

etc/app/vega_embed_footer.viz:

```
}
};

// Embed the visualization in the container with id `vis`
vegaEmbed('#vis', vlSpec);
</script>
</body>
</html>
```

Tests for these templates should be added to the makefile as part of the `test/inputs:` target using the standard `$(test_file)` recipe . The next component of our visualization is to create a template containing the Vega_Lite specification we created earlier.

```
test/outputs: \
  test/online_retail_II_last_6_months_filtered.csv \
  test_online_retail_II_last_6_months_filtered_002.csv \
  test_WEEKLY_TOP_SALES_RANK_001.html

test_WEEKLY_TOP_SALES_RANK_001.html: svc/static/WEEKLY_TOP_SALES_RANK_001.html
  @$(test_dependent_file)
```

etc/app/WEEKLY_TOP_SALES_RANK_001.vega

```
"title": "Weekly Top Sales Rank",
"mark": {"type": "bar", "tooltip": {"content": "data"}},
  "resolve": {"axis": {"x": "independent", "y": "independent"}},
  "encoding": {
    "facet": {"field": "preferred_description", "type": "ordinal", "columns":
    3, "sort": {"op": "sum", "field": "total_sales_revenue", "order":
    "descending"}},
    "x": {"field": "end_of_week_ssmtwtf", "type": "temporal", "title":
    "Period", "timeUnit": "month"},
    "y": {"field": "total_sales_revenue", "type": "quantitative", "title":
    "Value (GBP)", "aggregate": "sum"},
  "color": {"field": "preferred_description", "type": "nominal", "title":
  "Description", "sort": {"op": "sum", "field": "total_sales_revenue", "order":
  "descending"}}
```

All sub-components can now be assembled into a complete embedded Vega-Lite visualization. Add a new Make target and a recipe that introduces using the dependencies as parameters.

This target is built with a combination of patterns we've used in other recipes. It uses local variable assignment to reference the Vega visualization template we are using. The main functionality in the recipe used the cat command to assemble the separate pieces of the target file together.

```
# Publish ----------------------------------------------------------------------
svc/static/WEEKLY_TOP_SALES_RANK_001.json: INFO_WEEKLY_TOP_SALES_RANK_001
	@#<path/to/export_file.csv>(colon)(space)<view_name>
	@echo $(DTS)      [INFO] - Executing $< and exporting to $@
	@sqlite-utils query $(DBFILE) "SELECT * FROM $<" > $@

svc/static/WEEKLY_TOP_SALES_RANK_001.html: VIZTEMPLATE=etc/app/WEEKLY_TOP_SALES_RANK_001.vega
svc/static/WEEKLY_TOP_SALES_RANK_001.html: svc/static/WEEKLY_TOP_SALES_RANK_001.json
	@#<path/to/export_file.html>(colon)(space)VIZTEMPLATE=<path/to/viz_template.vega>
	@#<path/to/export_file.html>(colon)(space)<path/to/exported_file.json>
	@cat etc/app/vega_embed_header.viz > $@
	@echo "\"data\":{ \"values\":" >> $@
	@cat $< >> $@ && echo "}, " >> $@
	@cat $(VIZTEMPLATE) >> $@
	@cat etc/app/vega_embed_footer.viz >> $@
```

By including the test for the target html file, we automatically include it in our `make run` data pipeline.

Retrospective

With the creation of our Top Sales Rank visualization, we have completed all but one of the stories in this iteration.

- Migrated and automated the data pipeline for all data integration and visualization tasks.
- Performed several data analysis tasks, leveraging functionality built into the database.
- Implemented data cleaning tasks.
- Identified a few issues we may encounter in the future.
- Successfully created an advanced visualization, which easily identified many products with no monthly sales.

The final bullet point takes into account only the top 10 products per week. Due to this finding, defer any work on creating product groupings. Even within high-volume products, the majority have sporadic sales that point to a bigger question about inventory we cannot yet see.

IN ORDER TO FOCUS ON THE PRODUCTS WITH THE HIGHEST REVENUE.
AS A SALES MANAGER
I WANT A LIST OF THE TOP 10 PRODUCTS WITH SIMILAR PRODUCT ATTRIBUTES, BY TOTAL REVENUE, OVER THE LAST SIX MONTHS.

[X] FILTER OUT POSTAGE, MANUAL, ETC.
[X] PROVIDE TOP 10 PRODUCTS BY REVENUE IN AN EMAIL TO THE SALES MANAGER.
[X] PROVIDE A CHART OF PRODUCT SALES BY WEEK ONE THE LAST SIX MONTHS.

IN ORDER TO PROVIDE A SINGLE SOURCE OF INVOICE DATA
AS A SALES MANAGER
I WANT CONSOLIDATED DATA SET OF INVOICE DATA
AND NO DUPLICATE RECORDS
AND A RECORD OF CHANGES TO INVOICES OVER TIME
AND IDENTIFICATION OF POTENTIALLY MISSING DATA

[X] BUILD OUT A DATA SET WITH ALL GROSS DATA ERRORS REMOVED.

IN ORDER TO FOCUS ON THE PRODUCTS WITH THE HIGHEST REVENUE.
AS A SALES MANAGER
I WANT TO BE ABLE TO GROUP SIMILAR PRODUCTS.

[-] RESEARCH PRODUCT GROUPINGS, SUGGEST IDEAS.
[X] POC - ALIAS TABLE FOR PRODUCT DESCRIPTIONS.
[X] REVIEW TOP 10 DATA SET W/ GROUPINGS.

[133] See the Appendix for an example.

[134] Load Balancing (https://en.wikipedia.org/wiki/Load_balancing_(computing))

[135] A/B Testing (https://en.wikipedia.org/wiki/A/B_testing)

[136] Window Functions(https://sqlite.org/windowfunctions.html)

[137] Window Functions (https://sqlite.org/windowfunctions.html)

[138] Materalized views can be much more complicated than changing a CREATE VIEW to CREATE TABLE depending on the database platform. Unfortunately, every platform does this differently. Therefore, it is easier to implement and maintain a standard table.

[139] Markdown (https://en.wikipedia.org/wiki/Markdown)

[140] GitHub Flavored Markdown (https://github.github.com/gfm/)

[141] MediaWiki (https://www.mediawiki.org/wiki/MediaWiki)

[142] JSON (https://www.json.org/json-en.html)

[143] Vega Lite (https://vega.github.io/vega-lite/)

[144] Vega Editor (https://vega.github.io/editor/)

[145] Small Multiples (https://en.wikipedia.org/wiki/Small_multiple)

Chapter 6: Building the Data Discovery Platform

Feed yourselves with questioning,
That reason wonder may diminish,
How thus we met, and these things finish.
- William Shakespeare, As You Like It (Act V, Scene 4)

Up to this point, we shared all our analyses through email, print, and direct conversation. That level of sharing isn't scalable, nor does it allow for our customers to perform their own exploration. If they can't spend time with the data or are limited to asking predefined questions, they will never develop a good understanding of the facts buried in that data. Without understanding the facts, you can't make good decisions. As analysts, we never understand how to get the most value out of the data until our users actively engage and ask us for answers to their difficult questions. Sadly, if we can't answer difficult or complex questions, then we aren't adding value.

Typically, we would resort to using Excel for this user-driven ad-hoc analysis, but as we've seen, Excel can't perform the level of complex analysis easily done in SQL. Another shortcoming of Excel is that the underlying data can be either intentionally or unintentionally manipulated, and these errors are nearly impossible to identify. Sharing Excel requires distributing multiple copies of the file to many people and ensuring that everyone is working with the most up-to-date copy. This becomes impossible if we require people to migrate their custom analysis, functions, VBA code, charts, pivot tables, and PowerQuery data models from one persons version to another.

These issues can be addressed if you diligently separate your data tabs from your analysis tabs and you keep the data separate from the workbook but most people have not been trained to use Excel in this way.

Moving to a cloud-based spreadsheet application like Google Sheets or Office365 does provide a shared copy of the spreadsheet, but as soon as people add data sources and perform analysis by modifying it, you end up with a chaotic and unsupportable mess. Lastly, even if you build a well-engineered shared spreadsheet application, you are still constrained by practical file and record size limits.

In organizations where the reporting needs are well defined, platforms like Cumul.io[146], Chartio[147], Numerics[148], or Grafana[149] can be used to deliver dedicated dashboards. Each of these applications are geared toward curated data sets that change infrequently and last for a long time (e.g., Delivered in the Expand phase). Another obvious solution is to deploy an expensive ad-hoc visualization and analytics platform like Tableau[150], Looker[151], Power BI[152], QlikView[153], or Superset[154]. These platforms offer the obvious advantage of being fully featured, easy to use, and performant. They are a fantastic addition to organizations where the platform is well supported, there are prohibitions on directly accessing the data, but a significant amount of ad-hoc analysis still needs to be performed.

These BI applications hide another problem. Their high procurement and operational costs require positioning them as a shared corporate service managed by a centralized IT organization. Usually, there is only one additional organization with a clearly articulated business need signing up for the service. While other groups or individuals may be interested, they seldom have the skills or long term need supporting such a large investment without a significant engagement in training and ongoing support.

Thus, new teams get onboarded to the reporting tool, and over time, their initial use dramatically falls off. Then, the IT team is left holding the bag of unused reports and stale data; this is now an IT problem. The results are diminishing business value and growing technical debt, weighed down by either constant or growing expenses. Because *"Corporate IT owns the system"*, it's nearly impossible to hold the business users accountable for the value they assumed they would generate.

Finally, we could let the ad-hoc users access our database directly. IT, as the owner of these databases, usually has major complaints about this idea.

- What if someone executes a runaway query that locks other users out of the database?
- What if someone inadvertently (or maliciously) deletes a table?
- What if a user modifies a table or adds new data and "*messes up*" the database? Besides, how would they manage this data? You don't expect them to have access to our ETL and scheduler?
- What if a user shares data from "*our*" database and it's wrong? Won't we get the calls and be expected to fix it?

Even if you could successfully address these objections, giving users access to the database requires every user to have a good SQL development environment, adequate SQL skills, and a way to produce basic charts to gain visibility to the data structure.

What we need is an environment where users can quickly access the data they need to answer the questions they have without endangering the systems used to run the business.

The Data Discovery Platform

We can address most of these issues by shifting ownership and management of the data back to the people who are closest to the data. By keeping the scope small, the system simple, and robust, we can overcome the problems of balancing business value with capital and labor costs.

So far, we have a toolbox of simple-to-use tools to access and process data. We have a method to automate data processing that is so robust we can delete the solution at any time and easily rebuild it from scratch with a single command. We can even build complicated reports automatically. Most importantly, this system has an incredibly low operational cost and potentially high business value.[155]

We've laid the foundation for a better solution to these problems through adopting better practices like iterative development, automation, and open-source standards and practices. Unfortunately, we don't have much to show for it.

What we haven't done is share this data with our users in a way that encourages them to use the data and provide feedback. What we need is an application to:

- Expose our data through a web browser.
- Interface with other applications.
- Sort and filter data.
- Search data easily.
- Build simple charts.
- Support the necessary security requirements.
- Be easy to update and manage.
- Integrate with our data management toolbox.

Before continuing, we need to decide on our scope and set acceptance criteria to keep the work from getting out of control.

IN ORDER TO FOCUS ON THE PRODUCTS WITH THE HIGHEST REVENUE.
AS A SALES MANAGER
I WANT A CHART OF PRODUCT SALES BY WEEK OVER THE LAST SIX MONTHS. (ATTRIBUTES BY TOTAL REVENUE, OVER THE LAST SIX MONTHS)

[] REPORTS ARE AVAILABLE DURING NORMAL BUSINESS HOURS.
[] ACCESSIBLE THROUGH A WEB BROWSER.
[] REFLECTS THE MOST RECENT DATA AVAILABLE.

IN ORDER TO IDENTIFY ISSUES WITH THE DATA.
AS A SALES MANAGER RESPONSIBLE FOR THE QUALITY OF THE SALES DATA
I WANT TO BE ABLE TO IDENTIFY ISSUES WITH THE DATA.
AND A WAY TO DEMONSTRATE AND COMMUNICATE THOSE ISSUES.
AND A WAY TO QUICKLY PRIORITIZE AND FIX THOSE ISSUES.

[] PROVIDE VISIBILITY TO THE DATABASE.
[] PROVIDE THE ABILITY TO FILTER AND QUERY TABLES.
[] PROVIDE A WAY TO VISUALIZE THE DATA. (E.G., PRODUCTS HAVE A DIFFERENT COST FOR DIFFERENT CUSTOMERS. A CHART MIGHT HELP.)
[] IT CAN'T RUN ON SOMEONE'S LAPTOP!

Fortunately, there is an open-source application that meets all these criteria: Datasette.[156] It is a web-based, written in Python, for exploring and sharing data. It can publish any SQLite database online without the need to build a custom web application. Out of the box, it automatically exposes all the database tables and views with an easy-to-navigate set of pages and tables. All tables and queries are also exposed as CSV and JSON objects for easy integration with other systems and applications. The data is read-only by default, so the source data cannot be corrupted. It deploys with a single command on a developer's computer, a networked server, a cloud-hosted computer, or a container running in a serverless environment.

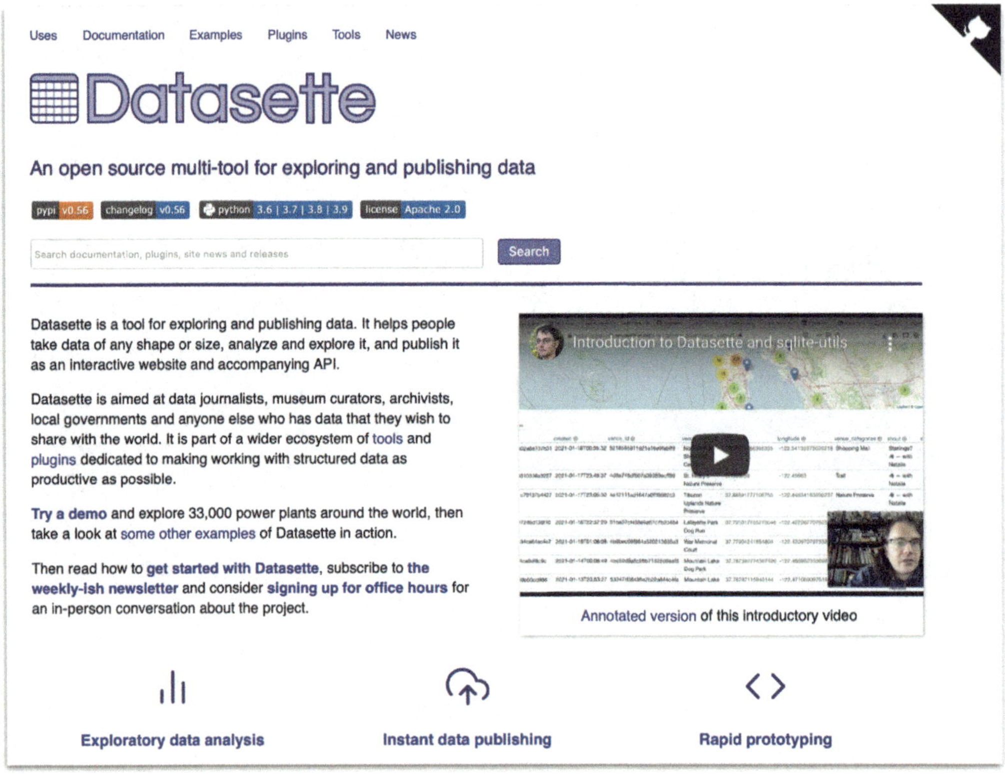

Datasette.io

Running Datasette

To understand how Datasette can be used to deliver the Data Discovery Platform, we'll briefly look at it running against the data in our database.

Datasette is started from a command line at the root of our project by executing `datasette svc/db/sales.db -o`.

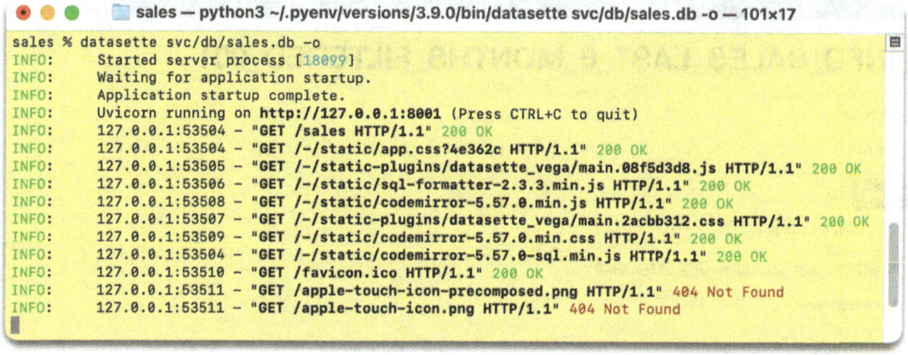

As the application begins, the log is written to the terminal window, providing similar real-time feedback to our makefile. Once the server is running, the -o command opens a web browser, and we see the database, tables, and views.

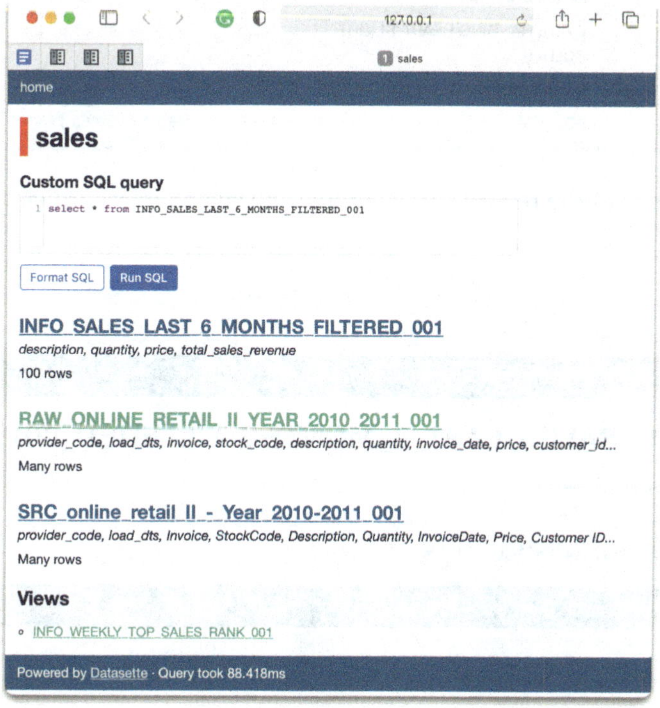

Let's take a quick tour of the Datasette application. If you select a table or view, the page shows the records in that table. Every column is sortable, and you can filter the data by selecting a column, filter type, and value with a form.

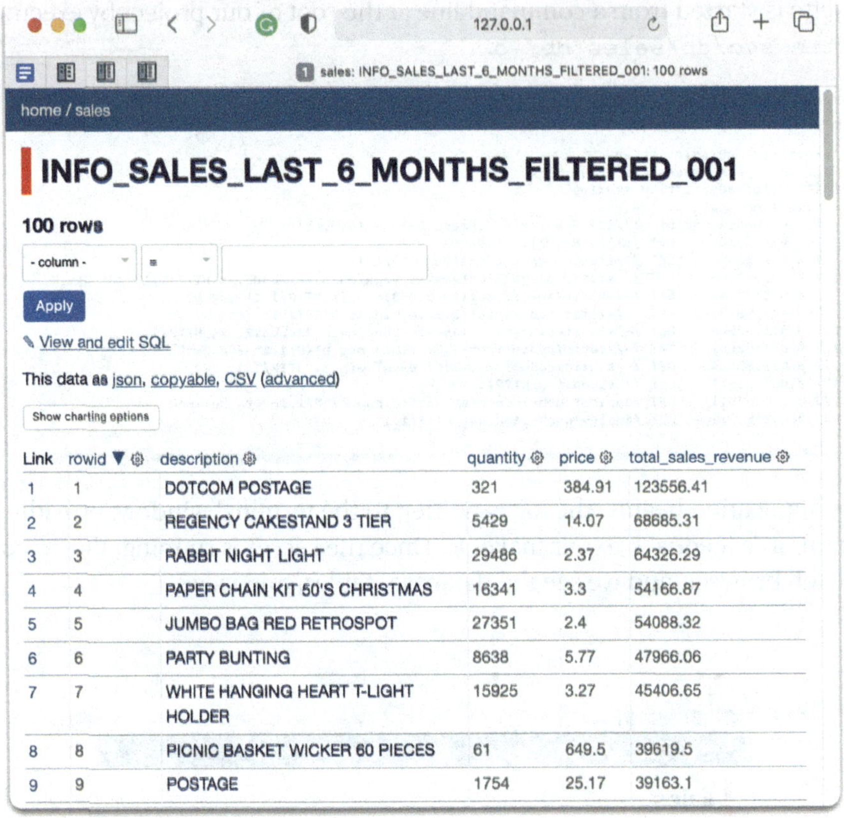

If you select one of the records, the window will switch to record view.

The table view also allows you to view and edit the select statement for the table. The SQL interface supports any valid SQLite statement, and if you include parameters in the query, they render on a form.

At the bottom of every table is the SQL statement used to create that table or view. For more complex queries, this will be an extremely helpful piece of automatic documentation and a great teaching tool to help people eventually write their own queries.

```
CREATE VIEW INFO_WEEKLY_TOP_SALES_RANK_001 AS

WITH CTE_BASE AS (
  SELECT DISTINCT
  provider_code,
  load_dts,
  --invoice as raw_invoice,
  REPLACE(invoice, 'C', '') AS invoice,
  stock_code,
  description,
  invoice_date,
  quantity,
  price,
```

Each table supports filtering the data by facets. Facets filter data by exposing a list of the distinct values in a column. This is equivalent to the slicer functionality in Excel, and it simplifies the process of finding records. However, as people use the data to answer more questions, be prepared to add new fields to the table to exposed new facets. Fortunately, each new field added or modified in the table is automatically included the next time the database is deployed.

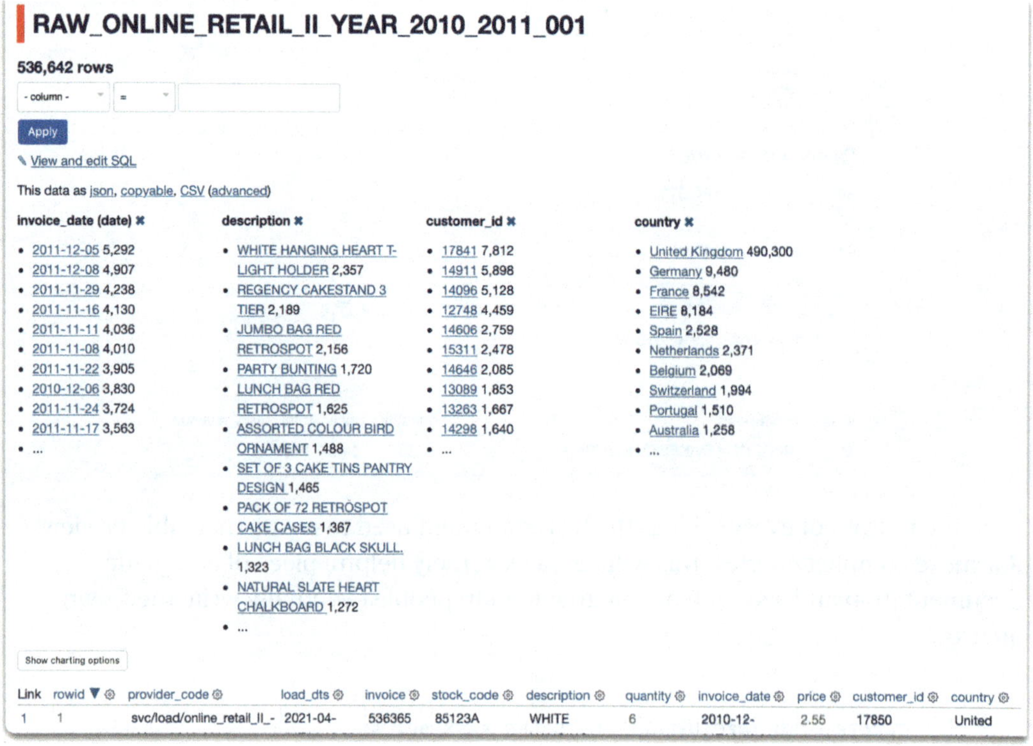

Every page includes either a form or link to export the underlying data in many JSON or delimited text file formats.

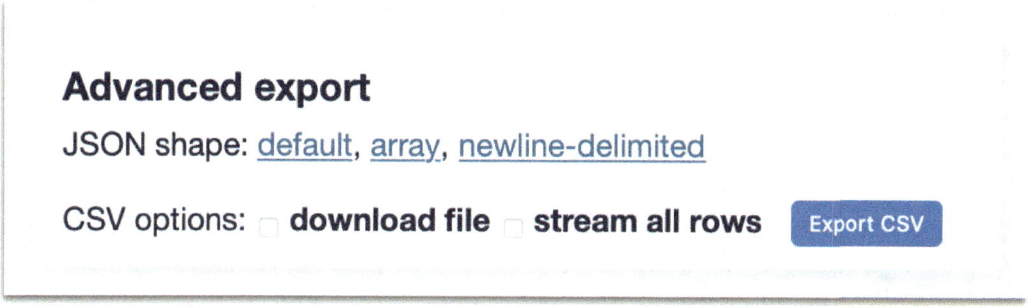

This JSON data can be used in other JavaScript applications by referencing the URL of the webpage.

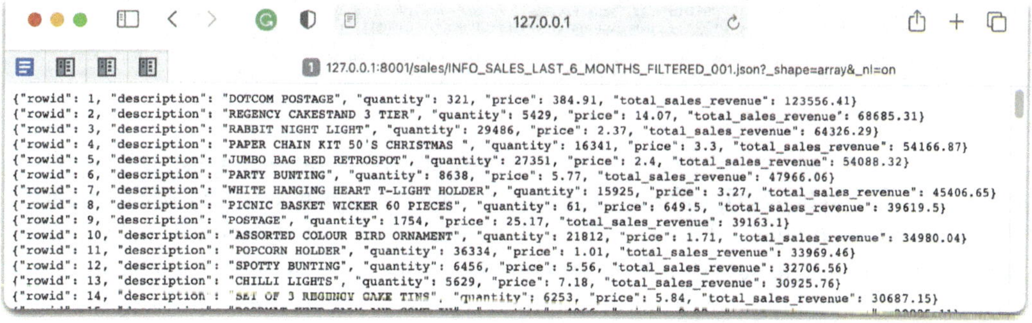

CSV files can be used to easily export any of the tables or views or as a table source in Excel or other applications that expect a CSV data source.

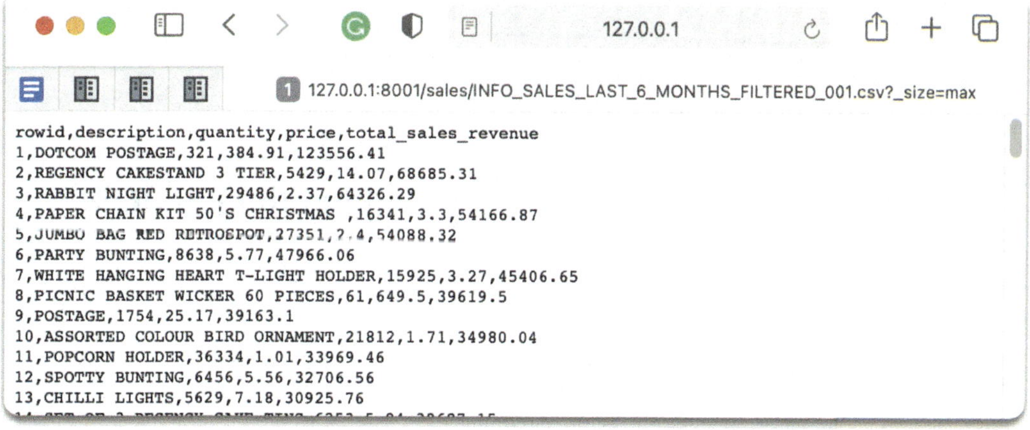

Exporting data has an added benefit of exposing all data through a consistent and easy-to-use API. By adding `.json` to the end of a URL for a table, any application can access any data set defined by a table or view. When we developed the visualization for sales data, we exported a JSON data set and then embedded it directly in our HTML page. Now that we can expose the same data set through a URL, we can replace the embedded data with data coming directly from the database. Other applications that consume invoice data can do the same. Later, we'll review specific examples of these use cases.

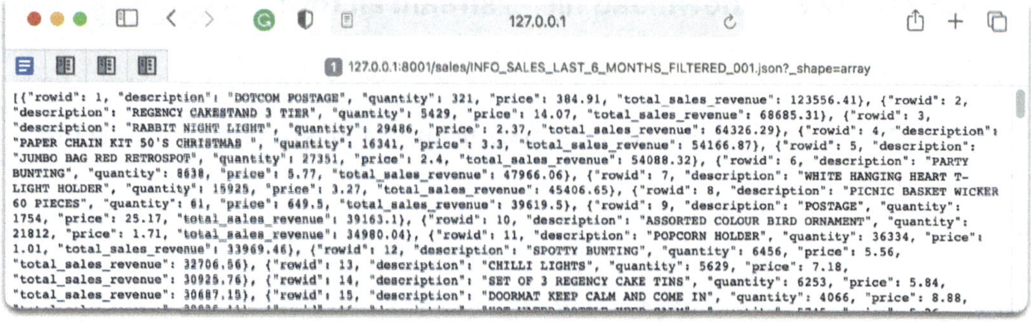

The final user-facing feature is to create ad-hoc charts on the web page. Datasette includes the Vega JavaScript library used earlier, but extends it to use a form to create charts based on the filtered data set. This encourages people to try new visualizations without exporting the data or asking for help. Because these are Vega-Lite charts, it is easy to open them in the Vega editor and then use that code as the basis for new standardized reporting.

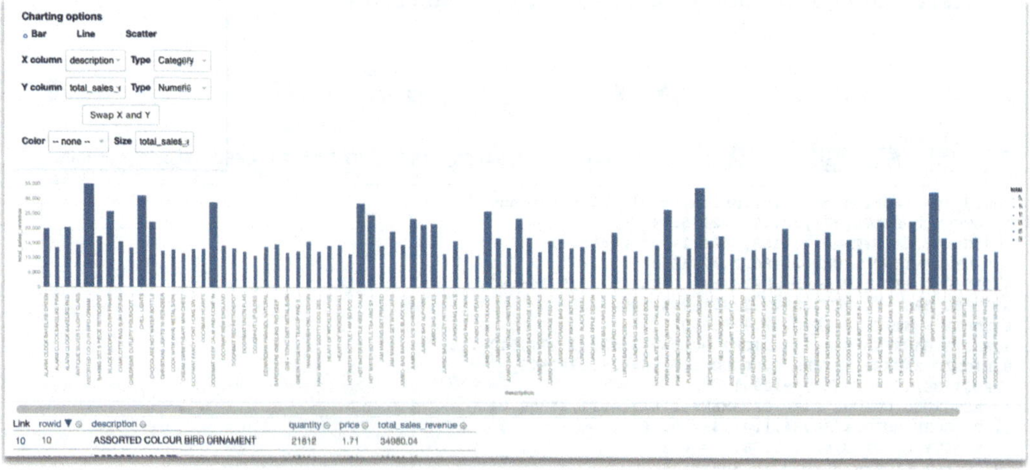

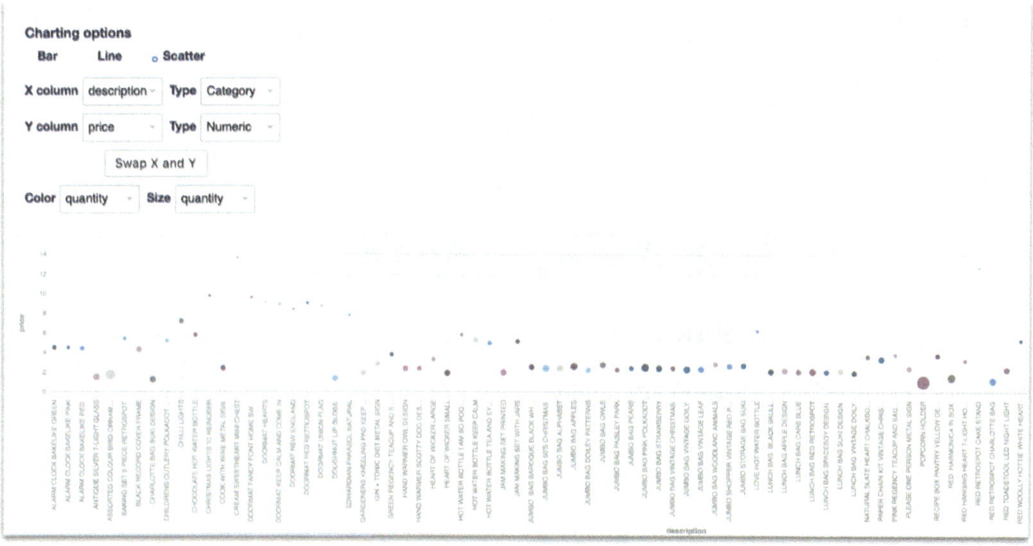

Serving the Data on our Local Network

By default, Datasette runs locally. The web server is only accessible from the computer running the application by executing the `datasette sales.db -o` command. Unfortunately, this isn't very practical. By specifying a specific host IP address, we can open the application on our local network.

```
datasette svc/db/sales.db --host 192.168.1.251 --port 8001 -o
```

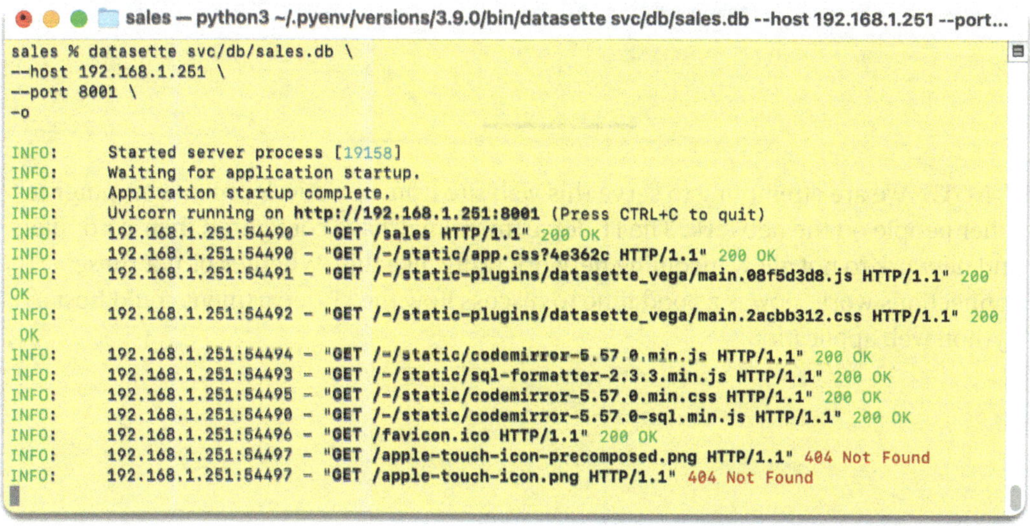

```
sales — python3 ~/.pyenv/versions/3.9.0/bin/datasette svc/db/sales.db --host 192.168.1.251 --port...
sales % datasette svc/db/sales.db \
--host 192.168.1.251 \
--port 8001 \
-o
INFO:     Started server process [19158]
INFO:     Waiting for application startup.
INFO:     Application startup complete.
INFO:     Uvicorn running on http://192.168.1.251:8001 (Press CTRL+C to quit)
INFO:     192.168.1.251:54490 - "GET /sales HTTP/1.1" 200 OK
INFO:     192.168.1.251:54490 - "GET /-/static/app.css?4e362c HTTP/1.1" 200 OK
INFO:     192.168.1.251:54491 - "GET /-/static-plugins/datasette_vega/main.08f5d3d8.js HTTP/1.1" 200
OK
INFO:     192.168.1.251:54492 - "GET /-/static-plugins/datasette_vega/main.2acbb312.css HTTP/1.1" 200
 OK
INFO:     192.168.1.251:54494 - "GET /-/static/codemirror-5.57.0.min.js HTTP/1.1" 200 OK
INFO:     192.168.1.251:54493 - "GET /-/static/sql-formatter-2.3.3.min.js HTTP/1.1" 200 OK
INFO:     192.168.1.251:54495 - "GET /-/static/codemirror-5.57.0.min.css HTTP/1.1" 200 OK
INFO:     192.168.1.251:54490 - "GET /-/static/codemirror-5.57.0-sql.min.js HTTP/1.1" 200 OK
INFO:     192.168.1.251:54496 - "GET /favicon.ico HTTP/1.1" 200 OK
INFO:     192.168.1.251:54497 - "GET /apple-touch-icon-precomposed.png HTTP/1.1" 404 Not Found
INFO:     192.168.1.251:54497 - "GET /apple-touch-icon.png HTTP/1.1" 404 Not Found
```

This means that we can now access our data from our phones or another computer on the network.

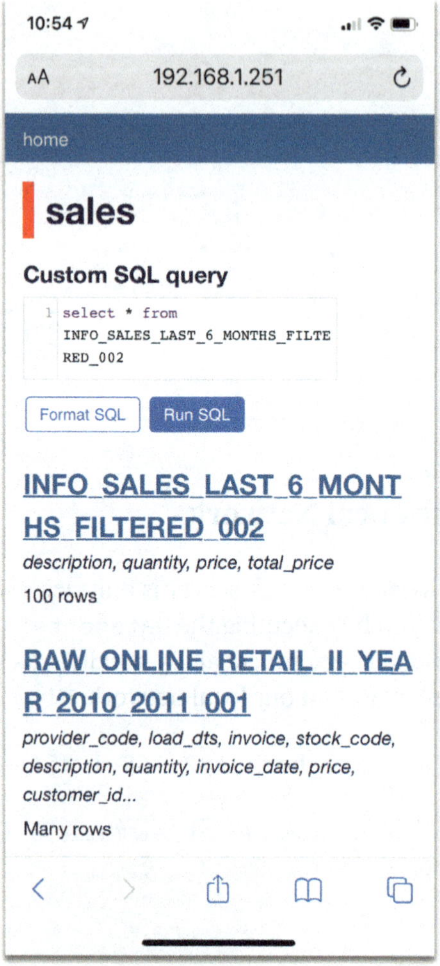

NOTE: We are attempting to serve this web site from our development computer to other people on the network. The IT department may have configured their computers and network to not allow incoming network traffic like this. Whether or not these connections work, now is a good time to discuss how the IT department could host a Python web application.

Integrating our Reporting

Fortunately, we don't have these problems yet! Our next step is to integrate the static visualizations we created earlier. Datasette serves static files and web pages by starting the server with the `--static` flag.

1. Stop the server with the `[ctrl]+[c]` keys.
2. Restart the server with this command: `datasette svc/db/sales.db --static static:svc/static/ -o`

We could serve the application from the same directory we use for development, but it is better to separate the development environment from the deployment environment. To do this, we will use the `opt/local/` directory and manually copy the database file from `svc/db/`. The next step is to create a `opt/local/static/` directory and copy our visualization HTML file and JSON data export. We can confirm these changes by restarting the server with the database in the new location.

```
datasette opt/local/sales.db --static static:opt/local/static/
--host 192.168.1.251 --port 8001 -o
```

```
sales — python3 ~/.pyenv/versions/3.9.0/bin/datasette opt/local/sales.db --static static:opt/local/static...
Usage: datasette serve [OPTIONS] [FILES]...
sales % datasette opt/local/sales.db \
--static static:opt/local/static/ \
--host 192.168.1.251 \
--port 8001 \
-o
INFO:     Started server process [30027]
INFO:     Waiting for application startup.
INFO:     Application startup complete.
INFO:     Uvicorn running on http://192.168.1.251:8001 (Press CTRL+C to quit)
INFO:     192.168.1.251:60527 - "GET /sales HTTP/1.1" 200 OK
INFO:     192.168.1.251:60527 - "GET /-/static/app.css?4e362c HTTP/1.1" 200 OK
INFO:     192.168.1.251:60529 - "GET /-/static-plugins/datasette_vega/main.08f5d3d8.js HTTP/1.1" 200 OK
INFO:     192.168.1.251:60530 - "GET /-/static-plugins/datasette_vega/main.2acbb312.css HTTP/1.1" 200 OK
INFO:     192.168.1.251:60531 - "GET /-/static/sql-formatter-2.3.3.min.js HTTP/1.1" 200 OK
INFO:     192.168.1.251:60532 - "GET /-/static/codemirror-5.57.0.min.js HTTP/1.1" 200 OK
INFO:     192.168.1.251:60533 - "GET /-/static/codemirror-5.57.0.min.css HTTP/1.1" 200 OK
INFO:     192.168.1.251:60527 - "GET /-/static/codemirror-5.57.0-sql.min.js HTTP/1.1" 200 OK
INFO:     192.168.1.251:60573 - "GET /static/WEEKLY_TOP_SALES_RANK_001.html HTTP/1.1" 200 OK
INFO:     192.168.1.251:60573 - "GET /favicon.ico HTTP/1.1" 200 OK
INFO:     192.168.1.251:60577 - "GET /static/WEEKLY_TOP_SALES_RANK_001.json HTTP/1.1" 200 OK
INFO:     192.168.1.251:60577 - "GET /favicon.ico HTTP/1.1" 200 OK
```

Confirm the serving of static files is working correctly by opening the URLs to both the visualization and JSON file. Note, this JSON file was the one we exported earlier, not the one we generated from the database.

```
http://192.168.1.251:8001/static/WEEKLY_TOP_SALES_RANK_001.html
```

```
http://192.168.1.251:8001/static/WEEKLY_TOP_SALES_RANK_001.json
```

If we try to access the view to generate the dynamic extract, we get a timeout error and a message to adjust the sql_time_limit_ms configuration options.

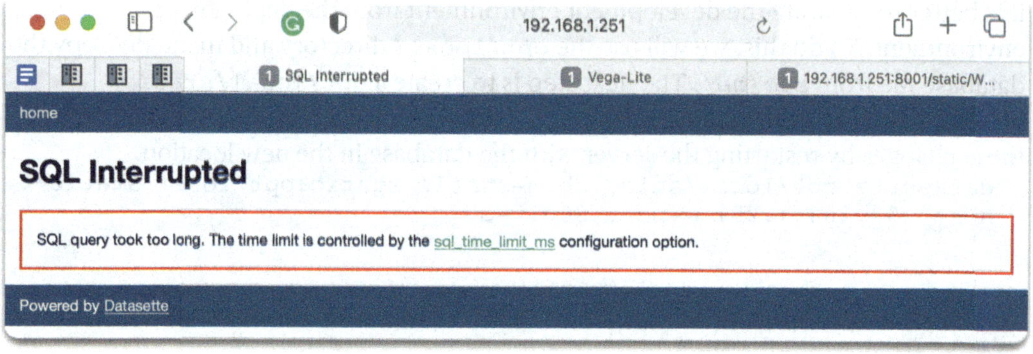

There are numerous configuration options to avoid these errors, and they are documented at (https://docs.datasette.io/en/stable/settings.html). After some trial and error testing, these settings get everything working properly.

```
datasette opt/local/sales.db \
--static static:opt/local/static/ \
--host 192.168.1.251 \
--port 8001 \
--setting num_sql_threads 3 \
--setting sql_time_limit_ms 5000 \
--setting max_returned_rows 5000 \
--setting default_page_size 1000 \
--setting facet_time_limit_ms 1000 \
--setting default_facet_size 10 \
--setting facet_suggest_time_limit_ms 1000 \
--setting allow_download on \
--setting max_csv_mb 0 \
-o
```

Accessing `http://192.168.1.251:8001/sales/INFO_WEEKLY_TOP_SALES_RANK_001.json?_shape=array` now returns an array formatted JSON document.

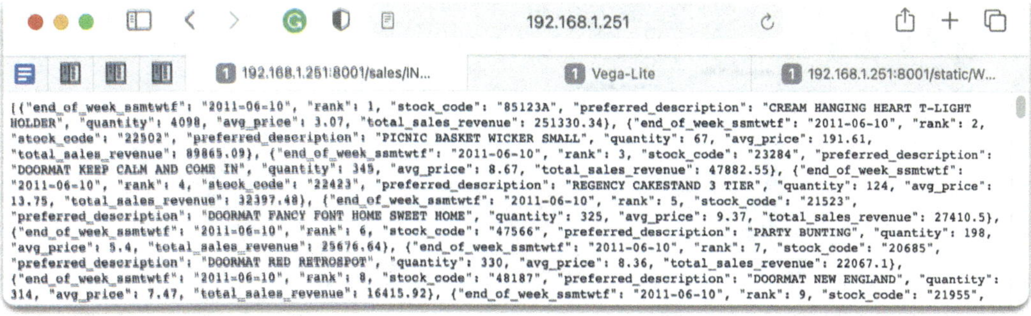

Modifying our Visualizations

The next step in the development process is linking the visualization to the Datasette JSON API. This allows dynamically generating the report without exporting the data first. The first step is to copy the `WEEKLY_TOP_SALES_RANK_001.html` file two times, renaming it `WEEKLY_TOP_SALES_RANK_002.html` and `WEEKLY_TOP_SALES_RANK_003.html`.

Open the `_002` file and replace the `"data"` and `"title"` objects with the following:

```
<!-- Embed Vega-Lite Definition Here -->
"data":{"url":"/sales/INFO_WEEKLY_TOP_SALES_RANK_001.json?
_shape=array"},
"title":"Weekly Top Sales Rank - JSON API call",
```

This file will now reference the data generated by the API each time the URL is opened.

Open the `_003` file and replace the `"data"` and `"title"` objects with the following:

```
<!-- Embed Vega-Lite Definition Here -->
"data":{"url":"/static/WEEKLY_TOP_SALES_RANK_001.json"},
"title":"Weekly Top Sales Rank - URL with a static JSON file",
```

This file will now reference the JSON file we exported earlier, replacing the data set we copied with the cat command.

Each URL can now be opened in a separate tab, and we can see they look identical.

`http://192.168.1.251:8001/static/WEEKLY_TOP_SALES_RANK_001.html`

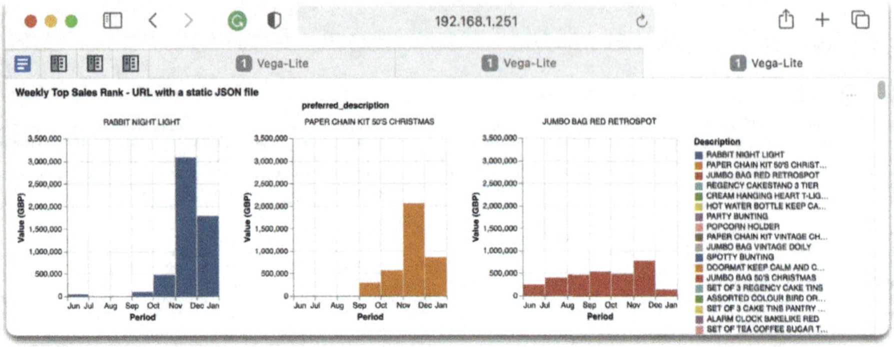

`http://192.168.1.251:8001/static/WEEKLY_TOP_SALES_RANK_002.html`

`http://192.168.1.251:8001/static/WEEKLY_TOP_SALES_RANK_003.html`

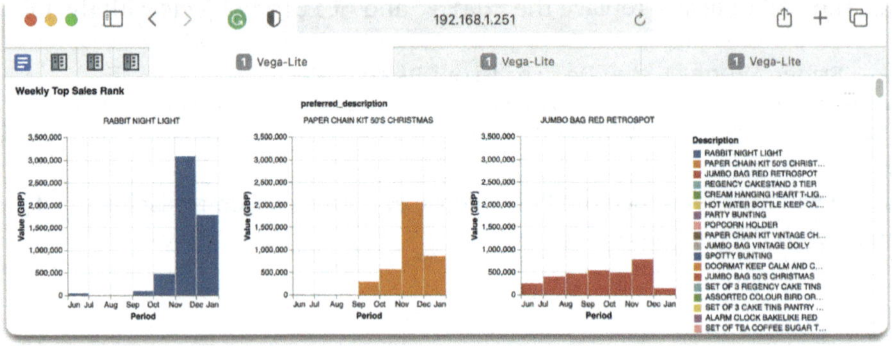

A Word About Performance

One obvious observation can be made from this experiment. The page accessing the API takes a significant amount of time to draw. Investigate this problem by opening the developer tools menu on the browser and reloading the pages.

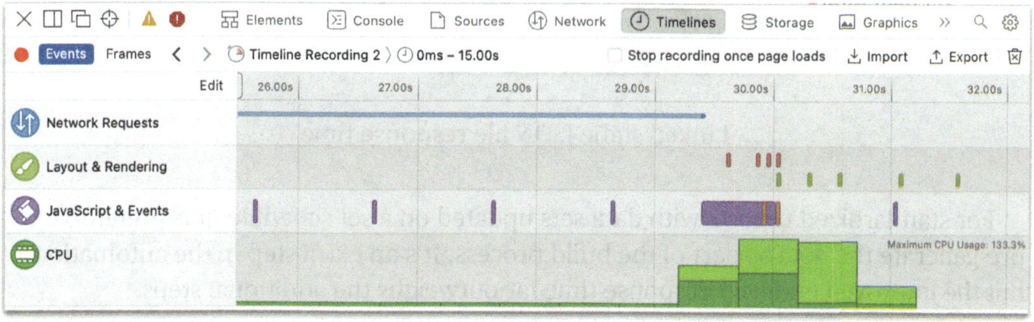

JSON API response time

It isn't pretty. The API takes around 30 seconds to return the data, as shown by the blue bar in the Network Requests row. While 30 seconds is an unacceptably long time, it's a good start. Keep in mind that at this early stage, we are assembling the plumbing and making sure water can flow from one end to another. You don't want to spend too much time perfecting one part of the solution when other parts are needing more attention.

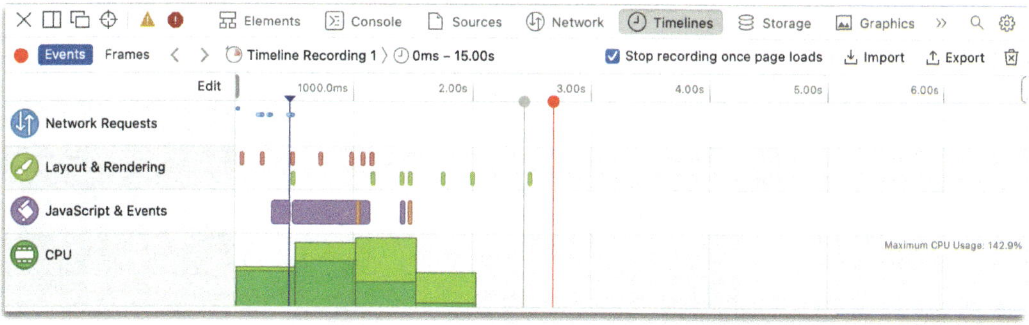

Embedded JSON data set response time

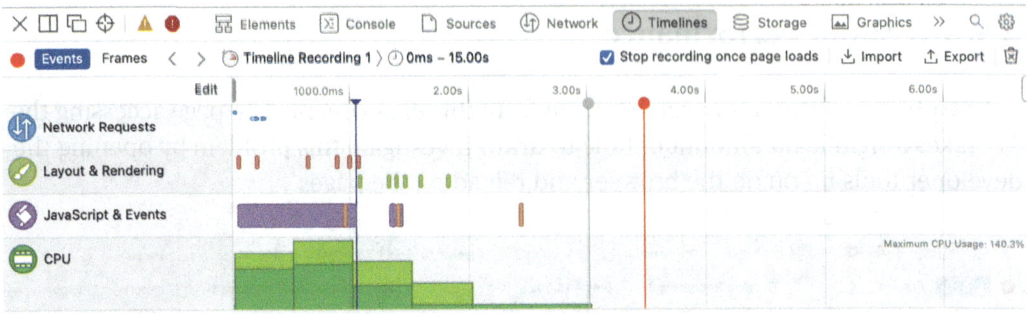

Linked static JSON file response time

For standardized reports with data sets updated on a set schedule, it is preferable to pre-generate the data as part of the build process. It's an extra step in the automation, but the improved end-user response time far outweighs the additional steps.

This little experiment illustrates a key part of the design process. If you look at the flow of the data from the source to the end-user, you are trying to minimize the time it takes to move from start to finish. Along the way, some steps take longer than others, and some are more visible to your customers. Any attempt to improve the process should start with identifying and improving this constraint.

One way to approach this problem is to segment those customers into multiple groups based on how they use the data. Consider your electric bill. The first group needs their utility bill delivered every month on the same day. The most important visualization is a simple month-over-month chart and a few additional metrics. Meet their needs with pre-generated standardized reports.

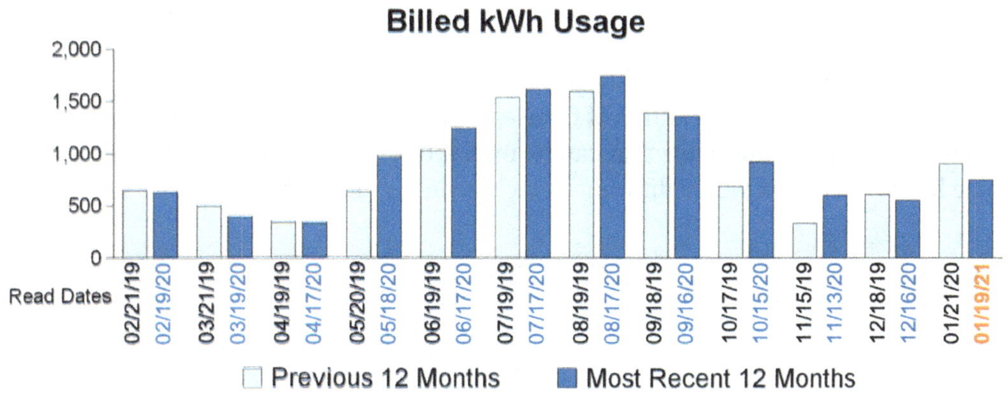

Billing Period Comparison

	Current	Previous	Last Year
Avg High Temperature	**67°F**	**74°F**	**63°F**
Avg Low Temperature	**39°F**	**46°F**	**40°F**
Billing Days	34	33	34
Avg Daily Usage (kWh)	22.00	16.79	26.65
Total kWh Usage	748.00	554.00	906.00
Demand (kW) *For Information Only*	-	-	-

Average Daily Cost*
$3.57

View more details at tep.com/myaccount or use the TEP mobile app.

**Average Daily Cost reflects current charges divided by billing days.*

The second group may require additional granularity to make decisions. An example in an electric bill is to include the previous twelve months. But even more useful is to include a chart for hourly usage over the last three months. This allows users to know when they are using the most electricity so they can look for opportunities to cut back. Do they need a button to click to drill into this information? No. If you want users to look at their energy consumption, make this information obvious, and include an hourly consumption bar chart with indicators of off-peak hours. This capability doesn't necessitate on-demand reporting.

The visualization is a great example of this in action. Our data set pre-calculates the top ten products by week over the last six months and then ranks these products by total sales volume from highest to lowest. The actual charts break down that number into months. Performing those calculations on-demand only adds to the total response time; if you add the time for a user to select the data set filters, it would take even longer. As developers, aim to balance the needs of the few users who want total freedom with delivering the most value to the most people as quickly as possible.

For the many, develop and deliver products to get the best information into users' hands as quickly as possible. For the few, give them free and full access to as many things as possible, as well as appropriate tools for the job and to let them play. The worst thing that can happen is they discover issues with the data for you to address.

Extending Datasette with plugins

One of the most useful features of Datasette as a Data Discovery platform are the additional plugin components that can be installed to add functionality for users. The table below lists a few we might want to include in our deployment.

Plugin	Description
datasette-vega	Datasette plugin for visualizing data using Vega.
datasette-copyable	Datasette plugin for outputting tables in formats suitable for copy and paste.
datasette-cluster-map	Datasette plugin that shows a map for any data with latitude/ longitude columns.
datasette-search-all	Datasette plugin for searching all searchable tables at once.
datasette-auth-passwords	Datasette plugin for searching all searchable tables at once. datasette-auth-passwords
datasette-backup	Once installed, you can download a SQL backup of any of your databases from: /-/ backup/dbname.sql.

Each of these can be installed as a Python package using the PIP package manager. This is the same process we used when setting up our development environment as described in the appendix (pip install <package> and/or pip install upgrade <package>).

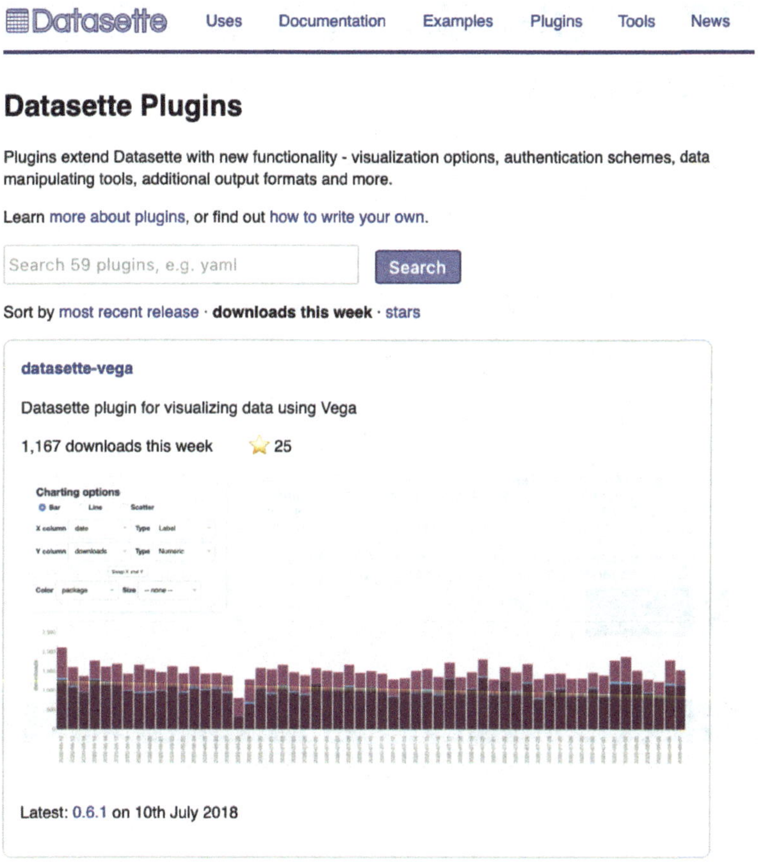

NOTE: Avoid the urge to install numerous plugins without having a firm understanding of how work. A number of them require changes to the database and additional configuration. Install additional features only when you understand the support and deployment requirements and people are ready for them. That being said, we'll use two plugins as a requirement for our initial deployment. When we create our deployment target for an external server, we need to make sure that we have installed all the necessary plugins.

The Copyable plugin,[157] makes it possible to copy and paste any data set directly from the web page without exporting the data first. Once the plugin is installed with pip (`pip install datasette-copyable`), restart the server, and the copyable option will be added to the export form.

Creating a Deployment

Up to this point, we have been starting Datasette from a rather complicated command line. Now that we are running from our `opt/local/` directory, we should begin taking advantage of some additional configuration options and settings. The first thing we need to refactor is to move our command-line settings into a settings file called `settings.json`.

Opt/local/settings.json:

```
{
    "default_page_size": 1000,
    "sql_time_limit_ms": 5000,
    "max_returned_rows": 5000,
    "num_sql_threads": 3,
    "allow_facet": true,
    "default_facet_size": 10,
    "facet_time_limit_ms": 1000,
    "facet_suggest_time_limit_ms": 500,
    "suggest_facets": true,
    "allow_download": true,
    "default_cache_ttl": 5,
    "default_cache_ttl_hashed": 31536000,
    "cache_size_kb": 0,
    "allow_csv_stream": true,
    "max_csv_mb": 0,
    "truncate_cells_html": 2048,
    "force_https_urls": false,
    "hash_urls": false,
    "template_debug": false,
    "base_url": "/"
}
```

This file contains a JSON array of all the application configuration options we can set when Datasette starts up. By moving the configuration out of the command line and into a file, we make it easier to consistently deploy the application and to make future modifications without modifying the start-up command.[158]

```
datasette serve opt/local/ --host 192.168.1.251 --port 8001
```

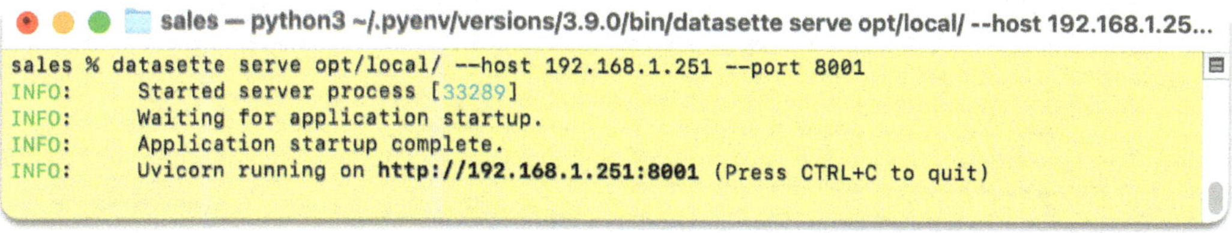

The next deployment feature is the Metadata file.[159] This is another JSON file within the deployment directory containing basic information about the web site and data.

opt/local/metadat.json:

```
{
  "license": "CC Attribution 4.0 License",
  "license_url": "http://creativecommons.org/licenses/by/4.0/",
  "source": "Building Data Products",
  "source_url": "https://github.com/",
  "title": "Sales Data Discovery Platform",
  "databases": {sales.db}
}
```

For the definition of complex metadata values, the JSON format with all of its brackets and quotation marks can become cumbersome. An alternative is to define the metadata using the YAML markup language.[160] The advantage of YAML is that it is easier for people to read and write than JSON.

Opt/local/metadata.yaml:

```
title: Sales Data Discovery Platform
license: CC Attribution 4.0 License
license_url: http://creativecommons.org/licenses/by/4.0/
source: Building Data Products
source_url: https://github.com/
databases:
  sales.db:
    source: online_retail_II.xlsx-Year_2010-2011
      tables:
        SRC_ONLINE_RETAIL_II_YEAR_2010_2011_001:
          source: svc/load/online_retail_II_-_Year_2010-2011.csv

```

One additional advantage of the YAML-based metadata file over the JSON file is that it is much easier to add HTML formatted text to be rendered when a page is loaded. For example, you can extend the metadata for the sales database to include as much descriptive information as possible.

```yaml
title: Sales Data Discovery Platform
license: CC Attribution 4.0 License
license_url: http://creativecommons.org/licenses/by/4.0/
source: Building Data Products
source_url: https://github.com/
databases:
  sales:
    source: Manual report - online_retail_II.xlsx-Year_2010-2011
    description_html: |-
       <strong>Description:</strong> Invoice data provided from a report.<br>
       <strong>Source:</strong> Manual extract<br>
       <strong>File:</strong> online_retail_II.xlsx-Year_2010-2011<br>
       <p></p>
       <a href = "mailto: sales.manager@example.com">Business Contact</a><br>
       <a href = "mailto: data.sales@example.com">Technical Contact</a>
```

We can use the same capability to link to our reports without needing to do any additional development. This buys us time to develop a more robust solution.

```yaml
title: Sales Data Discovery Platform
license: CC Attribution 4.0 License
license_url: http://creativecommons.org/licenses/by/4.0/
source: Building Data Products
source_url: https://github.com/
databases:
  sales:
    source: Manual report - online_retail_II.xlsx-Year_2010-2011
    description_html: |-
       <strong>Description:</strong> Invoice data provided from a report.<br>
       <strong>Source:</strong> Manual extract<br>
       <strong>File:</strong> online_retail_II.xlsx-Year_2010-2011<br>
       <p></p>
       <a href = "mailto: sales.manager@example.com">Business Contact</a><br>
       <a href = "mailto: data.sales@example.com">Technical Contact</a>
    tables:
      INFO_WEEKLY_TOP_SALES_RANK_001:
        description_html: |-
         <strong>Description:</strong> Sales revenue for the top 10 products in each week of the previc
         <strong>Source:</strong> Database view<br>
         <strong>Source table(s):</strong> INFO_SALES_LAST_6_MONTHS_FILTERED_002
         <p></p>
         <strong>Reports:</strong><br>
         <a href="http://192.168.1.251:8001/static/WEEKLY_TOP_SALES_RANK_001.html" target="_blank">Embe
         <a href="http://192.168.1.251:8001/static/WEEKLY_TOP_SALES_RANK_002.html" target="_blank">API
         <a href="http://192.168.1.251:8001/static/WEEKLY_TOP_SALES_RANK_003.html" target="_blank">Link
         <p></p>

```

The final configuration file we need to create is a `requirements.txt` file for our additional python modules and Datasette plugins. Rather than manually installing new modules, we want to automate this process with Make. The first step is to make a new text document in `opt/local/` listing all the python modules required by our solution.

opt/local/requirements.txt

```
# etc/server/local/requirements.txt
#
# pip install -r path/to/requirements.txt
#
csvkit >= 1.0.5
sqlite-utils >= 3.3
datasette >=0.54.1
datasette-vega >= 0.6.2
datasette-copyable >= 0.3.1
```

This file can be called by the pip package using the command `pip install -r opt/local/requirements.txt`. These packages can be updated with this command `pip install update -r opt/local/requirements.txt`. The update command will update any package dependencies in the requirements document. Be aware, changes in these packages may introduce bugs in your code; while rare, it is a possibility. You can address this by specifying a specific package version using the standard python comparison operators.

Operation	Description
==	Equal
>	Greater than
>=	Greater than or equal
<	Less than
<=	Less than or equal

NOTE: When we were working on getting Datasette running, and modifying the visualizations to use new data sources, we made a lot of changes without updating the automation. There is going to be a strong urge to update everything at once. Don't do it! Start by modifying the bare minimum and make sure that the system is working as we expect. Then add the new capabilities, one at a time, being sure to build in an appropriate level of testing.

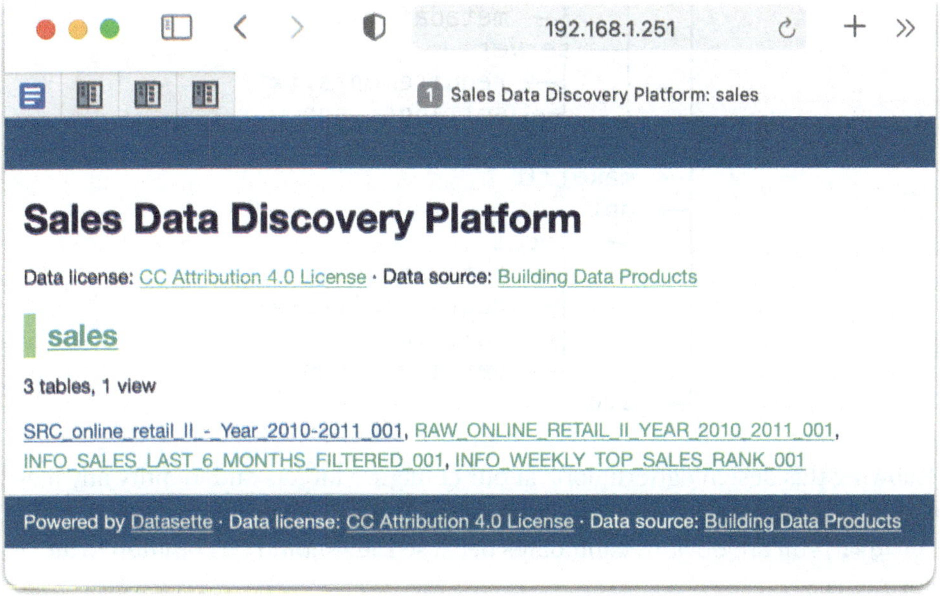

We now have a design decision to make. Currently, we are creating our static files and writing them to the `svc/` directory as part of the build process. We could repoint them to the `opt/` directory, but what if we need to deploy to multiple servers? Should the build process push the files into multiple deployment targets, or should the deployment targets pull in the files they need?

There is no one right answer, but the rule of modularity (where we write simple parts connected by clean interfaces) suggests using the build process to create the files and using the deploy process to assemble and configure everything needed, including moving them to the destination server(s).

```
.
├── etc
│   ├── app
│   │   └── metadata.yaml
│   ├── server
│   │   ├── requirements.txt
│   │   └── settings.json
│   └── sql
├── makefile
├── opt
│   └── local
│       ├── metadata.yaml
│       ├── requirements.txt
│       ├── sales.db
│       └── settings.json
└── svc
```

Following this design pattern, look at our configure targets and identify any files we should treat as prerequisites to the entire solution. The `requirements.txt` and `settings.json` are obvious candidates because they should be common to all deployments.

The tests for the configuration targets follow the same pattern as the targets we wrote to the visualization templates.

```
################################################################################
# Deployment configuration                                                     #
################################################################################
# Source files ---------------------------------------------------------------

test/shared/datasette: \
  etc/app/metadata.yaml \
  etc/server/requirements.txt \
  etc/server/settings.json

etc/app/metadata.yaml:
  @$(test_file)

etc/server/requirements.txt:
  @$(test_file)

etc/server/settings.json:
  @$(test_file)

```

NOTE: As with the other templates, we need to make sure we update the Build Tool to ensure these files are automatically written into the next project we initiate. Consider modifying these generic templates to provide enough structure to get started and obvious clues that these files need to be modified before they are put into production.

```
title: Modify etc/app/metadata.yml
license: ~
license_url: http://example.com/
source: Building Data Products
source_url: https://example.com/
databases:
  sales:
    source: ~
    description_html: |-
       <strong>Description:</strong> ~ <br>
       <strong>Source:</strong> ~ <br>
       <strong>Source table(s):</strong> ~ <p></p>
       <a href = "mailto: manager@example.com">~Business Contact</a><br>
       <a href = "mailto: tech@example.com">~Technical Contact</a>
    tables:
      table_001:
        description_html: |-
         <strong>Description:</strong> ~ <br>
         <strong>Source:</strong> ~ <br>
         <strong>Source table(s):</strong> ~ <p></p>
         <strong>Reports:</strong><br>
         <a href="http://example.com/path/to/file.html" target="_blank">~.html</a><br>
         <p></p>
```

Next, we need to create the targets for the local deployment by specifying the desired file locations.

```
###############################################################################
# Deployments                                                                 #
###############################################################################
# Local deployment ------------------------------------------------------------
test/local_config: build/local \
  opt/local/metadata.yaml \
  opt/local/requirements.txt \
  opt/local/settings.json \
  opt/local/sales.db \
  opt/local/static/WEEKLY_TOP_SALES_RANK_001.json \
  opt/local/static/WEEKLY_TOP_SALES_RANK_001.html \
  opt/local/static/WEEKLY_TOP_SALES_RANK_002.html \
  opt/local/static/WEEKLY_TOP_SALES_RANK_003.html
  @echo $(DTS)     [INFO] - Executing $@

opt/local/metadata.yaml:
  @$(test_file)

opt/local/requirements.txt:
  @$(test_file)

opt/local/settings.json:
  @$(test_file)

opt/local/sales.db:
  @$(test_file)

opt/local/static/WEEKLY_TOP_SALES_RANK_001.json:
  @$(test_file)

opt/local/static/WEEKLY_TOP_SALES_RANK_001.html:
  @$(test_file)

opt/local/static/WEEKLY_TOP_SALES_RANK_002.html:
  @$(test_file)

opt/local/static/WEEKLY_TOP_SALES_RANK_003.html:
  @$(test_file)
```

Once the file targets are defined, the `build/local:` target can be written to copy the files we need for the local deployment.

```
build/local:
	@echo $(DTS)	[INFO] - Executing $@
	@cp -f etc/app/metadata.yaml opt/local/metadata.yaml
	@cp -f etc/server/requirements.txt opt/local/requirements.txt
	@cp -f etc/server/settings.json opt/local/settings.json
	@cp -f svc/db/sales.db opt/local/sales.db
	@cp -f svc/static/WEEKLY_TOP_SALES_RANK_001.json opt/local/static/WEEKLY_TOP_SALES_RANK_001.json
	@cp -f svc/static/WEEKLY_TOP_SALES_RANK_001.html opt/local/static/WEEKLY_TOP_SALES_RANK_001.html
```

Don't forget to build an uninstall target. The combination of `build/local:` and `uninstall/local:` allows us to easily cycle through the test (fail) / build / test (pass) cycle without rerunning the entire `make all` process.

```
uninstall/local: ## Removes the build artifacts. "make uninstall/local"
	@echo $(DTS)	[INFO] - Executing $@.
	@rm -f opt/local/static/*
	@rm -f opt/local/*
```

Next, we need to create the build targets for the files we have in the proof of concept `svc/static/` directory. Our .json extract should be fine, but we will need to create two new HTML files for the new visualizations that pull from the different data sources and then create the corresponding targets.

First, we are going to rewrite the original recipe to create the WEEKLY_TOP_SALES_RANK_001 visualization to add a new variable for the report title. This will also require we remove the title line from the WEEKLY_TOP_SALES_RANK_001.vega file.

While we are at it, we should make another small change to the vega_embed_header.viz file in our project to reflect the current name of the product we are developing.

```
<html>
  <head>
    <title>Data Discovery Reporting</title>
    <meta charset="utf-8" />
```

```
svc/static/WEEKLY_TOP_SALES_RANK_001.html: VIZTITLE="Weekly Top Sales Rank - Embedded JSON dataset"
svc/static/WEEKLY_TOP_SALES_RANK_001.html: VIZTEMPLATE=etc/app/WEEKLY_TOP_SALES_RANK_001.vega
svc/static/WEEKLY_TOP_SALES_RANK_001.html: svc/static/WEEKLY_TOP_SALES_RANK_001.json
  @#<path/to/export_file.html>(colon)(space)VIZTEMPLATE=<path/to/viz_template.vega>
  @#<path/to/export_file.html>(colon)(space)<path/to/exported_file.json>
  @echo $(DTS)      [INFO] - Executing $@
  @cat etc/app/vega_embed_header.viz > $@
  @echo "\"data\":{ \"values\":" >> $@
  @cat $< >> $@ && echo "}, " >> $@
  @echo "\"title\":\"$(VIZTITLE)\"," >> $@
  @cat $(VIZTEMPLATE) >> $@
  @cat etc/app/vega_embed_footer.viz >> $@
```

```
"mark": {"type": "bar", "tooltip": {"content": "data"}},
  "resolve": {"axis": {"x": "independent", "y": "independent"}},
  "encoding": {
    "facet": {"field": "preferred_description", "type": "ordinal", "columns": 3,
    "x": {"field": "end_of_week_ssmtwtf", "type": "temporal", "title": "Period",
    "y": {"field": "total_sales_revenue", "type": "quantitative", "title": "Valu
  "color": {"field": "preferred_description", "type": "nominal", "title": "Descr

```

Setting all of this up to run can be done through a `deploy/local:` target with the `build/local:` target as a dependency to the `test/local_config:` target.

```
# Local deployment ----------------------------------------------------------------
.PHONY: deploy/local test_local_config build/local uninstall/local
deploy/local: test_local_config

test/local_config: build/local \
  opt/local/metadata.yaml \
```

Manual integration test

We're almost there! Unfortunately, with our new solution, we can't open the web pages without deploying the webserver.[161]

1. Rebuild the base application from scratch by executing `make uninstall && make uninstall/local && make`.
2. Build the deployment `make deploy/local`
3. Run the command to start up the server: `datasette serve opt/local/ --host 192.168.1.251 --port 8001 -o`
4. Open the INFO_WEEKLY_TOP_SALES_RANK_001 page: `http://192.168.1.251:8001/static/WEEKLY_TOP_SALES_RANK_001.html`

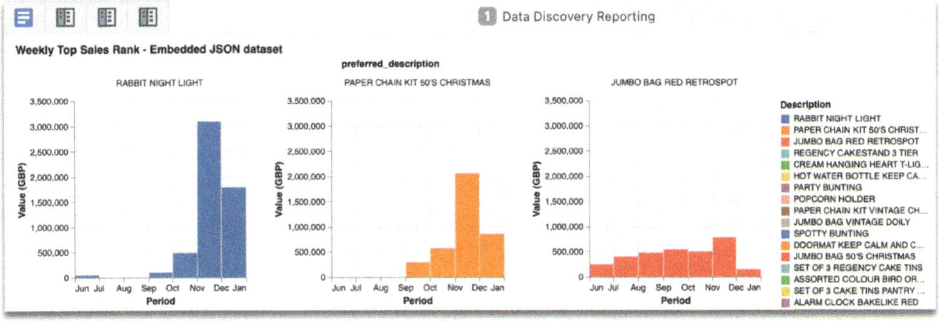

Starting the server

Having manually run a full integration test, it's time to automate the running of the local server. Looking at the command to start the server, we can easily replace the hard coded address with a few variables. The `$(shell ipconfig getifaddr en0)` command can be used to automatically assigns our IP address to the LOCAL_ADDRESS variable.

```
# Deployment variables
LOCAL_ADDRESS := $(shell /usr/sbin/ipconfig getifaddr en0) #192.168.1.251
LOCAL_PORT := 8001
```

These variables can be used to rewrite the command to make it possible to run with only a hard coded port. We can add the build and test targets as dependencies and simplify the `deploy/local:` target to be dependent on starting the server.

```
start/local: build/local test/local_config
	@echo $(DTS)	[INFO] - Starting server on http://$(strip $(LOCAL_ADDRESS)):$(LOCAL_PORT)
	@$(DATASETTE) serve $(LOCALDEPLOYMENTDIR) --host $(LOCAL_ADDRESS) --port $(LOCAL_PORT) -o
```

```
# Local deployment ------------------------------------------------------------
.PHONY: deploy/local test_local_config build/local uninstall/local start/local
deploy/local: start/local
	@echo $(DTS)	[INFO] - Executing $@
```

Integrating the other reports

Building the other two HTML files requires a simple change to the recipe we built for the WEEKLY_TOP_SALES_RANK_001.html file. We're substituting the path to the JSON file with a URL for the JSON document API exposed by Datasette.

```
svc/static/WEEKLY_TOP_SALES_RANK_002.html: VIZTITLE="Weekly Top Sales Rank - Embedded JSON API call"
svc/static/WEEKLY_TOP_SALES_RANK_002.html: VIZTEMPLATE=etc/app/WEEKLY_TOP_SALES_RANK_001.vega
svc/static/WEEKLY_TOP_SALES_RANK_002.html: VIZURL="/sales/INFO_WEEKLY_TOP_SALES_RANK_001.json?_shape=array"
svc/static/WEEKLY_TOP_SALES_RANK_002.html: INFO_SALES_LAST_6_MONTHS_FILTERED_001
	@#<path/to/export_file.html>(colon)(space)VIZTITLE=<report title>
	@#<path/to/export_file.html>(colon)(space)VIZTEMPLATE=<path/to/viz_template.vega>
	@#<path/to/export_file.html>(colon)(space)VIZURL=<path/to/viz_url.json?_shape=array>
	@#<path/to/export_file.html>(colon)(space)<source_table_template_name>
	@echo $(DTS)      [INFO] - Executing $@
	@cat etc/app/vega_embed_header.viz > $@
	@echo "\"data\":{\"url\":\"$(VIZURL)\"}, " >> $@
	@echo "\"title\":\"$(VIZTITLE)\"," >> $@
	@cat $(VIZTEMPLATE) >> $@
	@cat etc/app/vega_embed_footer.viz >> $@

svc/static/WEEKLY_TOP_SALES_RANK_003.html: VIZTITLE="Weekly Top Sales Rank - Link to static JSON
svc/static/WEEKLY_TOP_SALES_RANK_003.html: VIZTEMPLATE=etc/app/WEEKLY_TOP_SALES_RANK_001.vega
svc/static/WEEKLY_TOP_SALES_RANK_003.html: VIZURL="/static/WEEKLY_TOP_SALES_RANK_001.json"
svc/static/WEEKLY_TOP_SALES_RANK_003.html: INFO_SALES_LAST_6_MONTHS_FILTERED_001
	@#<path/to/export_file.html>(colon)(space)VIZTITLE=<report title>
	@#<path/to/export_file.html>(colon)(space)VIZTEMPLATE=<path/to/viz_template.vega>
	@#<path/to/export_file.html>(colon)(space)VIZURL=<path/to/viz_url.json?_shape=array>
	@#<path/to/export_file.html>(colon)(space)<source_table_template_name>
	@echo $(DTS)      [INFO] - Executing $@
	@cat etc/app/vega_embed_header.viz > $@
	@echo "\"data\":{\"url\":\"$(VIZURL)\"}, " >> $@
	@echo "\"title\":\"$(VIZTITLE)\"," >> $@
	@cat $(VIZTEMPLATE) >> $@
	@cat etc/app/vega_embed_footer.viz >> $@
```

These new files are added into the pipeline by adding them to the `test/outputs:` and `build/local:` targets.

```
test/outputs: \
  test/online_retail_II_last_6_months_filtered.csv \
  test_online_retail_II_last_6_months_filtered_002.csv \
  svc/static/WEEKLY_TOP_SALES_RANK_001.html \
  svc/static/WEEKLY_TOP_SALES_RANK_002.html \
  svc/static/WEEKLY_TOP_SALES_RANK_003.html
```

```
build/local:
	@echo $(DTS)     [INFO] - Executing $@
	@cp -f etc/app/metadata.yaml opt/local/metadata.yaml
	@cp -f etc/server/requirements.txt opt/local/requirements.txt
	@cp -f etc/server/settings.json opt/local/settings.json
	@cp -f svc/db/sales.db opt/local/sales.db
	@cp -f svc/static/WEEKLY_TOP_SALES_RANK_001.json opt/local/static/WEEKLY_TOP_SALES_RANK_001.json
	@cp -f svc/static/WEEKLY_TOP_SALES_RANK_001.html opt/local/static/WEEKLY_TOP_SALES_RANK_001.html
	@cp -f svc/static/WEEKLY_TOP_SALES_RANK_002.html opt/local/static/WEEKLY_TOP_SALES_RANK_002.html
	@cp -f svc/static/WEEKLY_TOP_SALES_RANK_003.html opt/local/static/WEEKLY_TOP_SALES_RANK_003.html
```

Finally, we can run a simple test to verify the webserver is running.

```
test/local:
	@$(if $(shell curl http://$(strip $(LOCAL_ADDRESS)):$(LOCAL_PORT) -fIs | head -n 1), \
	echo $(DTS)     [INFO] - http://$(strip $(LOCAL_ADDRESS)):$(LOCAL_PORT) - \
	$(shell curl http://$(strip $(LOCAL_ADDRESS)):$(LOCAL_PORT) -fIs | head -n 1), \
	echo $(DTS)     [FAIL] - $(strip $(LOCAL_ADDRESS)):$(LOCAL_PORT) is unavailable)
```

NOTE: This target needs to be executed from another terminal window, separate from the one running the webserver.

```
sales — -zsh — 77×5
sales % make test/local
2021-04-23T15:33:54-MST [INFO] - http://192.168.1.251:8001 - HTTP/1.1 200 OK
sales %
```

Deploying to Google Cloud

In addition to serving the data on our local network, we can publish the application to the public internet using one of many hosting providers. For example, we could publish to Google's CloudRun serverless hosting platform[162] with the following command.

```
datasette publish cloudrun --service=sales opt/local/sales.db
```

The process begins by building a compressed archive of the files in the `opt/local/` directory. This file is then bundled into a container with all of the files required by the Datasette application.

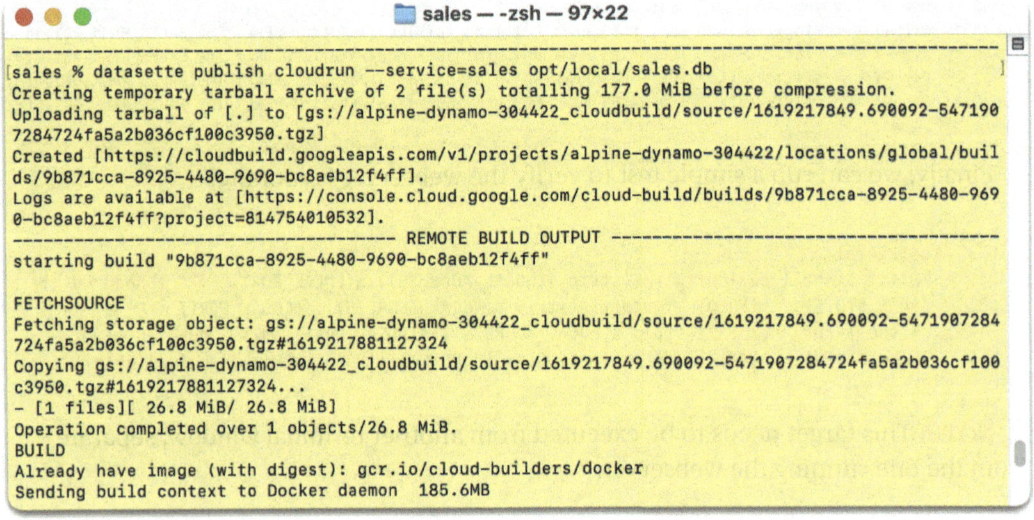


```
-------------------------------------------------------------------------------------------------
[sales % datasette publish cloudrun --service=sales opt/local/sales.db
Creating temporary tarball archive of 2 file(s) totalling 177.0 MiB before compression.
Uploading tarball of [.] to [gs://alpine-dynamo-304422_cloudbuild/source/1619217849.690092-547190
7284724fa5a2b036cf100c3950.tgz]
Created [https://cloudbuild.googleapis.com/v1/projects/alpine-dynamo-304422/locations/global/buil
ds/9b871cca-8925-4480-9690-bc8aeb12f4ff].
Logs are available at [https://console.cloud.google.com/cloud-build/builds/9b871cca-8925-4480-969
0-bc8aeb12f4ff?project=814754010532].
-------------------------------------- REMOTE BUILD OUTPUT ---------------------------------------
starting build "9b871cca-8925-4480-9690-bc8aeb12f4ff"

FETCHSOURCE
Fetching storage object: gs://alpine-dynamo-304422_cloudbuild/source/1619217849.690092-5471907284
724fa5a2b036cf100c3950.tgz#1619217881127324
Copying gs://alpine-dynamo-304422_cloudbuild/source/1619217849.690092-5471907284724fa5a2b036cf100
c3950.tgz#1619217881127324...
- [1 files][ 26.8 MiB/ 26.8 MiB]
Operation completed over 1 objects/26.8 MiB.
BUILD
Already have image (with digest): gcr.io/cloud-builders/docker
Sending build context to Docker daemon  185.6MB
```

Once the container is sent to the Google CloudRun service, it is deployed and all of the networking and access rules are implemented.

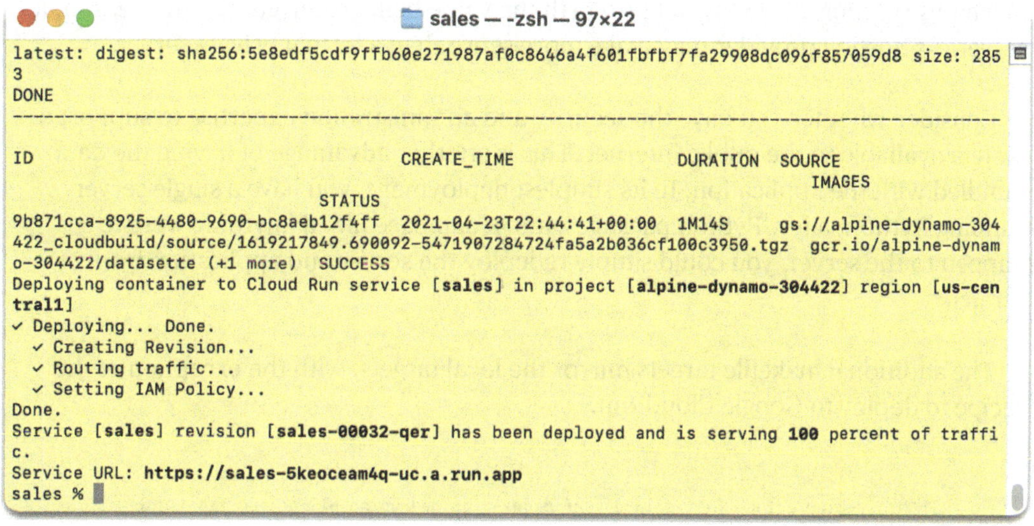

Finally, the console returns the URL to be used to access the server.

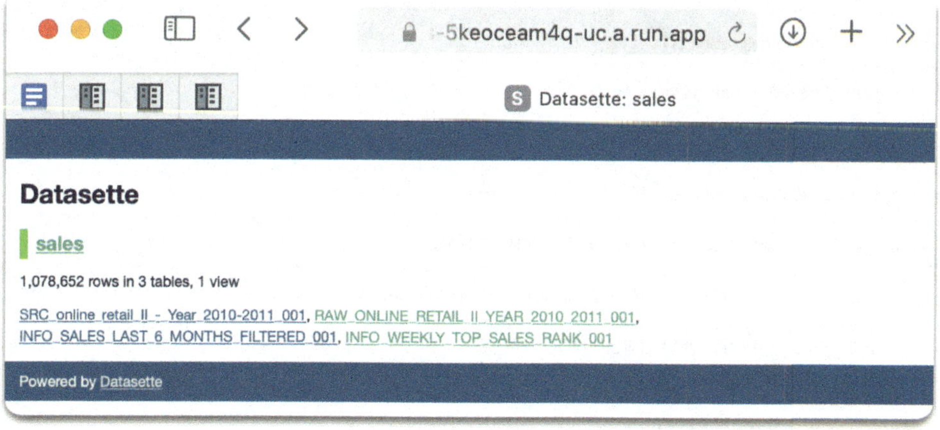

The advantages to using a hosting service like Google, is that they provide all the additional features you need, like monitoring, log management, security, and access to additional services as your needs grow.

However, each hosting platform operates differently and bills differently. For services with a low number of users accessing the application infrequently, you want a service that bills for actual utilization and has low storage cost. Paying for dedicated virtual machines running 24x7 may not be worth the value being received. For this reason, a serverless hosting provider may make more sense than a virtual private server.

Consider whether you have the security and administration expertise to support a system available to the public internet. This is another advantage of having the data bundled with the application. In its simplest deployment, you have a single server running Python, a few Python packages, and a database file. If anything were to happen to the server, you could simply redeploy the server and application from scratch.

The additional makefile targets mirror the local targets, with the exception of the recipe to deploy to Google CloudRun.

```
# Google CloudRun deployment --------------------------------------------------------
.PHONY: deploy/gcloud test_gcloud_config build/gcloud uninstall/gcloud start/gcl
deploy/gcloud: start/gcloud test/gcloud

test/gcloud_config: \

opt/gcloud/metadata.yaml:

opt/gcloud/requirements.txt:

opt/gcloud/settings.json:

opt/gcloud/sales.db:

opt/gcloud/static/WEEKLY_TOP_SALES_RANK_001.json:

opt/gcloud/static/WEEKLY_TOP_SALES_RANK_001.html:

opt/gcloud/static/WEEKLY_TOP_SALES_RANK_002.html:

opt/gcloud/static/WEEKLY_TOP_SALES_RANK_003.html:

build/gcloud:

uninstall/gcloud: ## Removes the build artifacts. "make uninstall/local"

start/gcloud: build/gcloud test/gcloud_config

test/gcloud:
```

The key target is `start/gcloud:` and the only significant difference is that instead of leveraging configuration files, we need to rely on command-line arguments for configuration.

```
start/gcloud: build/gcloud test/gcloud_config
	@echo $(INFO) - Starting server build on http://$(strip $(GCLOUD_URL))
	@$(DATASETTE) publish cloudrun --service=$(PROJECTNAME) \
	opt/$(notdir $@)/sales.db \
	-m opt/$(notdir $@)/metadata.yaml \
	--memory 2Gi \
	--install=datasette-vega \
	--install=datasette-copyable \
	--extra-options="--setting sql_time_limit_ms 5000"
```

Retrospective

By building and deploying the Data Discovery Platform, we have demonstrated the capability to expose any data set through an easy to use web site. This web site allows anyone with access the ability to query and filter the data through a web form or by executing SQL queries they have written. The Platform also lets anyone build simple charts to visualize the data. We have also demonstrated the ability to deploy the site locally and on external cloud services providers.

We also demonstrated a way to produce compelling data visualizations using the same automation infrastructure and code based configuration we use to manage the rest of the solution.

Most importantly, this chapter demonstrates the core "Building Data Products" design strategy.

1. Start with the data people are using and feel is valuable.
2. Quickly expose that data in a way that is easy to consume.
3. Provide a worry free mechanism to allow non-interactive users and technically sophisticated users the ability to interact with the data.
4. Provide a way to share data visualizations without additional infrastructure.
5. Provide a way to programmatically expose data to external systems.
6. Provide a method to clearly expose descriptive information about the data being exposed.
7. Provide a way to automate the updating of the system.

IN ORDER TO IDENTIFY ISSUES WITH THE DATA.
AS A SALES MANAGER RESPONSIBLE FOR THE QUALITY OF THE SALES DATA
I WANT TO BE ABLE TO IDENTIFY ISSUES WITH THE DATA.
AND A WAY TO DEMONSTRATE AND COMMUNICATE THOSE ISSUES.
AND A WAY TO QUICKLY PRIORITIZE AND FIX THOSE ISSUES.

[X] PROVIDE VISIBILITY TO THE DATABASE.
[X] PROVIDE THE ABILITY TO FILTER AND QUERY TABLES.
[X] PROVIDE A WAY TO VISUALIZE THE DATA. (E.G., PRODUCTS HAVE A DIFFERENT COST FOR DIFFERENT CUSTOMERS. A CHART MIGHT HELP.)
[X] IT CAN'T RUN ON SOMEONE'S LAPTOP!

IN ORDER TO FOCUS ON THE PRODUCTS WITH THE HIGHEST REVENUE.
AS A SALES MANAGER
I WANT A CHART OF PRODUCT SALES BY WEEK OVER THE LAST SIX MONTHS. (ATTRIBUTES BY TOTAL REVENUE, OVER THE LAST SIX MONTHS)

[X] REPORTS ARE AVAILABLE DURING NORMAL BUSINESS HOURS.
[X] ACCESSIBLE THROUGH A WEB BROWSER AS NEEDED.
[X] REFLECTS THE MOST RECENT DATA AVAILABLE.

146 Cumul.io (https://cumul.io/)

147 Chartio (https://chartio.com/)

148 Numerics (https://cynapse.com/numerics/)

[149] Grafana (https://grafana.com)

[150] Tableau (https://www.tableau.com/)

[151] Google Looker (https://looker.com/)

[152] Microsoft Power BI (https://powerbi.microsoft.com/)

[153] QlikView (https://www.qlik.com/)

[154] Apache Superset (https://superset.apache.org)

[155] Refer back to the discussion on Financial Levels to see the list of high value metrics. Start with these and then consider adding additional metrics.

[156] Datasette (https://datasette.io)

[157] datasette-copyable (https://datasette.io/plugins/datasette-copyable)

[158] Additional Datasette serve features are documented at (https://docs.datasette.io/en/latest/getting_started.html?highlight=serve#datasette-serve-help)

[159] Additional Metadata features are documented at (https://docs.datasette.io/en/latest/metadata.html#metadata)

[160] YAML (https://en.wikipedia.org/wiki/YAML)

[161] This is not entirely true, Datasette's testing interface can be called directly from the command line without starting the webserver.

[162] Google CloudRun (https://cloud.google.com/run)

Chapter 7: Building a database for the raw data

We now reach the home stretch in the development of our sales data and reporting solution. However, the next significant feature is invisible to the average user but structuring the underlying data to be easily updated, understandable, and correct is invaluable. The goal in this chapter is to improve the usability of the underlying database. This work centers around two stories. The first is to provide a solid, foundational analytical data set. The second story involves scheduling all our automation tasks to run without intervention.

IN ORDER TO CORRECT ISSUES WITH THE DATA.
AS A SALES MANAGER RESPONSIBLE FOR THE QUALITY OF THE SALES DATA
I WANT ACCESS TO AN ERROR-FREE DATA SET.
AND A WAY TO PERFORM ADDITIONAL ANALYTICS EASILY.
AND A SYSTEM THAT DOESN'T REQUIRE LONG DEVELOPMENT TIMES WHEN CHANGES ARE REQUIRED.

[ ] PROVIDE A BUSINESS-FOCUSED DATA SET WITH MINIMAL DATA QUALITY AND LOGIC ERRORS. USE EXISTING DATA FOR NOW.
[ ] IF A RECORD CHANGES, SAVE THAT HISTORY TO AID ANALYSIS.
[ ] DO NOT STORE DUPLICATE RECORDS.
[ ] IDENTIFY AND CORRECT ANOMALIES IN THE DATA WITHOUT DESTROYING THE ORIGINAL RECORD.
[ ] SUPPORT INCREMENTAL LOADING.

Staging and Raw Storage of Data

Normally, in a production environment, we receive updated data sets on a consistent schedule. However, we don't need to wait. We can simulate incremental data sets by splitting our source file into smaller pieces. As a side benefit, learning how to split source files comes in handy when tuning the data load process.

Rather than change the previous development, we treat these incremental loads as a new data feed. This means creating a new Source table to load the data into. Look at the file to see what fields we are dealing with.

online_retail_II_-_Year_2010-2011.csv

```
provider_code,load_dts,Invoice,StockCode,Description,Quantity,InvoiceDate,Price,Customer ID,Country
svc/load/online_retail_II_-_Year_2010-2011.csv,2021-04-26T13:31:54-MST,536365,85123A,WHITE HANGING HEART T-LI
svc/load/online_retail_II_-_Year_2010-2011.csv,2021-04-26T13:31:54-MST,536365,71053,WHITE METAL LANTERN,6,201
svc/load/online_retail_II_-_Year_2010-2011.csv,2021-04-26T13:31:54-MST,536365,84406B,CREAM CUPID HEARTS COAT
svc/load/online_retail_II_-_Year_2010-2011.csv,2021-04-26T13:31:54-MST,536365,84029G,KNITTED UNION FLAG HOT W
```

Previously, we relied on `csvkit` to delete and then recreate the Source table every time the data loaded. This works when the source data may change and comes from a single source with a consistent schedule. This drop and recreate process doesn't work with multiple simultaneous loads because each load erases the previous loads. One issue with this process is duplicate records in the table. Fortunately, we can eliminate these with a simple `SELECT DISTINCT` query.

Creating the target table

We must first design and create the table before the data can be loaded. Since this is a common task as we build out the solution, we will develop a utility in our makefile to do this consistently with each new source.

```
template/src_from_csv: ## Create source table from CSV template
	@# make template/src_from_csv CSVPATH=<path/to/file.csv>
	@echo $(DTS)     [INFO] - Creating script for SRC_$(notdir $(basename $(CSVPATH)))_###_create from $(CSVPATH)
	@if test -s $(CSVPATH); then echo [PASS] - $(CSVPATH) file exists; \
	else echo [FAIL] - $(CSVPATH) file does not exist; fi
	@$(SQLITE3) tmp/temp.db ".import --csv $(CSVPATH) SRC_$(notdir $(basename $(CSVPATH)))_###"
	@$(SQLITE3) tmp/temp.db ".schema SRC_$(notdir $(basename $(CSVPATH)))_###"
	@echo "--etc/sql/SRC_$(notdir $(basename $(CSVPATH)))_###_create.sql" \
	> etc/sql/SRC_$(notdir $(basename $(CSVPATH)))_###_create.sql
	@echo "------------------------------------------------------------------------" \
	>> etc/sql/SRC_$(notdir $(basename $(CSVPATH)))_###_create.sql
	@$(SQLITE3) tmp/temp.db ".schema SRC_$(notdir $(basename $(CSVPATH)))_###" \
	>> etc/sql/SRC_$(notdir $(basename $(CSVPATH)))_###_create.sql
	@rm tmp/temp.db
```

This target is similar to the other SQL query targets we've created and is executed with the following command:

```
make template/src_from_csv CSVPATH="svc/load/online_retail_II_-_Year_2010-2011.csv"
```

The recipe uses the `SQLite3` client to automatically load the data into a temporary database, inspect the schema of the newly created table and then it outputs the `CREATE TABLE` statement to the terminal window and creates a new file with the SQL code needed to create the new table in the `etc/sql/` directory.

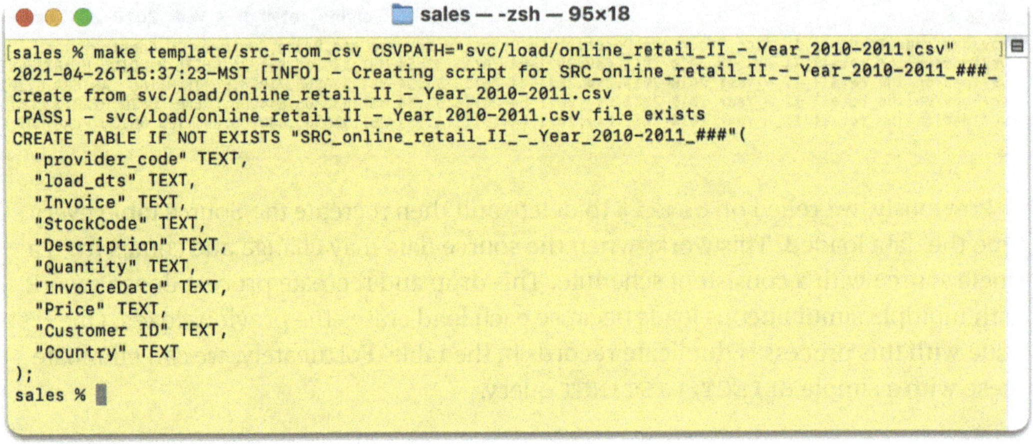

```
sales — -zsh — 95x18
sales % make template/src_from_csv CSVPATH="svc/load/online_retail_II_-_Year_2010-2011.csv"
2021-04-26T15:37:23-MST [INFO] - Creating script for SRC_online_retail_II_-_Year_2010-2011_###_
create from svc/load/online_retail_II_-_Year_2010-2011.csv
[PASS] - svc/load/online_retail_II_-_Year_2010-2011.csv file exists
CREATE TABLE IF NOT EXISTS "SRC_online_retail_II_-_Year_2010-2011_###"(
  "provider_code" TEXT,
  "load_dts" TEXT,
  "Invoice" TEXT,
  "StockCode" TEXT,
  "Description" TEXT,
  "Quantity" TEXT,
  "InvoiceDate" TEXT,
  "Price" TEXT,
  "Customer ID" TEXT,
  "Country" TEXT
);
sales %
```

```sql
--etc/sql/SRC_online_retail_II_-_Year_2010-2011_###_create.sql
-------------------------------------------------------------------------------------
CREATE TABLE IF NOT EXISTS "SRC_online_retail_II_-_Year_2010-2011_###"(
  "provider_code" TEXT,
  "load_dts" TEXT,
  "Invoice" TEXT,
  "StockCode" TEXT,
  "Description" TEXT,
  "Quantity" TEXT,
  "InvoiceDate" TEXT,
  "Price" TEXT,
  "Customer ID" TEXT,
  "Country" TEXT
);

```

Using this template, make a few small changes to rename the table properly. Remember, we do not change the table or field names in the Source table. This minimizes the decisions in development and reflects the composition of the original data, which simplifies debugging future defects.

```
--etc/sql/SRC_online_retail_II_-_Year_2010-2011_002_create.sql
------------------------------------------------------------------------------
CREATE TABLE IF NOT EXISTS "SRC_online_retail_II_-_Year_2010-2011_002"(
  "provider_code" TEXT,
  "load_dts" TEXT,
  "Invoice" TEXT,
  "StockCode" TEXT,
  "Description" TEXT,
  "Quantity" TEXT,
  "InvoiceDate" TEXT,
  "Price" TEXT,
  "Customer ID" TEXT,
  "Country" TEXT
);
```

This file can now be included in the configuration section of the makefile, following the standard pattern.

```
test/tables: \
  test_table/SRC_online_retail_II_-_Year_2010-2011_001 \
  test_table/RAW_ONLINE_RETAIL_II_YEAR_2010_2011_001 \
  test_table/INFO_SALES_LAST_6_MONTHS_FILTERED_001 \
  test_table/INFO_WEEKLY_TOP_SALES_RANK_001 \
  test_table/SRC_online_retail_II_-_Year_2010-2011_002

# SRC_online_retail_II_-_Year_2010-2011_002 ----
test_table/SRC_online_retail_II_-_Year_2010-2011_002: \
  SRC_online_retail_II_-_Year_2010-2011_002
  @$(test_table)

etc/sql/SRC_online_retail_II_-_Year_2010-2011_002_create.sql:
  @$(test_file)
```

Creating files to incrementally load

Now that we have the table, we split our file into multiple pieces to simulate multiple loads.

Create a new directory to store the new files. We want this separate from the normal load directory to make it easier to selectively copy these files into the `svc/load/` directory. We will manually copy one or more of these files as we test the solution.

```
mkdir -p svc/load/online_retail_II/ svc/load/
split_online_retail_II/
```

UNIX (like) operating systems were implemented from the beginning to treat everything as a file. As a result, there are numerous utilities to accomplish almost anything imaginable. The GNU split command[163] quickly splits any text file into multiple files based on either the number of lines in each file or a target file size.

Splitting a file by line number:

```
/usr/local/bin/gsplit -d -a 3 -l 50000 --additional-
suffix=".csv" \
  svc/load/online_retail_II_-_Year_2010-2011.csv \
  svc/load/split_online_retail_II/online_retail_II_-
_Year_2010-2011_
```

The `-d -a 3` parameter appends a three-digit numeric suffix to the output file name. `-l 50000` splits the file into 50,000 line chunks. The `—additional-suffix=".csv"` parameter adds `.csv` to the end of each file after it is created.

Splitting the file by size:

```
/usr/local/bin/gsplit -d -a 3 -b 10M --additional-suffix=".csv"
\
  svc/load/online_retail_II_-_Year_2010-2011.csv \
  svc/load/split_online_retail_II/online_retail_II_-
_Year_2010-2011_
```

The `-b 10M` parameter in this example splits the file into 10 megabyte (MB) files.

Either works for our use, but you might prefer one over the other, such as when splitting files to fit within email attachment limits or making files with a consistent row count to optimize database bulk insert performance.

To make this process easier to replicate, add a helper target to the makefile.

After running `make split/online_retail_II`, the target directory has several new files.

```
sales — -zsh — 95×16
sales % make split/online_retail_II
2021-04-27T10:32:35-MST [INFO] - Splitting svc/load/online_retail_II_-_Year_2010-2011.csv into
svc/load/split_online_retail_II/online_retail_II_-_Year_2010-2011__###
   50000 svc/load/split_online_retail_II/online_retail_II_-_Year_2010-2011_000.csv
   50000 svc/load/split_online_retail_II/online_retail_II_-_Year_2010-2011_001.csv
   50000 svc/load/split_online_retail_II/online_retail_II_-_Year_2010-2011_002.csv
   50000 svc/load/split_online_retail_II/online_retail_II_-_Year_2010-2011_003.csv
   50000 svc/load/split_online_retail_II/online_retail_II_-_Year_2010-2011_004.csv
   50000 svc/load/split_online_retail_II/online_retail_II_-_Year_2010-2011_005.csv
   50000 svc/load/split_online_retail_II/online_retail_II_-_Year_2010-2011_006.csv
   50000 svc/load/split_online_retail_II/online_retail_II_-_Year_2010-2011_007.csv
   50000 svc/load/split_online_retail_II/online_retail_II_-_Year_2010-2011_008.csv
   50000 svc/load/split_online_retail_II/online_retail_II_-_Year_2010-2011_009.csv
   41911 svc/load/split_online_retail_II/online_retail_II_-_Year_2010-2011_010.csv
  541911 total
sales %
```

Loading the Data

Our previous target to load data into the database assumed we were loading the data from a CSV file into a table once. The `csvsql` utility even created the table for us based on the fields in the file.

```
load_csv/SRC_online_retail_II_-_Year_2010-2011_001: \
  svc/load/online_retail_II_-_Year_2010-2011.csv
  @#load_csv/SRC_<csv_file_name>_001(colon)(space)<path/to/csv_file.csv>
  @echo $(DTS)     [INFO] - Loading data from $< into $(@F).$(DBNAME)
  @csvsql \
  --db sqlite:///$(DBFILE) \
  --create-if-not-exists --overwrite \
  --no-inference --no-constraints \
  --chunk-size 10000 \
  --tables $(@F) \
  --insert $<
```

Now that we are planning to load multiple files into the database table, we can't rely on this simple logic anymore. We need a system that can accommodate a number of possible file load scenarios.

1. There are multiple files in the same directory with the same columns.
2. There are no files in the directory.
3. There are multiple copies of the same file in the directory.
4. There are duplicate records in multiple files.
5. After files are loaded into the database, they are deleted from the load directory so they are not loaded again.

There are some assumptions we also need to make.

1. The target database table already exists. This was executed as part of the `test/tables:` target we implemented earlier.
2. We will call the file to be loaded `load.csv`.

We'll start with a new target to load the `load.csv` file.

```
552 svc/load/online_retail_II/load.csv:
553 	@echo $(DTS)      [INFO] - Loading csv files from $(realpath $(dir $@)) and loading into $@
554 
555 load/SRC_online_retail_II_-_Year_2010-2011_001: svc/load/online_retail_II/load.csv
556 	@#load/<SRC_target_table_name_###>(colon)(space)<path/to/csv_file/load.csv>
557 	@echo $(DTS)      [INFO] - Extracting data from $< and loading into $@
558 	@if test -s $<; \
559 	then $(SQLITE3) $(DBFILE) ".import --csv $< $(notdir $@)" ".quit"; \
560 	else echo $(DTS)      [WARNING] - $< file does not exist; fi
561 	@$(SQLITE3) $(DBFILE) \
562 	"SELECT COUNT(*) || ' records in $(notdir $@)' FROM [$(notdir $@)]" ".quit"
563 	@rm -f $<
```

The key to this target is the test for the existence of the `load.csv` file (lines 558-560). If this file exists, then import the CSV file into the table specified in the file name part of the target `($(notdir $@))`. If the `load.csv` file does not exist, a "WARNING" error is thrown because it is not necessarily a problem, nor unexpected to not have a file in the directory.

```
546 svc/load/online_retail_II/load.csv: .FORCE
547 	@#path/to/<source_reference_name_directory>/load.csv(colon)(space)
548 	@echo $(DTS)      [INFO] - Loading csv files from $(realpath $(dir $@)) and loading into $@
549 	@$(if $(abspath $(LIST_CSV)), cat $(abspath $(LIST_CSV)) >> $(addsuffix .tmp, $(basename $@))
550 	&& echo $(DTS)      [INFO] - Concatenating csv files [$(realpath $(LIST_CSV))] \
551 	&& wc -l $(addsuffix .tmp, $(basename $@)), \
552 	echo $(DTS)      [INFO] - no files to process in $(dir $@))
553 	@sort -u $(addsuffix .tmp, $(basename $@)) -o $@ || true
554 	@rm -f $(addsuffix .tmp, $(basename $@)) || true
555 	@find $(realpath $(dir $@)) -type f -not -name 'load.csv' -delete
556 	@wc -l $@ || true
```

Building this load file is complicated. The objective is to take one or more base files and combine them into one `load.csv` file.

We're going to use a new variable to hold a list of the CSV files in the directory. We can see this in action by manually expanding the find command in the `LIST_CSV` variable (line 549).

```
# Utility variables
DTS = $(shell date +%Y-%m-%dT%H:%M:%S-%Z)
LIST_CSV = $(shell find $(dir $@) -type f -name '*.csv' -not -name 'load.csv')
```

If we were to expand the command in the directory, it would return the names of the CSV files, excluding `load.csv`.

```
find svc/load/online_retail_II -type f -name '*.csv' -not -name
'load.csv'
```

```
sales — -zsh — 95×5
sales % find svc/load/online_retail_II -type f -name '*.csv' -not -name 'load.csv'
svc/load/online_retail_II/online_retail_II_-_Year_2010-2011_000.csv
svc/load/online_retail_II/online_retail_II_-_Year_2010-2011_001.csv
svc/load/online_retail_II/online_retail_II_-_Year_2010-2011_002.csv
sales %
```

Line 549 - If the file is in the `LIST_CSV` variable the use the `cat` utility to join the files together into a temporary file. If the files don't exist, throw a message that there are no file to process (Line 553).

Line 553 - Sort the lines in the temporary file and output the results to the `load.csv` file.

Line 554 - Delete the temporary file.

Line 555 - Delete the files not named `load.csv`.

Line 556 - Count the number of lines in the `load.csv` file.

Line 546 - Make only executes a target if the files it requires have changed since the last run. Generally, this is exactly the behavior you want. However, there are situations where you want the target to execute every time it is called, even if the files haven't changed. The `.FORCE:` dependency is a special make target that will force the target to run each time.

```
sales — -zsh — 95×10
sales % make svc/load/online_retail_II/load.csv
2021-04-27T14:00:37-MST [INFO] - Loading csv files from /Users/brianmcmillan/projects/sales/svc
/load/online_retail_II and loading into svc/load/online_retail_II/load.csv
2021-04-27T14:00:38-MST [INFO] - Concatenating csv files: [/Users/brianmcmillan/projects/sales/
svc/load/online_retail_II/online_retail_II_-_Year_2010-2011_000.csv /Users/brianmcmillan/projec
ts/sales/svc/load/online_retail_II/online_retail_II_-_Year_2010-2011_001.csv /Users/brianmcmill
an/projects/sales/svc/load/online_retail_II/online_retail_II_-_Year_2010-2011_002.csv]
  150000 svc/load/online_retail_II/load.tmp
  148644 svc/load/online_retail_II/load.csv
sales %
```

NOTE: Removing duplicate records is a relatively costly computation and we generally want to perform the most costly tasks as early as possible in order to reduce the number of records we need to process later. The sort with deduplicate commend (`sort -u`) is an unsophisticated but effective way to remove accomplish this. Executing this step as a standard part of every load process makes it easier to not care about having full or delta extracts from the source system. *"Just give us what you can, we don't care."*

Now, if we load a couple CSV files into the `svc/load/online_retail_II` directory and run the `load/SRC_online_retail_II_-_Year_2010-2011_001` target we can watch the process and ultimately, see the data being loaded into the `SRC_` table in the database.

```
sales — -zsh — 95×13
sales % make load/SRC_online_retail_II_-_Year_2010-2011_001
2021-04-27T14:23:17-MST [INFO] - Loading csv files from /Users/brianmcmillan/projects/sales/svc
/load/online_retail_II and loading into svc/load/online_retail_II/load.csv
2021-04-27T14:23:17-MST [INFO] - Concatenating csv files: [/Users/brianmcmillan/projects/sales/
svc/load/online_retail_II/online_retail_II_-_Year_2010-2011_000.csv /Users/brianmcmillan/projec
ts/sales/svc/load/online_retail_II/online_retail_II_-_Year_2010-2011_001.csv /Users/brianmcmill
an/projects/sales/svc/load/online_retail_II/online_retail_II_-_Year_2010-2011_002.csv]
  150000 svc/load/online_retail_II/load.tmp
  148644 svc/load/online_retail_II/load.csv
2021-04-27T14:23:19-MST [INFO] - Extracting data from svc/load/online_retail_II/load.csv and lo
ading into load/SRC_online_retail_II_-_Year_2010-2011_001
690554 records in SRC_online_retail_II_-_Year_2010-2011_001
sales %
```

The last step is to update the load: targets with this new flow.

```
# Load ------------------------------------------------------------------------
.PHONY: load load_csv/SRC_online_retail_II_-_Year_2010-2011_001 load/SRC_online_
load: \
  load_csv/SRC_online_retail_II_-_Year_2010-2011_001 \
  load/SRC_online_retail_II_-_Year_2010-2011_002
```

Running `make load` populates the new `SRC_..._002` table.

```
sales — -zsh — 170×1
sales % make load
2021-05-07T15:27:33-MST [INFO] - Loading data from svc/load/online_retail_II_-_Year_2010-2011.cs
2021-05-07T15:27:49-MST [INFO] - Loading csv files from /Users/brianmcmillan/projects/sales/svc/
2021-05-07T15:27:49-MST [INFO] - no files to process in svc/load/online_retail_II/
sort: No such file or directory
   99076 svc/load/online_retail_II/load.csv
2021-05-07T15:27:49-MST [INFO] - Extracting data from svc/load/online_retail_II/load.csv and loa
99076 records in SRC_online_retail_II_-_Year_2010-2011_002
sales %
```

Copying another group of files into the `online_retail_II/` directory and running `make load` again combines the separate CSV files into a deduplicated `load.csv` file which is then loaded into the STG_table in the database.

```
sales — -zsh — 170×1
sales % make load
2021-05-07T15:35:42-MST [INFO] - Loading data from svc/load/online_retail_II_-_Year_2010-2011.cs
2021-05-07T15:35:58-MST [INFO] - Loading csv files from /Users/brianmcmillan/projects/sales/svc/
2021-05-07T15:35:58-MST [INFO] - Concatenating csv files [/Users/brianmcmillan/projects/sales/sv
rianmcmillan/projects/sales/svc/load/online_retail_II/online_retail_II_-_Year_2010-2011_001.csv
l_II_-_Year_2010-2011_003.csv /Users/brianmcmillan/projects/sales/svc/load/online_retail_II/onli
svc/load/online_retail_II/online_retail_II_-_Year_2010-2011_004.csv]
  250000 svc/load/online_retail_II/load.tmp
  247938 svc/load/online_retail_II/load.csv
2021-05-07T15:36:00-MST [INFO] - Extracting data from svc/load/online_retail_II/load.csv and loa
347014 records in SRC_online_retail_II_-_Year_2010-2011_002
sales %
```

Storing Historical Data in a Satellite Table (SAT)

Our next objective is to take the records in the source table and load them into a table where we will be storing the history of all the loads. Unlike the source table, we will not be performing a simple append. If the record exists, why would we load it again? This *"append-only"* pattern has many benefits. Saving every unique record from every load gives us the ability to see each version of a record we have ever loaded. When it comes time to research defects in the data, having a table that efficiently saved past versions of the record will be invaluable. If we have multiple records where we expected one, we can see the history and make informed business logic decisions. For instance, we know we have multiple prices for a single invoice line item. Having the history allows us to implement business logic we can always change later. Another advantage of storing the record history is that we could recreate the state of the data at any point in the past.

In the Data Vault data modeling standard,[164] this type of append only table is called a Satellite table. This design pattern is similar to a Type 2 Dimensional table in Star Schema warehouse modeling. There is a lot to learn about the Data Vault 2.0 standard, but for our purposes, we are going to use the most basic design elements to help us quickly implement our database.

The benefit for us is the simplified and consistent table structure. There are only three core tables. The advantage of restricting the design to three basic tables is that we don't need to spend much time modeling our data. It's then possible to take an iterative approach and initially concern ourselves with building a single Satellite table for each Source table. We'll postpone the creation of the Hub and Link tables until we start applying the business logic necessary to meet our requirements.

Table	Feature	Benefits	Typical business question
Satellite (SAT)	Persistent record of all historical data changes.	Because we have history, we can always go back and change our minds if business logic changes.	How have the prices for a product changed over time?
Hub (HUB)	Stores all business keys for our important business entities.	Distinct list of key business entities.	How many customers do we have?

Table	Feature	Benefits	Typical business question
Link (LNK)	Stores all business keys for our important business relationships.	Distinct list of key business entity relationships.	Do we have customers with multiple locations?

Base Data Vault tables

The Satellite (SAT) is designed using the following process:

1. Write a SELECT query against the source table.
2. Rename the fields following following a consistent naming standard:
   A. Lowercase
   B. Change "CamelCase" to "underscore_separated"
   C. Where obvious, set data types for fields.
3. Create a new NULL field called "hash_diff".
4. Create a new NULL field called "load_dts".
5. Move the provider_code, hash_diff, load_dts, and insert_dts fields to the top of the query.
6. Name the table following a consistent table naming standard:
   A. The table name should be similar to the name of the Source table but convert all special characters to underscores.
   B. UPPER CASE all characters. This makes it easier to differentiate between TABLES and field_names in queries.
   C. Prefix the table name with SAT_. This makes it easier to identify the purpose of the table.
   D. Suffix the table name with _001 to identify this table as the first version of the data set.
   E. Add _load as an additional suffix to the file name.
   F. Add a consistent header block with the path to the file and file name.
7. Verify the query runs properly.
8. Save this file in etc/sql/.

```sql
-- sales/etc/sql/SAT_ONLINE_RETAIL_II_YEAR_2010_2011_001_load.sql
---------------------------------------------------------------------

SELECT
    provider_code
    ,CAST(NULL AS TEXT) AS hash_diff
    ,load_dts
    ,CAST(NULL AS TEXT) AS insert_dts
    ,Invoice AS invoice
    ,StockCode AS stock_code
    ,Description AS description
    ,CAST(Quantity AS NUMERIC) AS quantity
    ,InvoiceDate AS invoice_date
    ,CAST(Price AS NUMERIC) AS price
    ,"Customer ID" AS customer_id
    ,Country AS country
FROM [SRC_online_retail_II_-_Year_2010-2011_001]
```

Use these fields to create a new `CREATE TABLE` query.

```sql
-- sales/etc/sql/SAT_ONLINE_RETAIL_II_YEAR_2010_2011_001_create.sql
---------------------------------------------------------------------

CREATE TABLE IF NOT EXISTS SAT_ONLINE_RETAIL_II_YEAR_2010_2011_001 (
  provider_code TEXT
  ,hash_diff TEXT
  ,load_dts TEXT
  ,insert_dts TEXT
  ,invoice TEXT
  ,stock_code TEXT
  ,description TEXT
  ,quantity NUMERIC
  ,invoice_date TEXT
  ,price NUMERIC
  ,customer_id TEXT
  ,country TEXT
  ,PRIMARY KEY(provider_code, hash_diff)
  );
```

This creation script is added to the configuration section of the makefile the same as all the other tables.

```
test/tables: \
  test_table/SRC_online_retail_II_-_Year_2010-2011_001 \
  test_table/RAW_ONLINE_RETAIL_II_YEAR_2010_2011_001 \
  test_table/INFO_SALES_LAST_6_MONTHS_FILTERED_001 \
  test_table/INFO_WEEKLY_TOP_SALES_RANK_001 \
  test_table/SRC_online_retail_II_-_Year_2010-2011_002 \
  test_table/SAT_ONLINE_RETAIL_II_YEAR_2010_2011_001

# SAT_ONLINE_RETAIL_II_YEAR_2010_2011_001 ----
test_table/SAT_ONLINE_RETAIL_II_YEAR_2010_2011_001: \
  SAT_ONLINE_RETAIL_II_YEAR_2010_2011_001
  @$(test_table)

etc/sql/SAT_ONLINE_RETAIL_II_YEAR_2010_2011_001_create.sql:
  @$(test_file)

SAT_ONLINE_RETAIL_II_YEAR_2010_2011_001: \
  etc/sql/SAT_ONLINE_RETAIL_II_YEAR_2010_2011_001_create.sql
  @$(create_table)
```

Table joins

Now that we have data in our Stage table and have created a target Satellite table, we need to figure out how to identify the records in the Source which do not exist in the Satellite. This will require us to JOIN the two tables together. Before we write the code, it will be helpful to understand our options. The central concept of relational databases is Set Theory[165]. Logically, Set Theory is concerned with the relationships between sets of things. Think of a Venn Diagram[166] between two (or more) groups where we have one set to the left and one to the right.

In our case, we have two tables, the Source on the left side and the Satellite on the right. How can we group the records? The first set would be the records that are present in both tables. This is the standard INNER JOIN. This helps us filter our data down by filtering out all data not present in both tables.

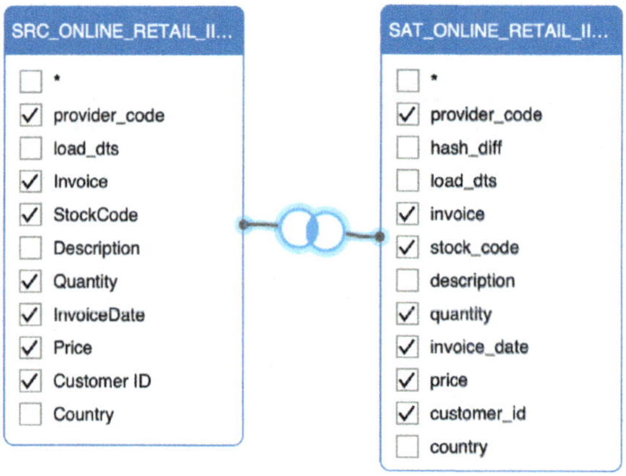

Inner Join

The next most common join type is the LEFT JOIN, where we select all the records in the left side table and the matching records in the right-hand table. This query is useful to add data from the right-hand table to the fields in the left-hand table. The RIGHT JOIN is a reversal of the tables. Select all the data on the right side and join in the data, where the keys match on the left table.

The keys are the fields used to join the two tables together. In most cases, the keys we join on are the matching primary keys in the tables. However, this does not need to be the case. We can join on any matching fields we choose.

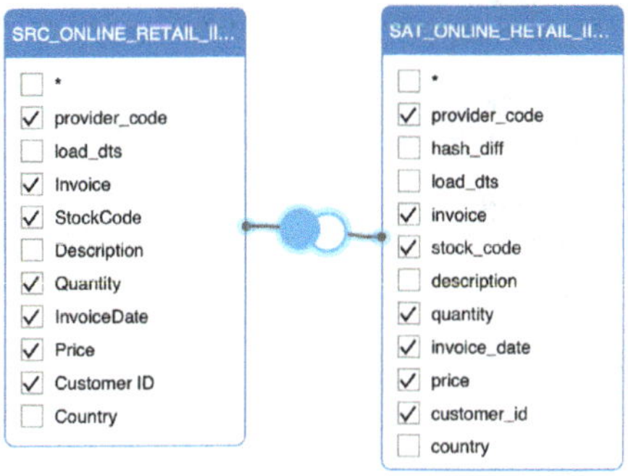

Left Join

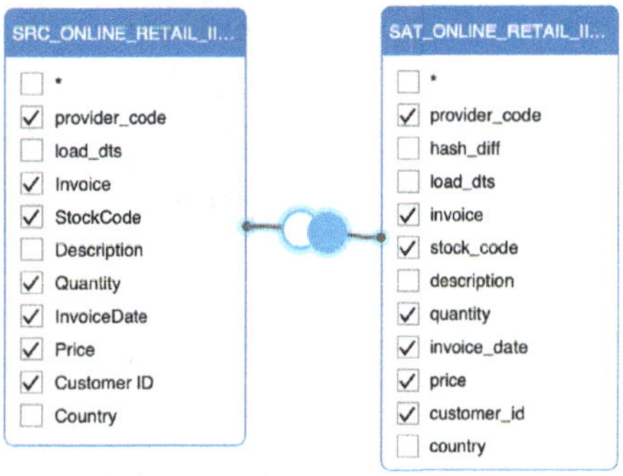

Right Join

By definition, primary keys identify the fields needed to make a unique record, and if they are shared between tables, we can be assured we will be maintaining a one-to-one relationship between the records. If we deviate from this, and we will, we need to be clear on how the join affects the record count of our new data set. It is easy to end up with more records than we intend.

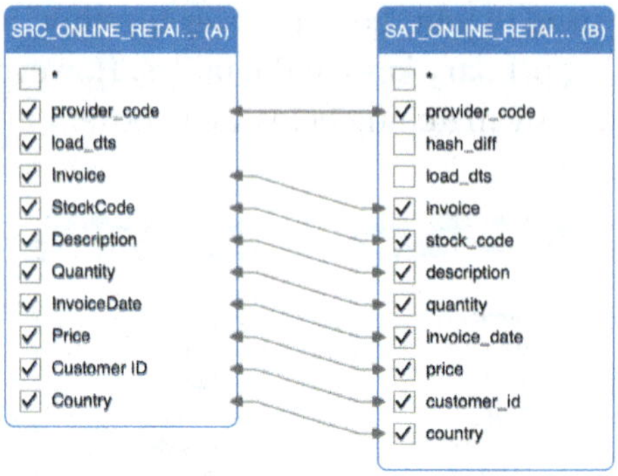

Joins across many fields

There are two other seldom used join types which are good to understand. The FULL OUTER JOIN combines both data sets. In effect, you are combining a LEFT JOIN and a RIGHT JOIN query. This can be handy if you need to compare all the records in two data sets together. You may have missing records on both the left and right sides. The CROSS JOIN generates all possible combinations of the records in both tables.

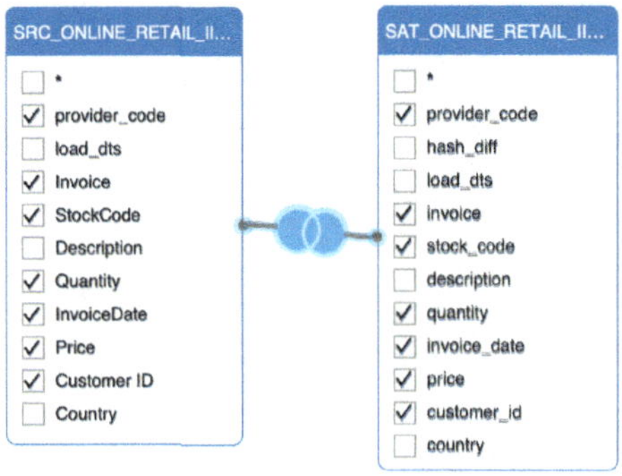

Full Outer Join

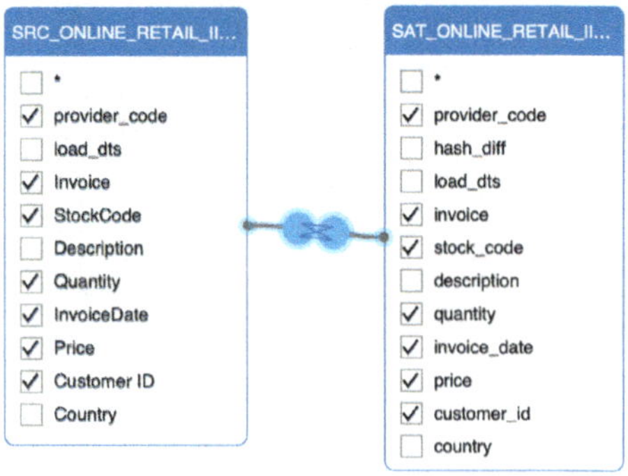

Cross Join

There are many variations on these, depending on how you specify the relationships between the tables. If you keep your data sets clear, and the data is well modeled, you may be able to get by with being able to confidently write only INNER JOINs, LEFT JOINs.

Consider the following query:

```
SELECT
    A.provider_code,
    A.load_dts,
    A.Invoice,
    A.StockCode,
    A.Description,
    A.Quantity,
    A.InvoiceDate,
    A.Price,
    A."Customer ID",
    A.Country,
    ----
    B.provider_code,
    B.invoice,
    B.stock_code,
    B.description,
    B.quantity,
    B.invoice_date,
    B.price,
    B.customer_id,
    B.country
FROM
    'SRC_online_retail_II_-_Year_2010-2011_001' AS A
    LEFT JOIN
    SAT_ONLINE_RETAIL_II_YEAR_2010_2011_001 AS B
    ON
        A.provider_code = B.provider_code AND
        A.provider_code = B.provider_code AND
        A.Invoice = B.invoice AND
        A.StockCode = B.stock_code AND
        A.Description = B.description AND
        A.Quantity = B.quantity AND
        A.InvoiceDate = B.invoice_date AND
        A.Price = B.price AND
        A."Customer ID" = B.customer_id AND
        A.Country = B.country;
```

Here, we are selecting all the data in the SRC_ table (the first table is considered the left side) with a LEFT JOIN to the SAT_ table on the right side. The ON statement defines the fields we use for the JOIN. Because we haven't loaded any data into the SAT_ table, it is empty.

Description	Quantity	InvoiceDate	Price	Customer ID	Country	provider_code(1)	invoice	stock_code	description	quantity
WHITE HANGING HEART T-LIGHT HOLDER	6	2010-12-01T08:26:00	2.55	17850	United Kingdom	(NULL)	(NULL)	(NULL)	(NULL)	(NULL)
WHITE METAL LANTERN	6	2010-12-01T08:26:00	3.39	17850	United Kingdom	(NULL)	(NULL)	(NULL)	(NULL)	(NULL)
CREAM CUPID HEARTS COAT HANGER	8	2010-12-01T08:26:00	2.75	17850	United Kingdom	(NULL)	(NULL)	(NULL)	(NULL)	(NULL)
KNITTED UNION FLAG HOT WATER BOTTLE	6	2010-12-01T08:26:00	3.39	17850	United Kingdom	(NULL)	(NULL)	(NULL)	(NULL)	(NULL)
RED WOOLLY HOTTIE WHITE HEART.	6	2010-12-01T08:26:00	3.39	17850	United Kingdom	(NULL)	(NULL)	(NULL)	(NULL)	(NULL)

Before we go further, we need to look at how we are defining the JOIN ON fields. Having to explicitly define each field is tedious and error-prone. One strategy could be to combine all the text fields into a long string and then join on that.

Using a huge concatenated key doesn't buy us much in reduced query complexity, and under the covers, it has a huge performance impact. The DataVault 2.0 standard introduced a variation on this concatenation technique, which balances simplicity with performance and, if done correctly, can significantly improve the overall data loading speed.

Determining whether a record is new

This is where the `hash_diff` field comes in. This field is created by concatenating the core data fields together after removing leading or trailing spaces and uppercasing the resulting data. This accommodates and differences in spacing and capitalization we may encounter.

```sql
-- sales/etc/sql/SAT_ONLINE_RETAIL_II_YEAR_2010_2011_001_load.sql
------------------------------------------------------------------
SELECT
    provider_code
    ,UPPER(TRIM(invoice)||','||
        TRIM(StockCode)||','||
        TRIM(Description)||','||
        TRIM(Quantity)||','||
        TRIM(InvoiceDate)||','||
        TRIM(Price)||','||
        TRIM("Customer ID")||','||
        TRIM(Country)) AS hash_diff
    ,load_dts
    ,CAST(NULL AS TEXT) AS insert_dts
    ,Invoice AS invoice
    ,StockCode AS stock_code
    ,Description AS description
    ,CAST(Quantity AS NUMERIC) AS quantity
    ,InvoiceDate AS invoice_date
    ,CAST(Price AS NUMERIC) AS price
    ,"Customer ID" AS customer_id
    ,Country AS country
FROM 'SRC_online_retail_II_-_Year_2010-2011_001'
```

provider_code	hash_diff	load_dts	insert_dts	invoice
svc/load/onlin...	536365,85123A,WHITE HANGING HEART T-LIGHT HOLDER,6,2010-12-01T08:26:00,2.55,17850,UNITED KINGDOM	2021-05-10T13:...	(NULL)	536365
svc/load/onlin...	536365,71053,WHITE METAL LANTERN,6,2010-12-01T08:26:00,3.39,17850,UNITED KINGDOM	2021-05-10T13:...	(NULL)	536365
svc/load/onlin...	536365,84406B,CREAM CUPID HEARTS COAT HANGER,8,2010-12-01T08:26:00,2.75,17850,UNITED KINGDOM	2021-05-10T13:...	(NULL)	536365
svc/load/onlin...	536365,84029G,KNITTED UNION FLAG HOT WATER BOTTLE,6,2010-12-01T08:26:00,3.39,17850,UNITED KINGDOM	2021-05-10T13:...	(NULL)	536365
svc/load/onlin...	536365,84029E,RED WOOLLY HOTTIE WHITE HEART.,6,2010-12-01T08:26:00,3.39,17850,UNITED KINGDOM	2021-05-10T13:...	(NULL)	536365
svc/load/onlin...	536365,22752,SET 7 BABUSHKA NESTING BOXES,2,2010-12-01T08:26:00,7.65,17850,UNITED KINGDOM	2021-05-10T13:...	(NULL)	536365

The next step is to apply a hashing algorithm to the string. We are going to use the SHA1 hash.[167] By applying a one-way hash to the core fields, we end up with a consistent 40 character representation of the entire record. The obvious benefit is that a 40 character string is smaller than a hundred-character string. The less obvious advantage comes into play when data is being loaded into tables.

In a traditional database, the primary key is a sequential key maintained by that instance of the database. In a typically normalized database, the primary table is an integer reference to the same integer in another table. These numbers do not have any meaning outside of the database where they were created.

These surrogate keys do not have any business meaning. A product ID in one database will not be the same in another database without a significant amount of work.[168]

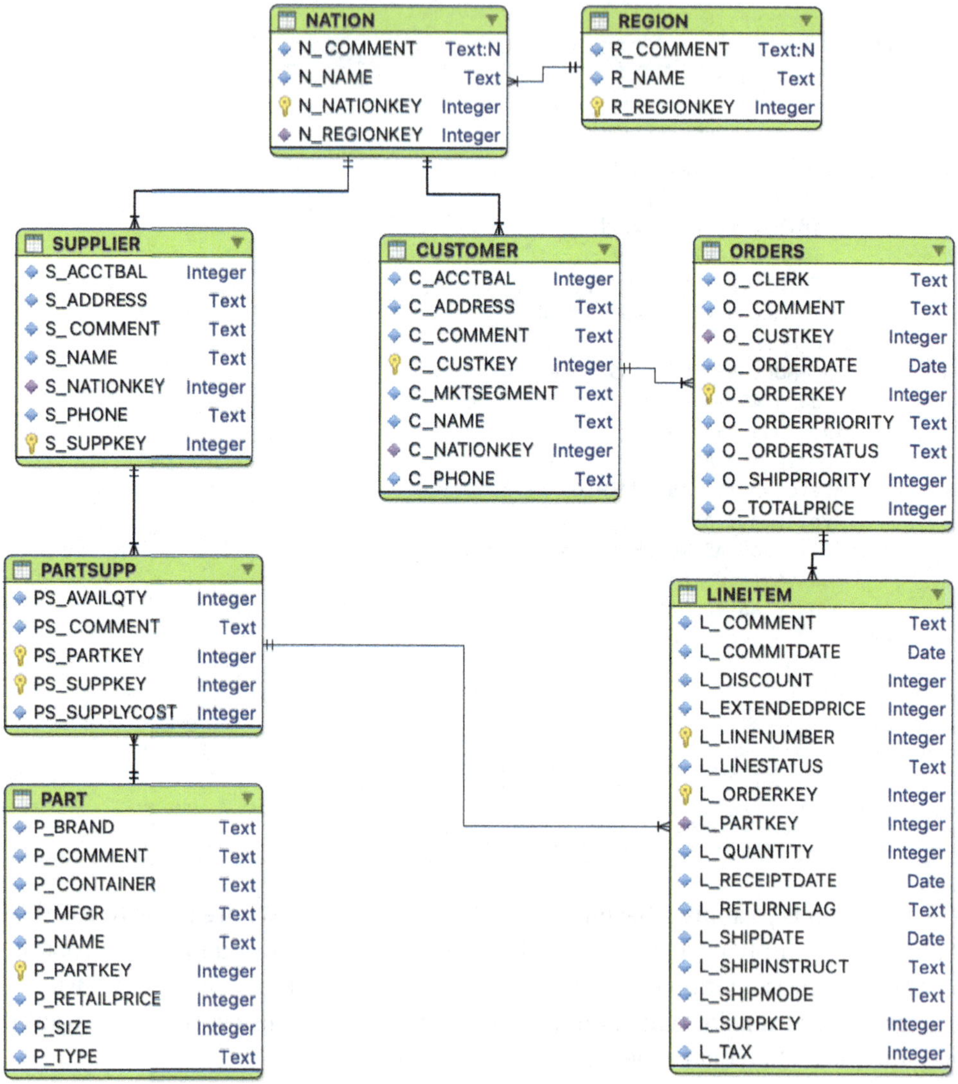

TPC-H schema

Using the TPC-H[169] schema example, to add the `L_ORDERKEY` to the `LINEITEM` table, we must first create the `O_ORDERKEY` in the ORDERS table. This imposes a strict sequence of operations we need to follow when adding and updating records in the database. In the case of the `LINEITEM` table, we need to update, or at least query, the `PARTSUPPLIER` and `ORDERS` tables before updating the table. If the `PARTSUPP` record does not exist, we need to reconcile the `SUPPLIER` and `PART` table before doing anything. With careful ETL work and creative views, we can make this easier, but it is intimidatingly complicated.[170]

Here is where the hash keys come into play. A hash key always generates the same value, given the same input. If you take a stock code (DCGS0003) and run it through the SHA1 algorithm, it will always return the same value (e7335d231204580c55e59c9d704240a83b04e221). This will be true on any platform, at any time.

The value is that you have separated the keys from the database and tied them explicitly to the data. Now, when you load data, you can load any table independently and in parallel with any other table. It also allows you to seamlessly move data between systems because the keys across the database will be consistent.

The worst case is that you will need to maintain a "same as" link table to map slight textural variations within the data and across systems. This is one huge advantage to adopting the Data Vault standard. The HUB, LINK, and SAT[ellite] tables provide a built-in Master Data Management capability from the start.

How does this work in practice? It starts with building out the concatenation of the data fields in the data set. The COALESCE statement converts NULL values into empty strings for consistency.

In SQLite, we need to load the SHA1 extension, either in our query or in the client software. This is one of many extensions that can be compiled to add functionality to the database.[171] Every database platform handles this differently, but a SHA1 hash generated by SQLite is portable to any other database. The same holds for hash keys generated by Java, Python, R, or any other language.

Validate that you can execute the SHA1 function after loading it into your client software and then execute the script.[172]

```sql
-- sales/etc/sql/SAT_ONLINE_RETAIL_II_YEAR_2010_2011_001_load.sql
--------------------------------------------------------------------
SELECT
    provider_code
    ,SHA1(UPPER(TRIM(COALESCE(invoice,''))||','||
        TRIM(COALESCE(StockCode,''))||','||
        TRIM(COALESCE(Description,''))||','||
        TRIM(COALESCE(Quantity,''))||','||
        TRIM(COALESCE(InvoiceDate,''))||','||
        TRIM(COALESCE(Price,''))||','||
        TRIM(COALESCE("Customer ID",''))||','||
        TRIM(COALESCE(Country,'')))
      ) AS hash_diff
    ,load_dts
    ,CAST(NULL AS TEXT) AS insert_dts
    ,Invoice AS invoice
    ,StockCode AS stock_code
    ,Description AS description
    ,CAST(Quantity AS NUMERIC) AS quantity
    ,InvoiceDate AS invoice_date
    ,CAST(Price AS NUMERIC) AS price
    ,"Customer ID" AS customer_id
    ,Country AS country
FROM 'SRC_online_retail_II_-_Year_2010-2011_001'
```

	provider _code	hash_diff	load_dts	insert_dts	invoice	stock_code	description	quantity
1	svc/load/...	6d0e815bb544188b03eb593019ec6d6b11fc6cb6	2021-05-10T13:41:4...	<NULL>	536365	85123A	WHITE ...	6
2	svc/load/...	bfdc21e3d58ee61fdd8b2360dc9f973dd4837173	2021-05-10T13:41:4...	<NULL>	536365	71053	WHITE ...	6
3	svc/load/...	28b29040b163d07620df60560e807620b010c09a	2021-05-10T13:41:4...	<NULL>	536365	84406B	CREAM ...	8
4	svc/load/...	85f9ac4a5edb7efddc99dad7c3d3f356c44ce221	2021-05-10T13:41:4...	<NULL>	536365	84029G	KNITTED ...	6
5	svc/load/...	92d1aa2dc93019633defe32197c9bcfa2e14d477	2021-05-10T13:41:4...	<NULL>	536365	84029E	RED ...	6

While in development, it is useful to be able to utilize the extensions from within the client software but when we are automating the queries, it is necessary to dynamically load them in when a query is run. To do this, add a `SELECT load_extension()` function to the top of the query.

```sql
-- sales/etc/sql/SAT_ONLINE_RETAIL_II_YEAR_2010_2011_001_load.sql
---------------------------------------------------------------------------
SELECT load_extension('/Users/brianmcmillan/projects/sales/etc/software/sqlite3/sha1');

SELECT
    provider_code
    ,SHA1(UPPER(TRIM(COALESCE(invoice,''))||','||
        TRIM(COALESCE(StockCode,''))||','||
        TRIM(COALESCE(Description,''))||','||
        TRIM(COALESCE(Quantity,''))||','||
        TRIM(COALESCE(InvoiceDate,''))||','||
        TRIM(COALESCE(Price,''))||','||
        TRIM(COALESCE("Customer ID",''))||','||
        TRIM(COALESCE(Country,'')))
      ) AS hash_diff
    ,load_dts
    ,CAST(NULL AS TEXT) AS insert_dts
    ,Invoice AS invoice
    ,StockCode AS stock_code
    ,Description AS description
    ,CAST(Quantity AS NUMERIC) AS quantity
    ,InvoiceDate AS invoice_date
    ,CAST(Price AS NUMERIC) AS price
    ,"Customer ID" AS customer_id
    ,Country AS country
FROM 'SRC_online_retail_II_-_Year_2010-2011_001'
```

Confirm the file executes and generates the hash_diff filed by executing the query from the terminal window.

```
sqlite3 svc/db/sales.db ".read etc/sql/
SAT_ONLINE_RETAIL_II_YEAR_2010_2011_001_load.sql" ".quit"
```

```
sales — -zsh — 208×9
csv|9fbac67e26072840c3b641c539e3cca0253a9be0|2021-05-10T13:41:45-MST||537781|22583|PACK OF 6 HANDBAG GIFT BOXES|1|2010-12-08
csv|e7c3928f933d3e380f8ebaaf270044758e7e2cb9|2021-05-10T13:41:45-MST||537781|22584|PACK OF 6 PANNETONE GIFT BOXES|1|2010-12-
csv|401a22684fe6bf41b8d5561ee8b95f50042e63fd|2021-05-10T13:41:45-MST||537781|21379|CAMPHOR WOOD PORTOBELLO MUSHROOM|1|2010-1
csv|bda77d3433f0c4e8b8ff4424e398b5303d413c2f|2021-05-10T13:41:45-MST||537781|21375|LARGE CAMPHOR WOOD FIELD MUSHROOM |1|2010
csv|de4f9d6a3e73e431cfe2819707ae2910931fccd6|2021-05-10T13:41:45-MST||537781|84247E|PACK/12 XMAS FUN CARD|1|2010-12-08T12:46
csv|fb7a7a7ddb64ffc70a705946bc99165582286ecf|2021-05-10T13:41:45-MST||537781|21205|MULTICOLOUR 3D BALLS GARLAND|1|2010-12-08
csv|6829ed48153ccfd1362674047a5967dcfde2f6b1|2021-05-10T13:41:45-MST||537781|21201|TROPICAL  HONEYCOMB PAPER GARLAND |1|2010
csv|3c992dafa5625fca9d086c9e8224752ac4d2cf57|2021-05-10T13:41:45-MST||537781|21355|TOAST ITS - I LOVE YOU |1|2010-12-08T12:4
csv|edbd08238bfee2e3f24bf59badcfd2fdd769065d|2021-05-10T13:41:45-MST||537781|22114|HOT WATER BOTTLE TEA AND SYMPATHY|1|2010-
```

Loading the Satellite Table

Now that we have introduced joins and hash keys, let's determine what data to update. There will be a lot of code to read. Take your time and don't step ahead until you have at least a general understanding of the data sets in each common table expression.[173]

```
FROM
    'SRC_online_retail_II_-_Year_2010-2011_001' AS A
    LEFT JOIN
    SAT_ONLINE_RETAIL_II_YEAR_2010_2011_001 AS B
    ON
         A.provider_code = B.provider_code AND
         (A.provider_code ||
         A.Invoice ||
         A.StockCode ||
         A.Description ||
         A.Quantity ||
         A.InvoiceDate ||
         A.Price ||
         A."Customer ID" ||
         A.Country)
         =
         (B.provider_code ||
         B.invoice ||
         B.stock_code ||
         B.description ||
         B.quantity ||
         B.invoice_date ||
         B.price ||
         B.customer_id ||
         B.country);
```

Defining the source

Step one is to set up our file with a useful header and reference to the SHA1 extension. We then create a CTE_SOURCE common table expression. The SELECT DISTINCT query will remove any duplicate records from the source table and a WHERE clause will filter the provider_code field to remove any extra header records from the CSV files. This will become the left side of our join.

```
-- sales/etc/sql/SAT_ONLINE_RETAIL_II_YEAR_2010_2011_001_load.sql
--------------------------------------------------------------------
SELECT load_extension('/Users/brianmcmillan/projects/sales/etc/software/sqlite3/sha1');

WITH CTE_SOURCE AS (
  SELECT DISTINCT
      provider_code
      ,SHA1(UPPER(TRIM(COALESCE(invoice,''))||','||
          TRIM(COALESCE(StockCode,''))||','||
          TRIM(COALESCE(Description,''))||','||
          TRIM(COALESCE(Quantity,''))||','||
          TRIM(COALESCE(InvoiceDate,''))||','||
          TRIM(COALESCE(Price,''))||','||
          TRIM(COALESCE("Customer ID",''))||','||
          TRIM(COALESCE(Country,'')))
        ) AS hash_diff
      ,load_dts
      ,CAST(NULL AS TEXT) AS insert_dts
      ,Invoice AS invoice
      ,StockCode AS stock_code
      ,Description AS description
      ,CAST(Quantity AS NUMERIC) AS quantity
      ,InvoiceDate AS invoice_date
      ,CAST(Price AS NUMERIC) AS price
      ,"Customer ID" AS customer_id
      ,Country AS country
  FROM 'SRC_online_retail_II_-_Year_2010-2011_001'
  WHERE provider_code != 'provider_code'
)
SELECT * FROM CTE_SOURCE;
```

Defining the Target

The target query references the SAT_ table. This query will become the right side of the join.

```
,
--SELECT * FROM CTE_SOURCE;

CTE_TARGET AS (
SELECT
    provider_code
    ,hash_diff
    ,load_dts
    ,insert_dts
    ,invoice
    ,stock_code
    ,description
    ,quantity
    ,invoice_date
    ,price
    ,customer_id
    ,country
FROM SAT_ONLINE_RETAIL_II_YEAR_2010_2011_001
)
SELECT * FROM CTE_TARGET;
```

Executing the query now returns no records because there are no records in the SAT_ table.

```
sales % sqlite3 svc/db/sales.db ".read etc/sql/SAT_ONLINE_RETAIL_II_YEAR_2010_2011_001_load.sql" ".quit"
sales %
```

Inserting the data

Inserting the data involves joining all the records in the CTE_SOURCE to the matching records in CTE_TARGET. The two data sets are matched with the A.provider_code and hash_diff fields. This will allow us to identify identical records from different data sources. When the source tables are supporting multiple data providers, this will become critically important.

```
CTE_INSERT AS (
SELECT
    A.provider_code
    ,A.hash_diff
    ----
    --,B.provider_code
    --,B.hash_diff
    ----
    ,A.load_dts
    ,strftime('%Y-%m-%dT%H:%M:%fZ', 'now') AS insert_dts
    ,A.invoice
    ,A.stock_code
    ,A.description
    ,A.quantity
    ,A.invoice_date
    ,A.price
    ,A.customer_id
    ,A.country
FROM CTE_SOURCE A
LEFT JOIN CTE_TARGET B
ON (
    A.provider_code = B.provider_code AND
    A.hash_diff = B.hash_diff
)
WHERE B.hash_diff IS NULL
)

SELECT * FROM CTE_INSERT;
```

The final statement in our query is the insert statement. When this query runs, it will add the records in the Source table that do not exist in the Satellite table.

```
INSERT INTO "SAT_ONLINE_RETAIL_II_YEAR_2010_2011_001" (
  provider_code
  ,hash_diff
  ,load_dts
  ,insert_dts
  ,invoice
  ,stock_code
  ,description
  ,quantity
  ,invoice_date
  ,price
  ,customer_id
  ,country
)
  SELECT
  provider_code
  ,hash_diff
  ,load_dts
  ,insert_dts
  ,invoice
  ,stock_code
  ,description
  ,quantity
  ,invoice_date
  ,price
  ,customer_id
  ,country
  FROM CTE_INSERT;
```

After the query runs, we can see the data is now loaded into the SAT_table.

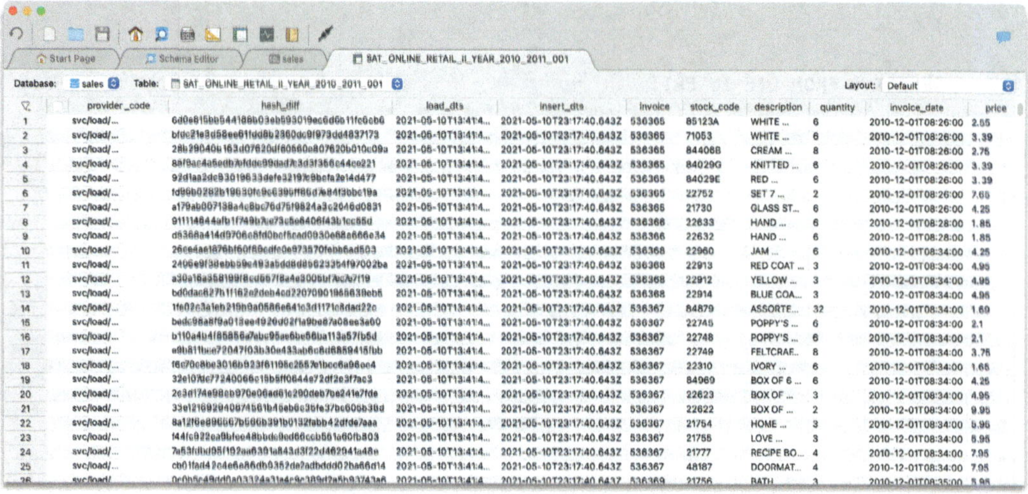

Cleaning the Stage Table

Now that we have data in the target Satellite table. We can selectively remove the data from the source table. One way we could accomplish this would be to issue a truncate table command on the Source table immediately after the load. This would delete all the data in the Source table, in most cases, this strategy is perfectly acceptable. The database will do a good job of locking the table to prevent writes while data is being deleted.

We are going to do something different. Following the rules of separation and modularity, we treat cleaning a Source table independently of any other process.

Source CTE

The source for this will be the the SAT table, and the target is the SRC table. We utilize a hidden field called rowid to simplify the delete statement.[174] This column is maintained internally by the database and can be leveraged as an internal reference to specific rows.

```
-- sales/etc/sql/SAT_ONLINE_RETAIL_II_YEAR_2010_2011_001_clean.sql
---------------------------------------------------------------------
SELECT load_extension('/Users/brianmcmillan/projects/sales/etc/software/sqlite3/sha1');

WITH CTE_SOURCE AS (
  SELECT
  rowid
  ,provider_code
  ,hash_diff
  FROM SAT_ONLINE_RETAIL_II_YEAR_2010_2011_001
)
SELECT * FROM CTE_SOURCE;
```

Validate the query by executing it from the command line.

```
sqlite3 svc/db/sales.db ".read etc/sql/
SAT_ONLINE_RETAIL_II_YEAR_2010_2011_001_clean.sql" ".quit"
```

Creating the target

Recalculate the hash_diff field for the SRC table, to match the statement used to in the SAT table load query.

```
,
--SELECT * FROM CTE_SOURCE;

CTE_TARGET AS (
SELECT
rowid
,provider_code
,SHA1(UPPER(
    TRIM(COALESCE(invoice, ''))||','||
    TRIM(COALESCE(StockCode, ''))||','||
    TRIM(COALESCE(Description, ''))||','||
    TRIM(COALESCE(Quantity, ''))||','||
    TRIM(COALESCE(InvoiceDate, ''))||','||
    TRIM(COALESCE(Price, ''))||','||
    TRIM(COALESCE("Customer ID", ''))||','||
    TRIM(COALESCE(Country, ''))
    )) AS hash_diff
FROM "SRC_online_retail_II_-_Year_2010-2011_001"
)

SELECT * FROM CTE_TARGET;
```

The CTE for the delete statement joins the two tables together and exposes the `rowid` field from the target table (SRC).

```
CTE_DELETE AS (
SELECT
A.rowid
FROM CTE_TARGET A
INNER JOIN CTE_SOURCE B
ON (
A.provider_code = B.provider_code AND
A.hash_diff = B.hash_diff
)
WHERE B.rowid IS NOT NULL
)

SELECT * FROM CTE_DELETE;
```

This generates a list of the records in the SRC table that have the same `provider_code` and `hash_diff` values in the SAT table.

```
541903
541904
541905
541906
541907
541908
541909
541910
sales %
```

The DELETE statement is straightforward. Take the list of records generated by the CTE_DELETE function and delete them from the SRC table.

```
DELETE FROM "SRC_online_retail_II_-_Year_2010-2011_001"
WHERE
rowid IN (SELECT rowid FROM CTE_DELETE) OR
provider_code = 'provider_code'
```

The results of this process can be verified by counting the number of records in both tables.

```
sqlite3 svc/db/sales.db "SELECT * FROM
'SRC_online_retail_II_-_Year_2010-2011_001'" ".quit"
```

```
sales % sqlite3 svc/db/sales.db "SELECT COUNT(*) FROM 'SRC_online_retail_II_-_Year_2010-2011_001'" ".quit"
0
sales % sqlite3 svc/db/sales.db "SELECT COUNT(*) FROM 'SAT_ONLINE_RETAIL_II_YEAR_2010_2011_001'" ".quit"
536642
sales %
```

A quick refactor

The load and clean file both used the `SRC_online_retail_II_-_Year_2010-2011_001` table which was populated with the original load process. We need to migrate these scripts to the new table using the `load.csv` process. Change the the table reference `FROM 'SRC_online_retail_II_-_Year_2010-2011_001'` to `FROM 'SRC_online_retail_II_-_Year_2010-2011_002'` in the load and clean files.

Building the automation

The automation is straightforward and follows the same pattern as every other query we've implemented.

```
test/tables: \
  test_table/SRC_online_retail_II_-_Year_2010-2011_001 \
  test_table/RAW_ONLINE_RETAIL_II_YEAR_2010_2011_001 \
  test_table/INFO_SALES_LAST_6_MONTHS_FILTERED_001 \
  test_table/INFO_WEEKLY_TOP_SALES_RANK_001 \
  test_table/SRC_online_retail_II_-_Year_2010-2011_002 \
  test_table/SAT_ONLINE_RETAIL_II_YEAR_2010_2011_001

# SAT_ONLINE_RETAIL_II_YEAR_2010_2011_001 ----
test_table/SAT_ONLINE_RETAIL_II_YEAR_2010_2011_001: \
  SAT_ONLINE_RETAIL_II_YEAR_2010_2011_001
  @$(test_table)

etc/sql/SAT_ONLINE_RETAIL_II_YEAR_2010_2011_001_create.sql:
  @$(test_file)

SAT_ONLINE_RETAIL_II_YEAR_2010_2011_001: \
  etc/sql/SAT_ONLINE_RETAIL_II_YEAR_2010_2011_001_create.sql
  @$(create_table)
```

Create a new recipe to execute a SQL query. This will be a variation of the `execute_sql_export_csv` and `create_table` macros.

```
define execute_sql
  @#<table_name>(colon)(space) <path/to/sql_file.sql> [<dependent_table_name(s)>]
  @echo $(DTS)     [INFO] - Executing $<
  @$(SQLITE3) $(DBFILE) ".read $<" ".quit"
endef
```

Use this macro to execute any sql query.

```
etc/sql/SAT_ONLINE_RETAIL_II_YEAR_2010_2011_001_load.sql:
  @$(test_file)

load/SAT_ONLINE_RETAIL_II_YEAR_2010_2011_001: \
  etc/sql/SAT_ONLINE_RETAIL_II_YEAR_2010_2011_001_load.sql \
  SRC_online_retail_II_-_Year_2010-2011_002 \
  SAT_ONLINE_RETAIL_II_YEAR_2010_2011_001 \
  load/SRC_online_retail_II_-_Year_2010-2011_002
  @$(execute_sql)

clean/SRC_online_retail_II_-_Year_2010-2011_002: \
  etc/sql/SAT_ONLINE_RETAIL_II_YEAR_2010_2011_001_clean.sql \
  load/SAT_ONLINE_RETAIL_II_YEAR_2010_2011_001
  @$(execute_sql)

metrics/SAT_ONLINE_RETAIL_II_YEAR_2010_2011_001: \
  SAT_ONLINE_RETAIL_II_YEAR_2010_2011_001
  @$(record_count_table)
```

This portion of the data pipeline can be executed by running the `clean/SRC…:` target. Adding this to the `transform:` target will incorporate it into the larger flow.

NOTE: Be sure to carefully look at the dependencies for each new target. It is very easy to miss one. Work deliberately and carefully look at the logs after each test run.

```
sales — -zsh — 115×11
sales % make clean/SRC_online_retail_II_-_Year_2010-2011_002
2021-05-11T10:09:25-MST [INFO] - Creating table SRC_online_retail_II_-_Year_2010-2011_002
2021-05-11T10:09:25-MST [INFO] - Creating table SAT_ONLINE_RETAIL_II_YEAR_2010_2011_001
2021-05-11T10:09:25-MST [INFO] - Executing etc/sql/SAT_ONLINE_RETAIL_II_YEAR_2010_2011_001_load.sql

2021-05-11T10:09:25-MST [INFO] - Executing etc/sql/SAT_ONLINE_RETAIL_II_YEAR_2010_2011_001_clean.sql

sales % make metrics/SAT_ONLINE_RETAIL_II_YEAR_2010_2011_001
2021-05-11T10:20:57-MST [INFO] - Creating table SAT_ONLINE_RETAIL_II_YEAR_2010_2011_001
2021-05-11T10:20:57-MST [INFO] - record count = 536642 records in SAT_ONLINE_RETAIL_II_YEAR_2010_2011_001.sales.db
sales %
```

```
transform: \
  svc/static/online_retail_II_last_6_months_filtered.csv \
  svc/static/online_retail_II_last_6_months_filtered_002.csv \
  clean/SRC_online_retail_II_-_Year_2010-2011_002
```

```
metrics: \
  metrics/online_retail_II_last_6_months_filtered.csv \
  metrics/online_retail_II_last_6_months_filtered_002.csv \
  metrics/SRC_online_retail_II_-_Year_2010-2011_001 \
  metrics/RAW_ONLINE_RETAIL_II_YEAR_2010_2011_001 \
  metrics/INFO_SALES_LAST_6_MONTHS_FILTERED_001 \
  metrics/SAT_ONLINE_RETAIL_II_YEAR_2010_2011_001
```

The entire flow can be retested by uninstalling and then rerunning the solution.

```
sales — -zsh — 115×55
sales % make
2021-05-11T13:15:39-MST [INFO] - Extracting data from svc/source/online_retail_II.xlsx [Year 2010-2011] into svc/lo
ad/online_retail_II_-_Year_2010-2011.csv
2021-05-11T13:16:38-MST [INFO] - Splitting svc/load/online_retail_II_-_Year_2010-2011.csv into svc/load/split_onlin
e_retail_II/online_retail_II_-_Year_2010-2011__###
   50000 svc/load/split_online_retail_II/online_retail_II_-_Year_2010-2011_000.csv
   50000 svc/load/split_online_retail_II/online_retail_II_-_Year_2010-2011_001.csv
   50000 svc/load/split_online_retail_II/online_retail_II_-_Year_2010-2011_002.csv
   50000 svc/load/split_online_retail_II/online_retail_II_-_Year_2010-2011_003.csv
   50000 svc/load/split_online_retail_II/online_retail_II_-_Year_2010-2011_004.csv
   50000 svc/load/split_online_retail_II/online_retail_II_-_Year_2010-2011_005.csv
   50000 svc/load/split_online_retail_II/online_retail_II_-_Year_2010-2011_006.csv
   50000 svc/load/split_online_retail_II/online_retail_II_-_Year_2010-2011_007.csv
   50000 svc/load/split_online_retail_II/online_retail_II_-_Year_2010-2011_008.csv
   50000 svc/load/split_online_retail_II/online_retail_II_-_Year_2010-2011_009.csv
   41911 svc/load/split_online_retail_II/online_retail_II_-_Year_2010-2011_010.csv
  541911 total
```

```
2021-05-11T10:37:18-MST [INFO] - Loading data from svc/load/online_retail_II_-_Year_2010-2011.csv into SRC_online_r
etail_II_-_Year_2010-2011_001.sales.db
2021-05-11T10:37:36-MST [INFO] - Executing etc/sql/online_retail_II_last_6_months_filtered.sql and exporting to svc
/static/online_retail_II_last_6_months_filtered.csv
2021-05-11T10:37:38-MST [INFO] - Creating table RAW_ONLINE_RETAIL_II_YEAR_2010_2011_001
2021-05-11T10:37:40-MST [INFO] - Executing etc/sql/online_retail_II_last_6_months_filtered_002.sql and exporting to
 svc/static/online_retail_II_last_6_months_filtered_002.csv
2021-05-11T10:37:41-MST [INFO] - Creating table SRC_online_retail_II_-_Year_2010-2011_002
2021-05-11T10:37:41-MST [INFO] - Creating table SAT_ONLINE_RETAIL_II_YEAR_2010_2011_001
2021-05-11T10:37:41-MST [INFO] - Executing etc/sql/SAT_ONLINE_RETAIL_II_YEAR_2010_2011_001_load.sql

2021-05-11T10:37:41-MST [INFO] - Executing etc/sql/SAT_ONLINE_RETAIL_II_YEAR_2010_2011_001_clean.sql

2021-05-11T10:37:41-MST [INFO] - Creating table INFO_SALES_LAST_6_MONTHS_FILTERED_001
2021-05-11T10:37:41-MST [INFO] - Creating table INFO_WEEKLY_TOP_SALES_RANK_001
2021-05-11T10:37:41-MST [INFO] - Executing INFO_WEEKLY_TOP_SALES_RANK_001 and exporting to svc/static/WEEKLY_TOP_SA
LES_RANK_001.json
2021-05-11T10:37:45-MST [INFO] - Executing svc/static/WEEKLY_TOP_SALES_RANK_001.html
2021-05-11T10:37:45-MST [INFO] - Executing svc/static/WEEKLY_TOP_SALES_RANK_002.html
2021-05-11T10:37:45-MST [INFO] - Executing svc/static/WEEKLY_TOP_SALES_RANK_003.html
2021-05-11T10:37:45-MST [INFO] - record count = 11 svc/static/online_retail_II_last_6_months_filtered.csv
2021-05-11T10:37:45-MST [INFO] - record count = 11 svc/static/online_retail_II_last_6_months_filtered_002.csv
2021-05-11T10:37:45-MST [INFO] - record count = 541910 records in SRC_online_retail_II_-_Year_2010-2011_001.sales.d
b
2021-05-11T10:37:45-MST [INFO] - record count = 536642 records in RAW_ONLINE_RETAIL_II_YEAR_2010_2011_001.sales.db
2021-05-11T10:37:45-MST [INFO] - record count = 100 records in INFO_SALES_LAST_6_MONTHS_FILTERED_001.sales.db
2021-05-11T10:37:45-MST [INFO] - record count = 0 records in SAT_ONLINE_RETAIL_II_YEAR_2010_2011_001.sales.db
2021-05-11T10:37:45-MST [INFO] - Executing documentation.
sales %
```

Looking at the log, notice that there are no records in the `SAT_ONLINE_RETAIL_II_YEAR_2010_2011_001` table. This is because we have not copied any CSV files into the `svc/load/online_retail_II/` directory.

Simulate a periodic load by copying a few files into that directory and then run the `make` command again.

```
b
2021-05-11T13:20:43-MST [INFO] - record count = 536642 records in RAW_ONLINE_RETAIL_II_YEAR_2010_2011_001.sales.db
2021-05-11T13:20:43-MST [INFO] - record count = 100 records in INFO_SALES_LAST_6_MONTHS_FILTERED_001.sales.db
2021-05-11T13:20:43-MST [INFO] - record count = 99075 records in SAT_ONLINE_RETAIL_II_YEAR_2010_2011_001.sales.db
2021-05-11T13:20:43-MST [INFO] - Executing documentation.
sales %
```

The final step is to deploy these new processes to our local environment by running `make deploy/local`.

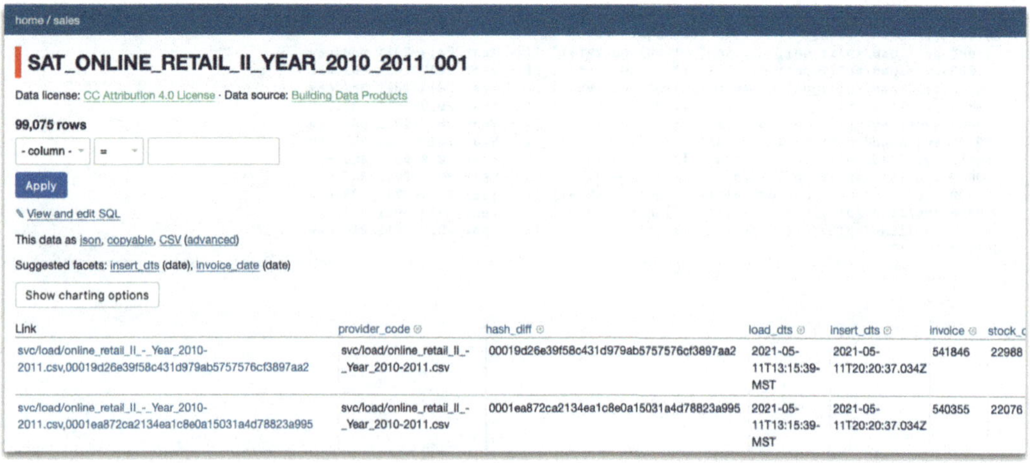

Identifying Business Keys

Now that we have a table to store our incremental loads, we can extend the solution by identifying the business keys found in the data set. A business key is an identifier for an important business entity. In this data set, they are invoice, stock code, customer, and country. We also have business keys that are part of the technical solution like the provider code.

These business keys will be used to link different data sets together in a primary and foreign key relationship. By pre-calculating the value of the keys as hashes, we can simplify and speed up the load process by enabling decoupled, parallel loads.

Pre-calculating these keys also makes it easier for others to consistently and accurately combine data sets without needing to generate their own unique set of surrogate keys within their system.

These keys may also break business users from the habit of using the integer values for actual business keys. An example in our data set would be referring to a customer as #13050 rather than by their actual name. A better solution would be to use a consistent business name.

Adding the business keys is a simple matter of calculating the hash key for each of these columns in the Satellite table. One tricky part of this step it deciding what to call these fields. You want to be as clear as possible and this may mean changing the name from the data set you are working with. The goal is to pick a name with broad business recognition. Hopefully, this will help steer the business toward developing a common vocabulary for core business data elements.

Best practice is to rename the entity as a "code" rather than an "id". This makes it easier to recognize that a thing may have many "codes" and what you call it may differ in various situations. The core changes to our create and load sql queries can be seen below.

NOTE: By Data Vault convention, we also add the suffix "_hkey" to identify the fields is a hash key.

SAT_ONLINE_RETAIL_II_YEAR_2010_2011_001_create.sql:

```sql
-- sales/etc/sql/SAT_ONLINE_RETAIL_II_YEAR_2010_2011_001_create.sql
-------------------------------------------------------------------

CREATE TABLE IF NOT EXISTS SAT_ONLINE_RETAIL_II_YEAR_2010_2011_001 (
  provider_code TEXT
  ,hash_diff TEXT
  ,load_dts TEXT
  ,insert_dts TEXT
  ,invoice TEXT
  ,stock_code TEXT
  ,description TEXT
  ,quantity NUMERIC
  ,invoice_date TEXT
  ,price NUMERIC
  ,customer_id TEXT
  ,country TEXT
  ----
  ,invoice_code_hkey TEXT
  ,stock_code_hkey TEXT
  ,customer_code_hkey TEXT
  ,country_code_hkey TEXT
  ,PRIMARY KEY(provider_code, hash_diff)
  );
```

SAT_ONLINE_RETAIL_II_YEAR_2010_2011_001_load.sql:

```sql
WITH CTE_SOURCE AS (
  SELECT DISTINCT
      provider_code
      ,SHA1(UPPER(TRIM(COALESCE(invoice,''))||','||
          TRIM(COALESCE(StockCode,''))||','||
          TRIM(COALESCE(Description,''))||','||
          TRIM(COALESCE(Quantity,''))||','||
          TRIM(COALESCE(InvoiceDate,''))||','||
          TRIM(COALESCE(Price,''))||','||
          TRIM(COALESCE("Customer ID",''))||','||
          TRIM(COALESCE(Country,'')))
        ) AS hash_diff
      ,load_dts
      ,CAST(NULL AS TEXT) AS insert_dts
      ,Invoice AS invoice
      ,StockCode AS stock_code
      ,Description AS description
      ,CAST(Quantity AS NUMERIC) AS quantity
      ,InvoiceDate AS invoice_date
      ,CAST(Price AS NUMERIC) AS price
      ,"Customer ID" AS customer_id
      ,Country AS country
      ----
      ,SHA1(UPPER(TRIM(COALESCE(invoice,'')))) AS invoice_code_hkey
      ,SHA1(UPPER(TRIM(COALESCE(StockCode,'')))) AS stock_code_hkey
      ,SHA1(UPPER(TRIM(COALESCE("Customer ID",'')))) AS customer_code_hkey
      ,SHA1(UPPER(TRIM(COALESCE(Country,'')))) AS country_code_hkey
  FROM 'SRC_online_retail_II_-_Year_2010-2011_002'
  WHERE provider_code != 'provider_code'
)
```

The technical implementation of the `_hkey` is the same as was used for the `hash_diff` field. The goal is to apply the same simple, consistent logic to remove obvious differences with the text being hashed.

The easiest way to execute this change would be to uninstall and re-make everything.

```
make uninstall && make
```

```
2021-05-11T17:12:52-MST [INFO] - Executing svc/static/WEEKLY_TOP_SALES_RANK_001.html
2021-05-11T17:12:53-MST [INFO] - Executing svc/static/WEEKLY_TOP_SALES_RANK_002.html
2021-05-11T17:12:53-MST [INFO] - Executing svc/static/WEEKLY_TOP_SALES_RANK_003.html
2021-05-11T17:12:53-MST [INFO] - record count = 11 svc/static/online_retail_II_last_6_months_filtered.csv
2021-05-11T17:12:53-MST [INFO] - record count = 11 svc/static/online_retail_II_last_6_months_filtered_002.csv
2021-05-11T17:12:53-MST [INFO] - record count = 541910 records in SRC_online_retail_II_-_Year_2010-2011_001.sales.db
2021-05-11T17:12:53-MST [INFO] - record count = 536642 records in RAW_ONLINE_RETAIL_II_YEAR_2010_2011_001.sales.db
2021-05-11T17:12:53-MST [INFO] - record count = 100 records in INFO_SALES_LAST_6_MONTHS_FILTERED_001.sales.db
2021-05-11T17:12:53-MST [INFO] - record count = 0 records in SAT_ONLINE_RETAIL_II_YEAR_2010_2011_001.sales.db
2021-05-11T17:12:53-MST [INFO] - Executing documentation.
sales %
```

If we copy and load a few CSV files into the `svc/load/online_retail_II/` directory we can verify the changes.

```
make transform && sqlite3 svc/db/sales.db "SELECT invoice,
invoice_code_hkey FROM "SAT_ONLINE_RETAIL_II_YEAR_2010_2011_001"
LIMIT 10;" ".quit"
```

Retrospective

Looking back at the Venn diagram of the primary responsibilities of Data and Analytics Engineers. Most of our efforts, aside from the development of the Top 10 Sales charts, are solidly within the role of Data Engineering.

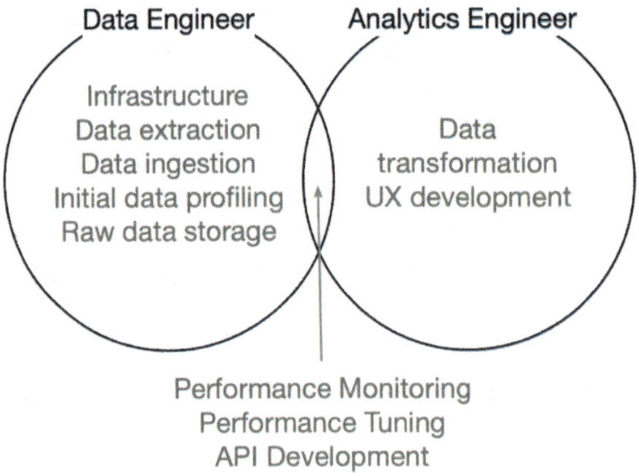

Now that we have a solid data set and initial infrastructure, it's time to focus on the data transformation activities and the construction of our analytical micro-warehouse.

---

163 Split (https://man7.org/linux/man-pages/man1/split.1.html)

164 Data Vault Alliance (https://datavaultalliance.com/about/what-is-datavault/)

165 Set Theory (https://en.wikipedia.org/wiki/Set_theory)

166 Venn diagram (https://en.wikipedia.org/wiki/Venn_diagram)

167 SHA1 (https://en.wikipedia.org/wiki/SHA-1)

168 In fact, there is an entire IT field dedicated to resolving these conflicts: Master Data Management. (https://www.gartner.com/en/information-technology/glossary/master-data-management-mdm). Yes, there is more to it than that, but 90% of the work is creating mappings between database surrogate keys.

169 TPC-H (http://www.tpc.org/tpch/)

170 This is why we have Database Administrators, Data Modelers, and ETL Developers. It's too complicated and specialized for any one developer to manage.

171 Compiling extensions is covered in the Appendix.

172 Valentina Studio: Select the database in the Schema Editor -> Right click -> Show Extensions -> [Add...] -> Select the extension (etc/software/sqlite3/[sha1.dylib] on macOS.

DB Browser for SQLite: Open the database -> Menu: Tools -> Load Extension -> Select the extension (etc/software/sqlite3/[sha1.dylib] on macOS.

SQLiteStudio: Open the database -> Menu: Tools -> Open extension manager -> Select the extension (etc/software/sqlite3/[sha1.dylib] on macOS -> Check Register in all databases -> Select the green check box to exit.

173 Construct as many steps as you need to use as you build out your query. Clarity is much more important than brevity and cleverness.

174 Not every database has a hidden row id field (MS SQL Server). This makes the process slightly more difficult to implement in tables without a single incremental primary key.

Chapter 8: The Analytics Database

This next step leverages the unique record analysis we performed on the data in an earlier iteration. That initial analysis identified a number of issues which we addressed by applying some filters and unsophisticated but sufficient business logic. This next pass will build on those decisions and start the process of building a more flexible analytics database.

IN ORDER TO CORRECT ISSUES WITH THE DATA.
AS A SALES MANAGER RESPONSIBLE FOR THE QUALITY OF THE SALES DATA
I WANT ACCESS TO AN ERROR-FREE DATA SET.
AND A WAY TO PERFORM ADDITIONAL ANALYTICS EASILY.
AND A SYSTEM THAT DOESN'T REQUIRE LONG DEVELOPMENT TIMES WHEN CHANGES ARE REQUIRED.

[] PROVIDE A BUSINESS-FOCUSED DATA SET WITH MINIMAL DATA QUALITY AND LOGIC ERRORS. USE EXISTING DATA FOR NOW.
[] IDENTIFY AND CORRECT ANOMALIES IN THE DATA WITHOUT DESTROYING THE ORIGINAL RECORD.
[X] IF A RECORD CHANGES, SAVE THAT HISTORY TO AID ANALYSIS.
[X] DO NOT STORE DUPLICATE RECORDS.
[X] SUPPORT INCREMENTAL LOADING.

```
IN ORDER TO IMPROVE FUTURE DEVELOPMENT EFFORTS
AS A SALES MANAGER RESPONSIBLE FOR IMPROVING OUR
ANALYTICS CAPABILITIES
I WANT A SYSTEM THAT IS EASY FOR ANALYSTS TO USE
AND CONSISTENTLY IMPLEMENTS STANDARD BUSINESS
LOGIC.

[] SINGLE PRODUCT NAME FOR EACH STOCK CODE
(SKU).
[] SINGLE PRICE AND QUANTITY FOR EACH INVOICE
LINE ITEM.
[] NO "C" IN INVOICE CODES FOR CANCELED LINE
ITEMS.
[] REIMPLEMENT PREVIOUS REPORTING W/ NEW DATA
SET.
```

```
IN ORDER TO MINIMIZE THE ONGOING SUPPORT BURDEN.
AS A SYSTEM
I WANT TO AUTOMATE ALL DATA MANAGEMENT TASKS.
AND

[] SCHEDULE MANAGEMENT TASKS WEEKLY.
[] SCHEDULE DEPLOYMENT REFRESHES WEEKLY.
```

So far, we've implemented a robust and efficient solution to store the raw source data, including the ability to look back at the data and review the history. The next step is to begin evolving our data set to address the data quality and business logic discrepancies we observed.

Finally, we need to automate the data pipelines by executing them on a schedule.

In our first pass, we decided to hard code in preliminary business logic for the sake of faster delivery. This time, we are going to take the results and produce additional tables built specifically for future analytics work.

Creating our First Business Satellite (BSAT)

In the Data Vault model, we have two types of Satellite tables. First there is a "Raw Satellite" containing the raw historical data. This is the Satellite table we just created. The second type of table is a "Business Satellite". This table is a variation of the Raw Satellite table that reflects the business logic necessary to derive value from the raw data.

The advantage to this multi tiered data model is that the Raw Satellite tables provide a persistent store of the source data we can always dip back into if we need to change the business logic in the future. This safety net allows us to iterate the design of the warehouse over time, without requiring long planning and modeling cycles. If we need to correct something, we can simply implement a newer version in parallel with the old version. As we become more comfortable with this safety net, we become more confident in our ability to experiment with our analysis.

This multitiered approach allows us to break free from the structure of the source data and focus on building data sets tailored to actual business needs. Not only can we support multiple version of business logic, we can support specific versions of the data for different business purposes.

The initial business satellite we will build will reflect our current understanding of the invoice data. We start here, not because it is easy to implement, but because it is critically important we get this portion of the analysis right.

Back when we performed our initial assessment of the invoice data, we noted that there were both invoices and stock codes with multiple prices and quantities. Rectifying these issues starts with writing a query to identify examples where this is true. This query will compare the raw prices and quantities against an aggregated value calculated over the invoice code and stock code. This can be accomplished with a series of window functions and many flags to aid in filtering the data.

Step one, as usual, is to develop the base data set.

```
-- sales/etc/sql/BSAT_INVOICES_001_load.sql
------------------------------------------------------------------------

SELECT
'sales/etc/sql/BSAT_INVOICES_001_load.sql' AS provider_code
,load_dts
,CASE WHEN invoice LIKE 'C%' THEN REPLACE(invoice, 'C', '') ELSE invoice END AS invoice_code
,DATE(invoice_date, 'UTC') AS invoice_date
,UPPER(stock_code) AS stock_code
,customer_id AS customer_code
,price
,quantity
,invoice_code_hkey
,stock_code_hkey
,customer_code_hkey
FROM SAT_ONLINE_RETAIL_II_YEAR_2010_2011_001
)
--,
SELECT * FROM CTE_BASE;
```

The first window function calculates the maximum quantity sold for every invoice code and stock code combination. The second calculates the minimum price on the same combination.

```
CTE_AGG AS (
  SELECT
    invoice_code
    ,stock_code
    ,invoice_date
    ,quantity
    ,MAX(quantity) OVER (PARTITION BY
        invoice_code
        ,stock_code
        ORDER BY
        invoice_date DESC
    ) AS max_quantity
    ,price
    ,MIN(price) OVER (PARTITION BY
        invoice_code
        ,stock_code
        ORDER BY
        invoice_date DESC
    ) AS min_price
    -----
    ,customer_code
    ,invoice_code_hkey
    ,stock_code_hkey
    ,customer_code_hkey
    ,provider_code
    ,load_dts
  FROM CTE_BASE
)
--,
SELECT * FROM CTE_AGG
```

We can then use these fields to flag the records where there are discrepancies, starting with the invoices where we see both issues.

```
SELECT
invoice_code
,stock_code
,invoice_date
,quantity
,max_quantity
,price
,min_price
,CASE WHEN price != min_price THEN 1 ELSE 0 END AS price_ne_flag
,CASE WHEN quantity != max_quantity THEN 1 ELSE 0 END AS quantity_ne_flag
,(CASE WHEN price != min_price THEN 1 ELSE 0 END) +
(CASE WHEN quantity != max_quantity THEN 1 ELSE 0 END) AS ne_flag
FROM CTE_AGG
WHERE ne_flag > 1
ORDER BY ne_flag DESC;
```

Looking at the results, it appears we should use the MAX(quantity) and MIN(price) values.

	invoice_code	stock_code	invoice_date	quantity	max_quantity	price	min_price	price_ne_flag	quantity_ne_flag	ne_flag
1	536544	21218	2010-12-01	1	2	8.47	3.75	1	1	2
2	536544	22844	2010-12-01	1	2	16.98	8.5	1	1	2
3	536544	22862	2010-12-01	1	2	8.47	4.25	1	1	2
4	536592	22467	2010-12-02	1	3	5.06	2.55	1	1	2
5	536876	22909	2010-12-03	2	6	1.66	0.85	1	1	2
6	536876	22952	2010-12-03	6	24	1.28	0.55	1	1	2
7	536876	84992	2010-12-03	3	24	1.28	0.55	1	1	2
8	537236	22073	2010-12-06	8	16	3.75	3.39	1	1	2
9	537237	22766	2010-12-06	1	2	5.91	2.95	1	1	2
10	537237	22862	2010-12-06	1	2	8.47	4.25	1	1	2

However, it isn't enough to check a few records. As a general rule, you should look at at least thirty records to have a minimum valid sample size. There is nothing magic about the 30 observation rule, but when you are evaluating a data set to decide the business logic, be sure you have looked at many randomly chosen examples before you code and deploy your assumptions.

```
SELECT
invoice
,stock_code
,invoice_date
,description
,quantity
,price
FROM "SAT_ONLINE_RETAIL_II_YEAR_2010_2011_001"
WHERE
    invoice LIKE '%536544'
    AND stock_code IN ('21218', '22844', '228662')
ORDER BY 1,2
```

	invoice_code	customer_code	invoice_date	stock_code	description	price	min_price	quantity	max_quantity	price_ne_flag	quantity_ne_flag	ne_flag
1	536544		2010-12-01	21218	RED SPOTTY ...	8.47	3.75	1	2	1	1	2
2	536544		2010-12-01	22844	VINTAGE ...	16.98	8.5	1	2	1	1	2
3	536544		2010-12-01	22862	LOVE HEART ...	8.47	4.25	1	2	1	1	2
4	536592		2010-12-02	22467	GUMBALL CO...	5.06	2.55	1	3	1	1	2
5	536876		2010-12-03	22909	SET OF 20 ...	1.66	0.85	2	6	1	1	2

Spot checking our assumptions:

	invoice	stock_code	invoice_date	description	quantity	price
1	536544	21218	2010-12-01T14:32:00	RED SPOTTY BISCUIT TIN	1	8.47
2	536544	21218	2010-12-01T14:32:00	RED SPOTTY BISCUIT TIN	2	3.75
3	536544	22844	2010-12-01T14:32:00	VINTAGE CREAM DOG FOOD CONTAINER	1	16.98
4	536544	22844	2010-12-01T14:32:00	VINTAGE CREAM DOG FOOD CONTAINER	2	8.5

	invoice	stock_code	invoice_date	description	quantity	price
1	536876	22909	2010-12-03T11:36:00	SET OF 20 VINTAGE CHRISTMAS NAPKINS	2	1.66
2	536876	22909	2010-12-03T11:36:00	SET OF 20 VINTAGE CHRISTMAS NAPKINS	6	0.85
3	536876	22952	2010-12-03T11:36:00	60 CAKE CASES VINTAGE CHRISTMAS	24	0.55
4	536876	22952	2010-12-03T11:36:00	60 CAKE CASES VINTAGE CHRISTMAS	6	1.28
5	536876	84992	2010-12-03T11:36:00	72 SWEETHEART FAIRY CAKE CASES	24	0.55
6	536876	84992	2010-12-03T11:36:00	72 SWEETHEART FAIRY CAKE CASES	3	1.28

	invoice	stock_code	invoice_date	description	quantity	price
1	536592	22467	2010-12-01T17:06:00	GUMBALL COAT RACK	1	5.06
2	536592	22467	2010-12-01T17:06:00	GUMBALL COAT RACK	3	2.55

	invoice	stock_code	invoice_date	description	quantity	price
1	576644	23355	2011-11-16T10:01:00	HOT WATER BOTTLE KEEP CALM	1	10.79
2	576644	23355	2011-11-16T10:01:00	HOT WATER BOTTLE KEEP CALM	1	12.46
3	576644	23355	2011-11-16T10:01:00	HOT WATER BOTTLE KEEP CALM	3	8.29

	invoice	stock_code	invoice_date	description	quantity	price
1	580727	22107	2011-12-05T17:17:00	PIZZA PLATE IN BOX	2	7.46
2	580727	22107	2011-12-05T17:17:00	PIZZA PLATE IN BOX	8	3.29
3	580727	22446	2011-12-05T17:17:00	PIN CUSHION BABUSHKA PINK	1	6.63
4	580727	22446	2011-12-05T17:17:00	PIN CUSHION BABUSHKA PINK	3	2.46
5	580727	22653	2011-12-05T17:17:00	BUTTON BOX	1	4.13
6	580727	22653	2011-12-05T17:17:00	BUTTON BOX	4	1.63
7	580727	23263	2011-12-05T17:17:00	SET OF 3 WOODEN HEART DECORATIONS	16	2.46
8	580727	23263	2011-12-05T17:17:00	SET OF 3 WOODEN HEART DECORATIONS	8	2.5

	invoice	stock_code	invoice_date	description	quantity	price
1	539492	21481	2010-12-20T10:14:00	FAWN BLUE HOT WATER BOTTLE	11	2.95
2	539492	21481	2010-12-20T10:14:00	FAWN BLUE HOT WATER BOTTLE	2	5.91
3	539492	22910	2010-12-20T10:14:00	PAPER CHAIN KIT VINTAGE CHRISTMAS	1	5.91
4	539492	22910	2010-12-20T10:14:00	PAPER CHAIN KIT VINTAGE CHRISTMAS	9	3.36

	invoice	stock_code	invoice_date	description	quantity	price
1	565378	20726	2011-09-02T15:16:00	LUNCH BAG WOODLAND	1	8.33
2	565378	20726	2011-09-02T15:16:00	LUNCH BAG WOODLAND	11	4.96
3	565378	20727	2011-09-02T15:16:00	LUNCH BAG BLACK SKULL.	1	8.33
4	565378	20727	2011-09-02T15:16:00	LUNCH BAG BLACK SKULL.	17	4.96

Fortunately, all these records follow the minimum price equals the maximum quantity observation. Therefore, we can have confidence in implementing this business logic.

We also need to recompute a new `invoice_code_hkey` because we stripped the "C" from the invoices that were canceled.

```sql
CTE_TARGET AS (
  SELECT DISTINCT
    SHA1(UPPER(
    TRIM(COALESCE(invoice_code, ''))||','||
    TRIM(COALESCE(stock_code, '')) ))AS invoice_hkey
    ,provider_code
    ,load_dts
    ----
    ,invoice_code
    ,stock_code
    ,invoice_date
    ,customer_code
    ,min_price AS price
    ,max_quantity AS quantity
    ,SHA1(UPPER(TRIM(COALESCE(invoice_code, '')))) AS invoice_code_hkey
    ,stock_code_hkey
    ,customer_code_hkey
  FROM CTE_AGG
)
```

	invoice_hkey	provider_code	load_dts	invoice_code	stock_code	invoice_date	customer_code	price	quantity	invoice_code_hkey
1	abb89fd4a6181cc...	sales/etc/sql/...	2021-05-11T17...	536365	21730	2010-12-01	17850	4.25	6	65105462a7e2003f760...
2	0b991de231def67...	sales/etc/sql/...	2021-05-11T17...	536365	22752	2010-12-01	17850	7.65	2	65105462a7e2003f760...
3	9c9294c8f06529...	sales/etc/sql/...	2021-05-11T17...	536365	71053	2010-12-01	17850	3.39	6	65105462a7e2003f760...
4	fc81d5b8bc9c878...	sales/etc/sql/...	2021-05-11T17...	536365	84029E	2010-12-01	17850	3.39	6	65105462a7e2003f760...
5	aa615de5ffebbf4c...	sales/etc/sql/...	2021-05-11T17...	536365	84029G	2010-12-01	17850	3.39	6	65105462a7e2003f760...

Because we are calculating a new hash key for the relationship of invoice to stock codes, we need to add the link to the SHA1 extensions, just like we did when we populated the SAT table.

```sql
-- sales/etc/sql/BSAT_INVOICES_001_load.sql
-------------------------------------------------------------
SELECT load_extension('/Users/brianmcmillan/projects/sales/etc/software/sqlite3/sha1');
```

This target data set can now be inserted into the database.

```
INSERT INTO BSAT_INVOICES_001 (
  invoice_hkey
  ,provider_code
  ,load_dts
  ,insert_dts
  ,invoice_code
  ,stock_code
  ,invoice_date
  ,customer_code
  ,price
  ,quantity
  ,invoice_code_hkey
  ,stock_code_hkey
  ,customer_code_hkey
)

SELECT
  invoice_hkey
  ,provider_code
  ,load_dts
  ,strftime('%Y-%m-%dT%H:%M:%fZ', 'now') AS insert_dts
  ,invoice_code
  ,stock_code
  ,invoice_date
  ,customer_code
  ,price
  ,quantity
  ,invoice_code_hkey
  ,stock_code_hkey
  ,customer_code_hkey
FROM CTE_TARGET
```

	invoice_hkey	provider_code	load_dts	insert_dts	invoice_code	stock_code	invoice_date	customer_code	price	quantity	invoice_code_hkey
1	abb89fd4a6181cce...	sales/etc/sql/...	2021-05-11...	2021-05-12T...	536365	21730	2010-12-01	17850	4.25	6	65105462a7e200...
2	0b991de231def678...	sales/etc/sql/...	2021-05-11...	2021-05-12T...	536365	22752	2010-12-01	17850	7.65	2	65105462a7e200...
3	9c9294c8f065290...	sales/etc/sql/...	2021-05-11...	2021-05-12T...	536365	71053	2010-12-01	17850	3.39	6	65105462a7e200...
4	fc81d5b8bc9c878...	sales/etc/sql/...	2021-05-11...	2021-05-12T...	536365	84029E	2010-12-01	17850	3.39	6	65105462a7e200...
5	aa615de5ffebbf4c...	sales/etc/sql/...	2021-05-11...	2021-05-12T...	536365	84029G	2010-12-01	17850	3.39	6	65105462a7e200...

Before we create the target BSAT table, we need to add a statement at the top of the load file to truncate the table before we load new data.

```
-- sales/etc/sql/BSAT_INVOICES_001_load.sql
-----------------------------------------------------------------
SELECT load_extension('/Users/brianmcmillan/projects/sales/etc/software/sqlite3/

DELETE FROM BSAT_INVOICES_001;

WITH
CTE_BASE AS (
```

The process we are using to load data into the Business tables is affectionately called *"Trunk'n Load"*. We first delete all the data in the table (Truncate), and then we insert the results we want (Load). This is a good initial strategy because it is so simple to manage. However, in situations where the database is being accessed frequently, there could be a time where someone needs the data in a table that is being updated. This is a failure mode to be aware of, but in practice, reporting systems can usually operate with periodic access issues during the update cycle.[175]

In our architecture, where most access is through an independently deployed, read-only instance of the database. This refresh cycle is perfectly acceptable, and if we incorporate red/green deployments, they will be invisible to the end-users of the database.

The create statement mirrors the fields in the create statement.

```
-- sales/etc/sql/BSAT_INVOICES_001_create.sql
------------------------------------------------------------------

CREATE TABLE IF NOT EXISTS BSAT_INVOICES_001 (
  invoice_hkey TEXT
  ,provider_code TEXT
  ,load_dts TEXT
  ,insert_dts TEXT
  ,invoice_code TEXT
  ,stock_code TEXT
  ,invoice_date TEXT
  ,customer_code TEXT
  ,price NUMERIC
  ,quantity NUMERIC
  ,invoice_code_hkey TEXT
  ,stock_code_hkey TEXT
  ,customer_code_hkey TEXT
  ,PRIMARY KEY (invoice_hkey, load_dts)
);
```

BSAT_INVOICES_001
invoice_hkey [TEXT]
provider_code [TEXT]
load_dts [TEXT]
insert_dts [TEXT]
invoice_code [TEXT]
stock_code [TEXT]
invoice_date [TEXT]
customer_code [TEXT]
price [NUMERIC]
quantity [NUMERIC]
invoice_code_hkey [TEXT]
stock_code_hkey [TEXT]
customer_code_hkey [TEXT]

The automation follows the usual patterns:

```
# BSAT_INVOICES_001 ----
test_table/BSAT_INVOICES_001: \
  SAT_ONLINE_RETAIL_II_YEAR_2010_2011_001
  @$(test_table)

etc/sql/BSAT_INVOICES_001_create.sql:
  @$(test_file)

BSAT_INVOICES_001: \
  etc/sql/BSAT_INVOICES_001_create.sql
  @$(create_table)
```

```
transform: \
  svc/static/online_retail_II_last_6_months_filtered.csv \
  svc/static/online_retail_II_last_6_months_filtered_002.csv \
  clean/SRC_online_retail_II_-_Year_2010-2011_002 \
  load/BSAT_INVOICES_001

# BSAT_INVOICES_001 ----
.PHONY: load/BSAT_INVOICES_001
etc/sql/BSAT_INVOICES_001_load.sql:
  @$(test_file)

load/BSAT_INVOICES_001: \
  etc/sql/BSAT_INVOICES_001_load.sql \
  SAT_ONLINE_RETAIL_II_YEAR_2010_2011_001 \
  BSAT_INVOICES_001 \
  load/SAT_ONLINE_RETAIL_II_YEAR_2010_2011_001
  @$(execute_sql)
```

```
metrics/BSAT_INVOICES_001: \
  BSAT_INVOICES_001
  @$(record_count_table)
```

After running the make command again, we can see that 531224 records were successfully loaded into the new `BSAT_INVOICES_001` table.

```
sales — -zsh — 116×16
2021-05-12T15:30:59-MST [INFO] - Creating table INFO_SALES_LAST_6_MONTHS_FILTERED_001
2021-05-12T15:30:59-MST [INFO] - Creating table INFO_WEEKLY_TOP_SALES_RANK_001
2021-05-12T15:30:59-MST [INFO] - Executing INFO_WEEKLY_TOP_SALES_RANK_001 and exporting to svc/static/WEEKLY_TOP_SAL
ES_RANK_001.json
2021-05-12T15:31:03-MST [INFO] - Executing svc/static/WEEKLY_TOP_SALES_RANK_001.html
2021-05-12T15:31:03-MST [INFO] - Executing svc/static/WEEKLY_TOP_SALES_RANK_002.html
2021-05-12T15:31:03-MST [INFO] - Executing svc/static/WEEKLY_TOP_SALES_RANK_003.html
2021-05-12T15:31:03-MST [INFO] - record count = 11 svc/static/online_retail_II_last_6_months_filtered.csv
2021-05-12T15:31:03-MST [INFO] - record count = 11 svc/static/online_retail_II_last_6_months_filtered_002.csv
2021-05-12T15:31:03-MST [INFO] - record count = 541910 records in SRC_online_retail_II_-_Year_2010-2011_001.sales.db
2021-05-12T15:31:03-MST [INFO] - record count = 536642 records in RAW_ONLINE_RETAIL_II_YEAR_2010_2011_001.sales.db
2021-05-12T15:31:03-MST [INFO] - record count = 100 records in INFO_SALES_LAST_6_MONTHS_FILTERED_001.sales.db
2021-05-12T15:31:03-MST [INFO] - record count = 536642 records in SAT_ONLINE_RETAIL_II_YEAR_2010_2011_001.sales.db
2021-05-12T15:31:03-MST [INFO] - record count = 531224 records in BSAT_INVOICES_001.sales.db
2021-05-12T15:31:03-MST [INFO] - Executing documentation.
sales %
```

Creating the Business Link Table (BLNK)

Figuring out how to choose a single description for each stock code is the next problem to tackle. Previously, we made a common table expression that used the description value from the latest invoice. This strategy worked fine, but now we want to derive a more accurate set of descriptions.

Why wouldn't we select the best name and insert it into the SAT table as we did in our initial analysis? We could do that, but if we decided we needed to adjust our logic, we would need to update each of the records. Admittedly, not an issue with the Trunk n' Load process, but by separating the relationship between the stock code and its description, we are declaring in the model that we may have other alternatives to the description we are presenting.

BLNK_STOCK_CODE_PREFERRED_DESCRIPTION_001
stock_code_hkey [TEXT]
provider_code [TEXT]
load_dts [TEXT]
insert_dts [TEXT]
preferred_description [TEXT]

As an example, we have many stock code descriptions, and the link table supports these many to one relationships. Or, we could derive a single preferred description and create a table named `BLNK_STOCK_CODE_PREFERRED_DESCRIPTION,` and it would be obvious to an analyst what is in the table. These business tables encourage you to develop multiple tables addressing specific analytical requirements. These tables can make the system much easier to use, because these business tables reduce the amount of custom query code someone needs to develop.

NOTE: This is a good reason to sit down with your users and review their code. When you see reused or complicated logic, consider reimplementing it as a new Business Hub, Link, or Satellite.

Link tables are used to define the relationships between entities. There are many possible relationship types. Some link types are naturally part of the data (e.g., a Bill of Material), some are reflections of the relationships we can derive from the data (e.g., Multiple descriptions and prices), and some are manually maintained separately from the data (e.g., Product categories).

Relationship type	Description	Example
Same-As link	A is also know as B	Preferred description
Hierachical link	A requires B	Bill of Materials
Non-Historized link	A at time 1 A at time 2	Non-updatable transaction history. Double entry accounting register.
Non-descriptive	A and B are related	Customer clicked on product offer
Computed aggregate links	A is related to (B, C, F)	Transaction Throughput ((Qty * Price) - Raw material cost)
Exploration Links	Computed links for business purposes only	Logical groupings to make analysis easier.

The structure of a Link table typically only consists of one or more href_keys. This provides the flexibility to define many-to-many relationships or many-to-one relationships in the same table. The exception to this is when the attribute can't stand on its own (e.g., serial number).

```sql
-- sales/etc/sql/BLNK_STOCK_CODE_PREFERRED_DESCRIPTION_001_create.sql
---------------------------------------------------------------------

CREATE TABLE IF NOT EXISTS BLNK_STOCK_CODE_PREFERRED_DESCRIPTION_001 (
stock_code_hkey TEXT
,provider_code TEXT
,load_dts TEXT
,insert_dts TEXT
,preferred_description TEXT
,PRIMARY KEY (stock_code_hkey)
);
```

The code below demonstrates a good example of a straightforward data cleansing task that might not be obvious to a less experienced or thorough developer. It does not affect a large number of records, but removing these defects improves the data quality, and these little fixes contribute to making your data products a better source of truth than one without these small improvements.

```sql
-- sales/etc/sql/BLNK_STOCK_CODE_PREFERRED_DESCRIPTION_001_load.sql
---------------------------------------------------------------------
SELECT load_extension('/Users/brianmcmillan/projects/sales/etc/software/sqlite3/

DELETE FROM BLNK_STOCK_CODE_PREFERRED_DESCRIPTION_001;

WITH
CTE_BASE AS (
SELECT DISTINCT
  stock_code_hkey
  ,UPPER(TRIM(COALESCE(stock_code, ''))) AS stock_code
  ,REPLACE(REPLACE(REPLACE(REPLACE(TRIM(UPPER(description))
    , 'N0', 'NO')
    , '  ', ' ')
    , '*', '')
    , 'VIPPASSPORT', 'VIP PASSPORT') AS description
FROM SAT_ONLINE_RETAIL_II_YEAR_2010_2011_001
WHERE description != ''
ORDER BY 1 ASC
)
--,
SELECT * FROM CTE_BASE;
```

If we run this query, we can see there are issues with the descriptions. There are stock codes with multiple descriptions and codes with descriptions of defects and not products.

	stock_code_hkey	stock_code	description
1	00050f32305a575e95847a97c029ad9e934cce7b	90132	LIGHT TOPAZ TEAL/AQUA COL NECKLACE
2	00201cc17c6d38a221744603ce75c9624c77c64d	22336	DOVE DECORATION PAINTED ZINC
3	00201cc17c6d38a221744603ce75c9624c77c64d	22336	DAMAGED
4	0055f6812c66283b3beedeafb1fac2f8a0468b23	22344	PARTY PIZZA DISH PINK POLKADOT
5	007343b9ccd9b031604915a07254101b92d14073	22902	TOTE BAG I LOVE LONDON

If we scroll down to the bottom of the list or sort ascending, we can also see stock codes that appear to represent something other than a product.

stock_code_hkey	stock_code	description
9227f861197e6e737f2f9812be6e9eee13226a10	90214Z	LETTER "Z" ...
9156cfc85cc7ca37c03f3359ba33ff204ed33d26	AMAZONFEE	AMAZON FEE
ae4f281df5a5d0ff3cad6371f76d5c29b6d953ec	B	ADJUST BAD...
373e157dc0362cdb0e62070935e6c85b582a63...	BANK ...	BANK ...
cb7d29f43f4a81ff1f3a1202c80293337faa7a0a	C2	CARRIAGE
af2af7a1808793831c6f88dea09d7291895b1870	CRUK	CRUK ...
50c9e8d5fc98727b4bbc93cf5d64a68db647f04f	D	DISCOUNT

One approach to these problems is to break them into smaller data sets we can independently validate and understand. These can then be reassembled into a set of data reflecting our business requirements.

Specifically, we will be using is to create separate CTEs for each group of stock code descriptions and a new field flagging whether the description text is invalid. These data sets will then be recombined and filtered down to a master list of descriptions we can consistently leverage in other queries.

```
CTE_FILTER_DOTCOM AS (
  SELECT
    stock_code
    ,description
    ,CASE WHEN
    description LIKE '%DOTCOM%'
    THEN 1 ELSE 0 END AS invalid_description_flag
  FROM CTE_BASE
  WHERE invalid_description_flag = 1
)
--,
SELECT *
FROM CTE_FILTER_DOTCOM A
INNER JOIN CTE_BASE B
ON (A.stock_code = B.stock_code)
```

	stock_code	description	invalid_description_flag	_code	stock_code	description
1	22016	DOTCOMGIFTSH...	1	01...	22016	DOTCOMGIFTSHOP ...
2	85172	DOTCOM SET	1	03...	85172	?SOLD AS SETS?
3	85172	DOTCOM SET	1	03...	85172	CHECK
4	85172	DOTCOM SET	1	03...	85172	DOTCOM SET
5	85172	DOTCOM SET	1	03...	85172	HYACINTH BULB T-...
6	85172	DOTCOM SET	1	03...	85172	WRONGLY SOLD AS ...
7	37340	SOLD AS SET ON ...	1	05...	37340	MULTICOLOUR SPRIN...
8	37340	SOLD AS SET ON ...	1	05...	37340	SOLD AS SET ON ...

In this query, we are comparing all descriptions containing the word "DOTCOM" (The left side of the join (A)) against the other descriptions with the same stock_code. What we're looking for on the right side are valid product names like "RED RETROSPOT PURSE". This query tells us we can safely mark descriptions containing %DOTCOM% as invalid. The same can be done for %AMAZON% and %EBAY%.

```sql
CTE_FILTER_AMAZON AS (
  SELECT
    stock_code
    ,description
    ,CASE WHEN
    description LIKE '%AMAZON%'
    THEN 1 ELSE 0 END AS invalid_description_flag
  FROM CTE_BASE
  WHERE invalid_description_flag = 1
)
,
```

```sql
CTE_FILTER_EBAY AS (
  SELECT
    stock_code
    ,description
    ,CASE WHEN
    description LIKE '%EBAY%'
    THEN 1 ELSE 0 END AS invalid_description_flag
  FROM CTE_BASE
  WHERE invalid_description_flag = 1
)
,
```

Unfortunately, the situation is different for the %GIFTSHOP% data set. The descriptions on the left side all appear to be valid, but when we look on the right side, at stock_code 22351, we can see the description of "GIVEN AWAY". Take note of this, and we'll address this when we start filtering the remaining invalid descriptions.

```sql
CTE_FILTER_GIFTSHOP AS (
  SELECT
    stock_code
    ,description
    ,CASE WHEN
    description LIKE '%GIFTSHOP%'
    THEN 0 ELSE 1 END AS invalid_description_flag
  FROM CTE_BASE
  WHERE invalid_description_flag = 0
)
,
```

	stock_code	description	invalid_description_flag	_code	stock_code	description
1	22016	DOTCOMGIFTSHOP GIFT VOUCHER £100.00	0	018...	22016	DOTCOMGIFTSHOP GIFT VOUCHER £100.00
2	GIFT_0001_10	DOTCOMGIFTSHOP GIFT VOUCHER £10.00	0	070...	GIFT_0001_10	DOTCOMGIFTSHOP GIFT VOUCHER £10.00
3	22206	MUG ,DOTCOMGIFTSHOP.COM	0	3af...	22206	MUG ,DOTCOMGIFTSHOP.COM
4	23001	TRAVEL CARD WALLET DOTCOMGIFTSHOP	0	53b...	23001	TRAVEL CARD WALLET DOTCOMGIFTSHOP
5	GIFT_0001_20	DOTCOMGIFTSHOP GIFT VOUCHER £20.00	0	70b...	GIFT_0001_20	DOTCOMGIFTSHOP GIFT VOUCHER £20.00
6	GIFT_0001_20	DOTCOMGIFTSHOP GIFT VOUCHER £20.00	0	70b...	GIFT_0001_20	TO PUSH ORDER THROUGHA S STOCK WAS
7	GIFT_0001_30	DOTCOMGIFTSHOP GIFT VOUCHER £30.00	0	73b...	GIFT_0001_30	DOTCOMGIFTSHOP GIFT VOUCHER £30.00
8	22351	DOTCOMGIFTSHOP TEA TOWEL	0	84c...	22351	DOTCOMGIFTSHOP TEA TOWEL
9	22351	DOTCOMGIFTSHOP TEA TOWEL	0	84c...	22351	GIVEN AWAY
10	GIFT_0001_50	DOTCOMGIFTSHOP GIFT VOUCHER £50.00	0	9ea...	GIFT_0001_50	DOTCOMGIFTSHOP GIFT VOUCHER £50.00
11	GIFT_0001_40	DOTCOMGIFTSHOP GIFT VOUCHER £40.00	0	a27...	GIFT_0001_40	DOTCOMGIFTSHOP GIFT VOUCHER £40.00

This step looks back at the right side of our previous data sets for additional descriptions we can filter out, progressively adding more until we've added all the non-product descriptions we can find. This is a laborious process, but by the end, we will have a better understanding of the types of non-conformances we see in the data than anyone else.

```
CTE_FILTER_BUS_SKU AS (
  SELECT
    stock_code
    ,description
    ,CASE WHEN
    stock_code LIKE 'S'
    OR stock_code LIKE 'POST'
    OR stock_code LIKE 'PADS'
    OR stock_code LIKE 'M'
    --OR stock_code LIKE 'GIFT_0001_%'
    OR (stock_code LIKE 'GIFT_0001_%' AND description LIKE 'DOTCOMGIFTSHOP%')
    OR stock_code LIKE 'DOT'
    OR stock_code LIKE 'D'
    OR stock_code LIKE 'CRUK'
    OR stock_code LIKE 'C2'
    OR stock_code LIKE 'BANK CHARGES'
    OR stock_code LIKE 'B'
    OR stock_code LIKE 'AMAZONFEE'
    OR stock_code LIKE '23574' --PACKING CHARGE
    OR stock_code LIKE '23444'
    THEN 0 ELSE 1 END AS invalid_description_flag
  FROM CTE_BASE
  WHERE invalid_description_flag = 0
)
--,
SELECT * FROM CTE_FILTER_BUS_SKU
```

	stock_code	description	invalid_description_flag
1	S	SAMPLES	0
2	GIFT_0001_10	DOTCOMGIFTSHOP GIFT VOUCHER £10.00	0
3	23444	NEXT DAY CARRIAGE	0
4	BANK CHARGES	BANK CHARGES	0
5	DOT	DOTCOM POSTAGE	0

The benefit of this attention to detail is that we are laying the groundwork to enable future analysis. These non-conformances represent reductions in our ability to deliver the right product, at the right time, to the right place. At this moment, we are concerned with filtering these issues out from the descriptions. In the future, we may leverage this analysis to determine whether we are delivering On Time and In Full.

TIP: Try changing the WHERE clause and look for text in the description field on the left side of the query (e.g. WHERE invalid_description_flag = 0). As we get closer to filtering out the bad data, searching through the base set will be more efficient. However, don't forget to change the filter back.

```
CTE_FILTER_DEFECTS AS (
  SELECT
    stock_code
    ,description
    ,CASE WHEN
    description LIKE '%WET%'
    OR description LIKE '%GIVEN AWAY%'
    OR description LIKE 'CHECK'
    OR description LIKE '%DAMAGE%'
    ...
    OR description LIKE '%CREDIT%'
    OR description LIKE '%TEMP FIX%'
    OR description LIKE '%MARKED AS%'
    THEN 1 ELSE 0 END AS invalid_description_flag
  FROM CTE_BASE
  WHERE invalid_description_flag = 1
  ORDER BY 2 DESC
)
,
-- SELECT *
-- FROM CTE_FILTER_DEFECTS A
-- INNER JOIN CTE_BASE B
-- ON (A.stock_code = B.stock_code)
```

179	20681	PINK POLKADOT CHILDRENS ...	0	20681	MIA
180	20681	PINK POLKADOT CHILDRENS ...	0	20681	PINK POLKADOT CHILDRENS UMBRELLA
181	20681	MIA	0	20681	MIA
182	20681	MIA	0	20681	PINK POLKADOT CHILDRENS UMBRELLA
183	20682	RED RETROSPOT CHILDRENS ...	0	20682	RED RETROSPOT CHILDRENS UMBRELLA
184	20684	STRAWBERRY DREAM CHILDS ...	0	20684	STRAWBERRY DREAM CHILDS UMBRELLA

The next step in preparing the data is to union all the stock codes with invalid descriptions together and to then check for duplicate stock_codes. They indicate we need to refine the descriptions further.

```
CTE_UNION_INVALID_DESC AS (
  SELECT * FROM CTE_FILTER_BUS_SKU
      UNION
  SELECT * FROM CTE_FILTER_DOTCOM
      UNION
  SELECT * FROM CTE_FILTER_AMAZON
      UNION
  SELECT * FROM CTE_FILTER_GIFTSHOP
      UNION
  SELECT * FROM CTE_FILTER_EBAY
      UNION
  SELECT * FROM CTE_FILTER_DEFECTS
)
,
```

Joining the combined data sets with the original base table validates our ability to identify the primary description for each stock_code in the base data set.

```
SELECT
A.stock_code
,A.description AS description
,B.description AS description2
,B.invalid_description_flag
FROM CTE_BASE A
LEFT JOIN CTE_UNION_INVALID_DESC B
    ON (
    A.stock_code = B.stock_code AND
    A.description = B.description
    );
```

	stock_code	description	description2	invalid_description_flag
1	10002	INFLATABLE POLITICAL GLOBE	<NULL>	<NULL>
2	10080	GROOVY CACTUS INFLATABLE	<NULL>	<NULL>
3	10080	CHECK	CHECK	1
4	10120	DOGGY RUBBER	<NULL>	<NULL>

However, there are still stock codes with multiple names. We'll decide to keep the longest name for now, under the assumption that it is more descriptive. At the same time, we will add back in the stock codes for the non-products.

	stock_code	description	invalid_description_flag
2144	23196	VINTAGE LEAF MAGNETIC NOTEPAD	0
2145	23196	RETRO LEAVES MAGNETIC NOTEPAD	0
2146	23196	RETO LEAVES MAGNETIC SHOPPING LIST	0
2147	23196	LEAVES MAGNETIC SHOPPING LIST	0
2148	23197	VEGETABLE MAGNETIC SHOPPING LIST	0
2149	23197	SKETCHBOOK MAGNETIC SHOPPING LIST	0

The next step is to combine the new descriptions with the list of all stock codes. If a code does not have a description, use the stock_code.

```
CTE_SINGLE_DESCRIPTION AS (
  SELECT
    stock_code
    ,description
  FROM (
    SELECT
      ROW_NUMBER() OVER (PARTITION BY
      stock_code
      ORDER BY
      LENGTH(description) DESC
      ) AS row_number
      ,stock_code
      ,description
    FROM (
      SELECT
        A.stock_code AS stock_code
        ,A.description AS description
        -- ,B.description AS description2
        -- ,B.invalid_description_flag
      FROM CTE_BASE A
      LEFT JOIN CTE_UNION_INVALID_DESC B
        ON (
        A.stock_code = B.stock_code AND
        A.description = B.description
        )
      WHERE B.invalid_description_flag IS NULL
    UNION
      SELECT
        stock_code
        ,description
      FROM CTE_UNION_INVALID_DESC
      WHERE invalid_description_flag = 0
    ) A
  ) B
  WHERE row_number = 1
  ORDER BY 1 DESC
)
--,
SELECT * FROM CTE_SINGLE_DESCRIPTION;
```

We are almost there! This next CTE derives a single description for each stock code.

```
CTE_DESC_ALL_SKUS AS (
  SELECT DISTINCT
    A.stock_code
    --,B.stock_code
    ,COALESCE(B.description, A.stock_code) AS description
  FROM CTE_BASE A
  LEFT JOIN CTE_SINGLE_DESCRIPTION B
  ON (A.stock_code = B.stock_code)
)
--,
SELECT * FROM CTE_DESC_ALL_SKUS;
```

	stock_code	description
1	90132	LIGHT TOPAZ TEAL/AQUA COL NECKLACE
2	22336	DOVE DECORATION PAINTED ZINC
3	22344	PARTY PIZZA DISH PINK POLKADOT
4	22902	TOTE BAG I LOVE LONDON
5	85135A	YELLOW DRAGONFLY HELICOPTER
6	21945	STRAWBERRIES DESIGN FLANNEL
7	20997	ROSE DU SUD CUSHION COVER

This small CTE assigns our earliest load timestamp to the stock code. This will then be joined into the main data set to align the load dates of the description to the stock code.

```
CTE_SKU_LOAD_DTS AS (
  SELECT DISTINCT
    stock_code
    ,MIN(load_dts) AS load_dts
  FROM SAT_ONLINE_RETAIL_II_YEAR_2010_2011_001
  GROUP BY stock_code
)
```

The target CTE joins everything together to be inserted into the table.

```
CTE_TARGET AS (
  SELECT
    SHA1(UPPER(TRIM(COALESCE(A.stock_code, '')))) AS stock_code_hkey
    ,'sales/etc/sql/BLNK_STOCK_CODE_PREFERRED_DESCRIPTION_001_load.sql' AS provider_code
    ,load_dts
    ,A.description AS preferred_description
  FROM CTE_DESC_ALL_SKUS A
  INNER JOIN CTE_SKU_LOAD_DTS B
  ON (A.stock_code = B.stock_code)
)
```

stock_code_hkey	provider _code	load_dts	preferred_description
00050f32305a575e95847a97c029ad9e934cce7b	sales/etc/sql/...	2021-05-11T17:11:2...	LIGHT TOPAZ TEAL/AQUA COL NECKLAC
00201cc17c6d38a221744603ce75c9624c77c64d	sales/etc/sql/...	2021-05-11T17:11:2...	DOVE DECORATION PAINTED ZINC
0055f6812c66283b3beedeafb1fac2f8a0468b23	sales/etc/sql/...	2021-05-11T17:11:2...	PARTY PIZZA DISH PINK POLKADOT
007343b9ccd9b031604915a07254101b92d14073	sales/etc/sql/...	2021-05-11T17:11:2...	TOTE BAG I LOVE LONDON
0073d0eb4fc430384b23466a110f524b453c4aee	sales/etc/sql/...	2021-05-11T17:11:2...	YELLOW DRAGONFLY HELICOPTER
007c8709462677fdc8e7ed5da878bb49aaf9e108	sales/etc/sql/...	2021-05-11T17:11:2...	STRAWBERRIES DESIGN FLANNEL
008de3806159187d76c997d147226c998d52f9d2	sales/etc/sql/...	2021-05-11T17:11:2...	ROSE DU SUD CUSHION COVER

```
INSERT INTO BLNK_STOCK_CODE_PREFERRED_DESCRIPTION_001 (
  stock_code_hkey
  ,provider_code
  ,load_dts
  ,insert_dts
  ,preferred_description
)
SELECT
  stock_code_hkey
  ,provider_code
  ,load_dts
  ,strftime('%Y-%m-%dT%H:%M:%fZ', 'now') AS insert_dts
  ,preferred_description
FROM CTE_TARGET;
```

The automation follows the usual pattern.

```
# BLNK_STOCK_CODE_PREFERRED_DESCRIPTION_001 ----
.PHONY: load/BLNK_STOCK_CODE_PREFERRED_DESCRIPTION_001
etc/sql/BLNK_STOCK_CODE_PREFERRED_DESCRIPTION_001_load.sql:
	@$(test_file)

load/BLNK_STOCK_CODE_PREFERRED_DESCRIPTION_001: \
	etc/sql/BLNK_STOCK_CODE_PREFERRED_DESCRIPTION_001_load.sql \
	SAT_ONLINE_RETAIL_II_YEAR_2010_2011_001 \
	BLNK_STOCK_CODE_PREFERRED_DESCRIPTION_001 \
	load/SAT_ONLINE_RETAIL_II_YEAR_2010_2011_001
	@$(execute_sql)

metrics/BLNK_STOCK_CODE_PREFERRED_DESCRIPTION_001: \
	BLNK_STOCK_CODE_PREFERRED_DESCRIPTION_001
	@$(record_count_table)
```

```
test/tables: \
  test_table/SRC_online_retail_II_-_Year_2010-2011_001 \
  test_table/RAW_ONLINE_RETAIL_II_YEAR_2010_2011_001 \
  test_table/INFO_SALES_LAST_6_MONTHS_FILTERED_001 \
  test_table/INFO_WEEKLY_TOP_SALES_RANK_001 \
  test_table/SRC_online_retail_II_-_Year_2010-2011_002 \
  test_table/SAT_ONLINE_RETAIL_II_YEAR_2010_2011_001 \
  test_table/BSAT_INVOICES_001 \
  test_table/BLNK_STOCK_CODE_PREFERRED_DESCRIPTION_001

# BLNK_STOCK_CODE_PREFERRED_DESCRIPTION_001 ----
test_table/BLNK_STOCK_CODE_PREFERRED_DESCRIPTION_001: \
  BLNK_STOCK_CODE_PREFERRED_DESCRIPTION_001
  @$(test_table)

etc/sql/BLNK_STOCK_CODE_PREFERRED_DESCRIPTION_001_create.sql:
  @$(test_file)

BLNK_STOCK_CODE_PREFERRED_DESCRIPTION_001: \
  etc/sql/BLNK_STOCK_CODE_PREFERRED_DESCRIPTION_001_create.sql
  @$(create_table)
```

Executing make builds and populates the table.

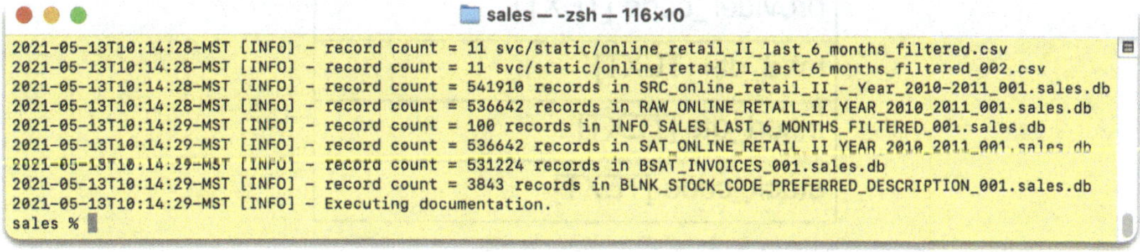

```
2021-05-13T10:14:28-MST [INFO] - record count = 11 svc/static/online_retail_II_last_6_months_filtered.csv
2021-05-13T10:14:28-MST [INFO] - record count = 11 svc/static/online_retail_II_last_6_months_filtered_002.csv
2021-05-13T10:14:28-MST [INFO] - record count = 541910 records in SRC_online_retail_II_-_Year_2010-2011_001.sales.db
2021-05-13T10:14:28-MST [INFO] - record count = 536642 records in RAW_ONLINE_RETAIL_II_YEAR_2010_2011_001.sales.db
2021-05-13T10:14:29-MST [INFO] - record count = 100 records in INFO_SALES_LAST_6_MONTHS_FILTERED_001.sales.db
2021-05-13T10:14:29-MST [INFO] - record count = 536642 records in SAT_ONLINE_RETAIL_II_YEAR_2010_2011_001.sales.db
2021-05-13T10:14:29-MST [INFO] - record count = 531224 records in BSAT_INVOICES_001.sales.db
2021-05-13T10:14:29-MST [INFO] - record count = 3843 records in BLNK_STOCK_CODE_PREFERRED_DESCRIPTION_001.sales.db
2021-05-13T10:14:29-MST [INFO] - Executing documentation.
sales %
```

Calculating the preferred description involved many steps and it takes a significant amount of time to complete (3-6 minutes). In the Exploration phase, this may be acceptable. In the future we may need to invest time refactoring this query to increase performance. Fortunately, we are materializing the results and the end users will not be exposed to any delays.

There are a number of things we can do to improve the performance. The place to start is by identify and optimize the longest running part of the query. Learning how to use the the query planner explain function will be critical as performance tuning becomes more important.

Creating our First Business HUB Table (Stock Codes)

Every organization has a set of core data entities that are critical to how they operate. For a wholesaler, these are stock codes, invoices, vendors. For a hospital, they are patients, providers, procedures, insurers. Every business type will have its own set, and these may change over time as the data analysis needs change.

In the Data Vault methodology, we use the Hub tables to store a distinct list of each of the core entities. One of the benefits of these tables is that by looking at the Hub tables alone, you can quickly determine the scope of the entire database.

We will start by creating stock code and invoice code Hubs. From these two tables alone, a user will know we have the interesting invoice and product data. While we may have fields for customer and country, by intentionally delaying exposing this data, we can help to set the expectation we are committing to standing behind this data.

BHUB_STOCK_CODES_001
stock_code_hkey [TEXT]
provider_code [TEXT]
load_dts [TEXT]
insert_dts [TEXT]
stock_code [TEXT]

By now the data pipeline development process and flow should be straight forward. See if you can comfortably follow the code without any additional discussion.

BHUB_STOCK_CODES_001_create.sql

```
-- sales/etc/sql/BHUB_STOCK_CODES_001_create.sql
------------------------------------------------------------
CREATE TABLE IF NOT EXISTS BHUB_STOCK_CODES_001 (
stock_code_hkey TEXT
,provider_code TEXT
,load_dts TEXT
,insert_dts TEXT
,stock_code TEXT
,PRIMARY KEY (stock_code_hkey)
);
```

BHUB_STOCK_CODES_001_load.sql

```
-- sales/etc/sql/BHUB_STOCK_CODES_001_load.sql
------------------------------------------------------------

DELETE FROM BHUB_STOCK_CODES_001;

WITH CTE_BASE AS (
SELECT DISTINCT
SHA1(UPPER(TRIM(COALESCE(A.stock_code, '')))) AS stock_code_hkey
,provider_code
,load_dts
,UPPER(TRIM(COALESCE(A.stock_code, ''))) AS stock_code
FROM SAT_ONLINE_RETAIL_II_YEAR_2010_2011_001 A
ORDER BY 4 ASC
)

INSERT INTO BHUB_STOCK_CODES_001 (
stock_code_hkey
,provider_code
,load_dts
,insert_dts
,stock_code
)
SELECT
stock_code_hkey
,provider_code
,load_dts
,strftime('%Y-%m-%dT%H:%M:%fZ', 'now') AS insert_dts
,stock_code
FROM CTE_BASE;
```

Makefile (Database and table tests)

```
transform: \
  svc/static/online_retail_II_last_6_months_filtered.csv \
  svc/static/online_retail_II_last_6_months_filtered_002.csv \
  clean/SRC_online_retail_II_-_Year_2010-2011_002 \
  load/BSAT_INVOICES_001 \
  load/BLNK_STOCK_CODE_PREFERRED_DESCRIPTION_001 \
  load/BHUB_STOCK_CODES_001 \

# BHUB_STOCK_CODES_001 ----
.PHONY: etc/sql/BHUB_STOCK_CODES_001_load.sql
etc/sql/BHUB_STOCK_CODES_001_load.sql:
  @$(test_file)

load/BHUB_STOCK_CODES_001: \
  etc/sql/BHUB_STOCK_CODES_001_load.sql \
  SAT_ONLINE_RETAIL_II_YEAR_2010_2011_001 \
  BHUB_STOCK_CODES_001 \
  load/SAT_ONLINE_RETAIL_II_YEAR_2010_2011_001
  @$(execute_sql)

metrics/BHUB_STOCK_CODES_001: \
  BHUB_STOCK_CODES_001
  @$(record_count_table)
```

Makefile (Transforms)

```
transform: \
  svc/static/online_retail_II_last_6_months_filtered.csv \
  svc/static/online_retail_II_last_6_months_filtered_002.csv \
  clean/SRC_online_retail_II_-_Year_2010-2011_002 \
  load/BSAT_INVOICES_001 \
  load/BLNK_STOCK_CODE_PREFERRED_DESCRIPTION_001 \
  load/BHUB_STOCK_CODES_001

# BHUB_STOCK_CODES_001 ----
.PHONY: load/BHUB_STOCK_CODES_001
etc/sql/BHUB_STOCK_CODES_001_load.sql:
  @$(test_file)

load/BHUB_STOCK_CODES_001: \
  etc/sql/BHUB_STOCK_CODES_001_load.sql \
  SAT_ONLINE_RETAIL_II_YEAR_2010_2011_001 \
  load/SAT_ONLINE_RETAIL_II_YEAR_2010_2011_001
  @$(execute_sql)

metrics/BHUB_STOCK_CODES_001: \
  BHUB_STOCK_CODES_001
  @$(record_count_table)
```

Makefile (Metrics)

```
metrics: \
  metrics/online_retail_II_last_6_months_filtered.csv \
  metrics/online_retail_II_last_6_months_filtered_002.csv \
  metrics/SRC_online_retail_II_-_Year_2010-2011_001 \
  metrics/RAW_ONLINE_RETAIL_II_YEAR_2010_2011_001 \
  metrics/INFO_SALES_LAST_6_MONTHS_FILTERED_001 \
  metrics/SAT_ONLINE_RETAIL_II_YEAR_2010_2011_001 \
  metrics/BSAT_INVOICES_001 \
  metrics/BLNK_STOCK_CODE_PREFERRED_DESCRIPTION_001 \
  metrics/BHUB_STOCK_CODES_001
```

sales — -zsh — 116×11

```
2021-05-13T11:52:13-MST [INFO] - record count = 11 svc/static/online_retail_II_last_6_months_filtered.csv
2021-05-13T11:52:13-MST [INFO] - record count = 11 svc/static/online_retail_II_last_6_months_filtered_002.csv
2021-05-13T11:52:13-MST [INFO] - record count = 541910 records in SRC_online_retail_II_-_Year_2010-2011_001.sales.db
2021-05-13T11:52:13-MST [INFO] - record count = 536642 records in RAW_ONLINE_RETAIL_II_YEAR_2010_2011_001.sales.db
2021-05-13T11:52:13-MST [INFO] - record count = 100 records in INFO_SALES_LAST_6_MONTHS_FILTERED_001.sales.db
2021-05-13T11:52:13-MST [INFO] - record count = 536642 records in SAT_ONLINE_RETAIL_II_YEAR_2010_2011_001.sales.db
2021-05-13T11:52:14-MST [INFO] - record count = 531224 records in BSAT_INVOICES_001.sales.db
2021-05-13T11:52:14-MST [INFO] - record count = 3843 records in BLNK_STOCK_CODE_PREFERRED_DESCRIPTION_001.sales.db
2021-05-13T11:52:14-MST [INFO] - record count = 3958 records in BHUB_STOCK_CODES_001.sales.db
2021-05-13T11:52:14-MST [INFO] - Executing documentation.
sales %
```

BHUB_INVOICE_CODES_001_create.sql

```
-- sales/etc/sql/BHUB_INVOICE_CODES_001_create.sql
----------------------------------------------------------

CREATE TABLE IF NOT EXISTS BHUB_INVOICE_CODES_001 (
invoice_code_hkey TEXT
,provider_code TEXT
,load_dts TEXT
,insert_dts TEXT
,invoice_code TEXT
,PRIMARY KEY (invoice_code_hkey)
);
```

BHUB_INVOICE_CODES_001_load.sql

```sql
-- sales/etc/sql/BHUB_INVOICE_CODES_001_load.sql
---------------------------------------------------------------

DELETE FROM BHUB_INVOICE_CODES_001;

WITH CTE_BASE AS (
SELECT DISTINCT
invoice_code_hkey
,provider_code
,load_dts
,CASE WHEN UPPER(TRIM(COALESCE(A.invoice, ''))) LIKE 'C%'
  THEN REPLACE(invoice, 'C', '')
  ELSE UPPER(TRIM(COALESCE(A.invoice, '')))
  END AS invoice_code
FROM SAT_ONLINE_RETAIL_II_YEAR_2010_2011_001 A
ORDER BY 4 ASC
)

INSERT INTO BHUB_INVOICE_CODES_001 (
invoice_code_hkey
,provider_code
,load_dts
,insert_dts
,invoice_code
)
SELECT
invoice_code_hkey
,provider_code
,load_dts
,strftime('%Y-%m-%dT%H:%M:%fZ', 'now') AS insert_dts
,invoice_code
FROM CTE_BASE;
```

Makefile (Database and table tests)

```
transform: \
  svc/static/online_retail_II_last_6_months_filtered.csv \
  svc/static/online_retail_II_last_6_months_filtered_002.csv \
  clean/SRC_online_retail_II_-_Year_2010-2011_002 \
  load/BSAT_INVOICES_001 \
  load/BLNK_STOCK_CODE_PREFERRED_DESCRIPTION_001 \
  load/BHUB_STOCK_CODES_001 \
  load/BHUB_INVOICE_CODES_001

# BHUB_INVOICE_CODES_001 ----
.PHONY: load/BHUB_INVOICE_CODES_001
etc/sql/BHUB_INVOICE_CODES_001_load.sql:
  @$(test_file)

load/BHUB_INVOICE_CODES_001: \
  etc/sql/BHUB_INVOICE_CODES_001_load.sql \
  SAT_ONLINE_RETAIL_II_YEAR_2010_2011_001 \
  BHUB_INVOICE_CODES_001 \
  load/SAT_ONLINE_RETAIL_II_YEAR_2010_2011_001
  @$(execute_sql)

metrics/BHUB_INVOICE_CODES_001: \
  BHUB_INVOICE_CODES_001
  @$(record_count_table)
```

Makefile (Transforms)

```
transform: \
  svc/static/online_retail_II_last_6_months_filtered.csv \
  svc/static/online_retail_II_last_6_months_filtered_002.csv \
  clean/SRC_online_retail_II_-_Year_2010-2011_002 \
  load/BSAT_INVOICES_001 \
  load/BLNK_STOCK_CODE_PREFERRED_DESCRIPTION_001 \
  load/BHUB_STOCK_CODES_001 \
  load/BHUB_INVOICE_CODES_001

# BHUB_INVOICE_CODES_001 ----
.PHONY: load/BHUB_INVOICE_CODES_001
etc/sql/BHUB_INVOICE_CODES_001_load.sql:
  @$(test_file)

load/BHUB_INVOICE_CODES_001: \
  etc/sql/BHUB_INVOICE_CODES_001_load.sql \
  SAT_ONLINE_RETAIL_II_YEAR_2010_2011_001 \
  load/SAT_ONLINE_RETAIL_II_YEAR_2010_2011_001
  @$(execute_sql)

metrics/BHUB_INVOICE_CODES_001: \
  BHUB_INVOICE_CODES_001
  @$(record_count_table)
```

Makefile (Metrics)

```
metrics: \
  metrics/online_retail_II_last_6_months_filtered.csv \
  metrics/online_retail_II_last_6_months_filtered_002.csv \
  metrics/SRC_online_retail_II_-_Year_2010-2011_001 \
  metrics/RAW_ONLINE_RETAIL_II_YEAR_2010_2011_001 \
  metrics/INFO_SALES_LAST_6_MONTHS_FILTERED_001 \
  metrics/SAT_ONLINE_RETAIL_II_YEAR_2010_2011_001 \
  metrics/BSAT_INVOICES_001 \
  metrics/BLNK_STOCK_CODE_PREFERRED_DESCRIPTION_001 \
  metrics/BHUB_STOCK_CODES_001 \
  metrics/BHUB_INVOICE_CODES_001
```

sales — -zsh — 116×12

```
2021-05-13T12:21:10-MST [INFO] - record count = 11 svc/static/online_retail_II_last_6_months_filtered.csv
2021-05-13T12:21:10-MST [INFO] - record count = 11 svc/static/online_retail_II_last_6_months_filtered_002.csv
2021-05-13T12:21:10-MST [INFO] - record count = 541910 records in SRC_online_retail_II_-_Year_2010-2011_001.sales.db
2021-05-13T12:21:10-MST [INFO] - record count = 536642 records in RAW_ONLINE_RETAIL_II_YEAR_2010_2011_001.sales.db
2021-05-13T12:21:10-MST [INFO] - record count = 100 records in INFO_SALES_LAST_6_MONTHS_FILTERED_001.sales.db
2021-05-13T12:21:10-MST [INFO] - record count = 536642 records in SAT_ONLINE_RETAIL_II_YEAR_2010_2011_001.sales.db
2021-05-13T12:21:10-MST [INFO] - record count = 531224 records in BSAT_INVOICES_001.sales.db
2021-05-13T12:21:10-MST [INFO] - record count = 3843 records in BLNK_STOCK_CODE_PREFERRED_DESCRIPTION_001.sales.db
2021-05-13T12:21:10-MST [INFO] - record count = 3958 records in BHUB_STOCK_CODES_001.sales.db
2021-05-13T12:21:10-MST [INFO] - record count = 25900 records in BHUB_INVOICE_CODES_001.sales.db
2021-05-13T12:21:10-MST [INFO] - Executing documentation.
sales %
```

Questions to ask yourself:

- What are the dependencies of the load/ targets?
- What task seems to take the longest?
- What happens if I run `make uninstall && make`?
- What does the directory structure look like now?
- Is it possible to identify and follow the flow in the `makefile_graph.png` file?

Refactoring INFO_WEEKLY_TOP_SALES_RANK

Now that we have a better data set at our disposal, we can reimplement the Vega-Lite reports. The place to start is to refamiliarize ourselves with the current reporting flow.

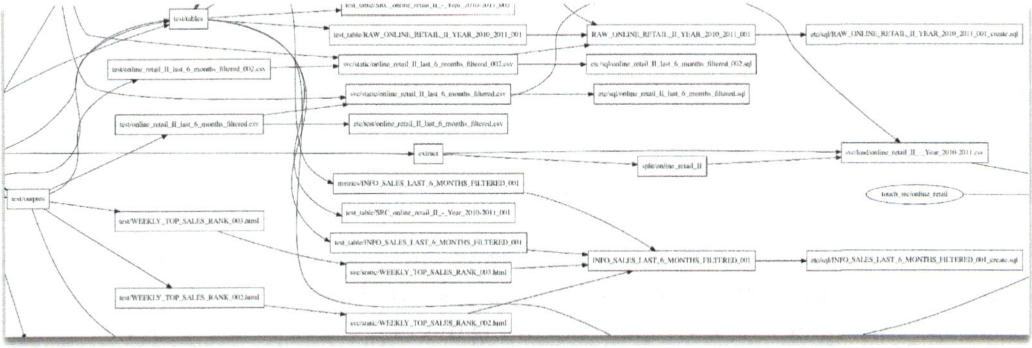

Unfortunately, our nice diagram isn't so useful anymore. Ideally, we would have the ability to isolate the flows into and out of a specific node. This could be something to add to the backlog as a supportability enhancement.

The easier alternative is to manually follow the makefile dependencies back to the view we used to generate our dynamic API call. We should start there because it was the report which took the longest to generate, and it did not require the creation of an external file. Hopefully, we will see a dramatic improvement in the rendering time of the report.

```
# ---- Tests outputs ----
test/outputs: \
  test/online_retail_II_last_6_months_filtered.csv \
  test/online_retail_II_last_6_months_filtered_002.csv \
  test/WEEKLY_TOP_SALES_RANK_001.html \
  test/WEEKLY_TOP_SALES_RANK_002.html \
  test/WEEKLY_TOP_SALES_RANK_003.html
```

The `svc/static/WEEKLY_TOP_SALES_RANK_002.html` file is our final output.

```
761 svc/static/WEEKLY_TOP_SALES_RANK_002.html: VIZTITLE="Weekly Top Sales Rank - JSON API call"
762 svc/static/WEEKLY_TOP_SALES_RANK_002.html: VIZTEMPLATE=etc/app/WEEKLY_TOP_SALES_RANK_001.vega
763 svc/static/WEEKLY_TOP_SALES_RANK_002.html: VIZURL="/sales/INFO_WEEKLY_TOP_SALES_RANK_001.json?_shape=array"
764 svc/static/WEEKLY_TOP_SALES_RANK_002.html: INFO_SALES_LAST_6_MONTHS_FILTERED_001
765   @#<path/to/export_file.html>(colon)(space)VIZTITLE=<report title>
766   @#<path/to/export_file.html>(colon)(space)VIZTEMPLATE=<path/to/viz_template.vega>
767   @#<path/to/export_file.html>(colon)(space)VIZURL=<path/to/viz_url.json?_shape=array>
768   @#<path/to/export_file.html>(colon)(space)<source_table_template_name>
769   @echo $(DTS)      [INFO] - Executing $@
770   @cat etc/app/vega_embed_header.viz > $@
771   @echo "\"data\":{\"url\":\"$(VIZURL)\"}, " >> $@
772   @echo "\"title\":\"$(VIZTITLE)\"," >> $@
773   @cat $(VIZTEMPLATE) >> $@
774   @cat etc/app/vega_embed_footer.viz >> $@
```

The `sales/INFO_WEEKLY_TOP_SALES_RANK_001.json` (line 763) refers to the target generating our data. In this case, it is a portion of the URL generating the JSON document we reference in the report. Following this dependency back leads to `INFO_SALES_LAST_6_MONTHS_FILTERED_001_create.sql`

```
# INFO_SALES_LAST_6_MONTHS_FILTERED_001 ----
test_table/INFO_SALES_LAST_6_MONTHS_FILTERED_001: \
  INFO_SALES_LAST_6_MONTHS_FILTERED_001
  @$(test_table)

etc/sql/INFO_SALES_LAST_6_MONTHS_FILTERED_001_create.sql:
  @$(test_file)

INFO_SALES_LAST_6_MONTHS_FILTERED_001: \
  etc/sql/INFO_SALES_LAST_6_MONTHS_FILTERED_001_create.sql
  @$(create_table)
```

What we want to do is create a new table, mirroring the `INFO_WEEKLY_TOP_SALES_RANK_001` view but built from the new business tables.

Here is the key portion of the original query:

```
--etc/sql/INFO_WEEKLY_TOP_SALES_RANK_001_create.sql
-----------------------------------------------------------
CREATE VIEW IF NOT EXISTS INFO_WEEKLY_TOP_SALES_RANK_001 AS

WITH CTE_BASE AS (
  SELECT DISTINCT
  provider_code,
  load_dts,
  --invoice as raw_invoice,
  REPLACE(invoice, 'C', '') AS invoice,
  stock_code,
  description,
  invoice_date,
  quantity,
  price,
  customer_id,
  country
  FROM RAW_ONLINE_RETAIL_II_YEAR_2010_2011_001
  WHERE
      invoice_date >= (
          SELECT DATE(MAX(invoice_date), '-6 months', 'localtime')
          FROM RAW_ONLINE_RETAIL_II_YEAR_2010_2011_001
          ) AND
      UPPER(description) NOT LIKE '%MANUAL%' AND
      UPPER(description) NOT LIKE '%POSTAGE%'
)
```

The code to reimplement the `INFO_WEEKLY_TOP_SALES_RANK_002` data set requires a few minimal changes for the base CTE to generate a similar data set.

```
      ,A.quantity
      ,A.price
  FROM BSAT_INVOICES_001 A
  LEFT JOIN BLNK_STOCK_CODE_PREFERRED_DESCRIPTION_001 B
  ON (A.stock_code_hkey = B.stock_code_hkey)
  WHERE
    invoice_date >= (
      SELECT DATE(MAX(invoice_date), '-6 months', 'localtime')
      FROM BSAT_INVOICES_001) AND
      UPPER(B.preferred_description) NOT LIKE '%MANUAL%' AND
      UPPER(B.preferred_description) NOT LIKE '%POSTAGE%'
    )
```

Another change is that we are populating a table rather than a view. By creating a table, we should see a significant reduction in the time to load the data set into the visualization template. This should perform fast enough to allow us to remove the old embedded and extract-based reports we created earlier. This requires the original SELECT query be changed to an INSERT statement and, of course, we need to create the code and automation to populate the new table.

```
INSERT INTO INFO_WEEKLY_TOP_SALES_RANK_002 (
  end_of_week_ssmtwtf
  ,rank
  ,stock_code
  ,preferred_description
  ,quantity
  ,avg_price
  ,total_sales_revenue
)

SELECT
    end_of_week_ssmtwtf,
    rank,
    stock_code,
    preferred_description,
    quantity,
    ROUND(avg_price, 2) AS avg_price,
    total_sales_revenue
FROM CTE_WEEKLY_TOP_SALES_RANK
WHERE rank <= 10
ORDER BY 1,2;
```

INFO_WEEKLY_TOP_SALES_RANK_002_create.sql

```
--etc/sql/INFO_WEEKLY_TOP_SALES_RANK_002_create.sql
------------------------------------------------------------
CREATE TABLE IF NOT EXISTS INFO_WEEKLY_TOP_SALES_RANK_002 (
end_of_week_ssmtwtf TEXT
,rank NUMERIC
,stock_code TEXT
,preferred_description TEXT
,quantity NUMERIC
,avg_price NUMERIC
,total_sales_revenue NUMERIC
);
```

Makefile (Database and table tests)

```
# INFO_WEEKLY_TOP_SALES_RANK_002_create.sql ----
test_table/INFO_WEEKLY_TOP_SALES_RANK_002: \
  INFO_WEEKLY_TOP_SALES_RANK_002
  @$(test_table)

etc/sql/INFO_WEEKLY_TOP_SALES_RANK_002_create.sql:
  @$(test_file)

INFO_WEEKLY_TOP_SALES_RANK_002: \
  etc/sql/INFO_WEEKLY_TOP_SALES_RANK_002_create.sql
  @$(create_table)
```

Makefile (Transforms)

```
# INFO_WEEKLY_TOP_SALES_RANK_002 ----
.PHONY: load/INFO_WEEKLY_TOP_SALES_RANK_002
etc/sql/INFO_WEEKLY_TOP_SALES_RANK_002_load.sql:
  @$(test_file)

load/INFO_WEEKLY_TOP_SALES_RANK_002: \
  etc/sql/INFO_WEEKLY_TOP_SALES_RANK_002_load.sql \
  INFO_WEEKLY_TOP_SALES_RANK_002 \
  load/BSAT_INVOICES_001 \
  load/BLNK_STOCK_CODE_PREFERRED_DESCRIPTION_001
  @$(execute_sql)

metrics/INFO_WEEKLY_TOP_SALES_RANK_002: \
  INFO_WEEKLY_TOP_SALES_RANK_002
  @$(record_count_table)
```

sales — -zsh — 116×13

```
2021-05-13T15:16:35-MST [INFO] - record count = 11 svc/static/online_retail_II_last_6_months_filtered.csv
2021-05-13T15:16:35-MST [INFO] - record count = 11 svc/static/online_retail_II_last_6_months_filtered_002.csv
2021-05-13T15:16:35-MST [INFO] - record count = 541910 records in SRC_online_retail_II_-_Year_2010-2011_001.sales.db
2021-05-13T15:16:35-MST [INFO] - record count = 536642 records in RAW_ONLINE_RETAIL_II_YEAR_2010_2011_001.sales.db
2021-05-13T15:16:35-MST [INFO] - record count = 100 records in INFO_SALES_LAST_6_MONTHS_FILTERED_001.sales.db
2021-05-13T15:16:35-MST [INFO] - record count = 536642 records in SAT_ONLINE_RETAIL_II_YEAR_2010_2011_001.sales.db
2021-05-13T15:16:35-MST [INFO] - record count = 531224 records in BSAT_INVOICES_001.sales.db
2021-05-13T15:16:35-MST [INFO] - record count = 3843 records in BLNK_STOCK_CODE_PREFERRED_DESCRIPTION_001.sales.db
2021-05-13T15:16:35-MST [INFO] - record count = 3958 records in BHUB_STOCK_CODES_001.sales.db
2021-05-13T15:16:35-MST [INFO] - record count = 25900 records in BHUB_INVOICE_CODES_001.sales.db
2021-05-13T15:16:35-MST [INFO] - record count = 270 records in INFO_WEEKLY_TOP_SALES_RANK_002.sales.db
2021-05-13T15:16:35-MST [INFO] - Executing documentation.
sales %
```

As a check, we can compare the two views by joining both tables together to include all the records in 001 that are not in 002, all the records in 002 that are not in 001, and all the shared records. This is a FULL JOIN. Unfortunately, SQLite does not implement this type of join, but (or because) it can be implemented by combining two LEFT JOINS.

```
SELECT *
  FROM (
    SELECT
      CASE WHEN A.total_sales_revenue != B.total_sales_revenue
        THEN 1 ELSE 0 END AS revenue_not_equal_flag
      ,A.end_of_week_ssmtwtf
      ,A.stock_code
      ,A.rank
      ,B.rank
      ,CAST(A.quantity AS INT) AS quantity
      ,B.quantity
      ,A.avg_price
      ,B.avg_price
      ,A.total_sales_revenue
      ,B.total_sales_revenue
      ,A.preferred_description
      ,B.preferred_description
    FROM INFO_WEEKLY_TOP_SALES_RANK_001 A
    LEFT JOIN INFO_WEEKLY_TOP_SALES_RANK_002 B
    ON (
      A.end_of_week_ssmtwtf = B.end_of_week_ssmtwtf
      AND A.stock_code = B.stock_code
      )
    WHERE A.stock_code = '85099B'

    UNION ALL

    SELECT
      CASE WHEN A.total_sales_revenue != B.total_sales_revenue
        THEN 1 ELSE 0 END AS revenue_not_equal_flag
      ,A.end_of_week_ssmtwtf
      ,A.stock_code
      ,A.rank
      ,B.rank
      ,CAST(A.quantity AS INT) AS quantity
      ,B.quantity
      ,A.avg_price
      ,B.avg_price
      ,A.total_sales_revenue
      ,B.total_sales_revenue
      ,A.preferred_description
      ,B.preferred_description
    FROM INFO_WEEKLY_TOP_SALES_RANK_002 A
    LEFT JOIN INFO_WEEKLY_TOP_SALES_RANK_001 B
    ON (
      A.end_of_week_ssmtwtf = B.end_of_week_ssmtwtf
      AND A.stock_code = B.stock_code
      )
    WHERE A.stock_code = '85099B' AND B.preferred_description IS NULL
  ) A
WHERE revenue_not_equal_flag = 1
ORDER BY end_of_week_ssmtwtf DESC
```

The first query returns all the records in _001 which do not exist in _002 and the records that exist in both. The second query exchanges the left and right sides ("A" and "B") and removes any records in 002 that do not exist in 001. The UNION ALL statement keeps any duplicate records.[176]

	revenue_not_equal_flag	of_week_ssr	tock_cod	rank	rank:1	quantity	quantity:1	avg_price	avg_price:1	total_sales_revenue	total_sales_revenue:1	rred_descr	description
1	1	2011-12-02	85099B	8	8	1049	1046	2.52	2.53	142716	140133	JUMBO ...	JUMBO ...
2	1	2011-11-25	85099B	10	10	753	751	2.42	2.42	83711	81926.6	JUMBO ...	JUMBO ...
3	1	2011-10-14	85099B	5	5	647	640	2.3	2.31	74430.9	70963.2	JUMBO ...	JUMBO ...
4	1	2011-10-07	85099B	1	1	2501	2500	2.21	2.23	315126	300475	JUMBO ...	JUMBO ...
5	1	2011-09-16	85099B	3	4	720	717	2.33	2.34	89078.4	85724.5	JUMBO ...	JUMBO ...
6	1	2011-08-12	85099B	1	1	1373	1371	2.36	2.37	126275	120388	JUMBO ...	JUMBO ...
7	1	2011-06-24	85099B	2	2	841	840	2.71	2.73	84436.4	82588.8	JUMBO ...	JUMBO ...

What this means for our analysis is that, as expected, the records we are using for our initial reports have changed. The next step will be to create a new Vega-Lite report using the data in the new table.

Creating and deploying the new report

Finally, the advantages of treating everything as code starts to pay off. Remake the project and deploy it locally. This serves as a reminder of what we need to accomplish before writing a new report. Look for the path to the JSON API for the new view.

```
make && make deploy/local
```

Link	rowid	end_of_week_ssmtwtf	rank	stock_code	description	quantity	avg_price	total_sales_revenue
1	1	2011-06-10	1	85123A	CREAM HANGING HEART T-LIGHT HOLDER	4206	3.23	367183.8
2	2	2011-06-10	2	22502	PICNIC BASKET WICKER 60 PIECES	135	67.61	200811.15
3	3	2011-06-10	3	47566	PARTY BUNTING	592	5.81	147840.16
4	4	2011-06-10	4	23284	DOORMAT KEEP CALM AND COME IN	349	9.36	65301.39
5	5	2011-06-10	5	22423	REGENCY CAKESTAND 3 TIER	181	13.81	65002.53

192.168.1.251:8001/sales/INFO_WEEKLY_TOP_SALES_RANK_002.json?_shape=array


```
[{"rowid": 1, "end_of_week_ssmtwtf": "2011-06-10", "rank": 1, "stock_code": "85123A", "description": "CREAM HANGING HEART T-LIGHT
HOLDER", "quantity": 4206, "avg_price": 3.23, "total_sales_revenue": 367183.8}, {"rowid": 2, "end_of_week_ssmtwtf": "2011-06-10",
"rank": 2, "stock_code": "22502", "description": "PICNIC BASKET WICKER 60 PIECES", "quantity": 135, "avg_price": 67.61,
"total_sales_revenue": 200811.15}, {"rowid": 3, "end_of_week_ssmtwtf": "2011-06-10", "rank": 3, "stock_code": "47566",
"description": "PARTY BUNTING", "quantity": 592, "avg_price": 5.81, "total_sales_revenue": 147840.16}, {"rowid": 4,
"end_of_week_ssmtwtf": "2011-06-10", "rank": 4, "stock_code": "23284", "description": "DOORMAT KEEP CALM AND COME IN", "quantity":
349, "avg_price": 9.36, "total_sales_revenue": 65301.39}, {"rowid": 5, "end_of_week_ssmtwtf": "2011-06-10", "rank": 5,
"stock_code": "22423", "description": "REGENCY CAKESTAND 3 TIER", "quantity": 181, "avg_price": 13.81, "total_sales_revenue":
65002.53}, {"rowid": 6, "end_of_week_ssmtwtf": "2011-06-10", "rank": 6, "stock_code": "85099B", "description": "JUMBO BAG RED
RETROSPOT", "quantity": 446, "avg_price": 2.95, "total_sales_revenue": 55290.62}, {"rowid": 7, "end_of_week_ssmtwtf": "2011-06-
10", "rank": 7, "stock_code": "20685", "description": "DOORMAT RED RETROSPOT", "quantity": 344, "avg_price": 10.05,
"total_sales_revenue": 44933.28}, {"rowid": 8, "end_of_week_ssmtwtf": "2011-06-10", "rank": 8, "stock_code": "23298",
"description": "BUNTING , SPOTTY", "quantity": 257, "avg_price": 5.51, "total_sales_revenue": 42461.54}, {"rowid": 9,
"end_of_week_ssmtwtf": "2011-06-10", "rank": 9, "stock_code": "21523", "description": "DOORMAT FANCY FONT HOME SWEET HOME",
"quantity": 332, "avg_price": 8.93, "total_sales_revenue": 38558.48}, {"rowid": 10, "end_of_week_ssmtwtf": "2011-06-10", "rank":
```


```
# ---- Tests outputs ----
test/outputs: \
  test/online_retail_II_last_6_months_filtered.csv \
  test/online_retail_II_last_6_months_filtered_002.csv \
  test/WEEKLY_TOP_SALES_RANK_001.html \
  test/WEEKLY_TOP_SALES_RANK_002.html \
  test/WEEKLY_TOP_SALES_RANK_003.html \
  test/WEEKLY_TOP_SALES_RANK_004.html

test/WEEKLY_TOP_SALES_RANK_004.html: svc/static/WEEKLY_TOP_SALES_RANK_004.html
  @$(test_dependent_file)
```

```
svc/static/WEEKLY_TOP_SALES_RANK_004.html: VIZTITLE="Weekly Top Sales Rank - JSON API call v2"
svc/static/WEEKLY_TOP_SALES_RANK_004.html: VIZTEMPLATE=etc/app/WEEKLY_TOP_SALES_RANK_001.vega
svc/static/WEEKLY_TOP_SALES_RANK_004.html: VIZURL="/sales/INFO_WEEKLY_TOP_SALES_RANK_002.json?_shape=array"
svc/static/WEEKLY_TOP_SALES_RANK_004.html: INFO_WEEKLY_TOP_SALES_RANK_002
  @#<path/to/export_file.html>(colon)(space)VIZTITLE=<report title>
  @#<path/to/export_file.html>(colon)(space)VIZTEMPLATE=<path/to/viz_template.vega>
  @#<path/to/export_file.html>(colon)(space)VIZURL=<path/to/viz_url.json?_shape=array>
  @#<path/to/export_file.html>(colon)(space)<source_table_template_name>
  @echo $(DTS)      [INFO] - Executing $@
  @cat etc/app/vega_embed_header.viz > $@
  @echo "\"data\":{\"url\":\"$(VIZURL)\"}, " >> $@
  @echo "\"title\":\"$(VIZTITLE)\"," >> $@
  @cat $(VIZTEMPLATE) >> $@
  @cat etc/app/vega_embed_footer.viz >> $@
```

Makefile target to generate the new report

Makefile deployment

```
test/local_config: \
  opt/local/metadata.yaml \
  opt/local/requirements.txt \
  opt/local/settings.json \
  opt/local/sales.db \
  opt/local/static/WEEKLY_TOP_SALES_RANK_001.json \
  opt/local/static/WEEKLY_TOP_SALES_RANK_001.html \
  opt/local/static/WEEKLY_TOP_SALES_RANK_002.html \
  opt/local/static/WEEKLY_TOP_SALES_RANK_003.html \
  opt/local/static/WEEKLY_TOP_SALES_RANK_004.html
  @echo $(DTS)      [INFO] - Executing $@

opt/local/static/WEEKLY_TOP_SALES_RANK_004.html:
  @$(test_file)
```

```
build/local:
	@echo $(DTS)      [INFO] - Executing $@
	@mkdir -p opt/$(notdir $@)/static
	@cp -f etc/app/metadata.yaml opt/local/metadata.yaml
	@cp -f etc/server/requirements.txt opt/local/requirements.txt
	@cp -f etc/server/settings.json opt/local/settings.json
	@cp -f svc/db/sales.db opt/local/sales.db
	@cp -f svc/static/WEEKLY_TOP_SALES_RANK_001.json opt/local/static/WEEKLY_TOP_SALES_RANK_001.json
	@cp -f svc/static/WEEKLY_TOP_SALES_RANK_001.html opt/local/static/WEEKLY_TOP_SALES_RANK_001.html
	@cp -f svc/static/WEEKLY_TOP_SALES_RANK_002.html opt/local/static/WEEKLY_TOP_SALES_RANK_002.html
	@cp -f svc/static/WEEKLY_TOP_SALES_RANK_003.html opt/local/static/WEEKLY_TOP_SALES_RANK_003.html
	@cp -f svc/static/WEEKLY_TOP_SALES_RANK_004.html opt/local/static/WEEKLY_TOP_SALES_RANK_004.html
```

After make deploy/local is rerun, we can see newly deployed report.

To link to the new report, we need to update the metadata for the new table and links.

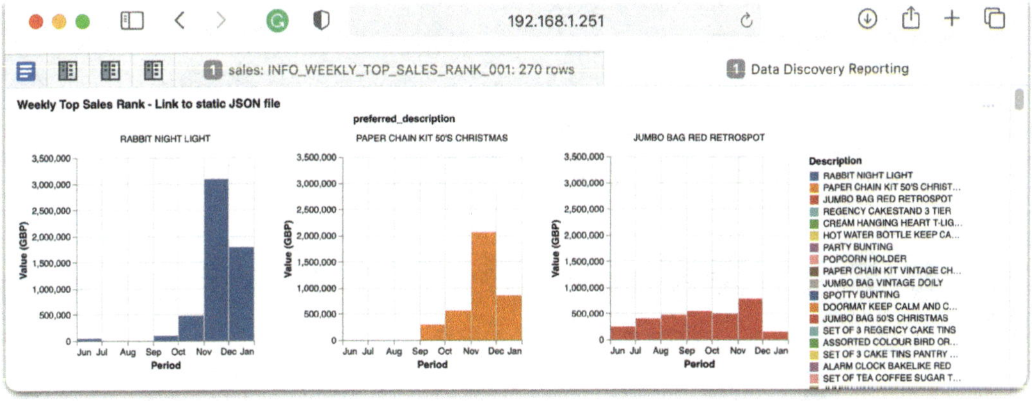


```
  tables:
    INFO_WEEKLY_TOP_SALES_RANK_001:
      description_html: |-
        <strong>Description:</strong> Sales revenue for the top 10 products in each week of the previous 6 months.<br>
        <strong>Source:</strong> Database view<br>
        <strong>Source table(s):</strong> INFO_SALES_LAST_6_MONTHS_FILTERED_002
        <p></p>
        <strong>Reports:</strong><br>
        <a href="http://192.168.1.251:8001/static/WEEKLY_TOP_SALES_RANK_001.html" target="_blank">Embedded JSON data set</a><br>
        <a href="http://192.168.1.251:8001/static/WEEKLY_TOP_SALES_RANK_002.html" target="_blank">API call</a><br>
        <a href="http://192.168.1.251:8001/static/WEEKLY_TOP_SALES_RANK_004.html" target="_blank">API call v2</a><br>
        <a href="http://192.168.1.251:8001/static/WEEKLY_TOP_SALES_RANK_003.html" target="_blank">Linked file</a>
        <p></p>
    INFO_WEEKLY_TOP_SALES_RANK_002:
      description_html: |-
        <strong>Description:</strong> Sales revenue for the top 10 products in each week of the previous 6 months.<br>
        <strong>Source:</strong> Database table<br>
        <strong>Source table(s):</strong> INFO_WEEKLY_TOP_SALES_RANK_002
        <p></p>
        <strong>Reports:</strong><br>
        <a href="http://192.168.1.251:8001/static/WEEKLY_TOP_SALES_RANK_004.html" target="_blank">Weekly Top Sales Rank</a><br>
        <p></p>
```

Redeploy with the command `make && make deploy/local`.

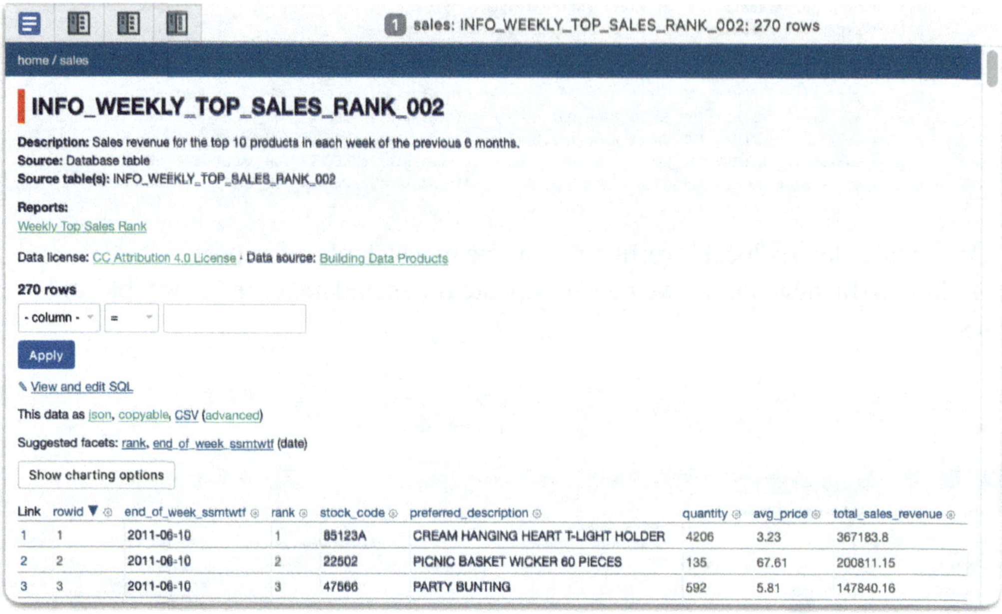

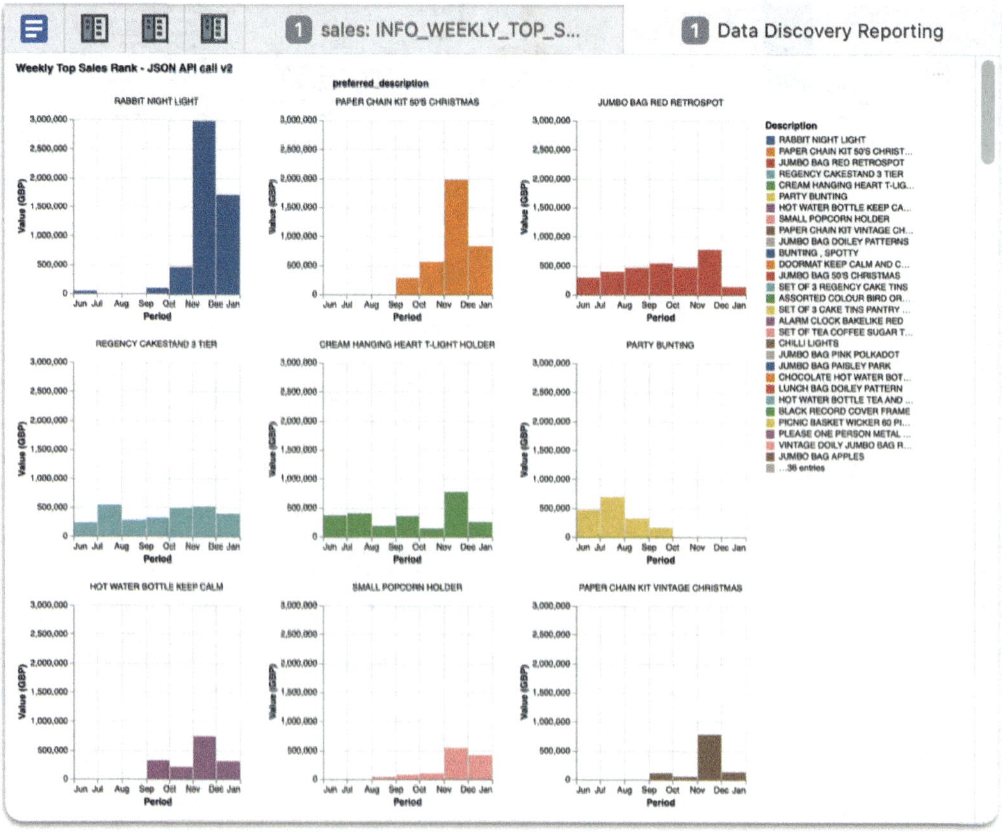

Comparing the two reports, they look very similar. Fixing the discrepancies in the prices, quantities, and descriptions didn't change the order of our top products, but it did change the values of the monthly sales slightly.

If we load the page with the developers' tools, we can verify that as you would expect, regenerating the data for the report and caching it in a database table reduces the load time down dramatically.

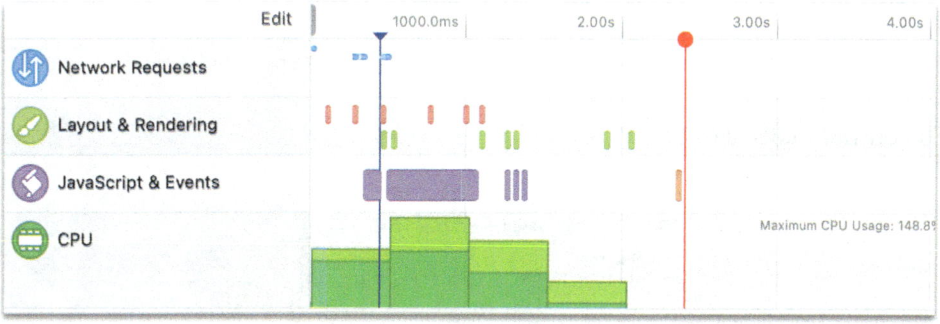

Scheduling Jobs

We used Make and the makefile targets to coordinate executing all the steps in the solution. However, we need to automatically execute our makefile on a schedule without our intervention. Fortunately, UNIX has a process to automatically execute commands on a schedule called cron[177] [178]

We can start exploring this utility by creating a new target in the makefile for testing.

```
foo:
  @echo $(shell date +%Y-%m-%dT%H:%M:%S-%Z) $(shell hostname) INFO - $@
```

The output looks like:

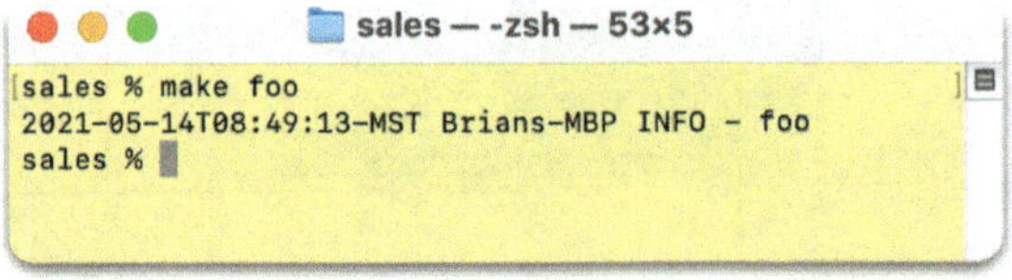

Our initial task will be to successfully schedule this target to run every minute. This will allow us to verify we have everything running properly.

The `cron` utility is managed by the `crontab` application. To add an entry, we can edit the file manually in the console with the nano editor.

```
env EDITOR=nano crontab -e
```

Add the following text to the file:

```
MAILTO=""
* * * * * /usr/bin/make -f /Users/brianmcmillan/projects/sales/makefile foo >> /Users/brianmcmillan/projects/sales/var/log/cron_log.txt 2>&1
```

Save and exit the editor: `[ctrl][o], [enter], [ctrl][x]`

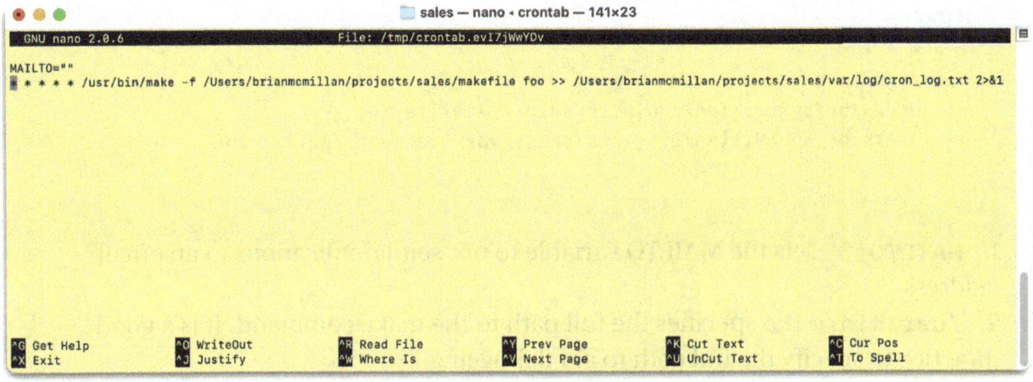

Verify the contents of the file are correct: `crontab -l` which will return the contents of the crontab file :

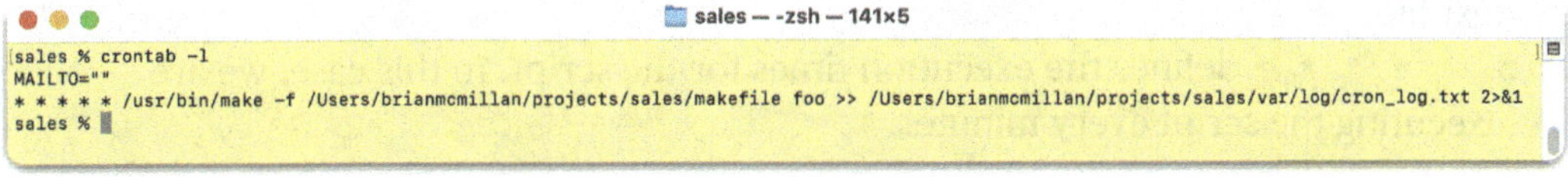

If you look in the `var/logs/` directory, there will soon be a file named `cron_log.txt`. After a waiting few minutes, open the file and check the contents.

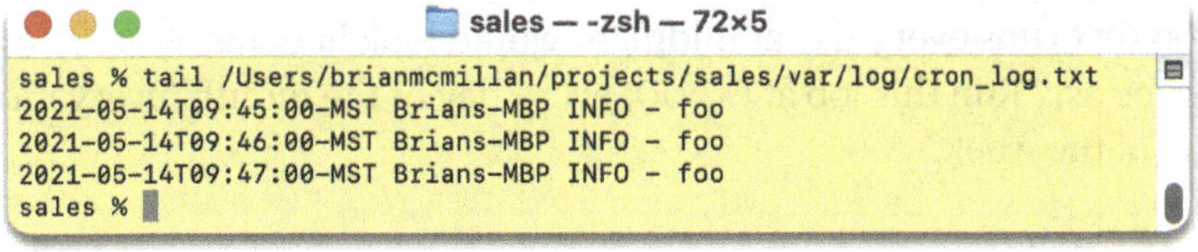

Let's step through the crontab file. Each separate crontab entry must be on a single line but for clarity we will reformat the entry to make it easier to read.

```
MAILTO=""
* * * * *
/usr/bin/make
-f /Users/brianmcmillan/projects/sales/makefile foo
>> /Users/brianmcmillan/projects/sales/var/log/cron_log.txt 2>&1
```

1. `MAILTO=""` sets the MAILTO variable to not send notifications to an email address.
2. `/usr/bin/make` specifies the full path to the make command. It is a good practice to specify the full path to aid debugging.
3. `-f /Users/brianmcmillan/projects/sales/makefile foo` defines the full path to the makefile you want to run. This will be handy if you want to split the makefile into multiple files as the project grows.
4. `>> /Users/brianmcmillan/projects/sales/var/log/cron_log.txt 2>&1` concatenates both the standard output and error (stdout and stderr) to the text file.
5. `* * * * *` defines the execution times for the script. In this case, we are executing the script every minute.

The format of this string is:

```
(Minute)<space>(Hour)<space>(Day of
Month)<space>(Month)<space>(Month Number)<space>(Day of Week)
```

A Cron Job that runs every day at midnight would look like this: `0 0 * * *`. You can read this recipe as, "Run this job at 00:00, every day of the month, every month, and on every day of the week."

The options for each position are:

Position	Description	Allowed value	Example
1	Minute	0 - 59	5 - Every 5 minutes
2	Hour	0 - 23	3 - At 3:00 AM
3	Day of Month	1 - 31	31 - last day of month
4	Month	1 - 12	3,6,9,12 - Every quarter
5	Day of week	0 - 6	Mon-Fri - Every weekday

The more common reporting schedules can be specified as:

Cron recipes	Description
/10 * * * *	Every 10 minutes
0 /1 * * *	Every hour
0 */4 * * *	Every 4 Hours
0 3 * * *	At 3:00am
0 3 * * 1	Every Monday at 3:00am
0 3 1 * *	1st of the month at 3:00am

As in the table above, there are modifiers you can use to specify ranges of the values. These can be combined to create any complicated execution schedule you might need. If you are having trouble creating the right combination, create multiple lines with different schedules. As they execute, the combined results will reflect a more complicated schedule.

A common example where this might be desired is when you want schedules to execute on the last day of the month. Because months are ending on the 28th - 31st day, you will need to create separate schedules for these months.

NOTE: Cron was designed to execute at the start of a period. In the example above, it is much easier to set a schedule for 00:00 on the first day of every month with `0 0 1 * *` or `@monthly`.

Range	Description
6-18	Range - 6:00am through 6:00pm
3,6,9,12	Lists - months 3, 6, 9, 12
*/3	Steps - every 3rd month

If the schedules can be kept simple, there are some special keywords you could use to simplify the specification.[179]

Simplified command	Crontab interval	Description
@yearly	0 0 1 1 *	At 00:00 on day-of-month 1 in January.
@monthly	0 0 1 * *	At 00:00 on day-of-month 1.
@weekly	0 0 * * 1	At 00:00 on Monday.
@daily	0 0 * * *	At 00:00 each day.
@hourly	0 * * * *	At minute 0, each hour.
@reboot	N/A	Run at startup

Instead of creating the crontab entries manually, we can create a file and then update the crontab with that.

```
MAILTO=""
*/2 * * * * /usr/bin/make -f /Users/brianmcmillan/projects/
sales/makefile foo >> /Users/brianmcmillan/projects/sales/var/
log/cron_log.txt 2>&1
```

This file is then loaded with this command:

```
crontab /Users/brianmcmillan/projects/sales/etc/cron/
crontab.txt
```

This can be verified by running the `crontab -l` command again and checking the log file. The job should now be running every two minutes.

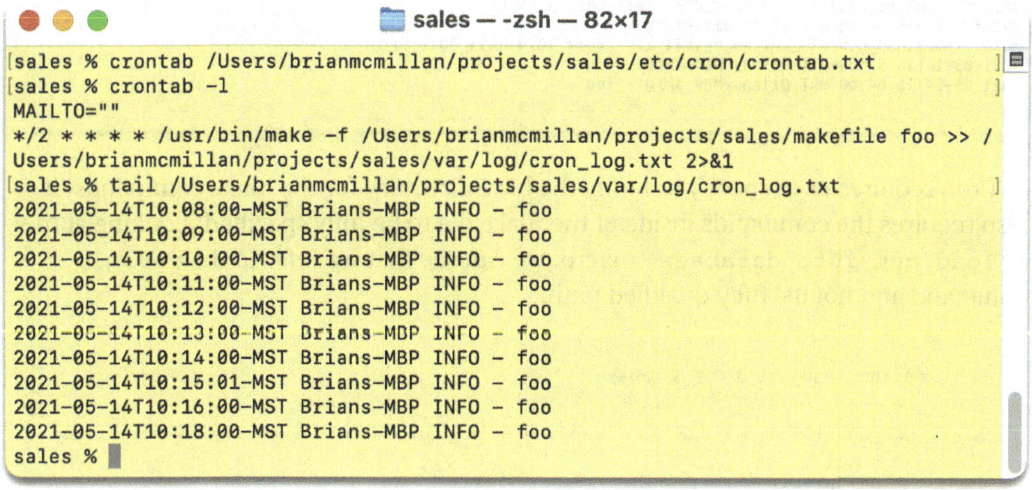

We can add the `run:` target to the `crontab.txt` file.Cron will now run the `foo:` target every two minutes and the `all:` target every 15 minutes.

```
MAILTO=""
*/2 * * * * /usr/bin/make -f /Users/brianmcmillan/projects/
sales/makefile foo >> /Users/brianmcmillan/projects/sales/var/
log/cron_log.txt 2>&1
*/15 * * * * /usr/bin/make -C /Users/brianmcmillan/projects/
sales/ -f makefile all >> /Users/brianmcmillan/projects/sales/
var/log/cron_log.txt 2>&1
```

NOTE: Up to this point, all of the commands we have been executing have run under our user ID. The cron command runs as the `root` user (unless specified). This changes the default directory used by `make`. The `-C` option resets the base directory for the make command. In this case, we specify the full directory path to our project.

Looking at the log file, we can see there appears to be an issue: `make: csvsql: No such file or directory`.

```
cron_log.txt
2021-05-14T10:48:00-MST Brians-MBP INFO - foo
2021-05-14T10:50:00-MST Brians-MBP INFO - foo
2021-05-14T10:50:00-MST [INFO] - Splitting svc/load/online_retail_II_-_Year_2010-2011.csv into svc/
load/split_online_retail_II/online_retail_II_-_Year_2010-2011__###
   50000 svc/load/split_online_retail_II/online_retail_II_-_Year_2010-2011_000.csv
   50000 svc/load/split_online_retail_II/online_retail_II_-_Year_2010-2011_001.csv
   50000 svc/load/split_online_retail_II/online_retail_II_-_Year_2010-2011_002.csv
   50000 svc/load/split_online_retail_II/online_retail_II_-_Year_2010-2011_003.csv
   50000 svc/load/split_online_retail_II/online_retail_II_-_Year_2010-2011_004.csv
   50000 svc/load/split_online_retail_II/online_retail_II_-_Year_2010-2011_005.csv
   50000 svc/load/split_online_retail_II/online_retail_II_-_Year_2010-2011_006.csv
   50000 svc/load/split_online_retail_II/online_retail_II_-_Year_2010-2011_007.csv
   50000 svc/load/split_online_retail_II/online_retail_II_-_Year_2010-2011_008.csv
   50000 svc/load/split_online_retail_II/online_retail_II_-_Year_2010-2011_009.csv
   41911 svc/load/split_online_retail_II/online_retail_II_-_Year_2010-2011_010.csv
  541911 total
2021-05-14T10:50:00-MST [INFO] - Loading data from svc/load/online_retail_II_-_Year_2010-2011.csv
into SRC_online_retail_II_-_Year_2010-2011_001.sales.db
make: csvsql: No such file or directory
make: *** [load_csv/SRC_online_retail_II_-_Year_2010-2011_001] Error 1
2021-05-14T10:52:00-MST Brians-MBP INFO - foo
2021-05-14T10:54:00-MST Brians-MBP INFO - foo
```

Cron requires us to specify not only the base directory for the make commands, it also requires the commands inside of the make file to be fully specified. Looking at the `$(load_csv_into_database)` macro, we can see that we refer to the `csvsql` command and not its' fully qualified path.

```
define load_csv_into_database
  @#load_csv/SRC_<csv_file_name>_001(colon)(space)<path/to/csv_file.csv>
  @echo $(DTS)      [INFO] - Loading data from $< into $(@F).$(DBNAME)
  @csvsql \
  --db sqlite:///$(DBFILE) \
```

Fortunately, this can be fixed by refactoring the makefile to use fully qualified paths for all of the non-standard commands. We specified these as variables but didn't reference them for the sake of readability. We now need to alter the commands to use a variable returning the fully qualified paths.

Add two new variables to the make file:

```
PYENVDIR := /Users/brianmcmillan/.pyenv/shims
CSVSQL := $(PYENVDIR)/csvsql
```

Change the `load_csv_into_database` macro to refer to the new variable.

```
define load_csv_into_database
  @#load_csv/SRC_<csv_file_name>_001(colon)(space)<path/to/csv_file.csv>
  @echo $(DTS)      [INFO] - Loading data from $< into $(@F).$(DBNAME)
  @$(CSVSQL) \
  --db sqlite:///$(DBFILE) \
```

When cron executes again, we no longer see this error in the log file. Unfortunately, we see an issue with the next command that was not using the variable. Now that we have a fix, we can refactor the remaining variables.

The `make info/variables` command can be used to confirm the fully qualified paths are being expanded correctly.

```
sales — -zsh — 79x15
-- Program paths -----------------------------------------------------
SHELL = /bin/bash
SQLITE3 = /usr/local/bin/sqlite3
GRAPHVIZDOT = /usr/local/bin/dot
SPLIT = /usr/local/bin/gsplit
PYENVDIR = /Users/brianmcmillan/.pyenv/shims
PYTHON3 = /Users/brianmcmillan/.pyenv/shims/python
PIP = /Users/brianmcmillan/.pyenv/shims/pip
IN2CSV = /Users/brianmcmillan/.pyenv/shims/in2csv
CSVSTACK = /Users/brianmcmillan/.pyenv/shims/csvstack
CSVSQL = /Users/brianmcmillan/.pyenv/shims/csvsql
SQLITEUTILS = /Users/brianmcmillan/.pyenv/shims/sqlite-utils
DATASETTE = /Users/brianmcmillan/.pyenv/shims/datasette
NODEGRAPH = /Users/brianmcmillan/.pyenv/shims/makefile2dot
-- Configuration paths (/etc) ----------------------------------------
```

Replace the commands in the file to utilize the new variables and wait for the cronjob to re-execute. Fortunately most of these commands are in the macros and there are only a small number of changes to be made.

Reload the crontab with the `crontab /Users/brianmcmillan/projects/sales/etc/cron/crontab.txt` command.

cron_log.txt

```
WEEKLY_TOP_SALES_RANK_001.json
2021-05-14T14:47:52-MST [INFO] - Executing svc/static/WEEKLY_TOP_SALES_RANK_001.html
2021-05-14T14:47:52-MST [INFO] - Executing svc/static/WEEKLY_TOP_SALES_RANK_002.html
2021-05-14T14:47:52-MST [INFO] - Executing svc/static/WEEKLY_TOP_SALES_RANK_003.html
2021-05-14T14:47:52-MST [INFO] - Executing svc/static/WEEKLY_TOP_SALES_RANK_004.html
2021-05-14T14:47:52-MST [INFO] - record count = 11 svc/static/online_retail_II_last_6_months_filtered.csv
2021-05-14T14:47:52-MST [INFO] - record count = 11 svc/static/online_retail_II_last_6_months_filtered_002.csv
2021-05-14T14:47:52-MST [INFO] - record count = 541910 records in SRC_online_retail_II_-_Year_2010-2011_001.sales.db
2021-05-14T14:47:52-MST [INFO] - record count = 536642 records in RAW_ONLINE_RETAIL_II_YEAR_2010_2011_001.sales.db
2021-05-14T14:47:52-MST [INFO] - record count = 100 records in INFO_SALES_LAST_6_MONTHS_FILTERED_001.sales.db
2021-05-14T14:47:52-MST [INFO] - record count = 536642 records in SAT_ONLINE_RETAIL_II_YEAR_2010_2011_001.sales.db
2021-05-14T14:47:52-MST [INFO] - record count = 531224 records in BSAT_INVOICES_001.sales.db
2021-05-14T14:47:52-MST [INFO] - record count = 3843 records in BLNK_STOCK_CODE_PREFERRED_DESCRIPTION_001.sales.db
2021-05-14T14:47:52-MST [INFO] - record count = 3958 records in BHUB_STOCK_CODES_001.sales.db
2021-05-14T14:47:52-MST [INFO] - record count = 25900 records in BHUB_INVOICE_CODES_001.sales.db
2021-05-14T14:47:52-MST [INFO] - record count = 270 records in INFO_WEEKLY_TOP_SALES_RANK_002.sales.db
2021-05-14T14:47:52-MST [INFO] - Executing documentation.
2021-05-14T14:48:00-MST Brians-MBP INFO - foo
```

While not necessarily what we want in production, 15 minutes will allow us to see the behavior of the schedule in a reasonable amount of time. Setting the production schedule can be done by setting the cron interval parameters to something matching the inflow of data and then reloading the file with the `crontab` command.

To schedule the publishing to Google, we can create a new schedule and add it to the crontab. In this example, the `deploy/gcloud:` target is run 30 minutes after the hour, every four hours.

```
30 */4 * * * /usr/bin/make -C /Users/brianmcmillan/projects/sales/ -f makefile deploy/gcloud >> /Users/brianmcmillan/projects/sales/var/log/cron_log.txt 2>&1
```

Each of these jobs logs its activity to the `cron_log.txt` file, and over time, this file will grow longer and longer, making it difficult to use for troubleshooting. To make this easier, we can create a new `LOG_ROTATE:` target.[180]

```
log_rotate:
	@echo $(DTS)	[INFO] - Executing $@
	@mv $(PROJECTLOGDIR)/cron_log.txt $(PROJECTLOGDIR)/cron_log_$(shell date +%Y-%m-%d).txt
```

This can be added to the crontab as:

```
@daily /usr/bin/make -C /Users/brianmcmillan/projects/sales/ -f makefile log_rotate >> /Users/brianmcmillan/projects/sales/var/log/cron_log.txt 2>&1
```

Our final crontab looks like:

```
MAILTO=""
#LOG_ROTATE - Rotate the log file every day.
@daily /usr/bin/make -C /Users/brianmcmillan/projects/sales/ -f makefile log_rotate >> /Users/brianmcmillan/projects/sales/var/log/cron_log.txt 2>&1
#Execute the data pipeline every hour
0 * * * * /usr/bin/make -C /Users/brianmcmillan/projects/sales/ -f makefile all >> /Users/brianmcmillan/projects/sales/var/log/cron_log.txt 2>&1
#deploy/gcloud every 6 hours, 30 min past the hour
30 */6 * * * /usr/bin/make -C /Users/brianmcmillan/projects/sales/ -f makefile deploy/gcloud >> /Users/brianmcmillan/projects/sales/var/log/cron_log.txt 2>&1
#deploy/local manually as needed
#0 */2 * * * /usr/bin/make -C /Users/brianmcmillan/projects/sales/ -f makefile deploy/gcloud >> /Users/brianmcmillan/projects/sales/var/log/cron_log.txt 2>&1
```

NOTE: An important thing to know about cron is that it is designed to work on systems that are always running. If we are running cron on our laptop and it is turned off, none of the scheduled jobs will run. They will execute the next time their schedules run. Ideally, our build process would be moved to a separate build server that is running 24x7.

Another alternative would be to use another scheduling utility like Anacron.[181] Anacron was designed to function in environments where the server running the jobs is expected to be off periodically. When the server is running, the jobs will start as soon as possible. One of the disadvantages to this program is that the lowest level of scheduling granularity is daily. Another alternative would be to mirror the periodic schedules with ones using the `@reboot` schedule.

Retrospective

We've completed everything! We built a new data set that addresses the errors discovered in our earlier analysis. This data set is held in a new set of tables following a simple analytics-focused data model. In the future, as we build out the sales data set, this model makes it easier to consistently build more reliable analyses. We proved this by refactoring the top sales report to use a new table that contains better product names, quantities, and prices.

On the technical side, we set up standard execution schedules for processing the data in the database and republishing the data discovery platform after these refreshes. We also logged the job executions to a common log for monitoring and troubleshooting.

> **IN ORDER TO** MINIMIZE THE ONGOING SUPPORT BURDEN.
> **AS A** SYSTEM
> **I WANT** TO AUTOMATE ALL DATA MANAGEMENT TASKS.
> AND
>
> [X] SCHEDULE MANAGEMENT TASKS WEEKLY.
> [X] SCHEDULE DEPLOYMENT REFRESHES WEEKLY.

> **IN ORDER TO** CORRECT ISSUES WITH THE DATA.
> **AS A** SALES MANAGER RESPONSIBLE FOR THE QUALITY OF THE SALES DATA
> **I WANT** ACCESS TO AN ERROR-FREE DATA SET.
> **AND** A WAY TO PERFORM ADDITIONAL ANALYTICS EASILY.
> **AND** A SYSTEM THAT DOESN'T REQUIRE LONG DEVELOPMENT TIMES WHEN CHANGES ARE REQUIRED.
>
> [X] PROVIDE A BUSINESS-FOCUSED DATA SET WITH MINIMAL DATA QUALITY AND LOGIC ERRORS. USE EXISTING DATA FOR NOW.
> [X] IDENTIFY AND CORRECT ANOMALIES IN THE DATA WITHOUT DESTROYING THE ORIGINAL RECORD.
> [X] IF A RECORD CHANGES, SAVE THAT HISTORY TO AID ANALYSIS.
> [X] DO NOT STORE DUPLICATE RECORDS.
> [X] SUPPORT INCREMENTAL LOADING.

```
IN ORDER TO IMPROVE FUTURE DEVELOPMENT EFFORTS
AS A SALES MANAGER RESPONSIBLE FOR IMPROVING OUR
ANALYTICS CAPABILITIES
I WANT A SYSTEM THAT IS EASY FOR ANALYSTS TO USE
AND CONSISTENTLY IMPLEMENTS STANDARD BUSINESS
LOGIC.

[X] SINGLE PRODUCT NAME FOR EACH STOCK CODE
(SKU).
[X] SINGLE PRICE AND QUANTITY FOR EACH INVOICE
LINE ITEM.
[X] NO "C" IN INVOICE CODES FOR CANCELED LINE
ITEMS.
[X] REIMPLEMENT PREVIOUS REPORTING W/ NEW DATA
SET.
```

---

175 Alternatively, load the data into a temporary table, drop the old table, and rename the temporary table with the same name as the old one. This will minimize the downtime without incurring the overhead of updating records in the old table.

176 This is how you implement a FULL OUTER JOIN query in SQLite.

177 cron (https://en.wikipedia.org/wiki/Cron)

178 man cron (https://man7.org/linux/man-pages/man8/cron.8.html)

179 Crontab Guru (https://crontab.guru/) is a great utility to help define cron specifications.

180 We could have used the UNIX logrotate utility but for simplicity we will create a simple rename recipe.

181 Anacron - (https://linux.die.net/man/8/anacron)

Chapter 9: Final iteration - Innovation and Planning

With the completion of these stories, it's tempting to declare success and start with the next development round. Don't do it! Take time to step away for a while. Take the afternoon off, relax, and give yourself time to let all this work settle in. Let things run for at least a few cycles to look for issues you might have missed.

After the quick break, this time should be focused on these activities:

1. Note any bugs and possible solutions.
2. Identify potential support refactoring opportunities. These are true refactors. They don't add new features. They make the code easier to support.
3. Identify potential performance issues and possible improvements.
4. Add to and update the documentation.
5. Identify feature enhancements.

In this Innovation and Planning phase,[182] focus on the technical side of the product rather than the customer or business side. By establishing a dedicated block of time to work through these issues, you make it easier to keep ahead of them. Over time, it becomes easier to integrate these activities into the day-to-day development flow. Early on, as the team establishes itself, having this dedicated time is critically important. Without it, it is too easy to plow ahead building user features while technical debt piles up and eventually overwhelms the product. It is a delicate balancing act, but establishing clear boundaries early goes a long way to keeping the amount of work manageable.

Start this process by brainstorming stories for each of these five categories and assign them rough priorities and values. Then from this list, create a few separate stories to work on in this iteration and a few to backlog for future iterations.

Determine the priority of a task by ranking them by their cost of delay.[183] [184] In this process, assign each story or desired outcome, three values. If you cannot assign actual monetary values, use proportional values across the set of deliverables. Good proportional scales could be a limited range (1-5, 1, 3, 5, 8, 13) or order of magnitude (1, 10, 100, 1000).

1. Urgency - How critical is it that this be done immediately?
2. Value - Is there hard or soft business value?
3. Duration - How long will this take? How confident are we in this estimate?

Bubble sort each deliverable by category. Based on the order, assign a value number (the modified Fibonacci sequence works well to break up any groupings) (1,2,3,5,8,13,21,34,55,89)[185].

The individual scores don't matter beyond prioritization. With this methodology, the highest value activities which can be completed in the shortest time receive the highest Cost of Delay divided by Duration scores ((Urgency * Value) / Duration).

Defects:

Description	Urgency	Value	Duration	Score
Dynamic command to shut down local server before restarting.	1	1	13	1

Refactors and Documentation:

Description	Urgency	Value	Duration	Score
Add metadata table to the db.	8	8	5	13
Add Entity relationship diagrams to the documentation.	13	13	8	21

Performance Enhancements:

Description	Urgency	Value	Duration	Score
Remove unused targets from the makefile.	3	3	1	9
Remove unnecessary tables from the deployed database.	5	5	3	8

Future Enhancements:

Description	Urgency	Value	Duration	Score
Research / POC access to product cost API.	34	21	21	34
Research non-conformance query.	21	34	34	21

Based on the Cost of Delay scoring, the prioritization looks like this:

1. Research / POC access to product cost API.
2. Research non-conformance query.
3. Add Entity relationship diagrams to the documentation.
4. Add metadata table to the db.
5. Remove unused targets from the makefile.
6. Remove unnecessary tables from the deployed database.
7. Dynamic command to shut down local server before restarting.

Executing Technical Improvements

This iteration is shorter and less formal. If the team feels like a basic task list sufficiently communicates progress, then this is a good time to experiment with less formality. Another strategy is executing a portion of the prioritized stories. This creates a smaller and more focused queue. In this example, focus on completing the first few tasks as quickly as possible. Once complete, start planning for future iterations.

The first two look like good candidates for a future development iteration. They have long durations, and most likely, many unknowns and potential issues. Therefore we should push these toward the bottom of the list for this short planning iteration.

The rest of the list look like good candidates. We'll pick the first three to start. Once complete, we start the planning process for future iterations.

Add Entity Relationship Diagrams

The problem with treating "everything as code" is that you miss out on the visual representation of the work you get with GUI based development tools. In database development, the cornerstone visualization tool is an Entity Relationship (ER) diagram.[186] These diagrams are a visual model of the entities, attributes, and relationships in the database. They are a useful reference when trying to understand the scope of a database and when developing new queries.

Traditionally, these diagrams are maintained by the data modeler and generated from a data modeling tool. Applications like ER/WIN[187] and ER/Studio[188] provide an extensive set of capabilities we can use to develop and manage complex data models.

However, these tools impose a specific workflow on the development of the database. This workflow funnels changes through the data modeler and their tools, thereby making the modeling and structuring of the database a separate development silo rather than a small, integrated, portion of the overall development and support workflow. In small, focused, systems like our micro-warehouse, this level of specialization isn't necessary.

What we need is a way to develop some simple visualizations of the structure of the database in order to make it easier for our users to understand the data and to develop their own analytics without being dependent on external specialists. This capability needs to be able to automatically reverse engineer the structure of the database at a level simple enough for a non-expert user to easily understand. This will require that we be able to modify the presentation to remove all but the most important information and relationships.

One issue we are going to encounter is that it isn't possible to automatically derive the relationships between the tables because we are not implementing the traditional primary key to foreign key constraints in the database. Analytics oriented data models require a great deal more flexibility to join tables, and if we were to build all of the possible relationships as constraints in the database, we are imposing a significant amount of unnecessary overhead in the system.

Fitting the creation of these diagrams into our "everything as code" development workflow is also an issue. We want to be able to have visibility to these diagrams as code in the same way we are treating the charts as code.

We will implement a simple system that automatically generates table information from the database which we will combine with simple relationships we will manually manage as part of the application configuration. Because these diagrams will be curated to assist our users, we will be building a few utility targets in the makefile to help us manage these diagrams but not automatically generating them each time we change the database.

For ease of use and simplicity. The first implementation will be to group the tables into the Data Vault logical schemas. This will make it easy to delineate groups of tables serving different purposes. We won't worry about defining relationships yet.

```
er_diagrams: svc/doc/raw_tables.pdf svc/doc/information_tables.pdf svc/doc/business_tables.pdf
	@echo $(DTS)     [INFO] - Executing $<
	@$(ERALCHEMY) -i sqlite:///$(DBFILE) -o etc/app/er_tables.er

svc/doc/raw_tables.pdf:
	@$(ERALCHEMY) -i sqlite:///$(DBFILE) -o $@ --include-tables \
	SRC_online_retail_II_-_Year_2010-2011_001 \
	SRC_online_retail_II_-_Year_2010-2011_002 \
	RAW_ONLINE_RETAIL_II_YEAR_2010_2011_001 \
	SAT_ONLINE_RETAIL_II_YEAR_2010_2011_001

svc/doc/information_tables.pdf:
	@$(ERALCHEMY) -i sqlite:///$(DBFILE) -o $@ --include-tables \
	INFO_SALES_LAST_6_MONTHS_FILTERED_001 \
	INFO_WEEKLY_TOP_SALES_RANK_002

svc/doc/business_tables.pdf:
	@$(ERALCHEMY) -i sqlite:///$(DBFILE) -o $@ --include-tables \
	BHUB_INVOICE_CODES_001 \
	BHUB_STOCK_CODES_001 \
	BLNK_STOCK_CODE_PREFERRED_DESCRIPTION_001 \
	BSAT_INVOICES_001
```

This produces a nice looking picture of the tables in both the configuration and documentation directories.

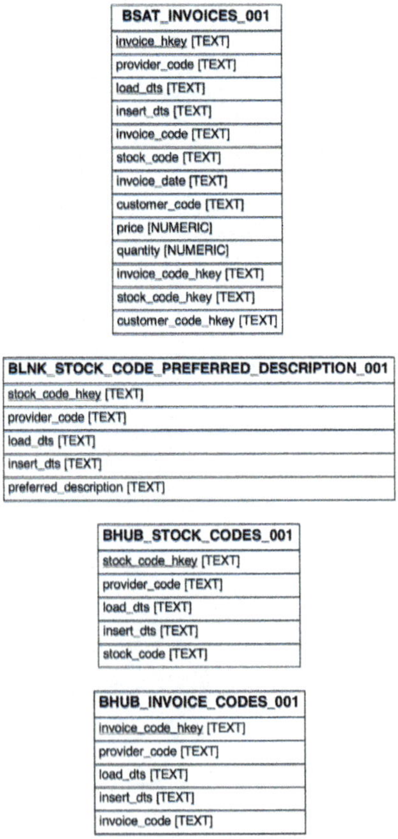

With the small number of tables grouped this way, it's easy to see how we might want to join these tables together. As the product becomes more complex we will want to provide some direction about how the tables are related by joining, in information about the relationships. These can be defined in a simple text file. With each line representing a single relationship in the form of:

```
<first_table>(space)<relationship type>(space)<second_table>
```

etc/app/er_business_relationships.txt:

```
BHUB_INVOICE_CODES_001 1--1 BSAT_INVOICES_001
BHUB_STOCK_CODES_001 1--+ BSAT_INVOICES_001
BLNK_STOCK_CODE_PREFERRED_DESCRIPTION_001 1--+ BSAT_INVOICES_001
BHUB_STOCK_CODES_001 1--1 BLNK_STOCK_CODE_PREFERRED_DESCRIPTION_001
```

Relationship code	Description
?	0 or 1
1	Exactly 1
*	0 or more
+	1 or more

In the model, `BHUB_INVOICE_CODES_001 1--1 BSAT_INVOICES_001` means there is a 1 to 1 relationship between the the invoice codes in the BHUB and BSAT tables. While the `BHUB_STOCK_CODES_001 1--+ BSAT_INVOICES_001` relationship means that each stock code in the BHUB table may be associated with one or more invoice codes.

Assembling this information into a new diagram requires modifying the `svc/doc/business_tables.pdf:` target to produce a textural representation of the tables that can be combined with the manually maintained relationship file.

```
svc/doc/business_tables.pdf: tmp/er_business.er
	@$(ERALCHEMY) -i $< -o $@
	@rm -f $<

tmp/er_business.er: tmp/er_business_tables.er etc/app/er_business_relationships.txt
	 @cat $^ > $@

etc/app/er_business_relationships.txt:
	@$(test_file)

tmp/er_business_tables.er:
	@$(ERALCHEMY) -i sqlite:///$(DBFILE) -o $@ --include-tables \
	BHUB_INVOICE_CODES_001 \
	BHUB_STOCK_CODES_001 \
	BLNK_STOCK_CODE_PREFERRED_DESCRIPTION_001 \
	BSAT_INVOICES_001
```

The final result is a set of diagrams for all of the tables in the database.

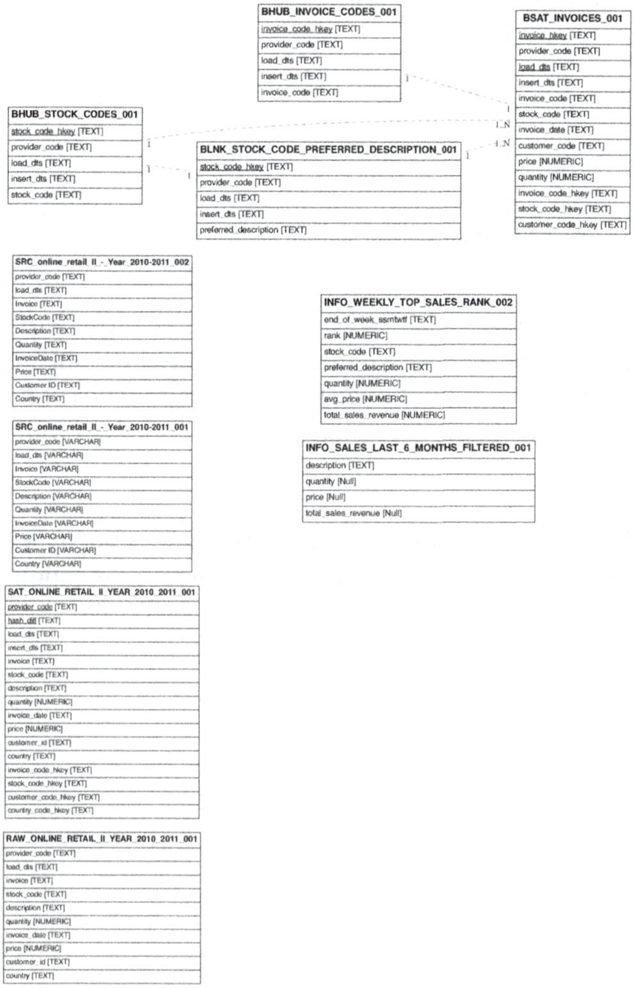

Add a Table Metadata Table to the Database

Another valuable feature to add would be the ability to search across the tables and columns in the database. Back when we were performing our initial data analysis, we used the `sqlite-utils analyze-tables data/db/sales.db` command to look at the data in a single table. We can use the same utility to analyze all the tables and then write the results into the database.

```
documentation: META_TABLES_001 ## Builds the documentation files for the build. (e.g. schema do
	@echo $(DTS)	[INFO] - Executing $@.
	@$(TREE) --prune > $(DOCUMENTATIONDIR)/directory_listing.txt
	@$(NODEGRAPH) --direction LR | $(GRAPHVIZDOT) -Tpng > $(DOCUMENTATIONDIR)/makefile_graph.png

META_TABLES_001:
	@$(SQLITE3) $(DBFILE) "DROP TABLE IF EXISTS '_analyze_tables_';" ".quit"
	@$(SQLITE3) $(DBFILE) "DROP TABLE IF EXISTS 'META_TABLES_001';" ".quit"
	@$(SQLITEUTILS) analyze-tables $(DBFILE) --save
	@$(SQLITE3) $(DBFILE) "ALTER TABLE '_analyze_tables_' RENAME TO 'META_TABLES_001';" ".quit"
```

This target populates a new table called META_TABLES_001 with the structural information about each table as well as two JSON columns containing the top 10 most common and least common values in each field. This makes it easy to preview the type of data in each column.

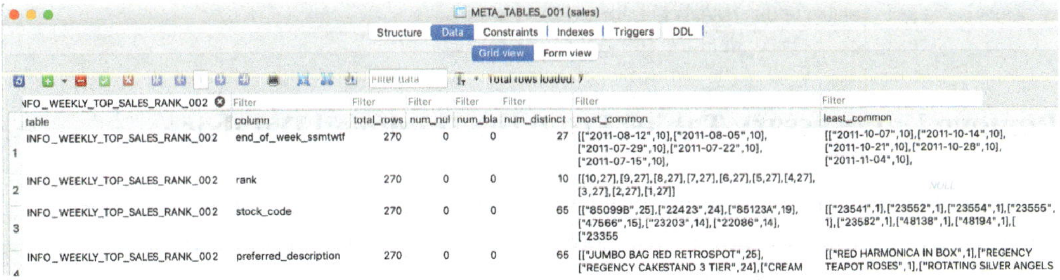

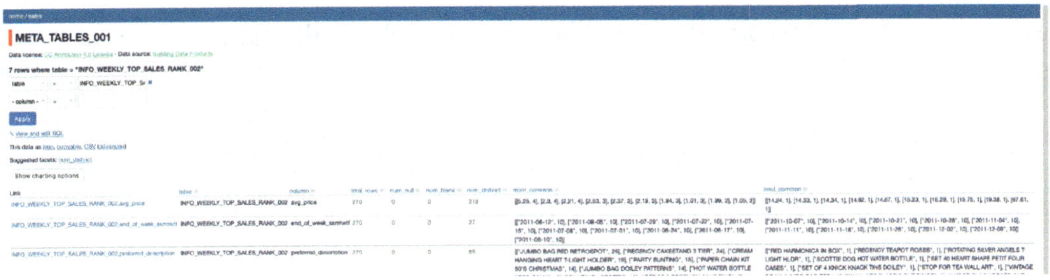

Remove Unused Targets From the Makefile.

Now that we have a complete data pipeline from the source files, to a new report, through a Data Discovery Platform. We can remove our old static reports from the makefile. This will leave us with our Data Vault tables and a single published report.

```
# ---- Tests outputs ----
test/outputs: \
  test/online_retail_II_last_6_months_filtered.csv \
  test/online_retail_II_last_6_months_filtered_002.csv \
  test/WEEKLY_TOP_SALES_RANK_001.html \
  test/WEEKLY_TOP_SALES_RANK_002.html \
  test/WEEKLY_TOP_SALES_RANK_003.html \
  test/WEEKLY_TOP_SALES_RANK_004.html
```

```
test/tables: \
  test_table/SRC_online_retail_II_-_Year_2010-2011_001 \
  test_table/RAW_ONLINE_RETAIL_II_YEAR_2010_2011_001 \
  test_table/INFO_SALES_LAST_6_MONTHS_FILTERED_001 \
  test_table/INFO_WEEKLY_TOP_SALES_RANK_001 \
  test_table/SRC_online_retail_II_-_Year_2010-2011_002 \
  test_table/SAT_ONLINE_RETAIL_II_YEAR_2010_2011_001 \
  test_table/BSAT_INVOICES_001 \
  test_table/BLNK_STOCK_CODE_PREFERRED_DESCRIPTION_001 \
  test_table/BHUB_STOCK_CODES_001 \
  test_table/BHUB_INVOICE_CODES_001 \
  test_table/INFO_WEEKLY_TOP_SALES_RANK_002
```

Remove Unnecessary Tables From the Deployed Database.

At the moment, our solution database has the old tables we used for our initial analysis. We've already removed the code we used to create and manage them, but we haven't deleted the tables from the database. The easiest way to do this is to manually delete the table from your query editing application. Alternatively, the `make uninstall && make` commands could be re run to rebuild the application from scratch.

Optimize the Database

Now that we've manually dropped the old, unused tables, we can perform a few database administration tasks to minimize the size of our file. These checks serve two purposes. First, they optimize the size of the database file by reorganizing the structure of the database on disk. Secondly, the optimize and integrity checks perform low-level optimizations to the database. By including this target as part of the make run process, we automate the optimization of the database every time we update the data.

```
compact_database:
	@$(SQLITE3) $(DBFILE) "PRAGMA optimize;" && echo $(DTS)    [INFO] - Optimizing database
	@$(SQLITE3) $(DBFILE) "PRAGMA auto_vacuum;" && echo $(DTS)    [INFO] - Vacuuming database
	@$(SQLITE3) $(DBFILE) "PRAGMA integrity_check;" && echo $(DTS)    [INFO] - Performing integrity check
```

Future Planning

Now that we've taken a bite out of our technical debt, let's plan for future iterations. Developing this list follows the same process we introduced in the innovation phase.

1. Develop high-level stories. These should be a mix of business value and enabling technology focused.
2. Determine the duration of an iteration (e.g., two weeks).
3. Score and rank the stories for urgency, business value, and duration.
4. Establish a cutoff point for the initial group (e.g., Top 3 first).
5. Select the stories with the highest Cost of Delay score within the cutoff point.
6. Starting with the most valuable parent story, break it down into smaller stories.
7. Add in placeholder stories for planned operational activities. Do not include stories for unplanned work.
8. Start working.

As a product owner, your responsibility is to develop high-level stories with clearly articulated business values. Where possible, work with the development team and customers ahead of time to break down these stories into smaller business features. Be critical about the expected outcomes. Focusing on outcomes makes it easier to discuss how to get there with the development team. Expect them to push back for more clarity, and be prepared to compromise.

As a developer, the obvious question is: how big should each of these sub-stories be? Following the earlier guideline, each of these stories should take 1-2 days to complete. Prioritize these stories by the order they need to be completed. In the case of multiple sub-stories that converge, it is helpful to physically lay them out using cards, sticky notes, or text boxes of the same size. With each box representing the same duration of work, it becomes obvious which story path will take the longest.

As the work progresses and the delivery process becomes more consistent, you can extend the planning window. When starting as a team, there isn't much value in planning out more than three weeks. This rolling three-week window encompasses two working weeks and a future buffer of work to be pulled ahead if the current queue is empty.

The product owner and a developer are responsible for keeping this queue full. The developer's responsibility is to represent the team and the technical debt. Ideally, this role rotates through the development team. Encouraging less-experienced developers to participate in this process quickly builds their business and technical planning abilities. With short iterations, any early misjudgments will be quickly resolved.

What should our product focus on next? Here we can step back into our business levels. Start by reviewing the yearly financial statements for the company.

REX INTERNATIONAL LIMITED — Page 6.

PROFIT AND LOSS ACCOUNT
for the year ended 31 October 2009

	Notes	2009 £	2008 £
TURNOVER	1e/2	7,462,098	6,032,837
COST OF SALES		(3,313,380)	(2,993,723)
GROSS PROFIT		4,148,718	3,039,114
DISTRIBUTION COSTS		(1,587,170)	(1,537,035)
ADMINISTRATIVE EXPENSES		(1,973,602)	(1,319,075)
OTHER OPERATING INCOME		43	54
OPERATING PROFIT	3	587,989	183,058
INTEREST RECEIVABLE		1,996	6,788
LOAN INTEREST PAYABLE		(34,317)	(93,454)
PROFIT ON ORDINARY ACTIVITIES BEFORE TAXATION		555,668	96,392
TAXATION	4	(99,977)	-
PROFIT FOR THE YEAR	10	455,691	96,392

2009 financial statement

REX INTERNATIONAL LIMITED			Page 6.
PROFIT AND LOSS ACCOUNT for the year ended 31 October 2010			
	Notes	2010 £	2009 £
TURNOVER	1e/2	8,907,773	7,462,098
COST OF SALES		(4,533,554)	(3,313,380)
GROSS PROFIT		4,374,219	4,148,718
DISTRIBUTION COSTS		(1,878,692)	(1,587,170)
ADMINISTRATIVE EXPENSES		(1,677,412)	(1,973,602)
OTHER OPERATING INCOME		223	43
OPERATING PROFIT	3	818,338	587,989
INTEREST RECEIVABLE		2,249	1,996
INTEREST PAYABLE		(18,760)	(34,317)
PROFIT ON ORDINARY ACTIVITIES BEFORE TAXATION		801,827	555,668
TAXATION	4	(215,117)	(99,977)
PROFIT FOR THE YEAR	10	586,710	455,691

2010 financial statement

Looking at the Net Profits from '08-'10 we can see that profits have been growing, there is a good chance we are in Level 4. A Level 4 company is characterized by these indicators:

- Net Profit is reliably and consistently improving.
- The focus is on orders and improving delivery execution.
- New opportunities are effectively assessed and implemented.
- Product mix decisions are effectively assessed and implemented.

Metrics to measure:

- Throughput growth
- On-time and in full deliveries
- Protective capacity on the constrained resource (CCR)
- Overall equipment effectiveness on the constrained resource
- Operational productivity ratio at the company level
- Free cash flow (Cash Velocity)

Metrics to ignore:

- Sales
- Traditional financial ratios (ROI, ROCE)
- Operating expense reduction
- Non-CCR utilization
- Manpower productivity

Looking at these indicators and metrics, we can have the most immediate impact with the following stories:

> **IN ORDER TO** IMPROVE DELIVERY EXECUTION
> **AS A** CUSTOMER
> **I WANT** TO RECEIVE THE ITEMS I ORDERED ON TIME
> **AND** WITHOUT ISSUES
>
> NOTES: WE CAN SEE THE DEFECTS IN THE RAW PRODUCT DESCRIPTION COLUMN.

> **IN ORDER TO** IMPROVE DELIVERY EXECUTION
> **AS A** SALES MANAGER
> **I WANT** TO MONITOR ON-TIME DELIVERIES BY PRODUCT
>
> NOTES: RATIO OF NON-CONFORMING INVOICES TO TOTAL INVOICES

IN ORDER TO IMPROVE DELIVERY EXECUTION
AS A SALES MANAGER
I WANT TO MONITOR IN FULL DELIVERIES BY CUSTOMER

NOTES: RATIO OF NON-CONFORMING INVOICES TO TOTAL INVOICES

IN ORDER TO IMPROVE DELIVERY EXECUTION
AS A SALES MANAGER
I WANT TO MONITOR IN FULL DELIVERIES BY PRODUCT

NOTES: RATIO OF NON-CONFORMING INVOICES TO TOTAL INVOICES

IN ORDER TO IMPROVE DELIVERY EXECUTION
AS A SALES MANAGER
I WANT TO MONITOR ON-TIME DELIVERIES BY CUSTOMER

NOTES: RATIO OF NON-CONFORMING INVOICES TO TOTAL INVOICES

IN ORDER TO IMPROVE THROUGHPUT
AS A SALES MANAGER
I WANT TO IDENTIFY THE PRODUCTS WITH THE HIGHEST THROUGHPUT

NOTES:
* THROUGHPUT = SALES REVENUE - RAW MATERIAL COST
* 1ST PASS RAW MATERIAL COST CAN BE ASSUMED TO BE THE LOWEST WHOLESALES COST / 2 UNTIL WE HAVE ACCESS TO THE PURCHASE DATA.

Rank and sort these stories using cost of delay divided by duration scores. The exercise helps us identify how to deliver the most value in the quickest time. At this moment, prioritize the throughput and in-full deliveries stories.

Description	Urgency	Value	Duration	Score
Highest Throughput	8	8	3	21
In Full Deliveries by product	5	3	1	15
In Full Deliveries by customer	3	1	2	2
On Time Deliveries by product	1	5	5	1
On Time Deliveries by customer	2	2	8	0.5

Break down the throughput story by identifying a few initial sub-stories. In order to deliver story 1.3, we must complete both 1.1. and 1.2. Which one should we finish first? Quickly calculate the cost of delay score for each. In the case of a tie, pick the story with the highest business value, and don't waste time overanalyzing.

Which one should we do first? We can quickly calculate the Cost of Delay score for each. In the case of a tie, pick the story with the highest business value and don't spend too much time over-analyzing.

```
1.2 (1)
IN ORDER TO IMPROVE THROUGHPUT
AS A SYSTEM
I WANT TO ESTIMATE SALES REVENUE FOR EACH
STOCK_CODE

GIVEN THE LAST SIX MONTHS OF SALES DATA
AND THE SALES PRICE FOR EACH INVOICE
AND THE SALES QUANTITY FOR EACH INVOICE
THEN CALCULATE THE SALES REVENUE (QTY. * PRICE)

SCORE: 2*1 / 1 = 2
```

```
1.1 (2)
IN ORDER TO IMPROVE THROUGHPUT
AS A SYSTEM
I WANT TO ESTIMATE RAW MATERIAL COST FOR EACH
STOCK_CODE

GIVEN THE LAST SIX MONTHS OF SALES DATA
AND THE LOWEST STOCK CODE PRICE FOR EACH INVOICE
AND THE WHOLESALE COST RATIO OF .5
THEN CALCULATE THE RAW MATERIAL COST

NOTE: DOES THIS VARY BY INVOICE?

SCORE: 1*2 / 2 = 1
```

```
1.3 (3)
IN ORDER TO IMPROVE THROUGHPUT
AS A SALES MANAGER
I WANT TO RESEARCH THE BEST VISUALIZATIONS FOR
THROUGHPUT.

GIVEN THROUGHPUT $ VALUE BY PRODUCT CODE
AND INVOICE CODE
AND CUSTOMER
THEN CREATE SOME POC VISUALIZATIONS WITH THE
DATA DISCOVERY PLATFORM VIZ. TOOL.

NOTE: RESULTS WILL DEFINE FUTURE STORIES.
```

In the list of metrics, we should ignore sales. Why is that? First, we talk about sales in several ways: number of units, total revenue, and various versions of profit contribution. Each is useful in particular contexts, but managing the number of units sold or total sales revenue bypasses the product cost. If we account for the costs associated with a sale, what do we subtract? Is it possible to easily describe the cost of goods sold (COGS) if you are not an accountant?

This is why we focus on a simple and effective version of throughput. If we focus on the sales revenue less the cost of the raw materials, we have a metric that is easy to understand. We can change the price to drive the sales volume. We can change the cost of the raw materials, or hold them steady. Together, they reflect the amount of money we make at a sufficient level to make decisions.[189]

Throughput becomes interesting when applied to the edges of our sales figures. If we agree that ((quantity * price) - raw material cost) is a useful representation of the sale's value, then we can use that same metric to assess the impact of defects and late orders. For example, if we have two products with similar defect levels but different throughput, focusing on the one with the higher throughput contribution has a greater bottom-line impact.

Focusing the metrics development efforts on being able to calculate Throughput should be the initial focus on any Business Intelligence effort because it provides the foundation to evaluate whether decisions are having, or are expected to have, positive impacts on the ability to make money now or into the future.

[182] SAFe Innovation and Planning (https://www.scaledagileframework.com/innovation-and-planning-iteration/)

[183] Black Swan Farming (https://blackswanfarming.com/cost-of-delay/)

[184] SAFe WSJF (https://www.scaledagileframework.com/wsjf/)

[185] Fibonacci number (https://en.wikipedia.org/wiki/Fibonacci_number)

[186] Entity Relationship diagram (https://en.wikipedia.org/wiki/Entity-relationship_model)

[187] erwin (https://erwin.com/products/erwin-data-modeler/)

[188] ER/Studio (https://www.idera.com/products/er-studio/enterprise-data-modeling)

[189] This is opposed to a more specific accounting definition of revenue, profit, and cost.

Epilogue

Introducing Data and Analytics Engineering to a diverse group of non-technical people requires broad exposure to specific technical skills and tools. More than that, everyone involved, needs to understand the larger philosophy of software development and business strategy to be effective.

Whether you focus on the difficulties of running a business faced with constant change and competition, or the simple fact that there are never enough hours in the day to get everything done. I hope you've found something useful. More than that, I hope you will have been exposed to new ways to think about problems.

Finally, I hope some aspect of the book piques your interest in some aspect of Data and Analytics Engineering or Business Management and this book becomes a steppingstone to years of investigation and experimentation.

What We've Covered:

- Technology projects fail because we don't understand the underlying issues specific to the general financial phase of our business.
- Based on that business phase as described by Throughput Economics, we can limit our focus to monitoring a small set of critical metrics.
- These metrics provide guidance to limit the scope of any improvement activity and eliminate the urge to do everything at once.

Now that we know what to measure, we can shift to defining goals of a valuable technological solution.

- Technological solutions have their own distinct phases which need to be managed in distinctly different ways.
- The 3X model and Wardley Maps can be used to identify the most appropriate approaches to defining scope, focus, value, appropriate skills, aptitudes, financing, planning, execution, and technological choices.

Even though our business and technology environment may be in an advanced level of maturity, every new product starts out in Exploration, using agile processes.

- What are the foundational principles and strategies of agile development?
- What are the core values needed to develop and support an effective team?
- What are the core practices that team can adopt to sustainably deliver the most value in the least amount of time?

Having a well rounded, diverse, multi-disciplinary development team means that everyone needs to have a basic understanding of the most important technological strategies in-play today.

- Microservices vs. monoliths.
- DevOps.
- Full stack development.
- Virtualization and containers.
- Data and analytics engineering.
- Evolution of data pipelines.

Throughout the process of building our Data Discovery Platform, we followed the agile processes of breaking deliverables into small, clearly scoped stories, with good acceptance criteria.

- What makes a good story?
- How do you know when you are done?
- Strategies for tracking and communication progress.
- How objectively prioritize the most valuable deliverables.
- How to ensure you have time to retire technical debt.

These business topics are critically important to being able to clearly articulate what needs to be done and how the team needs to act. The rest of the book covered how to build a foundational data product.

- Using shell scripts to execute tasks.
- Using GNU Make to automate everything.
- Break free from Excel with command line tools and SQL databases.
- Build a tool to bootstrap any data project.
- Build a set of end-to-end data management templates.

Then we built a fully automated system to extract, transform, load, provision, and deploy a database of actual sales data.

- Learned basic test driven development practices.
- Leveraged core features in GNU Make to minimize code duplication.
- Automated the creation of system documentation.
- Automated all aspects of the extract, load, and transformation process in a micro data warehouse.
- Learned how to publish and consume data APIs.
- Built a sophisticated sales report with a few lines of code.
- Leveraged open source tools to publish databases and reports locally and to Google's serverless hosting platform.
- Learned how to log the execution of the data pipeline.
- Learned how to schedule multiple processes.

In the prolog to the book, I told the story of my dad talking me to work to use the first personal computer they had ever purchased. The seed that was planted over those weekends was that big changes start small. They start with a few people, willing to take a chance and experiment. If you are lucky, one of those experiments can take off and completely replace the old way of doing things.

When should you start? As soon as things in the current world are looking good. When you are expanding and improving the current processes with established customers (e.g., In Expand) is the ideal time. Here you have adequate time to experiment with a few new options. Hopefully, this book has presented a framework to think about how to find the most valuable new opportunity.

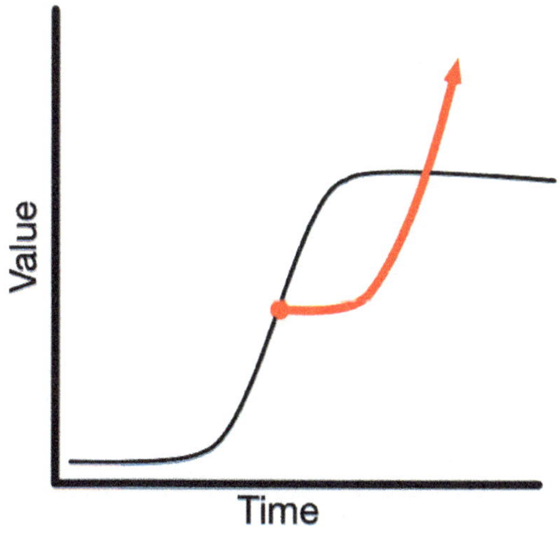

Appendix

Installing Software

All of the code examples were developed with MacOS but because it is UNIX based,

MacOS Installation

Install Xcode

```
xcode-select –install
```

There are a few permissions that must be reset in order to allow some of the software to be installed.

Make the `/usr/local/bin` directory writable by the current user.

```
sudo chown -R $(whoami) /usr/local/bin
```

```
chmod u+w /usr/local/bin
```

Installing the Brew package manager

The brew package manager makes it easier to manage UNIX software on a Mac. It will be used to manage the base software environment.

Website: https://brew.sh
Prerequisites: Ruby, Git
Install: `/bin/bash -c "$(curl -fsSL https://raw.githubusercontent.com/Homebrew/install/master/install.sh)"`

Validate: `brew doctor`
Update: `brew update`
Upgrade packages: `brew upgrade`
View Package information: `brew info <package>`

Install additional base packages:

```
brew install zlib tree sqlite aspell graphviz ImageMagick coreutils
```

Install Python 3
Website: https://www.python.org
Documentation: https://www.python.org/doc/

Rather than following the typical install process, we are going to install Python in using the pyenv program which will allow us to keep our development environment separate from the system version of Python. This will make it considerably easier to trouble shoot any issues in the future.

Install pyenv: `brew install pyenv`

From the Python website, identify the latest version of Python (https://www.python.org/downloads/).

Install the latest version of Python:
`pyenv install 3.9.0`

Set this version of Python as our global default:
`pyenv global 3.9.0`

Verify the version and path:
`pyenv version` returns `3.9.0 (set by /Users/brianmcmillan/.pyenv/version)`

Update the zshell configuration:
`echo -e 'if command -v pyenv 1>/dev/null 2>&1; then\n  eval "$(pyenv init -)"\nfi' >> ~/.zshrc`Reset the terminal: `reset`

Confirm the default Python location:
`which python` returns `/Users/brianmcmillan/.pyenv/shims/python`

Confirm the Python version:
`python -V` will return `python 3.9.0`

Confirm pip version:
`pip -V` will return `pip 20.2.3 from /Users/brianmcmillan/.pyenv/versions/3.9.0/lib/python3.9/site-packages/pip (python 3.9)`

Upgrade pip package manager:
`python3 -m pip install --upgrade pip`

Install additional python modules:
`python3 -m pip install makefile2dot pygraphviz eralchemy`

Upgrading pip:

```
/Users/brianmcmillan/.pyenv/versions/3.9.0/bin/python3 -m pip
install --upgrade pip
```

Listing installed pip packages:

```
pip list
```

Upgrading pip packages:

```
pip install upgrade <package-name>
```

Installing CSVKit

CSVKit is a general purpose set of command line tools to make it possible to easily work with CSV files, databases, and JSON files.

Repository: https://github.com/wireservice/csvkit
Documentation: https://csvkit.readthedocs.io/en/latest/#
Requirements: Python 3

Install: `pip install csvkit`

Datasette

Datasette is a tool for exploring and publishing data. It helps people take data of any shape or size, analyze and explore it, and publish it as an interactive website and accompanying API.

Datasette is aimed at data journalists, museum curators, archivists, local governments and anyone else who has data that they wish to share with the world. It is part of a wider ecosystem of tools and plugins dedicated to making working with structured data as productive as possible.

Repository: https://github.com/simonw/datasette
Documentation: https://docs.datasette.io/en/stable/
Requirements: Python 3

Install: `pip install datasette sqlite-utils datasette-vega`

SQLite

Small. Fast. Reliable. Choose any three.

SQLite is a C-language library that implements a small, fast, self-contained, high-reliability, full-featured, SQL database engine. SQLite is the most used database engine in the world. SQLite is built into all mobile phones and most computers and comes bundled inside countless other applications that people use every day.

The SQLite file format is stable, cross-platform, and backwards compatible and the developers pledge to keep it that way through the year 2050. SQLite database files are commonly used as containers to transfer rich content between systems and as a long-term archival format for data. There are over 1 trillion (1^12) SQLite databases in active use.

SQLite source code is in the public-domain and is free to everyone to use for any purpose.

Repository: https://www.sqlite.org/download.html
Documentation: https://www.sqlite.org/index.html
Requirements: None

Google Cloud SDK
Repository: https://cloud.google.com/sdk/
Documentation: https://cloud.google.com/sdk/docs/install

- Agree to the terms of service
- Set up contact and payment information
- Move the folder: `/google-cloud-sdk` to the root of your home directory.
- Open a terminal window in your home directory `cd ~`
- Run the install script and answer each prompts with the defaults `./google-cloud-sdk/install.sh`. Close the terminal when complete and then reopen a new terminal window in your home directory.
- Initialize the connection to Google Cloud: `./google-cloud-sdk/bin/gcloud init`
- Set the region `gcloud config set run/region us-central1`

Windows Installation

Over the years there have been numerous efforts to enable UNIX functionality within the Windows environment. [190] With the integration of a native hypervisor within windows,[191]Windows now supports the integration of virtual machines within the desktop operating system.

One clear advantage of this approach is that it makes it possible to have one or more development environments cleanly separated from the host operating system. Unlike the macOS, the installation within a virtual server can be completely deleted and reinstalled if needed. If the configuration steps were scripted, the provisioning steps could be included in the deployment pipeline.

Installing Windows Subsystem for Linux (WSL) requires Windows 10 Pro to enable support for the windows Hypervisor and the ability to run a virtual machine running Linux. We will be running the Debian[192] distribution of UNIX, but many other versions should work as well.

Preparing Windows 10 Pro

The first step in setting up our environment is to enable the hypervisor capability.

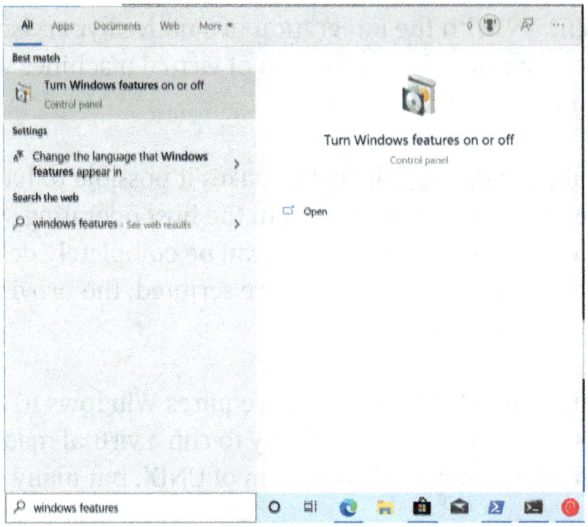

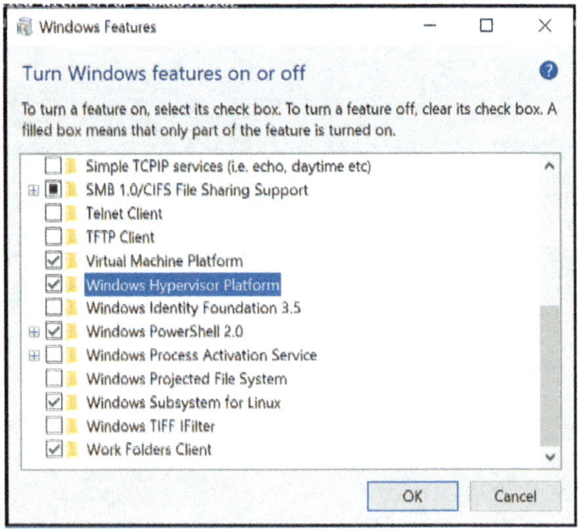

Once the feature is enabled, the Windows Subsystem for Linux (WSL)[193] can be enabled.

Open PowerShell as administrator.

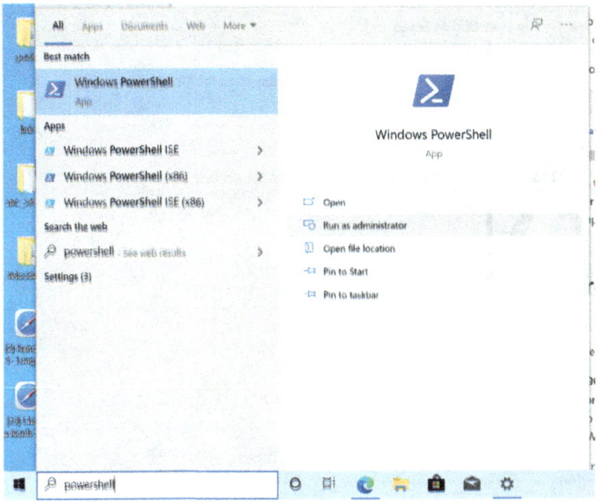

Run the following command: `dism.exe /online /enable-feature /featurename:Microsoft-Windows-Subsystem-Linux /all /norestar`

Now, enable support for virtual machines: `dism.exe /online /enable-feature /featurename:VirtualMachinePlatform /all /norestart` After

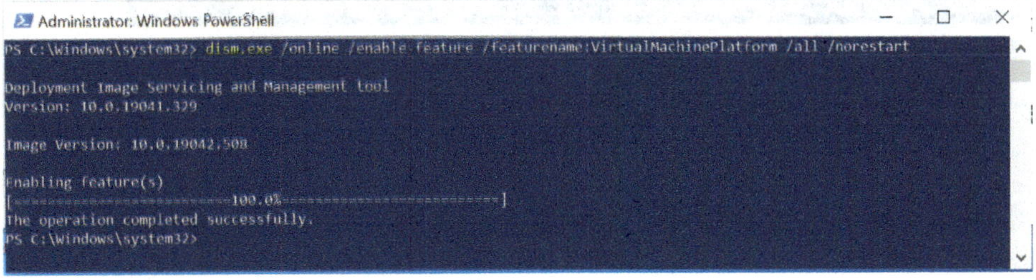

running the command, restart your computer.

Enabling WSL

Download the Linux kernel update package (https://docs.microsoft.com/en-us/windows/wsl/install-win10#manual-installation-steps) and run the installer.

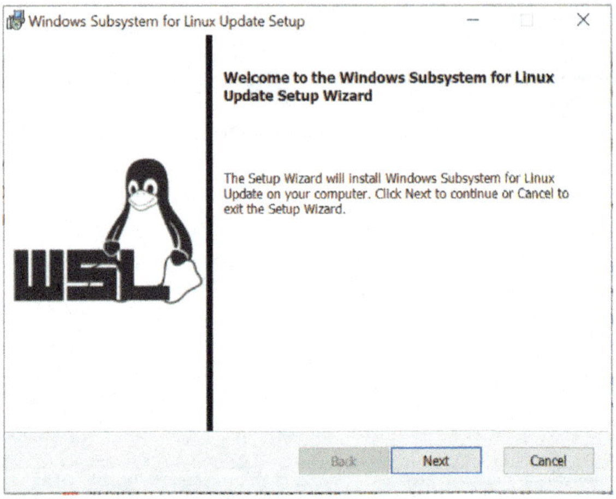

Set WSL2 as the default Linux environment: `wsl --set-default-version 2`

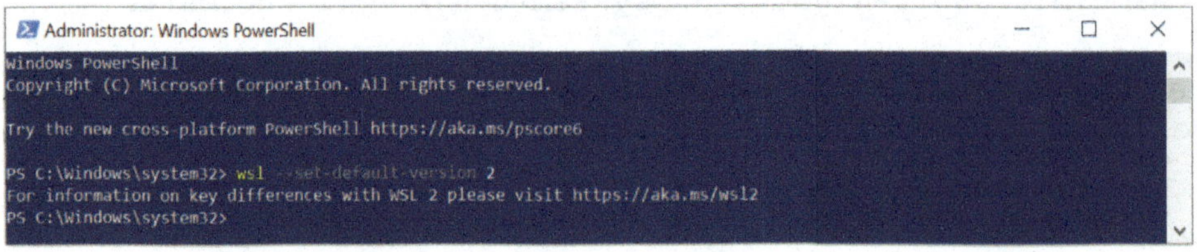

Install Windows Terminal

To make working within the UNIX environment we will install the Windows Terminal application from the Windows Store (https://aka.ms/terminal).

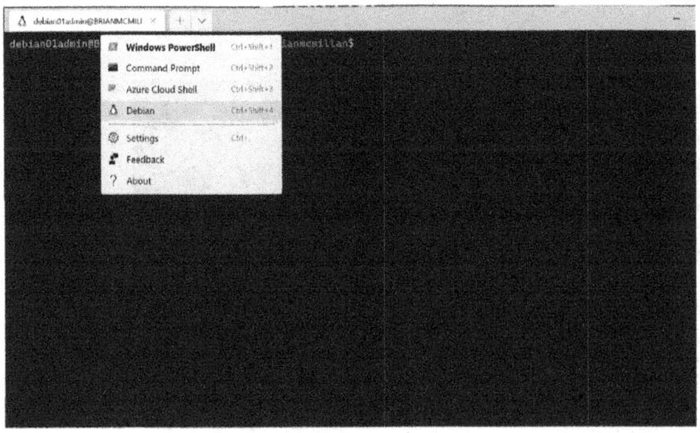

Install Debian

Download the Ubuntu Linux distribution from the Microsoft Store (https://aka.ms/wslstore).

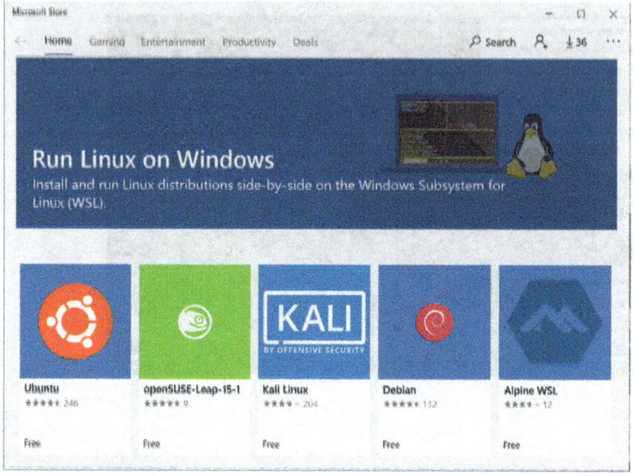

Select the Launch button, follow the instructions on the console window. This will include setting an administrator ID and password for Linux.

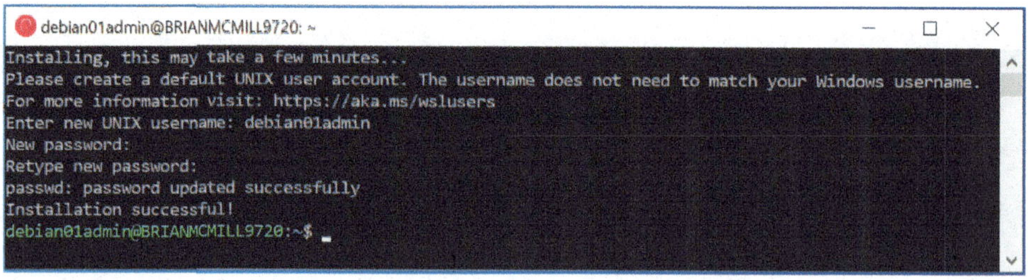

Update Linux packages:
```
sudo apt update && sudo apt upgrade
```

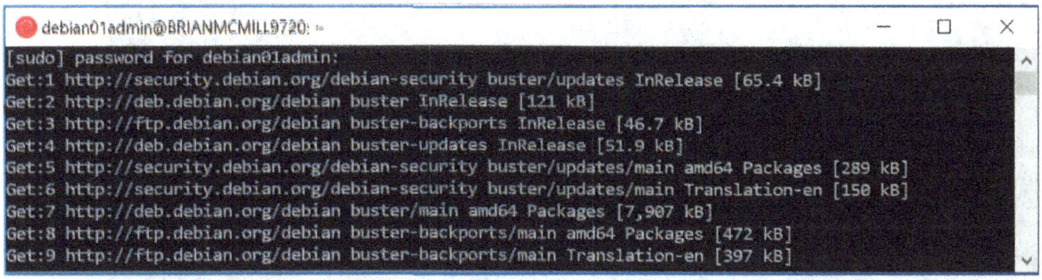

Configuring our software environment

Install the base set of non-standard utilities:

```
  sudo apt install unzip git aspell tree graphviz graphviz-dev
make curl wget python3-pip pkg-config libicu-dev libreadline-dev
```

Install the man pages for the standard utilities:

```
sudo apt install man-db manpages manpages-dev
```

Install additional python packages:

```
  sudo python3 -m pip install -U click==7.1.1 pygraphviz
makefile2dot eralchemy csvkit sqlite-utils datasette datasette-
vega datasette-copyable
```

Installing sqlite3 (https://sqlite.org/download.html):
Download the Precompiled Binaries for Linux file

```
cd ~/

wget https://sqlite.org/2021/sqlite-autoconf-3350500.tar.gz

tar xvfz sqlite-autoconf-3350500.tar.gz

cd sqlite-autoconf-3350500

./configure --prefix=/usr/local/

sudo make install
```

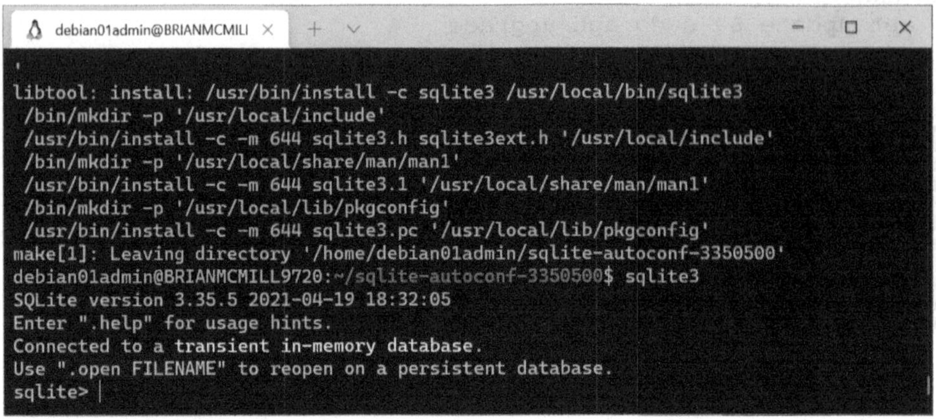

Verify the installation with the `which sqlite3` command. This should return `/usr/local/bin/sqlite3`. If you run the `sqlite3 –version` command, sqlite will return the version number (e.g., `3.35.5 2121-04-19 ...`

Installing the Google CloudSDK (https://cloud.google.com/sdk/).

Be sure you can access your gmail account. From a web browser, navigate to the install instructions (https://cloud.google.com/sdk/docs/install).

Select the Debian/Ubuntu tab. Follow the most recent install instructions on the web page. These are included for reference only.

```
echo "deb [signed-by=/usr/share/keyrings/cloud.google.gpg] https://packages.cloud.google.com/apt cloud-sdk main" | sudo tee -a /etc/apt/sources.list.d/google-cloud-sdk.list
```

```
sudo apt-get install apt-transport-https ca-certificates gnupg
```

```
curl https://packages.cloud.google.com/apt/doc/apt-key.gpg | sudo apt-key --keyring /usr/share/keyrings/cloud.google.gpg add -
```

```
sudo apt-get update && sudo apt-get install google-cloud-sdk
```

`gcloud init` and answer each prompts with the defaults. This will include setting up multi-factor authentication with gcloud.

At the final prompt, select *"Create a new project"* to initialize a new base project. The default name is OK to use.

Install the ATOM text editor

Run the AtomSetup-x64.exe application from the Download directory (https://atom.io). When it is finished running it will open to the Welcome page.

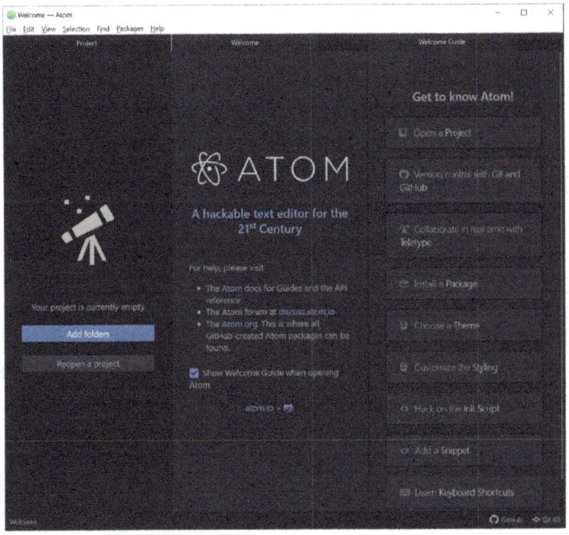

Important WSL commands

Shutdown WSL:

```
wsl.exe --shutdown
wsl.exe -t <DistroName>
```

Uninstall a distribution:

Windows search -> Debian -> Uninstall

Style Guides

A Style Guide serves a number of purposes. The practical benefit is that if code is written to follow a few basic rules, it will be easier to read and to understand when the code isn't working. the rules will make it easier to debug. Additionally, Style Guides are in important tool to train new developers by reinforcing the learning of learning good practices, many of which may not be immediately obvious. Most importantly, Style Guides, when collaboratively developed and maintained as living documents, serve to codify the practices of the development team. In effect, they become the laws and cultural practices the team follows.

As a set of laws and practices, they reinforce the principles and strategies adopted by the team. Ideally, the styles a team adopts should be just as simple as is necessary and no more. They should be open to modification as the team sees fit. If you choose to adopt a particular Style Guide, be prepared to modify it to suit your needs. Be skeptical of guides developed by teams doing other types of work, or guides developed by people working with other tools and systems. As an example, character limits on database fields and extensive abbreviation lists may be required by teams working with older databases but if your database allows you to use more descriptive names, you should be more descriptive. Better yet, avoid such proscriptive rule altogether.

The suggestions below are adapted from a number of sources and are intended as a starting point for guidance on developing data centric solutions.

Pay Attention to How You Name Things

- Use descriptive names that are understandable by the business.
- Use consistent and descriptive identifiers and names. Pick one: “female”, “FEMALE”, “F”
- Do not use abbreviations. "count" vs. "ct"
- Use the more natural collective term when describing groups. For example "staff" instead of "employees" or "people" instead of "individuals".
- Use the singular term when describing a single entity, "person", “company".
- Use consistent subject identifiers (business keys):
    - Human readable over sequence keys (George Schmerdnick not 123457)
    - Prefer hash keys over sequence keys for foreign keys and obfuscation.
- Primary and foreign keys should be hashes of the natural key(s) in the table rather than sequences. This significantly improves portability of the data across systems.
- Where possible avoid simply using id as the primary identifier for the table.
- For computed data (SUM() or AVG()) use the name you would give it were it a column defined in the schema. (e.g. sum_employee_count).
- Ensure the name is unique and does not exist as a reserved keyword.
- Use underscores where you would naturally include a space in the name ("first name" becomes "first_name").
- Only use letters, numbers, and underscores in names.
- Names must begin with a letter and may not end with an underscore.
- Avoid the use of multiple consecutive underscores, these can be hard to read.
- UPPERCASE for global variables, tables, databases, keywords.
- lowercase for local variables, fields, files, directories.
- Do not add a column with the same name as its table and vice versa.
- Do not use camelCase, it is very difficult to read.
- Do not use Hungarian notation (tbl_, sp_) to denote a type. NOTE: We’ve broken this rule with the Data Vault naming standards.
- If needed, append dates in YYYY-MM-DD format to facilitate sorting.
- Sequence suffixes should contain leading zero characters to facilitate sorting (001).
- If the files do not have legible names, consider placing them in a directory with a descriptive name.
- Carefully consider the cost of over specifying directories, schemas, additional databases. Start monolithic and then break things apart.
- Never give a table the same name as one of its columns and vice versa.
- Avoid, where possible, concatenating two table names together to create the name of a relationship table. Use a descriptive name instead, "supplier_catalog" over "part_supplier".

Treat Dates Carefully

- Use consistent dates.
- Store dates in ISO-8601 format,[194] or some derivation (YYYY-MM-DDTHH:MM:SS.SSSS+00:00).
- Avoid converting date strings into simple integer values (YYYYMMDD, YYYYDDMM). Use a numerical value like Julian or Epoch dates.

Strive for Legibility

- Include a header block in every file with at least the location and name of the file.
- Include comments in SQL code where necessary. Use the C style opening /* and closing */ where possible otherwise precede comments with -- and finish them with a new line.
- Make judicious use of white space and indentation to make code easier to read.
- Where possible, break code into small, independent, easy to understand sections.
  - Prefer Common Table Expressions over sub-queries.
  - Multiple tables with well defined scope scope
  - Prefer a functional approach over an object oriented / polymorphic / Entity Attribute Value (EVA) approach.
- Be as explicit as possible. Use the AS designator to clearly rename fields and tables rather than a space.
- White space: To make the code easier to read it is important that the correct complement of spacing is used. Do not crowd code or remove natural language spaces. Spaces should be used to line up the code so that the root keywords all end on the same character boundary. This forms a river down the middle making it easy for the readers eye to scan over the code and separate the keywords from the implementation detail.
- Always include spaces:
  - Before and after equals (" = ").
  - After commas (", ").
- Always include newlines/vertical space:
  - Before AND or OR.
  - After semicolons to separate queries for easier reading.
  - After each keyword definition.
  - After a comma when separating multiple columns into logical groups.
  - To separate code into related sections, which helps to ease the readability of large chunks of code.
- Keeping all the keywords aligned to the righthand side and the values left aligned to create a uniform gap down the middle of query. (e.g.; tables and fields in a JOIN statement).

Strive for Portability

- Default to treating data as text (001 not 1) rather than being reliant on the application functionality. As an example, Excel is notoriously inconsistent in how it interprets dates.
- Data should be exchangeable as either CSV or JSON. Prefer CSV.
- Try to use only standard SQL functions instead of vendor specific functions.
- If you must quote strings, use the SQL92 double quote standard.
- Avoid using stored procedures where possible. They limit portability across platforms and embed application business logic inside the database.

Query Syntax

Reserved words

- Always use uppercase for the reserved keywords like SELECT and WHERE.
- It is best to avoid the abbreviated keywords and use the full length ones where available (prefer ABSOLUTE to ABS).
- Do not use database server specific keywords where an ANSI SQL keyword already exists performing the same function. This helps to make code more portable.

Sorting and grouping

- Make use of BETWEEN where possible instead of combining multiple statements with AND.
- Similarly use IN() instead of multiple OR clauses.
- Where a value needs to be interpreted before leaving the database use the CASE expression. CASE statements can be nested to form more complex logical structures.
- Avoid the use of UNION clauses and temporary tables where possible. If the schema can be optimized to remove the reliance on these features then it most likely should be.

Create syntax

- When declaring schema information it is also important to maintain human readable code. To facilitate this ensure the column definitions are ordered and grouped where it makes sense to do so.
- Indent column definitions by four (4) spaces within the CREATE definition.

Choosing data types

- Where possible do not use vendor specific data types. These are not portable and may not be available in older versions of the same vendor's software.
- Only use REAL or FLOAT types where it is strictly necessary for floating point mathematics otherwise prefer NUMERIC and DECIMAL at all times. Floating point rounding errors are a nuisance!

Specifying default values

- The default value must be the same type as the column, if a column is declared a DECIMAL do not provide an INTEGER default value.
- Default values must follow the data type declaration and come before a NOT NULL statement.

Choosing keys

- The key should be unique to some degree.
- Consistency in terms of data type for the value across the schema and a lower likelihood of this changing in the future.
- Can the value be validated against a standard format (such as one published by ISO)? Encouraging conformity to point 2.
- Keeping the key as simple as possible whilst not being scared to use compound keys where necessary.
- Tables must have at least one key to be complete and useful.
- Specify the primary key first right after the CREATE TABLE statement.

Defining constraints

- Once the keys are decided it is possible to define them in the system using constraints along with field value validation.
- Constraints should be given a custom name excepting UNIQUE, PRIMARY KEY and FOREIGN KEY where the database vendor will generally supply sufficiently intelligible names automatically.
- Constraints should be defined directly beneath the column they correspond to. Indent the constraint so that it aligns to the right of the column name.
- If it is a multi-column constraint then consider putting it as close to both column definitions as possible and where this is difficult as a last resort include them at the end of the CREATE TABLE definition.
- If it is a table level constraint that applies to the entire table then it should also appear at the end.
- Use LIKE and SIMILAR TO constraints to ensure the integrity of strings where the format is known.
- Where the ultimate range of a numerical value is known it must be written as a range CHECK() to prevent incorrect values entering the database or the silent truncation of data too large to fit the column definition. In the least it should check that the value is greater than zero in most cases.
- CHECK() constraints should be kept in separate clauses to ease debugging.

Designs To Avoid

- Object oriented design principles do not effectively translate to relational database designs.
- Placing the value in one column and the units in another column. The column should make the units self evident to prevent the requirement to combine columns again later in the application (price_usd, price_eur). Use CHECK() to ensure valid data is inserted into the column.
- Entity Attribute Value (EVA) tables use a specialist product intended for handling such schema-less data instead.
- Splitting up data that should be in one table across many because of arbitrary concerns such as time-based archiving or location in a multi-national organization. Later queries must then work across multiple tables with UNION rather than just simply querying one table.

Attribution

SQL style guide by Simon Holywell (http://www.sqlstyle.guide)

Joe Celko's SQL Programming Style: (https://www.amazon.com/gp/product/0120887975/ref=as_li_ss_tl?ie=UTF8&linkCode=ll1&tag=treffynnon-20&linkId=9c88eac8cd420e979675c815771313d5)

SQL style guide issues on GitHub (https://github.com/treffynnon/sqlstyle.guide/issues)

Code Examples

Final Project Build Tool: Chapter 3

```
# ~/projects/projects/makefile
# Initialize a new data project
#
# make help
# make install PROJECTNAME=myproject
# make uninstall PROJECTNAME=myproject
#
##############################################################
# System variables and paths
SHELL := /bin/bash
ROOTDIR := $(shell pwd)

# Setup project
PROJECTNAME ?= test
PROJECTDIR := $(ROOTDIR)/$(PROJECTNAME)
SOURCEDIR := /src
SYSCONFIGDIR := /etc
SERVICEDIR := /svc
OPTIONALPKGDIR := /opt
LOCALSTATEDIR := /var
TEMPSTATEDIR := /tmp

# Utility variables
DTS = $(shell date +%Y-%m-%dT%H:%M:%S-%Z)

# Software variables
SQLITE_VERSION := 3350500
URL_SQLITE := "https://sqlite.org/2021/sqlite-amalgamation-$(SQLITE_VERSION).zip"
URL_EXTENSION_FUNCTIONS := "https://sqlite.org/contrib/download/extension-functions.c/download/extension-
functions.c?get=25"
URL_SHA1 := "https://www.sqlite.org/src/raw/c8f2253c8792ffab9517695ea7d88c079f0395a5505eefef5c8198fe184ed5ac?
at=sha1.c"
URL_PERCENTILE :="https://www.sqlite.org/src/raw/
b9086e223d583bdaf8cb73c98a6539d501a2fc4282654adbfea576453d82e691?at=percentile.c"

# Macros
define test_dir
	# tests the directory in the <first dependency>
	if ! test -d \$$<; \
	then echo $(DTS)	[FAIL] - \$$< does not exist; \
	else true; fi
endef

define test_file
	# tests the file in the <first dependency>
	if ! test -s \$$@; \
	then echo $(DTS)	[FAIL] - \$$@ does not exist; \
	else true; fi
endef

##############################################################
all: install check ## Executes the default make task. Initially, 'help'.
info: help info/variables ## Generates the informational files.
check: test/templates test/project test/project_dirs test/project_templates ## Executes all test suites.
installcheck: test/templates test/project test/project_dirs test/project_templates ## Run the project test
suite.
install: installdirs install/templates install/project_templates compile/sqlite3 ## Builds the project "make
install PROJECTNAME=<proj>".
uninstall: uninstalldirs ## Uninstalls the project.

.PHONY: installcheck
installcheck: ## Run the installation test suite.
	@echo $(DTS)	[INFO] - $@.

.PHONY: dist
dist: ## Create a distribution package.
	@echo $(DTS)	[INFO] - $@

.PHONY: help
help: ## List of all makefile tasks.
	@echo $(DTS)	[INFO] - $@
	@grep -E '^[a-zA-Z_-]+:.*?## .*$$' $(MAKEFILE_LIST) | \
	awk 'BEGIN {FS = ":.*?## "};\
	{printf "\033[36m%-20s\033[0m %s\n", $$1, $$2}'
```

```
.PHONY: info/variables
info/variables: ## List the variables in the makefile.
	@echo $(DTS)	[INFO] - $@
	@echo SHELL: $(SHELL)
	@echo ROOTDIR: $(ROOTDIR)
	@echo PROJECTNAME: $(PROJECTNAME)
	@echo PROJECTDIR: $(PROJECTDIR)
	@echo DTS: $(DTS)
	@echo SOURCEDIR: $(SOURCEDIR)
	@echo SYSCONFIGDIR: $(SYSCONFIGDIR)
	@echo SYSCONFIGDIR: $(SERVICEDIR)
	@echo OPTIONALPKGDIR: $(OPTIONALPKGDIR)
	@echo LOCALSTATEDIR: $(LOCALSTATEDIR)
	@echo TEMPSTATEDIR: $(TEMPSTATEDIR)
	@echo SQLITE_VERSION: $(SQLITE_VERSION)
	@echo URL_SQLITE: $(URL_SQLITE)
	@echo URL_EXTENSION_FUNCTIONS: $(URL_EXTENSION_FUNCTIONS)
	@echo URL_SHA1: $(URL_SHA1)
	@echo URL_PERCENTILE: $(URL_PERCENTILE)

################################################################################
# Tests                                                                        #
################################################################################
.PHONY: test/templates test/project test/project_dirs test/project_templates

test/templates:
	@if test -s $(ROOTDIR)/src/AUTHORS.md; \
		then echo $(DTS)	[PASS] - $(ROOTDIR)/src/AUTHORS.md file exists; \
		else echo $(DTS)	[FAIL] - $(ROOTDIR)/src/AUTHORS.md file does not exist; fi
	@if test -s $(ROOTDIR)/src/CHANGELOG.md; \
		then echo $(DTS)	[PASS] - $(ROOTDIR)/src/CHANGELOG.md file exists; \
		else echo $(DTS)	[FAIL] - $(ROOTDIR)/src/CHANGELOG.md file does not exist; fi
	@if test -s $(ROOTDIR)/src/LICENSE.md; \
		then echo $(DTS)	[PASS] - $(ROOTDIR)/src/LICENSE.md file exists; \
		else echo $(DTS)	[FAIL] - $(ROOTDIR)/src/LICENSE.md file does not exist; fi
	@if test -s $(ROOTDIR)/src/NEWS.md; \
		then echo $(DTS)	[PASS] - $(ROOTDIR)/src/NEWS.md file exists; \
		else echo $(DTS)	[FAIL] - $(ROOTDIR)/src/NEWS.md file does not exist; fi
	@if test -s $(ROOTDIR)/src/README.md; \
		then echo $(DTS)	[PASS] - $(ROOTDIR)/src/README.md file exists; \
		else echo $(DTS)	[FAIL] - $(ROOTDIR)/src/README.md file does not exist; fi
	@if test -s $(ROOTDIR)/src/crontab.txt; \
		then echo $(DTS)	[PASS] - $(ROOTDIR)/src/crontab.txt file exists; \
		else echo $(DTS)	[FAIL] - $(ROOTDIR)/src/crontab.txt file does not exist; fi
	@if test -s $(ROOTDIR)/src/data_sette_metadata.yaml; \
		then echo $(DTS)	[PASS] - $(ROOTDIR)/src/data_sette_metadata.yaml file exists; \
		else echo $(DTS)	[FAIL] - $(ROOTDIR)/src/data_sette_metadata.yaml file does not exist; fi
	@if test -s $(ROOTDIR)/src/data_sette_requirements.txt; \
		then echo $(DTS)	[PASS] - $(ROOTDIR)/src/data_sette_requirements.txt file exists; \
		else echo $(DTS)	[FAIL] - $(ROOTDIR)/src/data_sette_requirements.txt file does not exist; fi
	@if test -s $(ROOTDIR)/src/data_sette_settings.txt; \
		then echo $(DTS)	[PASS] - $(ROOTDIR)/src/data_sette_settings.txt file exists; \
		else echo $(DTS)	[FAIL] - $(ROOTDIR)/src/data_sette_settings.txt file does not exist; fi
	@if test -s $(ROOTDIR)/src/er_relationships.txt; \
		then echo $(DTS)	[PASS] - $(ROOTDIR)/src/er_relationships.txt file exists; \
		else echo $(DTS)	[FAIL] - $(ROOTDIR)/src/er_relationships.txt file does not exist; fi
	@if test -s $(ROOTDIR)/src/header.sql; \
		then echo $(DTS)	[PASS] - $(ROOTDIR)/src/header.sql file exists; \
		else echo $(DTS)	[FAIL] - $(ROOTDIR)/src/header.sql file does not exist; fi
	@if test -s $(ROOTDIR)/src/makefile_sqlite3; \
		then echo $(DTS)	[PASS] - $(ROOTDIR)/src/makefile_sqlite3 file exists; \
		else echo $(DTS)	[FAIL] - $(ROOTDIR)/src/makefile_sqlite3 file does not exist; fi
	@if test -s $(ROOTDIR)/src/vega_bar_chart.vega; \
		then echo $(DTS)	[PASS] - $(ROOTDIR)/src/vega_bar_chart.vega file exists; \
		else echo $(DTS)	[FAIL] - $(ROOTDIR)/src/vega_bar_chart.vega file does not exist; fi
	@if test -s $(ROOTDIR)/src/vega_line_chart.vega; \
		then echo $(DTS)	[PASS] - $(ROOTDIR)/src/vega_bar_chart.vega file exists; \
		else echo $(DTS)	[FAIL] - $(ROOTDIR)/src/vega_bar_chart.vega file does not exist; fi
	@if test -s $(ROOTDIR)/src/vega_scatter_chart.vega; \
		then echo $(DTS)	[PASS] - $(ROOTDIR)/src/vega_bar_chart.vega file exists; \
		else echo $(DTS)	[FAIL] - $(ROOTDIR)/src/vega_bar_chart.vega file does not exist; fi
	@if test -s $(ROOTDIR)/src/vega_embed_header.viz; \
		then echo $(DTS)	[PASS] - $(ROOTDIR)/src/vega_embed_header.viz file exists; \
		else echo $(DTS)	[FAIL] - $(ROOTDIR)/src/vega_embed_header.viz file does not exist; fi
	@if test -s $(ROOTDIR)/src/vega_embed_footer.viz; \
		then echo $(DTS)	[PASS] - $(ROOTDIR)/src/vega_embed_footer.viz file exists; \
		else echo $(DTS)	[FAIL] - $(ROOTDIR)/src/vega_embed_footer.viz file does not exist; fi

test/project: ## Test for a PROJECTNAME directory.
	@echo $(DTS)	[INFO] - $@
	@if test -d $(PROJECTDIR);\
	then echo $(DTS)	[PASS] - Project directory already exist;\
```

```
    else echo $(DTS)    [FAIL] - Missing project directory, run \"make install PROJECTNAME=\<proj\>\";\
    fi

test/project_dirs: ## Test for the existance of a directory_listing
    @echo $(DTS)    [INFO] - $@
    @if test -d $(ROOTDIR)$(SOURCEDIR);\
        then echo $(DTS)    [PASS] - Project directory $(ROOTDIR)$(SOURCEDIR) exists.;\
        else echo $(DTS)    [FAIL] - Project directory $(ROOTDIR)$(SOURCEDIR) does not exist;\
        fi
    @if test -d $(PROJECTDIR)$(SYSCONFIGDIR);\
        then echo $(DTS)    [PASS] - Project directory $(PROJECTDIR)$(SYSCONFIGDIR) exists.;\
        else echo $(DTS)    [FAIL] - Project directory $(PROJECTDIR)$(SYSCONFIGDIR) does not exist;\
        fi
    @if test -d $(PROJECTDIR)$(SYSCONFIGDIR)/app;\
        then echo $(DTS)    [PASS] - Project directory $(PROJECTDIR)$(SYSCONFIGDIR)/app exists.;\
        else echo $(DTS)    [FAIL] - Project directory $(PROJECTDIR)$(SYSCONFIGDIR)/app does not exist;\
        fi
    @if test -d $(PROJECTDIR)$(SYSCONFIGDIR)/cron;\
        then echo $(DTS)    [PASS] - Project directory $(PROJECTDIR)$(SYSCONFIGDIR)/cron exists.;\
        else echo $(DTS)    [FAIL] - Project directory $(PROJECTDIR)$(SYSCONFIGDIR)/cron does not exist;
\
        fi
    @if test -d $(PROJECTDIR)$(SYSCONFIGDIR)/server;\
        then echo $(DTS)    [PASS] - Project directory $(PROJECTDIR)$(SYSCONFIGDIR)/server exists.;\
        else echo $(DTS)    [FAIL] - Project directory $(PROJECTDIR)$(SYSCONFIGDIR)/server does not
exist;\
        fi
    @if test -d $(PROJECTDIR)$(SYSCONFIGDIR)/sql;\
        then echo $(DTS)    [PASS] - Project directory $(PROJECTDIR)$(SYSCONFIGDIR)/sql exists.;\
        else echo $(DTS)    [FAIL] - Project directory $(PROJECTDIR)$(SYSCONFIGDIR)/sql does not exist;\
        fi
    @if test -d $(PROJECTDIR)$(SYSCONFIGDIR)/test;\
        then echo $(DTS)    [PASS] - Project directory $(PROJECTDIR)$(SYSCONFIGDIR)/test exists.;\
        else echo $(DTS)    [FAIL] - Project directory $(PROJECTDIR)$(SYSCONFIGDIR)/test does not exist;
\
        fi
    @if test -d $(PROJECTDIR)$(OPTIONALPKGDIR);\
        then echo $(DTS)    [PASS] - Project directory $(PROJECTDIR)$(OPTIONALPKGDIR) exists.;\
        else echo $(DTS)    [FAIL] - Project directory $(PROJECTDIR)$(OPTIONALPKGDIR) does not exist;\
        fi
    @if test -d $(PROJECTDIR)$(OPTIONALPKGDIR)/local;\
        then echo $(DTS)    [PASS] - Project directory $(PROJECTDIR)$(OPTIONALPKGDIR)/local exists.;\
        else echo $(DTS)    [FAIL] - Project directory $(PROJECTDIR)$(OPTIONALPKGDIR)/local does not
exist;\
        fi
    @if test -d $(PROJECTDIR)$(OPTIONALPKGDIR)/local/static;\
        then echo $(DTS)    [PASS] - Project directory $(PROJECTDIR)$(OPTIONALPKGDIR)/local/static
exists.;\
        else echo $(DTS)    [FAIL] - Project directory $(PROJECTDIR)$(OPTIONALPKGDIR)/local/static does
not exist;\
        fi
    @if test -d $(PROJECTDIR)$(OPTIONALPKGDIR)/python;\
        then echo $(DTS)    [PASS] - Project directory $(PROJECTDIR)$(OPTIONALPKGDIR)/python exists.;\
        else echo $(DTS)    [FAIL] - Project directory $(PROJECTDIR)$(OPTIONALPKGDIR)/python does not
exist;\
        fi
    @if test -d $(PROJECTDIR)$(OPTIONALPKGDIR)/sqlite3;\
        then echo $(DTS)    [PASS] - Project directory $(PROJECTDIR)$(OPTIONALPKGDIR)/sqlite3 exists.;\
        else echo $(DTS)    [FAIL] - Project directory $(PROJECTDIR)$(OPTIONALPKGDIR)/sqlite3 does not
exist;\
        fi
    @if test -d $(PROJECTDIR)$(SOURCEDIR);\
      then echo $(DTS)    [PASS] - Project directory $(PROJECTDIR)$(SOURCEDIR) exists.;\
      else echo $(DTS)    [FAIL] - Project directory $(PROJECTDIR)$(SOURCEDIR) does not exist;\
      fi
    @if test -d $(PROJECTDIR)$(SOURCEDIR)/sqlite3;\
      then echo $(DTS)    [PASS] - Project directory $(PROJECTDIR)$(SOURCEDIR)/sqlite3 exists.;\
      else echo $(DTS)    [FAIL] - Project directory $(PROJECTDIR)$(SOURCEDIR)/sqlite3 does not exist;\
      fi
    @if test -d $(PROJECTDIR)$(SERVICEDIR);\
        then echo $(DTS)    [PASS] - Project directory $(PROJECTDIR)$(SERVICEDIR) exists.;\
        else echo $(DTS)    [FAIL] - Project directory $(PROJECTDIR)$(SERVICEDIR) does not exist;\
        fi
    @if test -d $(PROJECTDIR)$(SERVICEDIR)/analysis;\
        then echo $(DTS)    [PASS] - Project directory $(PROJECTDIR)$(SERVICEDIR)/analysis exists.;\
        else echo $(DTS)    [FAIL] - Project directory $(PROJECTDIR)$(SERVICEDIR)/analysis does not
exist;\
        fi
    @if test -d $(PROJECTDIR)$(SERVICEDIR)/db;\
        then echo $(DTS)    [PASS] - Project directory $(PROJECTDIR)$(SERVICEDIR)/db exists.;\
        else echo $(DTS)    [FAIL] - Project directory $(PROJECTDIR)$(SERVICEDIR)/db does not exist;\
        fi
    @if test -d $(PROJECTDIR)$(SERVICEDIR)/doc;\
```

```
            then echo $(DTS)     [PASS] - Project directory $(PROJECTDIR)$(SERVICEDIR)/doc exists.;\
            else echo $(DTS)     [FAIL] - Project directory $(PROJECTDIR)$(SERVICEDIR)/doc does not exist;\
            fi
    @if test -d $(PROJECTDIR)$(SERVICEDIR)/load;\
            then echo $(DTS)     [PASS] - Project directory $(PROJECTDIR)$(SERVICEDIR)/load exists.;\
            else echo $(DTS)     [FAIL] - Project directory $(PROJECTDIR)$(SERVICEDIR)/load does not exist;\
            fi
    @if test -d $(PROJECTDIR)$(SERVICEDIR)/source;\
            then echo $(DTS)     [PASS] - Project directory $(PROJECTDIR)$(SERVICEDIR)/source exists.;\
            else echo $(DTS)     [FAIL] - Project directory $(PROJECTDIR)$(SERVICEDIR)/source does not exist;
\
            fi
    @if test -d $(PROJECTDIR)$(SERVICEDIR)/static;\
            then echo $(DTS)     [PASS] - Project directory $(PROJECTDIR)$(SERVICEDIR)/static exists.;\
            else echo $(DTS)     [FAIL] - Project directory $(PROJECTDIR)$(SERVICEDIR)/static does not exist;
\
            fi
    @if test -d $(PROJECTDIR)$(TEMPSTATEDIR);\
            then echo $(DTS)     [PASS] - Project directory $(PROJECTDIR)$(TEMPSTATEDIR) exists.;\
            else echo $(DTS)     [FAIL] - Project directory $(PROJECTDIR)$(TEMPSTATEDIR) does not exist;\
            fi
    @if test -d $(PROJECTDIR)$(LOCALSTATEDIR);\
      then echo $(DTS)     [PASS] - Project directory $(PROJECTDIR)$(LOCALSTATEDIR) exists.;\
      else echo $(DTS)     [FAIL] - Project directory $(PROJECTDIR)$(LOCALSTATEDIR) does not exist;\
      fi
    @if test -d $(PROJECTDIR)$(LOCALSTATEDIR)/log;\
      then echo $(DTS)     [PASS] - Project directory $(PROJECTDIR)$(LOCALSTATEDIR)/log exists.;\
      else echo $(DTS)     [FAIL] - Project directory $(PROJECTDIR)$(LOCALSTATEDIR)/log does not exist;\
      fi

test/project_templates:
    @if test -s $(PROJECTDIR)/AUTHORS.md; \
            then echo $(DTS)     [PASS] - $(PROJECTDIR)/AUTHORS.md file exists; \
            else echo $(DTS)     [FAIL] - $(PROJECTDIR)/AUTHORS.md file does not exist; fi
    @if test -s $(PROJECTDIR)/CHANGELOG.md; \
            then echo $(DTS)     [PASS] - $(PROJECTDIR)/CHANGELOG.md file exists; \
            else echo $(DTS)     [FAIL] - $(PROJECTDIR)/CHANGELOG.md file does not exist; fi
    @if test -s $(PROJECTDIR)/LICENSE.md; \
            then echo $(DTS)     [PASS] - $(PROJECTDIR)/LICENSE.md file exists; \
            else echo $(DTS)     [FAIL] - $(PROJECTDIR)/LICENSE.md file does not exist; fi
    @if test -s $(PROJECTDIR)/NEWS.md; \
            then echo $(DTS)     [PASS] - $(PROJECTDIR)/NEWS.md file exists; \
            else echo $(DTS)     [FAIL] - $(PROJECTDIR)/NEWS.md file does not exist; fi
    @if test -s $(PROJECTDIR)/README.md; \
            then echo $(DTS)     [PASS] - $(PROJECTDIR)/README.md file exists; \
            else echo $(DTS)     [FAIL] - $(PROJECTDIR)/README.md file does not exist; fi
    @if test -s $(PROJECTDIR)$(SYSCONFIGDIR)/app/er_business_relationships.txt; \
            then echo $(DTS)     [PASS] - $(PROJECTDIR)$(SYSCONFIGDIR)/app/er_business_relationships.txt file
exists; \
            else echo $(DTS)     [FAIL] - $(PROJECTDIR)$(SYSCONFIGDIR)/app/er_business_relationships.txt file
does not exist; fi
    @if test -s $(PROJECTDIR)$(SYSCONFIGDIR)/app/metadata.yaml; \
            then echo $(DTS)     [PASS] - $(PROJECTDIR)$(SYSCONFIGDIR)/app/metadata.yaml file exists; \
            else echo $(DTS)     [FAIL] - $(PROJECTDIR)$(SYSCONFIGDIR)/app/metadata.yaml file does not exist;
fi
    @if test -s $(PROJECTDIR)$(SYSCONFIGDIR)/app/vega_embed_header.viz; \
            then echo $(DTS)     [PASS] - $(PROJECTDIR)$(SYSCONFIGDIR)/app/vega_embed_header.viz file exists;
\
            else echo $(DTS)     [FAIL] - $(PROJECTDIR)$(SYSCONFIGDIR)/app/vega_embed_header.viz file does
not exist; fi
    @if test -s $(PROJECTDIR)$(SYSCONFIGDIR)/app/vega_embed_footer.viz; \
            then echo $(DTS)     [PASS] - $(PROJECTDIR)$(SYSCONFIGDIR)/app/vega_embed_footer.viz file exists;
\
            else echo $(DTS)     [FAIL] - $(PROJECTDIR)$(SYSCONFIGDIR)/app/vega_embed_footer.viz file does
not exist; fi
    @if test -s $(PROJECTDIR)$(SYSCONFIGDIR)/app/vega_bar_chart.vega; \
            then echo $(DTS)     [PASS] - $(PROJECTDIR)$(SYSCONFIGDIR)/app/vega_bar_chart.vega file exists; \
            else echo $(DTS)     [FAIL] - $(PROJECTDIR)$(SYSCONFIGDIR)/app/vega_bar_chart.vega file does not
exist; fi
    @if test -s $(PROJECTDIR)$(SYSCONFIGDIR)/app/vega_line_chart.vega; \
            then echo $(DTS)     [PASS] - $(PROJECTDIR)$(SYSCONFIGDIR)/app/vega_line_chart.vega file exists;
\
            else echo $(DTS)     [FAIL] - $(PROJECTDIR)$(SYSCONFIGDIR)/app/vega_line_chart.vega file does not
exist; fi
    @if test -s $(PROJECTDIR)$(SYSCONFIGDIR)/app/vega_scatter_chart.vega; \
            then echo $(DTS)     [PASS] - $(PROJECTDIR)$(SYSCONFIGDIR)/app/vega_scatter_chart.vega file
exists; \
            else echo $(DTS)     [FAIL] - $(PROJECTDIR)$(SYSCONFIGDIR)/app/vega_scatter_chart.vega file does
not exist; fi
    @if test -s $(PROJECTDIR)$(SYSCONFIGDIR)/cron/crontab.txt; \
            then echo $(DTS)     [PASS] - $(PROJECTDIR)$(SYSCONFIGDIR)/cron/crontab.txt file exists; \
            else echo $(DTS)     [FAIL] - $(PROJECTDIR)$(SYSCONFIGDIR)/cron/crontab.txt file does not exist;
fi
```

```
	@if test -s $(PROJECTDIR)$(SYSCONFIGDIR)/server/requirements.txt; \
		then echo $(DTS)	[PASS] - $(PROJECTDIR)$(SYSCONFIGDIR)/server/requirements.txt file exists; \
		else echo $(DTS)	[FAIL] - $(PROJECTDIR)$(SYSCONFIGDIR)/server/requirements.txt file does not
exist; fi
	@if test -s $(PROJECTDIR)$(SYSCONFIGDIR)/server/settings.txt; \
		then echo $(DTS)	[PASS] - $(PROJECTDIR)$(SYSCONFIGDIR)/server/settings.txt file exists; \
		else echo $(DTS)	[FAIL] - $(PROJECTDIR)$(SYSCONFIGDIR)/server/settings.txt file does not
exist; fi
	@if test -s $(PROJECTDIR)$(SYSCONFIGDIR)/sql/header.sql; \
		then echo $(DTS)	[PASS] - $(PROJECTDIR)$(SYSCONFIGDIR)/sql/header.sql file exists; \
		else echo $(DTS)	[FAIL] - $(PROJECTDIR)$(SYSCONFIGDIR)/sql/header.sql file does not exist; fi
	@if test -s $(PROJECTDIR)$(SOURCEDIR)/sqlite3/makefile_sqlite3; \
		then echo $(DTS)	[PASS] - $(PROJECTDIR)$(SOURCEDIR)/sqlite3/makefile_sqlite3 file exists; \
		else echo $(DTS)	[FAIL] - $(PROJECTDIR)$(SOURCEDIR)/sqlite3/makefile_sqlite3 file does not
exist; fi
	@echo "----------------------------------------------------------------------------"
	@if test -s $(PROJECTDIR)$(OPTIONALPKGDIR)/sqlite3/sqlite3; \
		then echo $(DTS)	[PASS] - $(PROJECTDIR)$(OPTIONALPKGDIR)/sqlite3/sqlite3 file exists; \
		else echo $(DTS)	[FAIL] - $(PROJECTDIR)$(OPTIONALPKGDIR)/sqlite3/sqlite3 file does not exist;
fi
	@if test -s $(PROJECTDIR)$(OPTIONALPKGDIR)/sqlite3/sha1.dylib; \
		then echo $(DTS)	[PASS] - $(PROJECTDIR)$(OPTIONALPKGDIR)/sqlite3/sha1.dylib file exists; \
		else echo $(DTS)	[FAIL] - $(PROJECTDIR)$(OPTIONALPKGDIR)/sqlite3/sha1.dylib file does not
exist; fi
	@if test -s $(PROJECTDIR)$(OPTIONALPKGDIR)/sqlite3/percentile.dylib; \
		then echo $(DTS)	[PASS] - $(PROJECTDIR)$(OPTIONALPKGDIR)/sqlite3/percentile.dylib file
exists; \
		else echo $(DTS)	[FAIL] - $(PROJECTDIR)$(OPTIONALPKGDIR)/sqlite3/percentile.dylib file does
not exist; fi
	@if test -s $(PROJECTDIR)$(OPTIONALPKGDIR)/sqlite3/extension_functions.dylib; \
		then echo $(DTS)	[PASS] - $(PROJECTDIR)$(OPTIONALPKGDIR)/sqlite3/extension_functions.dylib
file exists; \
		else echo $(DTS)	[FAIL] - $(PROJECTDIR)$(OPTIONALPKGDIR)/sqlite3/extension_functions.dylib
file does not exist; fi

################################################################################
# Installation                                                                 #
################################################################################
.PHONY: installdirs install/templates install/project_templates

installdirs: ## Creates the project directories.
	@echo $(DTS)	[INFO] - Executing $@
	@mkdir -p $(ROOTDIR)/src \
	$(PROJECTNAME)$(SYSCONFIGDIR)/app \
	$(PROJECTNAME)$(SYSCONFIGDIR)/cron \
	$(PROJECTNAME)$(SYSCONFIGDIR)/server \
	$(PROJECTNAME)$(SYSCONFIGDIR)/sql \
	$(PROJECTNAME)$(SYSCONFIGDIR)/test \
	$(PROJECTNAME)$(OPTIONALPKGDIR)/local/static \
	$(PROJECTNAME)$(OPTIONALPKGDIR)/python \
	$(PROJECTNAME)$(OPTIONALPKGDIR)/sqlite3 \
	$(PROJECTNAME)$(SOURCEDIR)/sqlite3 \
	$(PROJECTNAME)$(SERVICEDIR)/analysis \
	$(PROJECTNAME)$(SERVICEDIR)/db \
	$(PROJECTNAME)$(SERVICEDIR)/doc \
	$(PROJECTNAME)$(SERVICEDIR)/load \
	$(PROJECTNAME)$(SERVICEDIR)/source \
	$(PROJECTNAME)$(SERVICEDIR)/static \
	$(PROJECTNAME)$(TEMPSTATEDIR) \
	$(PROJECTNAME)$(LOCALSTATEDIR)/log

install/templates: installdirs \
	src/AUTHORS.md \
	src/CHANGELOG.md \
	src/LICENSE.md \
	src/NEWS.md \
	src/README.md \
	src/header.sql \
	src/er_relationships.txt \
	src/vega_embed_header.viz \
	src/vega_embed_footer.viz \
	src/vega_bar_chart.vega \
	src/vega_line_chart.vega \
	src/vega_scatter_chart.vega \
	src/crontab.txt \
	src/data_sette_requirements.txt \
	src/data_sette_settings.txt \
	src/data_sette_metadata.yaml \
	src/makefile_sqlite3
	@echo $(DTS)	[INFO] - Executing $@

install/project_templates: install/templates
	@echo $(DTS)	[INFO] - Executing install/project_templates.
```

```
	@cp -f $(ROOTDIR)/src/AUTHORS.md $(PROJECTDIR)
	@cp -f $(ROOTDIR)/src/CHANGELOG.md $(PROJECTDIR)
	@cp -f $(ROOTDIR)/src/LICENSE.md $(PROJECTDIR)
	@cp -f $(ROOTDIR)/src/NEWS.md $(PROJECTDIR)
	@cp -f $(ROOTDIR)/src/README.md $(PROJECTDIR)
	@cp -f $(ROOTDIR)/src/er_relationships.txt $(PROJECTDIR)$(SYSCONFIGDIR)/app/
er_business_relationships.txt
	@cp -f $(ROOTDIR)/src/data sette_metadata.yaml $(PROJECTDIR)$(SYSCONFIGDIR)/app/metadata.yaml
	@cp -f $(ROOTDIR)/src/vega_embed_header.viz $(PROJECTDIR)$(SYSCONFIGDIR)/app/vega_embed_header.viz
	@cp -f $(ROOTDIR)/src/vega_embed_footer.viz $(PROJECTDIR)$(SYSCONFIGDIR)/app/vega_embed_footer.viz
	@cp -f $(ROOTDIR)/src/vega_bar_chart.vega $(PROJECTDIR)$(SYSCONFIGDIR)/app/vega_bar_chart.vega
	@cp -f $(ROOTDIR)/src/vega_line_chart.vega $(PROJECTDIR)$(SYSCONFIGDIR)/app/vega_line_chart.vega
	@cp -f $(ROOTDIR)/src/vega_scatter_chart.vega $(PROJECTDIR)$(SYSCONFIGDIR)/app/vega_scatter_chart.vega
	@cp -f $(ROOTDIR)/src/crontab.txt $(PROJECTDIR)$(SYSCONFIGDIR)/cron/crontab.txt
	@cp -f $(ROOTDIR)/src/data sette_requirements.txt $(PROJECTDIR)$(SYSCONFIGDIR)/server/requirements.txt
	@cp -f $(ROOTDIR)/src/data sette_settings.txt $(PROJECTDIR)$(SYSCONFIGDIR)/server/settings.txt
	@cp -f $(ROOTDIR)/src/header.sql $(PROJECTDIR)$(SYSCONFIGDIR)/sql/header.sql
	@cp -f $(ROOTDIR)/src/makefile_sqlite3  $(PROJECTNAME)$(SOURCEDIR)/sqlite3/makefile_sqlite3

.PHONY: uninstalldirs
uninstalldirs: ## Removes the project directories. "make uninstall PROJECTNAME=<proj>"
	@echo $(DTS)     [INFO] - Executing uninstalldirs.
	@rm -r $(PROJECTNAME) && echo $(DTS)     [WARNING] - Removing project directory
	@rm -r $(ROOTDIR)/src && echo $(DTS)     [WARNING] - Removing /src directory

###############################################################################
# Compile software                                                            #
###############################################################################

compile/sqlite3: install/project_templates
	@echo $(DTS)     [INFO] - Executing $@
	@$(shell make -C $(PROJECTNAME)$(SOURCEDIR)/sqlite3 -f makefile_sqlite3 all)
	@mv -f $(PROJECTNAME)$(SOURCEDIR)/sqlite3/sqlite3 $(PROJECTNAME)$(OPTIONALPKGDIR)/sqlite3/sqlite3
	@mv -f $(PROJECTNAME)$(SOURCEDIR)/sqlite3/sha1.dylib $(PROJECTNAME)$(OPTIONALPKGDIR)/sqlite3/sha1.dylib
	@mv -f $(PROJECTNAME)$(SOURCEDIR)/sqlite3/percentile.dylib $(PROJECTNAME)$(OPTIONALPKGDIR)/sqlite3/
percentile.dylib
	@mv -f $(PROJECTNAME)$(SOURCEDIR)/sqlite3/extension_functions.dylib $(PROJECTNAME)$(OPTIONALPKGDIR)/
sqlite3/extension_functions.dylib

###############################################################################
# File templates                                                              #
###############################################################################
src/AUTHORS.md:
	@echo $(DTS)     [INFO] - Executing $@
	@echo "# Authors" >> $@
	@echo "| Name | Role | Email | Phone |" >> $@
	@echo "|:--|:--|:--|:--|" >> $@
	@echo "| Prospero | Lead Sorcerer | prince@milan.com | 555-444-3333 |" >> $@
	@echo "| Miranda | Prospero's daughter | princess@milan.com | 555-444-2222 |" >> $@
	@echo "| Caliban | Slave of Prospero | mooncalf@island.net | 555-867-5000 |" >> $@
	@echo "| Ariel | Spirit | spirit@island.net | 555-867-5309 |" >> $@

src/CHANGELOG.md:
	@echo $(DTS)     [INFO] - Executing $@
	@echo "# Change Log" >> $@
	@echo "YYYY-MM-DD  Jane Doe  <mailto:johndoe@example.com>" >> $@
	@echo "* file1.txt (function): Lorem ipsum dolor sit amet" >> $@
	@echo "* file1.txt (unrelated_change): Lorem ipsum dolor sit amet" >> $@

src/LICENSE.md:
	@echo $(DTS)     [INFO] - Executing $@
	@echo "# MIT License" >> $@
	@echo "Copyright (c) [year] [fullname]" >> $@
	@echo " " >> $@
	@echo "Permission is hereby granted, free of charge, to any person obtaining a copy" >> $@
	@echo "of this software and associated documentation files (the "Software"), to deal" >> $@
	@echo "in the Software without restriction, including without limitation the rights" >> $@
	@echo "to use, copy, modify, merge, publish, distribute, sublicense, and/or sell" >> $@
	@echo "copies of the Software, and to permit persons to whom the Software is" >> $@
	@echo "furnished to do so, subject to the following conditions:" >> $@
	@echo " " >> $@
	@echo "The above copyright notice and this permission notice shall be included in all" >> $@
	@echo "copies or substantial portions of the Software." >> $@
	@echo " " >> $@
	@echo "THE SOFTWARE IS PROVIDED "AS IS", WITHOUT WARRANTY OF ANY KIND, EXPRESS OR" >> $@
	@echo "IMPLIED, INCLUDING BUT NOT LIMITED TO THE WARRANTIES OF MERCHANTABILITY," >> $@
	@echo "FITNESS FOR A PARTICULAR PURPOSE AND NONINFRINGEMENT. IN NO EVENT SHALL THE" >> $@
	@echo "AUTHORS OR COPYRIGHT HOLDERS BE LIABLE FOR ANY CLAIM, DAMAGES OR OTHER" >> $@
	@echo "LIABILITY, WHETHER IN AN ACTION OF CONTRACT, TORT OR OTHERWISE, ARISING FROM," >> $@
	@echo "OUT OF OR IN CONNECTION WITH THE SOFTWARE OR THE USE OR OTHER DEALINGS IN THE" >> $@
	@echo "SOFTWARE." >> $@

src/NEWS.md:
```

```
	@echo $(DTS)	[INFO] - Executing $@
	@echo "# News" >> $@
	@echo "## YYYY-MM-DD" >> $@
	@echo "Lorem ipsum dolor sit amet, consectetur adipiscing elit, sed do eiusmod tempor." >> $@
	@echo " " >> $@
	@echo "## YYYY-MM-DD" >> $@
	@echo "Lorem ipsum dolor sit amet, consectetur adipiscing elit, sed do eiusmod tempor." >> $@
	@echo " " >> $@
	@echo "## YYYY-MM-DD" >> $@
	@echo "Lorem ipsum incididunt ut labore et dolore magna aliqua. Bibendum arcu vitae." >> $@
src/README.md:
	@echo $(DTS)	[INFO] - Executing $@
	@echo " # Project Name" >> $@
	@echo " ## Brief Description" >> $@
	@echo " Lorem ipsum dolor sit amet, consectetur adipiscing elit, sed do eiusmod tempor." >> $@
	@echo " " >> $@
	@echo " ## Project Status" >> $@
	@echo " Lorem ipsum dolor sit amet, consectetur adipiscing elit, sed do eiusmod tempor." >> $@
	@echo " " >> $@
	@echo " ## Problem Statement" >> $@
	@echo " Lorem ipsum dolor sit amet, consectetur adipiscing elit, sed do eiusmod tempor." >> $@
	@echo " " >> $@
	@echo " ## Usage" >> $@
	@echo " Lorem ipsum dolor sit amet, consectetur adipiscing elit, sed do eiusmod tempor." >> $@
	@echo " ## Screen Shots" >> $@
	@echo " /docs/images/36-200x200.jpg" >> $@
	@echo " " >> $@
	@echo " ## Support" >> $@
	@echo " Lorem ipsum dolor sit amet, consectetur adipiscing elit, sed do eiusmod tempor." >> $@
	@echo " " >> $@
	@echo " ## Roadmap" >> $@
	@echo " Lorem ipsum dolor sit amet, consectetur adipiscing elit, sed do eiusmod tempor." >> $@
	@echo " " >> $@
	@echo " ## How you can help" >> $@
	@echo " Lorem ipsum dolor sit amet, consectetur adipiscing elit, sed do eiusmod tempor." >> $@
	@echo " " >> $@
	@echo "----" >> $@
	@echo " " >> $@
	@echo " ## For developers" >> $@
	@echo " #### Prerequisites" >> $@
	@echo " Lorem ipsum dolor sit amet, consectetur adipiscing elit, sed do eiusmod tempor." >> $@
	@echo " " >> $@
	@echo " #### Installation" >> $@
	@echo " Lorem ipsum dolor sit amet, consectetur adipiscing elit, sed do eiusmod tempor." >> $@
	@echo " " >> $@
	@echo " #### Usage" >> $@
	@echo " Lorem ipsum dolor sit amet, consectetur adipiscing elit, sed do eiusmod tempor." >> $@
	@echo " " >> $@
	@echo " ### License" >> $@
	@echo " [MIT](https://choosealicense.com/licenses/mit/)" >> $@

src/header.sql:
	@echo $(DTS)	[INFO] - Executing $@
	@echo "--etc/sql/<file_name>_###_<action>.sql" >> $@
	@echo "-------------------------------------------------------------------------------" >> $@

src/er_relationships.txt:
	@echo $(DTS)	[INFO] - Executing $@
	@echo "<table 1> 1--1 <table 2>" >> $@
	@echo "1 - Exactly one" >> $@
	@echo "? - 0 or 1" >> $@
	@echo "* - 0 or more" >> $@
	@echo "+ - 1 or more" >> $@

src/vega_embed_header.viz:
	@echo $(DTS)	[INFO] - Executing $@
	@echo " <!DOCTYPE html>" >> $@
	@echo " <html>" >> $@
	@echo "   <head>" >> $@
	@echo "     <title>Data Discovery Reporting</title>" >> $@
	@echo "     <meta charset="utf-8" />" >> $@
	@echo "     <script src="https://cdn.jsdelivr.net/npm/vega@5.17.0"></script>" >> $@
	@echo "     <script src="https://cdn.jsdelivr.net/npm/vega-lite@4.17.0"></script>" >> $@
	@echo "     <script src="https://cdn.jsdelivr.net/npm/vega-embed@6.12.2"></script>" >> $@
	@echo " " >> $@
	@echo "     <style media="screen">" >> $@
	@echo "       /* Add space between Vega-Embed links  */" >> $@
	@echo "       .vega-actions a {" >> $@
	@echo "         margin-right: 5px;" >> $@
	@echo "       }" >> $@
	@echo "     </style>" >> $@
	@echo "   </head>" >> $@
```

```
	@echo "   <body>" >> $@
	@echo "      <!-- Container for the visualization -->" >> $@
	@echo "      <div id="vis"></div>" >> $@
	@echo "      <script>" >> $@
	@echo "        // Assign the specification to a local variable vlSpec." >> $@
	@echo "        var vlSpec = {" >> $@
	@echo "          $schema: 'https://vega.github.io/schema/vega-lite/v4.json'," >> $@
	@echo " <!-- Embed Vega-Lite Definition Here -->" >> $@

src/vega_embed_footer.viz:
	@echo $(DTS)    [INFO] - Executing $@
	@echo "}" >> $@
	@echo "};" >> $@
	@echo " " >> $@
	@echo "// Embed the visualization in the container with id "vis"" >> $@
	@echo "vegaEmbed('#vis', vlSpec);" >> $@
	@echo "</script>" >> $@
	@echo "</body>" >> $@
	@echo "</html>" >> $@

src/vega_bar_chart.vega:
	@echo $(DTS)    [INFO] - Executing $@
	@echo "  "mark": "bar"," >> $@
	@echo "  "encoding": {" >> $@
	@echo "    "x": {"field": "end_of_week_ssmtwtf", "type": "temporal", "bin": false}," >> $@
	@echo "    "y": {"field": "total_sales_revenue", "type": "quantitative", "bin": false}," >> $@
	@echo "    "tooltip": {"sfield": "_tooltip_summary", "type": "ordinal"}" >> $@
	@echo "  }" >> $@

src/vega_line_chart.vega:
	@echo $(DTS)    [INFO] - Executing $@
	@echo "  "mark": "line"," >> $@
	@echo "  "encoding": {" >> $@
	@echo "    "x": {"field": "end_of_week_ssmtwtf", "type": "temporal", "bin": false}," >> $@
	@echo "    "y": {"field": "total_sales_revenue", "type": "quantitative", "bin": false}," >> $@
	@echo "    "tooltip": {"field": "_tooltip_summary", "type": "ordinal"}" >> $@
	@echo "  }" >> $@

src/vega_scatter_chart.vega:
	@echo $(DTS)    [INFO] - Executing $@
	@echo "  "mark": "circle"," >> $@
	@echo "  "encoding": {" >> $@
	@echo "    "x": {"field": "end_of_week_ssmtwtf", "type": "temporal", "bin": false}," >> $@
	@echo "    "y": {"field": "total_sales_revenue", "type": "quantitative", "bin": false}," >> $@
	@echo "    "tooltip": {"field": "_tooltip_summary", "type": "ordinal"}" >> $@
	@echo "  }" >> $@

src/crontab.txt:
	@echo $(DTS)    [INFO] - Executing $@
	@echo "MAILTO=""" >> $@
	@echo "#LOG_ROTATE - Rotate the log file every day." >> $@
	@echo "@daily /usr/bin/make -C </path/to/project/> -f makefile log_rotate >> </path/to/project>/var/
log/cron_log.txt 2>&1" >> $@
	@echo "#Execute the data pipeline every hour" >> $@
	@echo "#*/15 * * * * /usr/bin/make -C </path/to/project/> -f makefile all >> </path/to/project>/var/
log/cron_log.txt 2>&1" >> $@
	@echo "#deploy/local manually as needed" >> $@
	@echo "#0 */2 * * * /usr/bin/make -C </path/to/project/> -f makefile deploy/local >> </path/to/
project>/var/log/cron_log.txt 2>&1" >> $@

src/data sette_requirements.txt:
	@echo $(DTS)    [INFO] - Executing $@
	@echo "csvkit >= 1.0.5" >> $@
	@echo "sqlite-utils >= 3.3" >> $@
	@echo "datasette >=0.54.1" >> $@
	@echo "datasette-vega >= 0.6.2" >> $@
	@echo "datasette-copyable >= 0.3.1" >> $@

src/data sette_settings.txt:
	@echo $(DTS)    [INFO] - Executing $@
	@echo " {" >> $@
	@echo "      "default_page_size": 1000," >> $@
	@echo "      "sql_time_limit_ms": 5000," >> $@
	@echo "      "max_returned_rows": 5000," >> $@
	@echo "      "num_sql_threads": 3," >> $@
	@echo "      "allow_facet": true," >> $@
	@echo "      "default_facet_size": 10," >> $@
	@echo "      "facet_time_limit_ms": 1000," >> $@
	@echo "      "facet_suggest_time_limit_ms": 500," >> $@
	@echo "      "suggest_facets": true," >> $@
	@echo "      "allow_download": true," >> $@
	@echo "      "default_cache_ttl": 5," >> $@
	@echo "      "default_cache_ttl_hashed": 31536000," >> $@
```

```
	@echo "      "cache_size_kb": 0," >> $@
	@echo "      "allow_csv_stream": true," >> $@
	@echo "      "max_csv_mb": 0," >> $@
	@echo "      "truncate_cells_html": 2048," >> $@
	@echo "      "force_https_urls": false," >> $@
	@echo "      "hash_urls": false," >> $@
	@echo "      "template_debug": false," >> $@
	@echo "      "base_url": "/"" >> $@
	@echo " }         " >> $@

src/data sette_metadata.yaml:
	@echo $(DTS)    [INFO] - Executing $@
	@echo "title: Modify etc/app/metadata.yml" >> $@
	@echo "license: ~" >> $@
	@echo "license_url: http://example.com/" >> $@
	@echo "source: Building Data Products" >> $@
	@echo "source_url: https://example.com/" >> $@
	@echo "databases:" >> $@
	@echo "  sales:" >> $@
	@echo "    source: ~" >> $@
	@echo "    description_html: |-" >> $@
	@echo "       <strong>Description:</strong> ~ <br>" >> $@
	@echo "       <strong>Source:</strong> ~ <br>" >> $@
	@echo "       <strong>Source table(s):</strong> ~ <p></p>" >> $@
	@echo "       <a href = "mailto: manager@example.com">~Business Contact</a><br>" >> $@
	@echo "       <a href = "mailto: tech@example.com">~Technical Contact</a>" >> $@
	@echo "    tables:" >> $@
	@echo "      table_001:" >> $@
	@echo "        description_html: |-" >> $@
	@echo "         <strong>Description:</strong> ~ <br>" >> $@
	@echo "         <strong>Source:</strong> ~ <br>" >> $@
	@echo "         <strong>Source table(s):</strong> ~ <p></p>" >> $@
	@echo "         <strong>Reports:</strong><br>" >> $@
	@echo "         <a href="http://example.com/path/to/file.html" target="_blank">~.html</a><br>" >> $@
	@echo "         <p></p> " >> $@

src/makefile_sqlite3:
	@echo $(DTS)    [INFO] - Executing $@
	@#echo "URL_SQLITE:=\"https://sqlite.org/2021/sqlite-amalgamation-$(SQLITE_VERSION).zip\"" >> $@
	@#echo "URL_EXTENSION_FUNCTIONS:="https://sqlite.org/contrib/download/extension-functions.c/download/
extension-functions.c?get=25"" >> $@
	@#echo "URL_SHA1:="https://www.sqlite.org/src/raw/
c8f2253c8792ffab9517695ea7d88c079f0395a5505eefef5c8198fe184ed5ac?at=sha1.c"" >> $@
	@#echo "URL_PERCENTILE:="https://www.sqlite.org/src/raw/
b9086e223d583bdaf8cb73c98a6539d501a2fc4282654adbfea576453d82e691?at=percentile.c"" >> $@
	@#echo " " >> $@
	# Utility variables
	@echo " " >> $@
	@echo "all: sqlite3 sha1.dylib extension_functions.dylib percentile.dylib clean" >> $@
	@echo " " >> $@
	@echo "sqlite-amalgamation.zip:" >> $@
	@echo " @curl -o sqlite-amalgamation-$(SQLITE_VERSION).zip \"$(URL_SQLITE)\"" >> $@
	@echo " @unzip -oq sqlite-amalgamation-$(SQLITE_VERSION).zip" >> $@
	@echo " " >> $@
	@echo "sqlite3: sqlite-amalgamation.zip" >> $@
	@echo " @gcc -Os -I. \\" >> $@
	@echo " -DSQLITE_DEFAULT_FILE_PERMISSIONS=0644 \\" >> $@
	@echo " -DSQLITE_DEFAULT_LOCKING_MODE=0 \\" >> $@
	@echo " -DSQLITE_ENABLE_API_ARMOR \\" >> $@
	@echo " -DSQLITE_ENABLE_COLUMN_METADATA \\" >> $@
	@echo " -DSQLITE_ENABLE_DBSTAT_VTAB \\" >> $@
	@echo " -DSQLITE_ENABLE_FTS4 \\" >> $@
	@echo " -DSQLITE_ENABLE_FTS5 \\" >> $@
	@echo " -DSQLITE_ENABLE_GEOPOLY \\" >> $@
	@echo " -DSQLITE_ENABLE_JSON1 \\" >> $@
	@echo " -DSQLITE_ENABLE_RBU \\" >> $@
	@echo " -DSQLITE_ENABLE_RTREE \\" >> $@
	@echo " -DSQLITE_ENABLE_STAT4 \\" >> $@
	@echo " -DSQLITE_ENABLE_MATH_FUNCTIONS \\" >> $@
	@echo " -DSQLITE_OMIT_DEPRECATED \\" >> $@
	@echo " -DSQLITE_OMIT_TRACE \\" >> $@
	@echo " -DSQLITE_SOUNDEX \\" >> $@
	@echo " -DSQLITE_THREADSAFE=2 \\" >> $@
	@echo " -DHAVE_USLEEP \\" >> $@
	@echo " -DHAVE_READLINE \\" >> $@
	@echo " -DSQLITE_DEFAULT_FOREIGN_KEYS=0 \\" >> $@
	@echo " -DSQLITE_DQS=0 \\" >> $@
	@echo " -DSQLITE_ENABLE_EXPLAIN_COMMENTS \\" >> $@
	@echo " sqlite-amalgamation-$(SQLITE_VERSION)/shell.c \\" >> $@
	@echo " sqlite-amalgamation-$(SQLITE_VERSION)/sqlite3.c \\" >> $@
	@echo " -ldl -lreadline -lncurses -o sqlite3" >> $@
	@echo " " >> $@
	@echo "extension-functions.c:" >> $@
```

```
@echo " @curl -o extension-functions.c \"$(URL_EXTENSION_FUNCTIONS)\"" >> $@
@echo " " >> $@
@echo "sha1.c:" >> $@
@echo " @curl -o sha1.c \"$(URL_SHA1)\"" >> $@
@echo " " >> $@
@echo "percentile.c:" >> $@
@echo " @curl -o percentile.c \"$(URL_PERCENTILE)\"" >> $@
@echo " " >> $@
@echo "extension_functions.dylib: extension-functions.c" >> $@
@echo " @gcc -fno-common -dynamiclib extension-functions.c -o extension_functions.dylib #macos" >> $@
@echo " @#gcc -fPIC -lm -shared extension-functions.c -o lextension_functions.so #linux" >> $@
@echo " " >> $@
@echo "sha1.dylib: sha1.c" >> $@
@echo " @gcc -fno-common -dynamiclib sha1.c -o sha1.dylib #macos" >> $@
@echo " @#gcc -fPIC -lm -shared sha1.c -o sha1.dylib #linux" >> $@
@echo " " >> $@
@echo "percentile.dylib: percentile.c" >> $@
@echo " @gcc -fno-common -dynamiclib percentile.c -o percentile.dylib #macos" >> $@
@echo " @#gcc -fPIC -lm -shared percentile.c -o percentile.dylib #linux" >> $@
@echo " " >> $@
@echo "clean:" >> $@
@echo " @rm -fr *.zip *.c sqlite-amalgamation-*" >> $@
@echo " " >> $@
@echo "uninstall:" >> $@
@echo " @rm -f *.c" >> $@
@echo " @rm -f *.dylib" >> $@
@echo " @rm -f *.dll" >> $@
@echo " @rm -f *.so" >> $@
```

Example Project Makefile

```
# ~/projects/<project_name>/makefile
# Execute the data pipeline for a project.
#
# make all                  Executes the default make task.
# make info                 Generates the informational files.
# make check                Executes all test suites.
# make installcheck         Run the project test suite.
# make install              Builds the database and application structure.
# make uninstall            Uninstalls the project.
# make run                  Executes the data pipelines.
# make help                 List of all makefile tasks.
# make documentation        Builds the documentation files for the build. (e.g. schema docs, data flow
diagrams)
# make uninstalldirs        Removes the project directories. "make uninstall"
# make installcheck         Run the installation test suite.
#
##############################################################
# Program locations (which <utility>)
SHELL := /bin/bash
SQLITE3 := /usr/local/bin/sqlite3
SPLIT := /usr/local/bin/gsplit
TREE := /usr/local/bin/tree
CURL := /usr/bin/curl
GRAPHVIZDOT := /usr/local/bin/dot
GCLOUD := /Users/brianmcmillan/google-cloud-sdk/bin/gcloud
PYENVDIR := /Users/brianmcmillan/.pyenv/shims
PYTHON3 := $(PYENVDIR)/python
PIP := $(PYENVDIR)/pip
IN2CSV := $(PYENVDIR)/in2csv
SQL2CSV := $(PYENVDIR)/sql2csv
CSVSTACK := $(PYENVDIR)/csvstack
CSVSQL := $(PYENVDIR)/csvsql
SQLITEUTILS := $(PYENVDIR)/sqlite-utils
NODEGRAPH := $(PYENVDIR)/makefile2dot
DATASETTE := $(PYENVDIR)/datasette
ERALCHEMY := $(PYENVDIR)/eralchemy

# Utility variables
DTS = $(shell date +%Y-%m-%dT%H:%M:%S-%Z)
LIST_CSV = $(shell find $(dir $@) -type f -name '*.csv' -not -name 'load.csv')

# Deployment variables
LOCAL_ADDRESS := $(shell /usr/sbin/ipconfig getifaddr en0) #192.168.1.251
LOCAL_PORT := 8001

##############################################################################
# Macros                                                                     #
##############################################################################
define test_dir
	# tests the directory in the <first dependency>
	if ! test -d $<; \
	then echo $(DTS)	[FAIL] - $< does not exist; \
	else true; fi
endef

define test_file
	# tests the file in the <first dependency>
	if ! test -s $@; \
	then echo $(DTS)	[FAIL] - $@ does not exist; \
	else true; fi
endef

define test_dependent_file
	# tests the file in the <first dependency>
	if ! test -s $<; \
	then echo $(DTS)	[FAIL] - $< does not exist; \
	else true; fi
endef

define test_table
	@#test_table/<table_name>(colon)
	@if ! test $(@F) = $(shell $(SQLITE3) $(DBFILE) ".tables $(@F)" ".quit"); \
	then echo [FAIL] - $(@F) table does not exist; \
	else true; fi
endef

define test_database
	@#test_databse(colon)(space)<path/to/database.db>
```

```
	@echo $(DTS)	[INFO] - DB $(shell $(SQLITE3) $< ".databases")
endef

define file_compare
	@#<target>(colon)(space)<file_1> <file_2>
	@cmp -s $(word 1,$^) $(word 2,$^) || \
	echo $(DTS)	[FAIL] - $(word 2,$^) not equal to $(word 1,$^).
endef

define record_count_csv
	@#metrics/<csv_file.csv>(colon)(space)PATH = "<path/to/file.csv>"
	@#metrics/<csv_file.csv>(colon)(space)
	@echo $(DTS)	[INFO] - record count = $(shell wc -l < $(PATH)) $(PATH)
endef

define record_count_table
	@#record_count/<table name>(colon)(space)<path/to/database.db>
	echo $(DTS)	[INFO] - record count = $(shell $(SQLITE3) $< \
	"SELECT COUNT(*) || ' records in $(@F).$(notdir $<)' FROM [$(@F)]" ".quit")
endef

define update_file_modified_date
	@#touch_src/<generalized_file_identifier>(colon)(space)<path/to/file.xyz>
	@touch $^ && echo [INFO] - Manually updating [$^] file date.
endef

define extract_csv_from_excel
	@#<path/to/csv_file.csv>(colon)(space)TABNAME = "<name of XLS worksheet>"
	@#<path/to/csv_file.csv>(colon)(space)<path/to/source/excel_file.xlsx>
	@echo $(DTS)	[INFO] - Extracting data from $< [$(TABNAME)] into $@
	@$(IN2CSV) -f xlsx --sheet $(TABNAME) $< > $@
	@$(CSVSTACK) -n load_dts -g $(DTS) $@ > tmp/$(@F)_1.tmp
	@$(CSVSTACK) -n provider_code -g $@ tmp/$(@F)_1.tmp > tmp/$(@F)_2.tmp
	@mv tmp/$(@F)_2.tmp $@
	@rm tmp/$(@F)_1.tmp
	@$(test_file)
endef

define execute_sql_export_csv
	@#<path/to/export_file.csv>(colon)(space)<path/to/query.sql>
	@echo $(DTS)	[INFO] - Executing $< and exporting to $@
	@$(SQL2CSV) --db sqlite:///$(DBFILE) $< > $@
endef

define load_csv_into_database
	@#load_csv/SRC_<csv_file_name>_001(colon)(space)DBNAME=<database_name>
	@#load_csv/SRC_<csv_file_name>_001(colon)(space)<path/to/csv_file.csv>
	@echo $(DTS)	[INFO] - Executing $@
	@$(CSVSQL) \
	--db sqlite:///$(DBFILE) \
	--create-if-not-exists --overwrite \
	--no-inference --no-constraints \
	--chunk-size 10000 \
	--tables $(@F) \
	--insert $<
endef

define create_table
	@#<table_name>(colon)(space)<path/to/<table_name>_create.sql>
	@echo $(DTS)	[INFO] - Creating table $@
	@$(SQLITE3) $(DBFILE) ".read $<" ".quit"
endef

define execute_sql
	@#<table_name>(colon)(space) <path/to/sql_file.sql> [<dependent_table_name(s)>]
	@echo $(DTS)	[INFO] - Executing $<
	@$(SQLITE3) $(DBFILE) ".read $<" ".quit"
endef

define vega_report_from_api
	@#<path/to/export_file.html>(colon)(space)VIZTITLE=<report title>
	@#<path/to/export_file.html>(colon)(space)VIZTEMPLATE=<path/to/viz_template.vega>
	@#<path/to/export_file.html>(colon)(space)VIZURL=<path/to/viz_url.json?_shape=array>
	@#<path/to/export_file.html>(colon)(space)<source_table_name>
	@echo $(DTS)	[INFO] - Executing $@
	@cat etc/app/vega_embed_header.viz > $@
	@echo "\"data\":{\"url\":\"$(VIZURL)\"}, " >> $@
	@echo "\"title\":\"$(VIZTITLE)\"," >> $@
	@cat $(VIZTEMPLATE) >> $@
	@cat etc/app/vega_embed_footer.viz >> $@
endef

define vega_report_from_file
```

```
	@#<path/to/export_file.html>(colon)(space)VIZTITLE=<report title>
	@#<path/to/export_file.html>(colon)(space)VIZTEMPLATE=<path/to/viz_template.vega>
	@#<path/to/export_file.html>(colon)(space)<source_file_name>
	@echo $(DTS)	[INFO] - Executing $@
	@cat etc/app/vega_embed_header.viz > $@
	@echo "\"data\":{ \"values\":" >> $@
	@cat $< >> $@ && echo "}, " >> $@
	@echo "\"title\":\"$(VIZTITLE)\"," >> $@
	@cat $(VIZTEMPLATE) >> $@
	@cat etc/app/vega_embed_footer.viz >> $@
endef

define table_metadata
	@#table_metadata(colon)(space)<path/to/database.db>"
	@echo $(DTS)	[INFO] - Executing $@
	@$(SQLITE3) $(<) "DROP TABLE IF EXISTS '_analyze_tables_';" ".quit"
	@$(SQLITE3) $(<) "DROP TABLE IF EXISTS 'META_TABLES_001';" ".quit"
	@$(SQLITEUTILS) analyze-tables $(<) --save
	@$(SQLITE3) $(<) "ALTER TABLE '_analyze_tables_' RENAME TO 'META_TABLES_001';" ".quit"
endef

define sql_template_from_csv
	@#make template/src_from_csv CSVPATH=<path/to/file.csv>
	@echo $(DTS)	[INFO] - Creating script for SRC_$(notdir $(basename $(CSVPATH)))_###_create from $
(CSVPATH)
	@if test -s $(CSVPATH); then echo [PASS] - $(CSVPATH) file exists; \
	else echo [FAIL] - $(CSVPATH) file does not exist; fi
	@$(SQLITE3) tmp/temp.db ".import --csv $(CSVPATH) SRC_$(notdir $(basename $(CSVPATH)))_###"
	@$(SQLITE3) tmp/temp.db ".schema SRC_$(notdir $(basename $(CSVPATH)))_###"
	@echo "--etc/sql/SRC_$(notdir $(basename $(CSVPATH)))_###_create.sql" \
	> etc/sql/SRC_$(notdir $(basename $(CSVPATH)))_###_create.sql
	@echo "-------------------------------------------------------------------------------" \
	>> etc/sql/SRC_$(notdir $(basename $(CSVPATH)))_###_create.sql
	@$(SQLITE3) tmp/temp.db ".schema SRC_$(notdir $(basename $(CSVPATH)))_###" \
	>> etc/sql/SRC_$(notdir $(basename $(CSVPATH)))_###_create.sql
	@rm tmp/temp.db
endef

define er_diagram
	@#<path/to/diagram.type>(colon)(space)REL_FILE="<path/to/relationship_file.txt>"
	@#<path/to/diagram.type>(colon)(space)<table_name(s)>"
	@#Types can be er, pdf, png, dot
	@echo $(DTS)	[INFO] - Executing $@
	@$(ERALCHEMY) -i sqlite:///$(DBFILE) -o tmp/$(@F).er
	@cat tmp/$(@F).er $(REL_FILE) > tmp/$(@F)_2.er || true
	@$(ERALCHEMY) -i tmp/$(@F)_2.er -o $@
	@rm -f tmp/$(@F)*.er
endef

define log_rotate
	@#log_rotate:(colon)(space)<path/to/logfile>
	@echo $(DTS)	[INFO] - Executing $@
	@mv $< $(basename($<))_$(shell date +%Y-%m-%d).txt
endef

define compact_database
	@#compact_database(colon)(space)<path/to/database.db>
	@echo $(DTS)	[INFO] - Executing $@
	@$(SQLITE3) $< "PRAGMA optimize;" && echo $(DTS)	[INFO] - Optimizing database
	@$(SQLITE3) $< "PRAGMA auto_vacuum;" && echo $(DTS)	[INFO] - Vacuuming database
	@$(SQLITE3) $< "PRAGMA integrity_check;" && echo $(DTS)	[INFO] - Performing integrity check
endef

define help
	@echo $(DTS)	[INFO] - Executing $@
	@grep -E '^[a-zA-Z_-]+:.*?## .*$$' $(MAKEFILE_LIST) | \
	awk 'BEGIN {FS = ":.*?## "};\
	{printf "\033[36m%-20s\033[0m %s\n", $$1, $$2}'
endef

define split_csv
	@#<split/file_group_description>(colon)(space) path/to/source_file.csv
	@echo $(DTS)	[INFO] - Splitting $< into $(TARGETDIR)$(TARGETNAME)_###
	@mkdir -p svc/load/$(@F)/ svc/load/split_$(@F)/
	@$(SPLIT) -d -a 3 -l 50000 --additional-suffix=".csv" \
	$< svc/load/split_$(@F)/$(basename $(<F))_
	@wc -l svc/load/split_$(@F)/*.csv
endef

###############################################################################
all: run ## Executes the default make task.
info: help info/variables documentation ## Generates the informational files.
check: test/inputs test/outputs ## Executes all test suites.
```

```
installcheck: test/inputs ## Run the project test suite.
install: test/inputs ## Builds the database and application structure.
uninstall: uninstalldirs ## Uninstalls the project.
run: test/inputs build/local table_metadata documentation metrics ## Executes the data pipelines.
deploy: deploy/local ##Deploys local web server.

.PHONY: all info check installcheck install uninstall run deploy help documentation \
	table_metadata uninstalldirs log_rotate compact_database info/variables template/src_from_csv

.FORCE:

help: ## List of all makefile tasks.
	@$(help)

documentation: svc/doc/directory_listing.txt svc/doc/makefile_graph.png svc/doc/er_diagram.pdf ## Builds the documentation files for the build. (e.g. schema docs, data flow diagrams)

table_metadata: svc/db/online_retail.db
	@$(table_metadata)

svc/doc/directory_listing.txt: .FORCE
	@echo $(DTS)    [INFO] - Executing $@
	@$(TREE) --prune > svc/doc/directory_listing.txt

svc/doc/makefile_graph.png: .FORCE
	@echo $(DTS)    [INFO] - Executing $@
	@$(NODEGRAPH) --direction LR | $(GRAPHVIZDOT) -Tpng > $@

svc/doc/er_diagram.pdf: REL_FILE=""
svc/doc/er_diagram.pdf:      DBFILE=svc/db/online_retail.db
svc/doc/er_diagram.pdf: svc/db/online_retail.db
	@$(er_diagram)

uninstalldirs: ## Removes the project directories. "make uninstall"
	@echo $(DTS)    [INFO] - Executing $@
	@rm -rf svc/db/* svc/doc/* svc/load/* svc/static/* opt/local/static/* opt/local/*

log_rotate: <path/to/log_file> ## Rotates log files.
	@$(log_rotate)

compact_database: svc/db/online_retail.db ## Database maintenance scripts.
	@$(compact_database)

info/variables: ## List the variables in the makefile.
	@echo $(DTS)    [INFO] - Executing $@
	@echo "-- Program paths -----------------------------------------------------"
	@echo SHELL = $(SHELL)
	@echo SQLITE3 = $(SQLITE3)
	@echo GRAPHVIZDOT = $(GRAPHVIZDOT)
	@echo SPLIT = $(SPLIT)
	@echo TREE = $(TREE)
	@echo GCLOUD = $(GCLOUD)
	@echo PYENVDIR = $(PYENVDIR)
	@echo PYTHON3 = $(PYTHON3)
	@echo PIP = $(PIP)
	@echo IN2CSV = $(IN2CSV)
	@echo CSVSTACK = $(CSVSTACK)
	@echo CSVSQL = $(CSVSQL)
	@echo SQLITEUTILS = $(SQLITEUTILS)
	@echo DATASETTE = $(DATASETTE)
	@echo NODEGRAPH = $(NODEGRAPH)
	@echo ERALCHEMY = $(ERALCHEMY)
	@echo "----------------------------------------------------------------------"

.PHONY: template/src_from_csv
template/src_from_csv: ## Create source table from CSV template (make template/src_from_csv CSVPATH=<path/to/file.csv).
	@$(sql_template_from_csv)

################################################################################
# Tests                                                                        #
################################################################################
.PHONY: test/inputs test/outputs test/database metrics metrics/SRC_online_retail_II_001

test/inputs: svc/source/online_retail_II.xlsx

test/outputs: test/database
	@echo $(DTS)    [INFO] - Executing $@

test/database: svc/db/online_retail.db
	$(test_database)

metrics: metrics/SRC_online_retail_II_001 metrics/META_TABLES_001
```

```
metrics/SRC_online_retail_II_001: svc/db/online_retail.db
	@$(record_count_table)

metrics/META_TABLES_001: svc/db/online_retail.db
	@$(record_count_table)

##############################################################################
# Project Pipeline                                                           #
##############################################################################
.PHONY: load_csv/SRC_online_retail_II_001 build/local deploy/local

svc/source/online_retail_II.xlsx: PATH="https://archive.ics.uci.edu/ml/machine-learning-databases/00502/
online_retail_II.xlsx"
svc/source/online_retail_II.xlsx:
	@echo $(DTS)    [INFO] - Executing $@
	@$(CURL) -o $@ $(PATH)

svc/load/online_retail_II_-_Year_2010-2011.csv: TABNAME = "Year 2010-2011"
svc/load/online_retail_II_-_Year_2010-2011.csv: svc/source/online_retail_II.xlsx
	@$(extract_csv_from_excel)

load_csv/SRC_online_retail_II_001: DBFILE=svc/db/online_retail.db
load_csv/SRC_online_retail_II_001: svc/load/online_retail_II_-_Year_2010-2011.csv
	@$(load_csv_into_database)

svc/db/online_retail.db: load_csv/SRC_online_retail_II_001

build/local: svc/db/online_retail.db
	@echo $(DTS)      [INFO] - Executing $@
	@mkdir -p opt/$(notdir $@)/static
	@cp -f etc/app/metadata.yaml opt/local/metadata.yaml
	@cp -f etc/server/requirements.txt opt/local/requirements.txt
	@cp -f etc/server/settings.txt opt/local/settings.txt
	@cp -f $< opt/local/$(<F)

deploy/local: build/local
	@echo $(DTS)      [INFO] - Starting server on http://$(strip $(LOCAL_ADDRESS)):$(LOCAL_PORT)
	@$(DATASETTE) serve opt/local/ --host $(LOCAL_ADDRESS) --port $(LOCAL_PORT) -o
```

Final Makefile: Chapter 8

```
# ~/projects/sales/makefile
# Execute the data pipeline for a project.
#
# make all                  Executes the default make task.
# make info                 Generates the informational files.
# make check                Executes all test suites.
# make installcheck         Run the project test suite.
# make install              Builds the database and application structure.
# make uninstall            Uninstalls the project.
# make run                  Executes the data pipelines.
# make help                 List of all makefile tasks.
# make documentation        Builds the documentation files for the build. (e.g. schema docs, data flow
diagrams)
# make uninstalldirs        Removes the project directories. "make uninstall"
# make installcheck         Run the installation test suite.
#
################################################################
# Program locations (which <utility>)
SHELL := /bin/bash
SQLITE3 := /usr/local/bin/sqlite3
SPLIT := /usr/local/bin/gsplit
TREE := /usr/local/bin/tree
GRAPHVIZDOT := /usr/local/bin/dot
GCLOUD := /Users/brianmcmillan/google-cloud-sdk/bin/gcloud
PYENVDIR := /Users/brianmcmillan/.pyenv/shims
PYTHON3 := $(PYENVDIR)/python
PIP := $(PYENVDIR)/pip
IN2CSV := $(PYENVDIR)/in2csv
SQL2CSV := $(PYENVDIR)/sql2csv
CSVSTACK := $(PYENVDIR)/csvstack
CSVSQL := $(PYENVDIR)/csvsql
SQLITEUTILS := $(PYENVDIR)/sqlite-utils
NODEGRAPH := $(PYENVDIR)/makefile2dot
DATASETTE := $(PYENVDIR)/datasette
ERALCHEMY := $(PYENVDIR)/eralchemy

# Project directory paths
ROOTDIR := $(shell pwd)
PROJECTDIR := $(ROOTDIR)
PROJECTNAME := $(notdir $(ROOTDIR))
# /etc
SYSCONFIGDIR := $(PROJECTDIR)/etc
APPCONFIGDIR := $(PROJECTDIR)/etc/app
SCHEDULECONFIGDIR := $(PROJECTDIR)/etc/cron
SERVERCONFIGDIR := $(PROJECTDIR)/etc/server
SQLDIR := $(PROJECTDIR)/etc/sql
TESTSDIR := $(PROJECTDIR)/etc/test
# /opt
OPTIONALPKGDIR := $(PROJECTDIR)/opt
LOCALDEPLOYMENTDIR := $(PROJECTDIR)/opt/local
PYTHONSCRIPTS := $(PROJECTDIR)/opt/python
LOCALSQLITE3 := $(PROJECTDIR)/opt/sqlite3
# /src
SOURCEDIR := $(PROJECTDIR)/src
SQLITESRCDIR := $(PROJECTDIR)/src/sqlite3
# /srv
SERVICEDIR := $(PROJECTDIR)/svc
CUSTOMERFILEDIR := $(PROJECTDIR)/svc/source
LOADFILEDIR := $(PROJECTDIR)/svc/load
STATICFILEDIR := $(PROJECTDIR)/svc/static
DOCUMENTATIONDIR := $(PROJECTDIR)/svc/doc
DATABASEDIR := $(PROJECTDIR)/svc/db
# /tmp /var
TEMPSTATEDIR := $(PROJECTDIR)/tmp
LOCALSTATEDIR := $(PROJECTDIR)/var
PROJECTLOGDIR := $(LOCALSTATEDIR)/log
# Project files
DBNAME := $(PROJECTNAME).db
DBFILE := $(DATABASEDIR)/$(PROJECTNAME).db
LOGFILE := $(PROJECTLOGDIR)/$(PROJECTNAME).log

# Utility variables
DTS = $(shell date +%Y-%m-%dT%H:%M:%S-%Z)
LIST_CSV = $(shell find $(dir $@) -type f -name '*.csv' -not -name 'load.csv')

# Deployment variables
LOCAL_ADDRESS := $(shell /usr/sbin/ipconfig getifaddr en0) #192.168.1.251
LOCAL_PORT := 8001
```

```
GCLOUD_URL := https://sales-5keoceam4q-uc.a.run.app #UNKNOWN until first run.

# Macros
define test_dir
	# tests the directory in the <first dependency>
	if ! test -d $<; \
	then echo $(DTS)    [FAIL] - $< does not exist; \
	else true; fi
endef

define test_file
	# tests the file in the <first dependency>
	if ! test -s $@; \
	then echo $(DTS)    [FAIL] - $@ does not exist; \
	else true; fi
endef

define test_dependent_file
	# tests the file in the <first dependency>
	if ! test -s $<; \
	then echo $(DTS)    [FAIL] - $< does not exist; \
	else true; fi
endef

define test_table
	@#test_table/<table_name>(colon)
	@if ! test $(@F) = $(shell $(SQLITE3) $(DBFILE) ".tables $(@F)" ".quit"); \
	then echo [FAIL] - $(@F) table does not exist; \
	else true; fi
endef

define test_database
	@#test/<database name.db>(colon)(space)<path/to/database.db>
	@echo $(DTS)    [INFO] - DB $(shell $(SQLITE3) $< ".databases")
endef

define file_compare
	@#<target>(colon)(space)<file_1> <file_2>
	@cmp -s $(word 1,$^) $(word 2,$^) || \
	echo $(DTS)    [FAIL] - $(word 2,$^) not equal to $(word 1,$^).
endef

define record_count_csv
	@#metrics/<csv_file.csv>(colon)(space)PATH = "<path/to/file.csv>"
	@#metrics/<csv_file.csv>(colon)(space)
	@echo $(DTS)     [INFO] - record count = $(shell wc -l < $(PATH)) $(PATH)
endef

define record_count_table
	@#record_count/<table name>(colon)(space)
	@echo $(DTS)     [INFO] - record count = $(shell $(SQLITE3) $(DBFILE) \
	"SELECT COUNT(*) || ' records in $(@F).$(notdir $(DBFILE))' FROM [$(@F)]" ".quit")
endef

define update_file_modified_date
	@#touch_src/<generalized_file_identifier>(colon)(space)<path/to/file.xyz>
	@touch $^ && echo [INFO] - Manually updating [$^] file date.
endef

define extract_csv_from_excel
	@#<path/to/csv_file.csv>(colon)(space)TABNAME = "<name of XLS worksheet>"
	@#<path/to/csv_file.csv>(colon)(space)<path/to/source/excel_file.xlsx>
	@echo $(DTS)     [INFO] - Extracting data from $< [$(TABNAME)] into $@
	@$(IN2CSV) -f xlsx --sheet $(TABNAME) $< > $@
	@$(CSVSTACK) -n load_dts -g $(DTS) $@ > $(TEMPSTATEDIR)/$(@F)_1.tmp
	@$(CSVSTACK) -n provider_code -g $@ $(TEMPSTATEDIR)/$(@F)_1.tmp > $(TEMPSTATEDIR)/$(@F)_2.tmp
	@mv $(TEMPSTATEDIR)/$(@F)_2.tmp $@
	@rm $(TEMPSTATEDIR)/$(@F)_1.tmp
	@$(test_file)
endef

define execute_sql_export_csv
	@#<path/to/export_file.csv>(colon)(space)<path/to/query.sql>
	@echo $(DTS)     [INFO] - Executing $< and exporting to $@
	@$(SQL2CSV) --db sqlite:///$(DBFILE) $< > $@
endef

define load_csv_into_database
	@#load_csv/SRC_<csv_file_name>_001(colon)(space)<path/to/csv_file.csv>
	@echo $(DTS)     [INFO] - Loading data from $< into $(@F).$(DBNAME)
	@$(CSVSQL) \
	--db sqlite:///$(DBFILE) \
	--create-if-not-exists --overwrite \
```

```
    --no-inference --no-constraints \
    --chunk-size 10000 \
    --tables $(@F) \
    --insert $<
endef

define create_table
    @#<table_name>(colon)(space)<path/to/<table_name>_create.sql>
    @echo $(DTS)    [INFO] - Creating table $@
    @$(SQLITE3) $(DBFILE) ".read $<" ".quit"
endef

define execute_sql
    @#<table_name>(colon)(space) <path/to/sql_file.sql> [<dependent_table_name(s)>]
    @echo $(DTS)    [INFO] - Executing $<
    @$(SQLITE3) $(DBFILE) ".read $<" ".quit"
endef

define vega_report_from_api
    @#<path/to/export_file.html>(colon)(space)VIZTITLE=<report title>
    @#<path/to/export_file.html>(colon)(space)VIZTEMPLATE=<path/to/viz_template.vega>
    @#<path/to/export_file.html>(colon)(space)VIZURL=<path/to/viz_url.json?_shape=array>
    @#<path/to/export_file.html>(colon)(space)<source_table_name>
    @echo $(DTS)     [INFO] - Executing $@
    @cat etc/app/vega_embed_header.viz > $@
    @echo "\"data\":{\"url\":\"$(VIZURL)\"}, " >> $@
    @echo "\"title\":\"$(VIZTITLE)\"," >> $@
    @cat $(VIZTEMPLATE) >> $@
    @cat etc/app/vega_embed_footer.viz >> $@
endef

define vega_report_from_file
    @#<path/to/export_file.html>(colon)(space)VIZTITLE=<report title>
    @#<path/to/export_file.html>(colon)(space)VIZTEMPLATE=<path/to/viz_template.vega>
    @#<path/to/export_file.html>(colon)(space)<source_file_name>
    @echo $(DTS)     [INFO] - Executing $@
    @cat etc/app/vega_embed_header.viz > $@
    @echo "\"data\":{ \"values\":" >> $@
    @cat $< >> $@ && echo "}, " >> $@
    @echo "\"title\":\"$(VIZTITLE)\"," >> $@
    @cat $(VIZTEMPLATE) >> $@
    @cat etc/app/vega_embed_footer.viz >> $@
endef

##############################################################################
all: run documentation ## Executes the default make task.
info: help info/variables test/dirs test/solution_files documentation ## Generates the informational files.
check: test/outputs test/tables test/db metrics ## Executes all test suites.
installcheck: test/dirs test/inputs test/solution_files test/db ## Run the project test suite.
install: test/db test/tables ## Builds the database and application structure.
uninstall: uninstalldirs ## Uninstalls the project.
run: test/inputs extract transform test/tables test/outputs metrics compact_database ## Executes the data
pipelines.

.PHONY: help documentation uninstalldirs installcheck .FORCE log_rotate compact_database

.FORCE:

help: ## List of all makefile tasks.
    @echo $(DTS)    [INFO] - Executing $@.
    @grep -E '^[a-zA-Z_-]+:.*?## .*$$' $(MAKEFILE_LIST) | \
    awk 'BEGIN {FS = ":.*?## "};\
    {printf "\033[36m%-20s\033[0m %s\n", $$1, $$2}'

documentation: run META_TABLES_001 ## Builds the documentation files for the build. (e.g. schema docs, data
flow diagrams)
    @echo $(DTS)    [INFO] - Executing $@.
    @$(TREE) --prune > $(DOCUMENTATIONDIR)/directory_listing.txt
    @$(NODEGRAPH) --direction LR | $(GRAPHVIZDOT) -Tpng > $(DOCUMENTATIONDIR)/makefile_graph.png

META_TABLES_001:
    @$(SQLITE3) $(DBFILE) "DROP TABLE IF EXISTS '_analyze_tables_';" ".quit"
    @$(SQLITE3) $(DBFILE) "DROP TABLE IF EXISTS 'META_TABLES_001';" ".quit"
    @$(SQLITEUTILS) analyze-tables $(DBFILE) --save
    @$(SQLITE3) $(DBFILE) "ALTER TABLE '_analyze_tables_' RENAME TO 'META_TABLES_001';" ".quit"

er_diagrams: svc/doc/raw_tables.pdf svc/doc/information_tables.pdf svc/doc/business_tables.pdf svc/doc/
meta_tables.pdf
    @echo $(DTS)    [INFO] - Executing $<
    @$(ERALCHEMY) -i sqlite:///$(DBFILE) -o etc/app/er_tables.er

svc/doc/raw_tables.pdf:
    @$(ERALCHEMY) -i sqlite:///$(DBFILE) -o $@ --include-tables \
```

```
	SRC_online_retail_II_-_Year_2010-2011_002 \
	RAW_ONLINE_RETAIL_II_YEAR_2010_2011_001 \
	SAT_ONLINE_RETAIL_II_YEAR_2010_2011_001

svc/doc/information_tables.pdf:
	@$(ERALCHEMY) -i sqlite:///$(DBFILE) -o $@ --include-tables \
	INFO_WEEKLY_TOP_SALES_RANK_002

svc/doc/meta_tables.pdf:
	@$(ERALCHEMY) -i sqlite:///$(DBFILE) -o $@ --include-tables \
	META_TABLES_001

svc/doc/business_tables.pdf: tmp/er_business.er
	@$(ERALCHEMY) -i $< -o $@
	@rm -f $^

tmp/er_business.er: tmp/er_business_tables.er etc/app/er_business_relationships.txt
		@cat $^ > $@

etc/app/er_business_relationships.txt:
	@$(test_file)

tmp/er_business_tables.er:
	@$(ERALCHEMY) -i sqlite:///$(DBFILE) -o $@ --include-tables \
	BHUB_INVOICE_CODES_001 \
	BHUB_STOCK_CODES_001 \
	BLNK_STOCK_CODE_PREFERRED_DESCRIPTION_001 \
	BSAT_INVOICES_001

uninstalldirs: uninstall/online_retail_II uninstall/local uninstall/gcloud ## Removes the project
directories. "make uninstall"
	@echo $(DTS)	[INFO] - Executing $@.
	@rm -f svc/db/*
	@rm -f svc/doc/*
	@rm -f svc/load/*
	@rm -f svc/static/*

installcheck: ## Run the installation test suite.
	@echo $(DTS)	[INFO] - Executing $@.

log_rotate:
	@echo $(DTS)	[INFO] - Executing $@
	@mv $(PROJECTLOGDIR)/cron_log.txt $(PROJECTLOGDIR)/cron_log_$(shell date +%Y-%m-%d).txt

compact_database:
	@$(SQLITE3) $(DBFILE) "PRAGMA optimize;" && echo $(DTS)	[INFO] - Optimizing database
	@$(SQLITE3) $(DBFILE) "PRAGMA auto_vacuum;" && echo $(DTS)	[INFO] - Vacuuming database
	@$(SQLITE3) $(DBFILE) "PRAGMA integrity_check;" && echo $(DTS)	[INFO] - Performing integrity check

.PHONY: template/src_from_csv
template/src_from_csv: ## Create source table from CSV template.
	@#make template/src_from_csv CSVPATH=<path/to/file.csv>
	@echo $(DTS)	[INFO] - Creating script for SRC_$(notdir $(basename $(CSVPATH)))_###_create from $
(CSVPATH)
	@if test -s $(CSVPATH); then echo [PASS] - $(CSVPATH) file exists; \
	else echo [FAIL] - $(CSVPATH) file does not exist; fi
	@$(SQLITE3) tmp/temp.db ".import --csv $(CSVPATH) SRC_$(notdir $(basename $(CSVPATH)))_###"
	@$(SQLITE3) tmp/temp.db ".schema SRC_$(notdir $(basename $(CSVPATH)))_###"
	@echo "--etc/sql/SRC_$(notdir $(basename $(CSVPATH)))_###_create.sql" \
	> etc/sql/SRC_$(notdir $(basename $(CSVPATH)))_###_create.sql
	@echo "---------------------------------------------------------------------------" \
	>> etc/sql/SRC_$(notdir $(basename $(CSVPATH)))_###_create.sql
	@$(SQLITE3) tmp/temp.db ".schema SRC_$(notdir $(basename $(CSVPATH)))_###" \
	>> etc/sql/SRC_$(notdir $(basename $(CSVPATH)))_###_create.sql
	@rm tmp/temp.db

.PHONY: info/variables
info/variables: ## List the variables in the makefile.
	@echo $(DTS)	[INFO] - Executing $@.
	@echo "-- Program paths ----------------------------------------------------"
	@echo SHELL = $(SHELL)
	@echo SQLITE3 = $(SQLITE3)
	@echo GRAPHVIZDOT = $(GRAPHVIZDOT)
	@echo SPLIT = $(SPLIT)
	@echo TREE = $(TREE)
	@echo GCLOUD = $(GCLOUD)
	@echo PYENVDIR = $(PYENVDIR)
	@echo PYTHON3 = $(PYTHON3)
	@echo PIP = $(PIP)
	@echo IN2CSV = $(IN2CSV)
	@echo CSVSTACK = $(CSVSTACK)
	@echo CSVSQL = $(CSVSQL)
	@echo SQLITEUTILS = $(SQLITEUTILS)
```

```
	@echo DATASETTE = $(DATASETTE)
	@echo NODEGRAPH = $(NODEGRAPH)
	@echo ERALCHEMY = $(ERALCHEMY)
	@echo "-- Configuration paths (/etc) ----------------------------------------"
	@echo SYSCONFIGDIR = $(SYSCONFIGDIR)
	@echo APPCONFIGDIR = $(APPCONFIGDIR)
	@echo SCHEDULECONFIGDIR = $(SCHEDULECONFIGDIR)
	@echo SERVERCONFIGDIR = $(SERVERCONFIGDIR)
	@echo SQLDIR = $(SQLDIR)
	@echo TESTSDIR = $(TESTSDIR)
	@echo "-- Optional packages / deployment paths (/opt) ----------------------"
	@echo OPTIONALPKGDIR = $(OPTIONALPKGDIR)
	@echo LOCALDEPLOYMENTDIR = $(LOCALDEPLOYMENTDIR)
	@echo PYTHONSCRIPTS = $(PYTHONSCRIPTS)
	@echo LOCALSQLITE3 = $(LOCALSQLITE3)
	@echo "-- Source code paths (/src) -----------------------------------------"
	@echo SOURCEDIR = $(SOURCEDIR)
	@echo SQLITESRCDIR = $(SQLITESRCDIR)
	@echo "-- Services paths (/svc) --------------------------------------------"
	@echo SERVICEDIR = $(SERVICEDIR)
	@echo CUSTOMERFILEDIR = $(CUSTOMERFILEDIR)
	@echo LOADFILEDIR = $(LOADFILEDIR)
	@echo STATICFILEDIR = $(STATICFILEDIR)
	@echo DOCUMENTATIONDIR = $(DOCUMENTATIONDIR)
	@echo DATABASEDIR = $(DATABASEDIR)
	@echo "-- Temporary storage paths (/tmp /var) ------------------------------"
	@echo TEMPSTATEDIR = $(TEMPSTATEDIR)
	@echo LOCALSTATEDIR = $(LOCALSTATEDIR)
	@echo PROJECTLOGDIR = $(PROJECTLOGDIR)
	@echo "-- Project directory paths ------------------------------------------"
	@echo ROOTDIR = $(ROOTDIR)
	@echo PROJECTDIR = $(PROJECTDIR)
	@echo PROJECTNAME= $(PROJECTNAME)
	@echo DBNAME= $(DBNAME)
	@echo DBFILE= $(DBFILE)
	@#echo LOGFILE= $(LOGFILE)
	@echo "---------------------------------------------------------------------"

.PHONY: test/dirs ROOTDIR PROJECTDIR PROJECTNAME SYSCONFIGDIR APPCONFIGDIR \
SCHEDULECONFIGDIR SERVERCONFIGDIR SQLDIR TESTSDIR OPTIONALPKGDIR \
LOCALDEPLOYMENTDIR PYTHONSCRIPTS LOCALSQLITE3 SOURCEDIR SQLITESRCDIR SERVICEDIR \
CUSTOMERFILEDIR LOADFILEDIR STATICFILEDIR DOCUMENTATIONDIR DATABASEDIR \
TEMPSTATEDIR LOCALSTATEDIR PROJECTLOGDIR

test/dirs: ROOTDIR PROJECTDIR PROJECTNAME SYSCONFIGDIR APPCONFIGDIR \
SCHEDULECONFIGDIR SERVERCONFIGDIR SQLDIR TESTSDIR OPTIONALPKGDIR \
LOCALDEPLOYMENTDIR PYTHONSCRIPTS LOCALSQLITE3 SOURCEDIR SQLITESRCDIR SERVICEDIR \
CUSTOMERFILEDIR LOADFILEDIR STATICFILEDIR DOCUMENTATIONDIR DATABASEDIR \
TEMPSTATEDIR LOCALSTATEDIR PROJECTLOGDIR
	@echo $(DTS)    [INFO] - Executing $@.

ROOTDIR: $(ROOTDIR)
	@$(test_dir)
PROJECTDIR: $(PROJECTDIR)
	@$(test_dir)
SYSCONFIGDIR: $(SYSCONFIGDIR)
	@$(test_dir)
APPCONFIGDIR: $(APPCONFIGDIR)
	@$(test_dir)
SCHEDULECONFIGDIR: $(SCHEDULECONFIGDIR)
	@$(test_dir)
SERVERCONFIGDIR: $(SERVERCONFIGDIR)
	@$(test_dir)
SQLDIR: $(SQLDIR)
	@$(test_dir)
TESTSDIR: $(TESTSDIR)
	@$(test_dir)
OPTIONALPKGDIR: $(OPTIONALPKGDIR)
	@$(test_dir)
LOCALDEPLOYMENTDIR: $(LOCALDEPLOYMENTDIR)
	@$(test_dir)
PYTHONSCRIPTS: $(PYTHONSCRIPTS)
	@$(test_dir)
LOCALSQLITE3: $(LOCALSQLITE3)
	@$(test_dir)
SOURCEDIR: $(SOURCEDIR)
	@$(test_dir)
SQLITESRCDIR: $(SQLITESRCDIR)
	@$(test_dir)
SERVICEDIR: $(SERVICEDIR)
	@$(test_dir)
CUSTOMERFILEDIR: $(CUSTOMERFILEDIR)
	@$(test_dir)
```

```
LOADFILEDIR: $(LOADFILEDIR)
	@$(test_dir)
STATICFILEDIR: $(STATICFILEDIR)
	@$(test_dir)
DOCUMENTATIONDIR: $(DOCUMENTATIONDIR)
	@$(test_dir)
DATABASEDIR: $(DATABASEDIR)
	@$(test_dir)
TEMPSTATEDIR: $(TEMPSTATEDIR)
	@$(test_dir)
LOCALSTATEDIR: $(LOCALSTATEDIR)
	@$(test_dir)
PROJECTLOGDIR: $(PROJECTLOGDIR)
	@$(test_dir)

test/solution_files: SHELL PYTHON3 PIP SQLITE3 IN2CSV CSVSTACK SQLITEUTILS \
SPLIT TREE GRAPHVIZDOT NODEGRAPH
	@echo $(DTS)	[INFO] - Executing $@.

SHELL: $(SHELL)
	@$(test_dependent_file)
PYTHON3: $(PYTHON3)
	@$(test_dependent_file)
PIP: $(PIP)
	@$(test_dependent_file)
SQLITE3: $(SQLITE3)
	@$(test_dependent_file)
IN2CSV: $(IN2CSV)
	@$(test_dependent_file)
CSVSTACK: $(CSVSTACK)
	@$(test_dependent_file)
SQLITEUTILS: $(SQLITEUTILS)
	@$(test_dependent_file)
SPLIT: $(SPLIT)
	@$(test_dependent_file)
TREE: $(TREE)
	@$(test_dependent_file)
GRAPHVIZDOT: $(GRAPHVIZDOT)
	@$(test_dependent_file)
GCLOUD: $(GCLOUD)
	@$(test_dependent_file)
NODEGRAPH: $(NODEGRAPH)
	@$(test_dependent_file)

#.PHONY: dist
#dist: ## Create a distribution package.
#	@echo $(DTS)	[INFO] - Executing $@.

################################################################################
# Deployment configuration                                                     #
################################################################################
# Source files -----------------------------------------------------------------
.PHONY: test/shared/datasette

# ---- Datasette ----------------------------------------------------------------
test/shared/datasette: \
	etc/app/metadata.yaml \
	etc/server/requirements.txt \
	etc/server/settings.json

etc/app/metadata.yaml:
	@$(test_file)

etc/server/requirements.txt:
	@$(test_file)

etc/server/settings.json:
	@$(test_file)

# ---- Vega ---------------------------------------------------------------------
etc/app/vega_embed_header.viz:
	@$(test_file)

etc/app/vega_embed_footer.viz:
	@$(test_file)

################################################################################
# Configure Database                                                           #
################################################################################
# Database and table tests------------------------------------------------------
.PHONY: test/db test/sales.db test/tables \
	test_table/SRC_online_retail_II_-_Year_2010-2011_002 \
	test_table/SAT_ONLINE_RETAIL_II_YEAR_2010_2011_001
```

```
test/db: test/sales.db

test/sales.db: svc/db/sales.db
	$(test_database)

svc/db/sales.db:

test/tables: \
	test_table/SRC_online_retail_II_-_Year_2010-2011_002 \
	test_table/SAT_ONLINE_RETAIL_II_YEAR_2010_2011_001 \
	test_table/BSAT_INVOICES_001 \
	test_table/BLNK_STOCK_CODE_PREFERRED_DESCRIPTION_001 \
	test_table/BHUB_STOCK_CODES_001 \
	test_table/BHUB_INVOICE_CODES_001 \
	test_table/INFO_WEEKLY_TOP_SALES_RANK_002

# INFO_WEEKLY_TOP_SALES_RANK_002_create.sql ------------------------------------
test_table/INFO_WEEKLY_TOP_SALES_RANK_002: \
	INFO_WEEKLY_TOP_SALES_RANK_002
	@$(test_table)

etc/sql/INFO_WEEKLY_TOP_SALES_RANK_002_create.sql:
	@$(test_file)

INFO_WEEKLY_TOP_SALES_RANK_002: \
	etc/sql/INFO_WEEKLY_TOP_SALES_RANK_002_create.sql
	@$(create_table)

# BHUB_INVOICE_CODES_001_create.sql --------------------------------------------
test_table/BHUB_INVOICE_CODES_001: \
	BHUB_INVOICE_CODES_001
	@$(test_table)

etc/sql/BHUB_INVOICE_CODES_001_create.sql:
	@$(test_file)

BHUB_INVOICE_CODES_001: \
	etc/sql/BHUB_INVOICE_CODES_001_create.sql
	@$(create_table)

# BHUB_STOCK_CODES_001_create.sql ----------------------------------------------
test_table/BHUB_STOCK_CODES_001: \
	BHUB_STOCK_CODES_001
	@$(test_table)

etc/sql/BHUB_STOCK_CODES_001_create.sql:
	@$(test_file)

BHUB_STOCK_CODES_001: \
	etc/sql/BHUB_STOCK_CODES_001_create.sql
	@$(create_table)

# BLNK_STOCK_CODE_PREFERRED_DESCRIPTION_001 ------------------------------------
test_table/BLNK_STOCK_CODE_PREFERRED_DESCRIPTION_001: \
	BLNK_STOCK_CODE_PREFERRED_DESCRIPTION_001
	@$(test_table)

etc/sql/BLNK_STOCK_CODE_PREFERRED_DESCRIPTION_001_create.sql:
	@$(test_file)

BLNK_STOCK_CODE_PREFERRED_DESCRIPTION_001: \
	etc/sql/BLNK_STOCK_CODE_PREFERRED_DESCRIPTION_001_create.sql
	@$(create_table)

# BSAT_INVOICES_001 ------------------------------------------------------------
test_table/BSAT_INVOICES_001: \
	SAT_ONLINE_RETAIL_II_YEAR_2010_2011_001
	@$(test_table)

etc/sql/BSAT_INVOICES_001_create.sql:
	@$(test_file)

BSAT_INVOICES_001: \
	etc/sql/BSAT_INVOICES_001_create.sql
	@$(create_table)

# SAT_ONLINE_RETAIL_II_YEAR_2010_2011_001 --------------------------------------
test_table/SAT_ONLINE_RETAIL_II_YEAR_2010_2011_001: \
	SAT_ONLINE_RETAIL_II_YEAR_2010_2011_001
	@$(test_table)

etc/sql/SAT_ONLINE_RETAIL_II_YEAR_2010_2011_001_create.sql:
```

```
	@$(test_file)

SAT_ONLINE_RETAIL_II_YEAR_2010_2011_001: \
	etc/sql/SAT_ONLINE_RETAIL_II_YEAR_2010_2011_001_create.sql
	@$(create_table)

# SRC_online_retail_II_-_Year_2010-2011_002 -----------------------------------
test_table/SRC_online_retail_II_-_Year_2010-2011_002: \
	SRC_online_retail_II_-_Year_2010-2011_002
	@$(test_table)

etc/sql/SRC_online_retail_II_-_Year_2010-2011_002_create.sql:
	@$(test_file)

SRC_online_retail_II_-_Year_2010-2011_002: \
	etc/sql/SRC_online_retail_II_-_Year_2010-2011_002_create.sql
	@$(create_table)

################################################################################
# Project Pipeline                                                             #
################################################################################
.PHONY: test/inputs test/outputs
# ---- Tests inputs ----
test/inputs: \
	svc/source/online_retail_II.xlsx

svc/source/online_retail_II.xlsx:
	@$(test_file)

touch_src/online_retail: svc/source/online_retail_II.xlsx
	@$(update_file_modified_date)

# ---- Tests outputs ----
test/outputs: \
	test/WEEKLY_TOP_SALES_RANK_004.html

test/WEEKLY_TOP_SALES_RANK_004.html: svc/static/WEEKLY_TOP_SALES_RANK_004.html
	@$(test_dependent_file)

# Extract ----------------------------------------------------------------------
.PHONY: extract split/online_retail_II uninstall/online_retail_II
extract: split/online_retail_II

svc/load/online_retail_II_-_Year_2010-2011.csv: TABNAME = "Year 2010-2011"
svc/load/online_retail_II_-_Year_2010-2011.csv: svc/source/online_retail_II.xlsx
	@$(extract_csv_from_excel)

split/online_retail_II: SOURCEDIR="svc/load/$(@F)/"
split/online_retail_II: TARGETDIR="svc/load/split_$(@F)/"
split/online_retail_II: TARGETNAME="$(basename $(<F))_"
split/online_retail_II: svc/load/online_retail_II_-_Year_2010-2011.csv
	@#<split/file_group_description>(colon)(space) path/to/source_file.csv
	@echo $(DTS)     [INFO] - Splitting $< into $(TARGETDIR)$(TARGETNAME)_###
	@mkdir -p $(SOURCEDIR) $(TARGETDIR)
	@/usr/local/bin/gsplit -d -a 3 -l 50000 --additional-suffix=".csv" \
	$< $(TARGETDIR)/$(TARGETNAME)
	@wc -l $(TARGETDIR)*.csv

uninstall/online_retail_II:
	@echo $(DTS)    [INFO] - Executing $@
	@rm -r $(LOADFILEDIR)/$(@F) || true
	@rm -r $(LOADFILEDIR)/split_$(@F) || true

# Load -------------------------------------------------------------------------
.PHONY: load load/SRC_online_retail_II_-_Year_2010-2011_002
load: load/SRC_online_retail_II_-_Year_2010-2011_002

load/SRC_online_retail_II_-_Year_2010-2011_002: svc/load/online_retail_II/load.csv
	@#load/<SRC_target_table_name_###>(colon)(space)<path/to/csv_file/load.csv>
	@echo $(DTS)     [INFO] - Extracting data from $< and loading into $@
	@if test -s $<; \
	then $(SQLITE3) $(DBFILE) ".import --csv $< $(notdir $@)" ".quit"; \
	else echo $(DTS)     [WARNING] - $< file does not exist; fi
	@$(SQLITE3) $(DBFILE) \
	"SELECT COUNT(*) || ' records in $(notdir $@)' FROM [$(notdir $@)]" ".quit"
	@rm -f $<

svc/load/online_retail_II/load.csv: .FORCE
	@#path/to/<source_reference_name_directory>/load.csv(colon)(space)
	@echo $(DTS)     [INFO] - Loading csv files from $(realpath $(dir $@)) and loading into $@
	@$(if $(abspath $(LIST_CSV)), cat $(abspath $(LIST_CSV)) >> $(addsuffix .tmp, $(basename $@)) \
	&& echo $(DTS)     [INFO] - Concatenating csv files [$(realpath $(LIST_CSV))] \
	&& wc -l $(addsuffix .tmp, $(basename $@)), \
```

```
	echo $(DTS)	[INFO] - no files to process in $(dir $@))
	@sort -u $(addsuffix .tmp, $(basename $@)) -o $@ || true
	@rm -f $(addsuffix .tmp, $(basename $@)) || true
	@find $(realpath $(dir $@)) -type f -not -name 'load.csv' -delete
	@wc -l $@ || true

# Transform ---------------------------------------------------------------------
.PHONY: transform metrics load/SAT_ONLINE_RETAIL_II_YEAR_2010_2011_001 \
	clean/SRC_online_retail_II_-_Year_2010-2011_002 load/BSAT_INVOICES_001 \
	load/BLNK_STOCK_CODE_PREFERRED_DESCRIPTION_001 load/BHUB_STOCK_CODES_001 \
	load/BHUB_INVOICE_CODES_001 load/INFO_WEEKLY_TOP_SALES_RANK_002
	metrics/SAT_ONLINE_RETAIL_II_YEAR_2010_2011_001 metrics/BSAT_INVOICES_001 \
	metrics/BLNK_STOCK_CODE_PREFERRED_DESCRIPTION_001 metrics/BHUB_STOCK_CODES_001 \
	metrics/BHUB_INVOICE_CODES_001 metrics/INFO_WEEKLY_TOP_SALES_RANK_002

transform: \
	load/SAT_ONLINE_RETAIL_II_YEAR_2010_2011_001 \
	clean/SRC_online_retail_II_-_Year_2010-2011_002 \
	load/BSAT_INVOICES_001 \
	load/BLNK_STOCK_CODE_PREFERRED_DESCRIPTION_001 \
	load/BHUB_STOCK_CODES_001 \
	load/BHUB_INVOICE_CODES_001 \
	load/INFO_WEEKLY_TOP_SALES_RANK_002

metrics: \
	metrics/SAT_ONLINE_RETAIL_II_YEAR_2010_2011_001 \
	metrics/BSAT_INVOICES_001 \
	metrics/BLNK_STOCK_CODE_PREFERRED_DESCRIPTION_001 \
	metrics/BHUB_STOCK_CODES_001 \
	metrics/BHUB_INVOICE_CODES_001 \
	metrics/INFO_WEEKLY_TOP_SALES_RANK_002

# INFO_WEEKLY_TOP_SALES_RANK_002 ----------------------------------------------
.PHONY: load/INFO_WEEKLY_TOP_SALES_RANK_002
etc/sql/INFO_WEEKLY_TOP_SALES_RANK_002_load.sql:
	@$(test_file)

load/INFO_WEEKLY_TOP_SALES_RANK_002: \
	etc/sql/INFO_WEEKLY_TOP_SALES_RANK_002_load.sql \
	INFO_WEEKLY_TOP_SALES_RANK_002 \
	load/BSAT_INVOICES_001 \
	load/BLNK_STOCK_CODE_PREFERRED_DESCRIPTION_001
	@$(execute_sql)

metrics/INFO_WEEKLY_TOP_SALES_RANK_002: \
	INFO_WEEKLY_TOP_SALES_RANK_002
	@$(record_count_table)

# BHUB_INVOICE_CODES_001 ------------------------------------------------------
.PHONY: load/BHUB_INVOICE_CODES_001
etc/sql/BHUB_INVOICE_CODES_001_load.sql:
	@$(test_file)

load/BHUB_INVOICE_CODES_001: \
	etc/sql/BHUB_INVOICE_CODES_001_load.sql \
	SAT_ONLINE_RETAIL_II_YEAR_2010_2011_001 \
	BHUB_INVOICE_CODES_001 \
	load/SAT_ONLINE_RETAIL_II_YEAR_2010_2011_001
	@$(execute_sql)

metrics/BHUB_INVOICE_CODES_001: \
	BHUB_INVOICE_CODES_001
	@$(record_count_table)

# BHUB_STOCK_CODES_001 --------------------------------------------------------
.PHONY: load/BHUB_STOCK_CODES_001
etc/sql/BHUB_STOCK_CODES_001_load.sql:
	@$(test_file)

load/BHUB_STOCK_CODES_001: \
	etc/sql/BHUB_STOCK_CODES_001_load.sql \
	SAT_ONLINE_RETAIL_II_YEAR_2010_2011_001 \
	BHUB_STOCK_CODES_001 \
	load/SAT_ONLINE_RETAIL_II_YEAR_2010_2011_001
	@$(execute_sql)

metrics/BHUB_STOCK_CODES_001: \
	BHUB_STOCK_CODES_001
	@$(record_count_table)

# BLNK_STOCK_CODE_PREFERRED_DESCRIPTION_001 -----------------------------------
.PHONY: load/BLNK_STOCK_CODE_PREFERRED_DESCRIPTION_001
etc/sql/BLNK_STOCK_CODE_PREFERRED_DESCRIPTION_001_load.sql:
```

```
	@$(test_file)

load/BLNK_STOCK_CODE_PREFERRED_DESCRIPTION_001: \
	etc/sql/BLNK_STOCK_CODE_PREFERRED_DESCRIPTION_001_load.sql \
	SAT_ONLINE_RETAIL_II_YEAR_2010_2011_001 \
	BLNK_STOCK_CODE_PREFERRED_DESCRIPTION_001 \
	load/SAT_ONLINE_RETAIL_II_YEAR_2010_2011_001
	@$(execute_sql)

metrics/BLNK_STOCK_CODE_PREFERRED_DESCRIPTION_001: \
	BLNK_STOCK_CODE_PREFERRED_DESCRIPTION_001
	@$(record_count_table)

# BSAT_INVOICES_001 ------------------------------------------------------------
.PHONY: load/BSAT_INVOICES_001
etc/sql/BSAT_INVOICES_001_load.sql:
	@$(test_file)

load/BSAT_INVOICES_001: \
	etc/sql/BSAT_INVOICES_001_load.sql \
	SAT_ONLINE_RETAIL_II_YEAR_2010_2011_001 \
	BSAT_INVOICES_001 \
	load/SAT_ONLINE_RETAIL_II_YEAR_2010_2011_001
	@$(execute_sql)

metrics/BSAT_INVOICES_001: \
	BSAT_INVOICES_001
	@$(record_count_table)

# SAT_ONLINE_RETAIL_II_YEAR_2010_2011_001 --------------------------------------
.PHONY: load/SAT_ONLINE_RETAIL_II_YEAR_2010_2011_001 \
	clean/SRC_online_retail_II_-_Year_2010-2011_002

etc/sql/SAT_ONLINE_RETAIL_II_YEAR_2010_2011_001_load.sql:
	@$(test_file)

load/SAT_ONLINE_RETAIL_II_YEAR_2010_2011_001: \
	etc/sql/SAT_ONLINE_RETAIL_II_YEAR_2010_2011_001_load.sql \
	SRC_online_retail_II_-_Year_2010-2011_002 \
	SAT_ONLINE_RETAIL_II_YEAR_2010_2011_001 \
	load/SRC_online_retail_II_-_Year_2010-2011_002
	@$(execute_sql)

clean/SRC_online_retail_II_-_Year_2010-2011_002: \
	etc/sql/SAT_ONLINE_RETAIL_II_YEAR_2010_2011_001_clean.sql \
	load/SAT_ONLINE_RETAIL_II_YEAR_2010_2011_001
	@$(execute_sql)

metrics/SAT_ONLINE_RETAIL_II_YEAR_2010_2011_001: \
	SAT_ONLINE_RETAIL_II_YEAR_2010_2011_001
	@$(record_count_table)

################################################################################
# Publish                                                                      #
################################################################################
# Vega-Lite reports ------------------------------------------------------------
etc/app/WEEKLY_TOP_SALES_RANK_001.vega:
	@$(test_file)

svc/static/WEEKLY_TOP_SALES_RANK_004.html: VIZTITLE="Weekly Top Sales Rank - JSON API call v2"
svc/static/WEEKLY_TOP_SALES_RANK_004.html: VIZTEMPLATE=etc/app/WEEKLY_TOP_SALES_RANK_001.vega
svc/static/WEEKLY_TOP_SALES_RANK_004.html: VIZURL="/sales/INFO_WEEKLY_TOP_SALES_RANK_002.json?_shape=array"
svc/static/WEEKLY_TOP_SALES_RANK_004.html: INFO_WEEKLY_TOP_SALES_RANK_002
	$(vega_report_from_api)

################################################################################
# Deployments                                                                  #
################################################################################
# Local deployment -------------------------------------------------------------
.PHONY: deploy/local test/local_config build/local uninstall/local start/local test/local
deploy/local: start/local test/local
	@echo $(DTS)	[INFO] - Executing $@

test/local_config: \
	opt/local/metadata.yaml \
	opt/local/requirements.txt \
	opt/local/settings.json \
	opt/local/sales.db \
	opt/local/static/WEEKLY_TOP_SALES_RANK_004.html
	@echo $(DTS)	[INFO] - Executing $@

build/local:
	@echo $(DTS)	[INFO] - Executing $@
```

```
	@mkdir -p opt/$(notdir $@)/static
	@cp -f etc/app/metadata.yaml opt/local/metadata.yaml
	@cp -f etc/server/requirements.txt opt/local/requirements.txt
	@cp -f etc/server/settings.json opt/local/settings.json
	@cp -f svc/db/sales.db opt/local/sales.db
	@cp -f svc/static/WEEKLY_TOP_SALES_RANK_004.html opt/local/static/WEEKLY_TOP_SALES_RANK_004.html

opt/local/metadata.yaml:
	@$(test_file)

opt/local/requirements.txt:
	@$(test_file)

opt/local/settings.json:
	@$(test_file)

opt/local/sales.db:
	@$(test_file)

opt/local/static/WEEKLY_TOP_SALES_RANK_004.html:
	@$(test_file)

uninstall/local: ## Removes the build artifacts. "make uninstall/local"
	@echo $(DTS)     [INFO] - Executing $@
	@rm -r opt/local/static || true
	@rm -f opt/local/* || true

start/local: build/local test/local_config
	@echo $(DTS)      [INFO] - Starting server on http://$(strip $(LOCAL_ADDRESS)):$(LOCAL_PORT)
	@$(DATASETTE) serve $(LOCALDEPLOYMENTDIR) --host $(LOCAL_ADDRESS) --port $(LOCAL_PORT) -o

test/local:
	@echo $(DTS)     [INFO] - Executing $@
	@$(if $(shell curl http://$(strip $(LOCAL_ADDRESS)):$(LOCAL_PORT) -fIs | head -n 1), \
	echo $(DTS)     [INFO] - http://$(strip $(LOCAL_ADDRESS)):$(LOCAL_PORT) - \
	$(shell curl http://$(strip $(LOCAL_ADDRESS)):$(LOCAL_PORT) -fIs | head -n 1), \
	echo $(DTS)     [FAIL] - $(strip $(LOCAL_ADDRESS)):$(LOCAL_PORT) is unavailable)

# Google CloudRun deployment ---------------------------------------------------
.PHONY: deploy/gcloud test/gcloud_config build/gcloud uninstall/gcloud start/gcloud test/gcloud
deploy/gcloud: start/gcloud test/gcloud
	@echo $(DTS)      [INFO] - Executing $@

test/gcloud_config: \
	opt/gcloud/metadata.yaml \
	opt/gcloud/requirements.txt \
	opt/gcloud/settings.json \
	opt/gcloud/sales.db \
	opt/gcloud/static/WEEKLY_TOP_SALES_RANK_004.html
	@echo $(DTS)      [INFO] - Executing $@

opt/gcloud/metadata.yaml:
	@$(test_file)

opt/gcloud/requirements.txt:
	@$(test_file)

opt/gcloud/settings.json:
	@$(test_file)

opt/gcloud/sales.db:
	@$(test_file)

opt/gcloud/static/WEEKLY_TOP_SALES_RANK_004.html:
	@$(test_file)

build/gcloud:
	@echo $(DTS)     [INFO] - Executing $@
	@mkdir -p opt/$(notdir $@)/static
	@cp -f svc/db/sales.db opt/$(notdir $@)/sales.db
	@cp -f etc/app/metadata.yaml opt/$(notdir $@)/metadata.yaml
	@cp -f etc/server/requirements.txt opt/$(notdir $@)/requirements.txt
	@cp -f etc/server/settings.json opt/$(notdir $@)/settings.json
	@cp -f svc/static/WEEKLY_TOP_SALES_RANK_004.html opt/$(notdir $@)/static/WEEKLY_TOP_SALES_RANK_004.html

uninstall/gcloud: ## Removes the build artifacts. "make uninstall/local"
	@echo $(DTS)     [INFO] - Executing $@
	@rm -r opt/gcloud/static || true
	@rm -r opt/gcloud || true

start/gcloud: build/gcloud test/gcloud_config
	@echo [INFO] - Starting server build on http://$(strip $(GCLOUD_URL))
	@$(DATASETTE) publish cloudrun --service=$(PROJECTNAME) \
```

```
	opt/$(notdir $@)/sales.db \
	-m opt/$(notdir $@)/metadata.yaml \
	--memory 2Gi \
	--install=datasette-vega \
	--install=datasette-copyable \
	--extra-options="--setting sql_time_limit_ms 10000"

test/gcloud:
	@$(if $(shell curl $(strip $(GCLOUD_URL)) -fIs | head -n 1), \
	echo [PASS] - $(strip $(GCLOUD_URL)) - $(shell curl $(strip $(GCLOUD_URL)) -fIs | head -n 1), \
	echo [FAIL] - $(strip $(GCLOUD_URL)) is unavailable)
```

---

190 Cygwin (https://www.cygwin.com)

191 Hyper-V (https://en.wikipedia.org/wiki/Hyper-V)
Installing Hyper-V (https://docs.microsoft.com/en-us/virtualization/hyper-v-on-windows/about/)

192 Debian UNIX (https://www.debian.org)

193 WSL installation (https://docs.microsoft.com/en-us/windows/wsl/install-win10#manual-installation-steps)

194 ISO-8601 (https://en.wikipedia.org/wiki/ISO_8601)

About the Author

Over the last two decades, Brian McMillan has been lucky to have participated in the birth, growth, maturation, and closure of over a dozen major data products at significant multinational IT and defense companies. While an Enterprise Architect by title, his passion is really in discovering how to make data useful to any business. He lives with his wife and pet snake in Tucson, AZ.

Made in United States
North Haven, CT
10 November 2026

22088887R00246